The Slow Failure

History *of* Ireland *and the* Irish Diaspora

James S. Donnelly, Jr.
Thomas Archdeacon

SERIES EDITORS

The Slow Failure

Population Decline and
Independent Ireland, 1922–1973

Mary E. Daly

The University of Wisconsin Press

This book was published with the support of
the Anonymous Fund for the Humanities
of the University of Wisconsin–Madison.

The University of Wisconsin Press
1930 Monroe Street
Madison, Wisconsin 53711

www.wisc.edu/wisconsinpress/

3 Henrietta Street
London WC2E 8LU, England

Library of Congress Cataloging-in-Publication Data
Daly, Mary E.
The slow failure : population decline and
independent Ireland, 1922–1973 / Mary E. Daly.
p.   cm. — (History of Ireland and the Irish diaspora)
Includes bibliographical references and index.
ISBN 0-299-21290-4 (cloth: alk. paper)
1. Ireland — Population — History — 20th century.
2. Ireland — Emigration and immigration — History — 20th century.
3. Ireland — History — 1922–
I. Title.   II. Series.
HB3589.D35 2006
304.6′2′094170904 — dc22   2005005458

To my nieces and nephews

EDOUARD
SARA
MATTHEW
IAN
EMILY
LAURA

Contents

Tables

Acknowledgments

This book could not have been written without the assistance of many librarians and archivists. I would like to express my thanks to the staff of the National Archives, especially to Tom Quinlan and Catríona Crowe for tracking down elusive files; to Bernard Meehan and Stuart Ó Seanóir in the Manuscripts Room at Trinity College Dublin who listed sections of the Arnold Marsh Papers so that I could have access to them; to David Sheehy in the Dublin Diocesan Archives for his expertise and good company over lunch; to Seamus Helferty and the staff in the University College Dublin Archives for providing a peaceful retreat in a busy campus; and to another oasis on the UCD campus, the archives of the Department of Irish Folklore. My debt to Tony Eklof, Anne Cooney, and the staff in the Official Publications section of UCD Library for continuing to provide the most user-friendly environment in a large library cannot be overstated. Philip Hannan facilitated my access to the Fianna Fáil

Archives (now in UCD); Gary Ansbro of the Department of Foreign Affairs opened the door to records in the consular section of the Department of Foreign Affairs. My thanks, too, to Siobhán Fitzpatrick, Bernie Cunningham, and Petra Schnabel in the Library of the Royal Irish Academy. Gerry Hughes of the Economic and Social Research Institute gave me a copy of his unpublished estimates for net emigration; David Doyle, a colleague in the School of History and Archives, answered numerous queries and directed me toward several valuable sources; my thanks also to Jim Donnelly, Trevor Parkhill, Kevin O'Rourke, Michael Laffan, Michael Kennedy, Conor Ward, Susannah Riordan, and Cormac Ó Gráda.

This book gained enormously from my association with an outstanding group of graduate students and postdoctoral scholars: Marie Coleman, Catherine Cox, Caitríona Clear, Maurice Curtis, Mark Duncan, Lindsey Earner-Byrne, Gerry Fee, Tom Feeney, Diarmaid Ferriter, Patricia Harkin, William Murphy, Margaret Ó hÓgartaigh, and Paul Rouse. Two other graduate students, Rob Somerville-Woodward and Aideen Foley, helped with research on Irish provincial newspapers.

The initial research for this project was carried out during a one-year President's Fellowship awarded by University College Dublin, which was supplemented by a semester's leave granted by the Combined Departments of History (now the School of History and Archives).

I can never adequately express my gratitude to the most important people in my life: P. J., Paul, Elizabeth, Nicholas, and Alice.

The book is dedicated to six young people whose lives epitomize a new phase in Irish demography: Edouard and Sara Crowley, of French Irish parentage, live in Paris; Mathew Crowley lives in Brussels with his Irish parents; and Ian, Emily, and Laura Crowley, of Scottish and Irish parentage, are growing up in Dublin.

Abbreviations

D Ag	Department of Agriculture Files
DDA	Dublin Diocesan Archives
DE	Department of the Environment
DFA	Department of Foreign Affairs
DIC	Department of Industry and Commerce
DLGPH	Department of Local Government and Public Health
DT	Department of an Taoiseach
EEC	European Economic Community
ERI	Economic Research Institute
ESRI	Economic and Social Research Institute
EU	European Union
IHS	*Irish Historical Studies*
JSSISI	*Journal of the Statistical and Social Inquiry Society of Ireland*
MP	Member of Parliament
NAEW	National Archives of England and Wales

NAI   National Archives of Ireland
NIEC   National Industrial and Economic Council
OECD   Organization for Economic Cooperation and Development
OEEC   Organization for European Economic Cooperation
PDDE   Published Debates Dáil Éireann
PDSE   Published Debates Seanad Éireann
TCD   Trinity College Dublin, Manuscripts Room
TD   Teachta Dála
UCD   University College Dublin
UCDA   University College Dublin Archives

The Slow Failure

1

The Pathology of Irish Demographic History

In 2004 the population of the Republic of Ireland was in excess of four million for the first time since 1871.[1] The population of the island of Ireland is now at approximately the same figure as in the mid-1860s. Ireland[2] is the only country in the developed world whose population is below the level of the mid-nineteenth century and the only country where reports on the census returns draw comparisons with figures from more than a century ago.[3]

However, the current rate of population growth in Ireland, north and south, is significantly greater than elsewhere in Europe, and the average age of the population is well below that of the European Union. Between 1996 and 2002 the population of Ireland rose by 4 percent to 3,917,336; in 2001 the population of Northern Ireland was 1,685,267, an increase of 5 percent since 1995.[4] Over the past ten years the population of every Irish county has increased; in some counties, such as Leitrim, this was the first recorded increase in the population since the famine. Annual immigration averaged 25,500 during the years 1996–2002; a record 66,900 immigrated in 2000. Of the estimated 50,000 who immigrated in 2003, only one-third are returning immigrants; for the first time in almost three hundred years, a sizeable number of foreigners are settling in Ireland.[5]

The current picture of a rising population and substantial net immigration is a direct consequence of Ireland's economic prosperity. Between 1851 and 1961, every census recorded a fall in the population in the area that constitutes the Republic of Ireland (with the exception of the years 1946–51, when the population rose by 5,000). By 1961 the population was 10 percent below the 1911 figure, and probably lower than in 1800.[6] The long-term decline in population ended in the 1960s, and since then every census with the exception of 1986 has shown a rise in population.[7]

Liam Kennedy, writing in 1994, noted that "Irish population history is very different from that of other western societies, and therein lies its fascination."[8] The distinctive features of Ireland's population history include not only the long-term population decline but also emigration persisting over many decades, a low rate of marriage and late age of marriage, high marital fertility, and a very late transition to smaller families. Large families, few job opportunities for teenagers and women, and the high rate of emigration among young adults resulted in a high dependency ratio that reduced Irish living standards.[9]

Although no other European country experienced a catastrophe of the order of the great famine, other countries and regions in Europe did experience many of the same aspects of the late-nineteenth-century Irish population story—heavy emigration, late marriages, a high rate of permanent celibacy, and a declining rural population. But until recently, very few accounts of Irish emigration have noted, for example, that Britain was also a country of emigrants or that Germany, the Scandinavian countries, and Italy experienced a significant volume of emigration at some stage during the nineteenth century.[10] In the preface to his 1997 book, *The Vanishing Irish*, which deals with population change in rural Ireland from 1850 to 1914, Tim Guinnane remarked that "some aspects of Irish depopulation were unusual but . . . the basic forces leading to depopulation were similar to those at work all across Europe in the late nineteenth century."[11]

Guinnane pointed out that by the late nineteenth century some areas in Portugal, Austria, and Germany had celibacy rates that were comparable to, or even higher than, Ireland's. In 1911 marital fertility in parts of Bavaria was comparable to the level in Ireland, and there was substantial rural depopulation in New England, Scotland, and England.[12] Refuting the crude argument that Catholicism deterred men and women from marrying, Guinnane noted the high marriage rate in Quebec, a strongly Catholic province. It is now increasingly recognized that the Irish were not alone in resorting to sexual abstinence and celibacy in order to control fertility.[13] The peculiarity of Ireland's population history has undoubtedly been overstated, but in making this point, it is important not to go to the other extreme of denying what *was* unique.

Ireland's demographic profile is no longer exceptional. With a net reproduction rate below replacement level, Ireland now conforms to the European pattern of one- or two-child (or childless) families. The marriage rate is five per thousand, which is lower than it was during the 1940s and 1950s when the lack of marriages was a matter of great concern, but many of today's single adults are in long-term sexual relationships, which was not the case in the 1950s. In the Irish Republic the proportion of married women working outside the home has risen steadily during the past twenty years, although it remains below the European Union (EU) average. Only one male worker in ten now earns a living in farming, compared with 57 percent in 1926 and 43 percent in 1961, and immigration has replaced emigration as a cause of concern. The population is aging, but more slowly than in other European countries.

Accounting for Population Decline, 1851–1922: Irish Exceptionalism

The most unique feature in Ireland's population history is the long, drawn-out decline in population. Ireland was the only European country in modern times to experience a century or more of static or declining population.[14] This is a fundamentally political observation, because if Ireland were to be regarded as a region of the British Isles, rather than a separate nation, its demographic history would appear

less remarkable. By the late nineteenth century, a substantial migration from the countryside to the city meant that many regions in Europe were experiencing a decline in the rural population. In Ireland
most of the migration from the countryside to the city took the form
of a movement from rural Ireland to British and American cities.[15]
National statistics provide one mechanism for defining a nation.[16] In
1888 Thomas Grimshaw, the Irish registrar general, stated that "national statistics, to be of any value must be comparable with the nation itself, that is, the people."[17] Although Ireland was officially a part
of the United Kingdom until 1922, from 1841 the population census
offered one of the most obvious means of measuring progress or re-
gression. The census, together with the annual agricultural statistics,
provided the primary statistical index of national well-being until
the early twentieth century, when the newly established Department
of Agriculture and Technical Instruction began to compile data on
imports and exports.

The widely held impression that the Irish population continued
to decline for a century after the famine is essentially a partitionist
image, since the population of the island of Ireland rose between
1926 and 1951; indeed, the six counties that constituted the Northern
Ireland state after 1922 recorded a population increase in every census after 1891. But there is no evidence that politicians or civil servants in Dublin ever considered the more favorable demographic
outcome in Northern Ireland and the factors that might have
brought it about (principally a more urbanized and industrialized
economy).[18] The government of Northern Ireland was much more
conscious of the contrasting fortunes of the two Irelands.[19] The report on the 1926 Northern Ireland census noted that the population
had increased since 1891 and that the rate of increase accelerated
between 1911 and 1926 despite numerous casualties during the 1914–
18 war. It also remarked on the "not inconsiderable" migration from
the Irish Free State to Northern Ireland.[20] The 1951 Northern Ireland
census pointed out that the rate of population growth between 1911
and 1951 was greater than in Scotland or Wales, and it highlighted the
disparity in performance between both parts of Ireland to the extent
of noting that while the population of the twenty-six counties had
increased between 1821 and 1841, the decline that set in after that date

lasted until 1946. While the population trends in Northern Ireland were undoubtedly healthier than in independent Ireland, it is also the case that the exodus from rural areas—whether to cities in Northern Ireland or to Britain—attracted much less concern than in the Irish Republic, and the government of Northern Ireland was willing to assist emigration to Canada and Australia, reflecting the different political significance that was attached to emigration and rural decline.[21]

In the years between the great famine and the foundation of the Irish state, nationalist Ireland placed the responsibility for Ireland's population decline firmly at Britain's door. Nationalist interpretations of population decline contained both economic and noneconomic elements, and the two were often combined. Kerby Miller, a leading historian of Irish emigration to the United States, has written at length about the Irish tendency to view emigration "as forced exile," with emigrants as "unwilling and tragic political exiles."[22] According to Miller, even before the famine Irish nationalist leaders had begun to recast the traditional motifs of political exile—such as the Flight of the Earls and the Wild Geese—to include mass emigration. Furthermore, they had "conceptualized an ideal Irish society from which emigration was unnecessary and inappropriate."[23]

Another variant of this argument saw emigration, together with the famine, as part of the long-standing British conspiracy against the Irish race, a mechanism for subduing or killing Irish nationalism and finally conquering Ireland. According to Irish nationalist M.P., William O'Neill Daunt,

> In the days of Elizabeth and Cromwell there were sanguinary raids against the people, and troops were employed in destroying the green corn and carrying off the cattle in order to starve out the Irish race. The people perished because their means of support were destroyed or abstracted. And the people of our own time perish or emigrate precisely because their means of support are taken away from them—not, indeed, by the coarse, rude methods of a former age, but by the equally effectual methods devised by modern statesmanship. The Union, with its consequent drain of Irish wealth in absentee taxes and absentee rental, and its destruction of the nascent manufacturing industries of Ireland by irresistible British competition,

achieves the thinning out of our race which was formerly wrought by the sword. It deprives Ireland of the means of supporting the Irish; and it thus effectively replaces the murderous policy of Elizabeth and Cromwell. The work once performed by military violence is now accomplished by an economic process, and under legal, peaceful, and constitutional forms.[24]

This conspiracy theory fitted neatly with the nationalist interpretation of Irish economic history: that Britain's policy of free trade was designed to wipe out Irish industry and transform agriculture from labor-intensive tillage farming to extensive cattle grazing, releasing surplus labor in order to provide the expanding British economy with a ready supply of cheap workers. As George O'Brien noted, "Such was the effect of the ruin of Irish industries on Ireland. It also had effects on Great Britain, both of a very different kind. Many of the operatives thrown out of employment in Ireland migrated to Great Britain in search of work, and their presence proved an important benefit to England at a period when she was in urgent need of cheap labour."[25]

An editorial in the *Cork Examiner* in 1891, quoted by the American historian Arnold Schrier, stated that the decrease in population "in a large measure, if not wholly, may be attributed with certainty to the want of manufactures, the absence of that business enterprise which a paternal Government would do much to foster . . . and to the oppressive laws which reduced tenant farmers to a condition of continuous and hopeless struggle, and the labourers to a permanent and degrading destitution. . . . And we are convinced that the beneficial influence of Irish self-government will in no direction be more conspicuous than in the cessation of the fearful drain on the population of the country, which has been doing its deadly work for the past half-century."[26] Some members of the first Dáil, too, were of the opinion that the decline in population should be cited to justify Ireland's claim to self-government:

An official document from the Dáil, contrasting Ireland, Czecho Slovaks and Poland might be used, showing how while under Austrian and Russian rule these two countries increased in population and wealth. This not to excuse Austrian or Russian rule in these two countries but to make it clear to the world that the case of Ireland against England surpasses by far the case of any other country in Europe, against foreign domination. Several men might perhaps be needed to draw this up, but a reliable statistician is essential. . . . In any discussion regarding Ulster, it should be always pointed out that prosperity is fictitious. Show the continued decline of her population since 1845 especially in the Protestant counties year by year. Antrim, Down, Derry and Armagh, decline every year. See Census and Registrar General's figures. Contrast the decline in these counties with the *increase* in the others which are industrial.[27]

When Dáil Éireann applied to the Paris Peace Conference for recognition as a sovereign independent state, one of the justifications given in the supporting memorandum was the "atrocious and intolerable results in Ireland" of English rule, including "a depopulation unexampled in any other country, howsoever badly governed." There was a litany of other economic woes as well, including the destruction of Irish industry, overtaxation, the failure to develop Ireland's natural resources, and the drain of capital from the country.[28]

References to overtaxation and the destruction of Irish industry implied that emigration was caused by factors that were specific to Ireland. Thus the obvious remedy for a falling population was self-government, regardless of whether the protagonist favored radical economic policies or a more moderate approach. For the Home Rule leader Charles Stewart Parnell, the solution to emigration was to resettle people from the west on the larger holdings and more fertile eastern land, to develop the waste lands of rural Ireland, and to exploit the country's industrial resources.[29] Most nationalists believed, as Parnell did, that Irish economic development should be based on natural resources (which were believed to be plentiful) and intensively worked, small family farms This image was constructed from several sources, including Sir Robert Kane's *The Industrial Resources of Ireland* (1844) and romantic memories of prefamine Ireland, with its spade cultivation based on the potato. The evidence to support this economic model was rather flawed: there was a tendency to exaggerate the wealth and the economic potential of Irish indigenous resources, and unreal expectations were fuelled by the belief that Britain had retarded the development of Irish resources.[30] The conviction that Ireland's manifest destiny was to be a country of small farmers busily engaged in cultivation presumed that high rents and extortionist landlords were the major cause of rural poverty. This analysis, however, failed to take account of the difficulties in trying to provide a decent livelihood on the small farms and poor soil that characterized a substantial proportion of the Irish countryside.

Nationalist Ireland favored explanations and solutions for emigration and population decline that were politically determined and specific to Ireland. In contrast, the census commissioners, economists, statisticians, or quasi economists associated with the Irish administration were more likely to accept the primacy of economic forces and to assume that labor would migrate from agricultural Ireland to manufacturing areas in Britain. They were also more likely to suggest that emigration and population decline might actually be a good thing because it brought about a higher standard of living. The report on the 1841 census noted that the rate of increase in the population appeared to have slowed down considerably and that emigration had "operated to a very great extent." The report went on to state that "Ireland is an agricultural country, and devoid of the means of providing employment for its rapidly growing population equally profitable with that afforded by manufacturing countries. A valuable outlet for its excessive numbers is therefore to be found in the manufactories of England and Scotland."[31]

By 1871 this message was being argued with even greater force:

> The circumstances of the population, in respect of means of livelihood, which obtained for Ireland between 1841 and 1851, may be regarded as wholly at an end, through the conjoint action of the potato failure, the repeal of the corn laws, the emigration movement, and the consequent reduction of the population. So far from the working of these agencies having been spent in 1861, they are in progress, although in gradually slackening progress, still. A period must be reached in course of time, when Ireland in the absence of disturbing causes beyond human calculation, will have a normal industrial prosperity, a normal increase in population, and a normal check upon that increase by a more or less regulated emigration. That period, however, does not seem to be determinable by the most far-reaching conjecture.[32]

In 1848, with the famine as yet unabated, the economist W. N. Hancock anticipated the modern argument that emigration has brought about a substantial convergence between Irish wage rates and those in Britain and the United States when he predicted that emigration would bring about an increase in wages for those who remained in Ireland.[33] During the remainder of the nineteenth century, the members of the Statistical and Social Inquiry Society of Ireland (who tended to be drawn from the ranks of senior civil servants, lawyers, and academics), sat through numerous papers charting improvements in housing, literacy, or per capita savings in banks and post offices, all seen as indicators that the Irish economy was improving. The presidential address to the society in 1888 by Thomas Grimshaw, the registrar-general, suggested that "want of sufficient emigration before the Irish crisis [he was referring to the famine] had been the cause of great, rapid and unexampled decay which has only been stayed by emigration." The decline in population since the famine, according to Grimshaw, reflected the country's dependence on agriculture and the lack of alternative employment. He conceded that some people might regard a declining population as evidence of national decay, but he was of the opinion that the Irish economy had made remarkable advances since the famine.[34] Such an analysis, expounded with greater or less rigor (often less) recurs in many presidential addresses to the society up to 1920. This theme was particularly favored by men like Grimshaw, who occupied senior positions in the Irish administration, and it would not be unrealistic to regard this as the official line.

A more pessimistic point of view can also be found within the ranks of the Statistical and Social Inquiry Society, most graphically from Denis Caulfield Heron, professor of political economy and jurisprudence at Queen's University Belfast and member of Parliament (MP) for county Tipperary from 1870 to 1874. In 1862 Heron asserted that "a progressive decrease in population and in the production of wealth is a sign that something is not right in the legal and social conditions of a country." He also claimed that emigration had removed "the best educated, the most energetic of the peasantry,"[35] an argument that was to crop up in discussions of emigration for many years to come (most recently during the 1980s). In 1902 the president of the Society, Irish Land Commissioner, W. F. Bailey, concluded that "there may have been an excessive population in Ireland in 1844 while the population at the present day may be much less than the country is capable of supporting in comfort."[36]

Bailey's comments reflect a growing concern about the continuing decline in population, which may have been influenced by the plethora of literature and commentary on population decline in France and Britain's new-found worries about the quality of its population.[37] There was also an increasing resort to more complex explanations for Ireland's population crisis. According to the French writer L. Paul-Dubois, whose 1908 book *Contemporary Ireland* carried a foreword by Tom Kettle (which would appear to give it the imprimatur of the Irish Parliamentary Party), the cause of emigration was a lack of national industry, lack of trade, a general destitution that was aggravated by heavy taxation, and "the narrowness of life and the lack of openings. 'You cannot rise in Ireland,' that is the dominant feeling. An equal amount of work does not produce equal results. In order to succeed you must begin by leaving the country. 'To get up you must get out.'" These difficulties stemmed from Ireland's political condition: "misgovernment and political oppression are the keystone of the situation." But Paul-Dubois's explanations also contained a strong cultural dimension. He suggested that "a man must have risen a degree or two above his neighbour before he feels a desire to emigrate. He must have emerged from the doubt and despair around him and have become imbued with the wish to rise and to try his fortune."[38]

Almost all of the nationalist explanations for Ireland's declining population contain a cultural element, as do some of the more "unionist" interpretations. The journalist and Catholic Irish Irelander D. P. Moran, for example, was of the opinion that the restoration of the Irish language would curb emigration. By creating a cultural cordon sanitaire between Ireland and the rest of the world, the Irish people might be prevented from becoming aware of foreign living standards. Moran tended to blame emigration on psychological factors, such as a lack of self-reliance.[39] Lack of self-reliance could obviously be regarded as a consequence of Ireland's lack of independence. Similarly Paul-Dubois's reference to the dearth of opportunities for self-advancement in Ireland could be explained, at least in part, by the fact that a disproportionate number of senior positions in public administration and business were held by Englishmen and Scotsmen or by representatives of the Anglo-Irish gentry.[40]

Nationalists also tended to query the material benefits of emigration. John Francis Maguire described an emigrant household where the wife was "the daughter of a decent farmer in West Carbery, county Cork," and her husband, a former tenant in the area. They had emigrated in search of "a future of comfort and independence," only to find themselves relying on "the precarious employment of a day-labourer" and the grim living conditions of a New York tenement.[41] According to Patrick Maume, Sinn Féin founder Arthur Griffith equated emigration with suicide. "He saw emigrants—as did many nationalists—as rushing to moral and economic ruin, deceived by fallacious reports of prosperity overseas." Griffith believed that an Irish government should ban emigration.[42]

Irish nationalists paid little attention to the decline in the marriage and birth rates before 1920; their main concern was with emigration. Yet one of the most striking features of postfamine population was a more than doubling of the proportion of men and women who never married, from 10 percent of men and 12 percent of women in 1841 to 27 and 25 percent, respectively, by 1911. Insofar as the reasons for the decline in the marriage rate were considered, they were believed to be similar to those responsible for emigration, in other words, falling employment in rural Ireland, an inadequate number of smallholdings, failure to exploit waste land, lack of investment, and so forth. However, Frenchman Paul-Dubois wrote about "a weak and exhausted race . . . an abnormal and extreme reduction in the rate of births and marriages . . . [and] the marked increase of mental disease during the last fifty years," which was, he claimed, particularly pronounced in the areas that were dominated by cattle-grazing latifundia.[43] If we omit the reference to cattle-grazing latifundia, Paul-Dubois's statement seems to relate more to concerns about falling fertility in fin de siècle France than to Ireland. References to mental disease, which was often seen as a consequence of emigration—in later years it was more likely to be associated with celibacy—became common around the turn of the century,[44] as did allegations that emigration was creaming off the elite of the Irish population; these obviously reflect the growing concern with eugenics.[45]

These statements echo the cultural pessimism that was characteristic around the turn of the century, but they can also be regarded as linear descendants of the descriptions given by foreigners who visited Ireland in earlier centuries, which tended to highlight the primitive, uncivilized aspects of Irish life.[46] The anecdotal evidence given by many witnesses to the Poor Law commission is the most specific instance where these views influenced the interpretation of Irish demography. Many witnesses suggested that teenage marriages and pregnancies were extremely common in Ireland during the 1830s, but the 1841 census refutes this.[47] K. H. Connell used the evidence given to the Poor Law commission to present a picture of a prefamine peasantry who were listless and lacking in self-respect. He suggested that the pattern of early and frequent marriages, which he regarded as a characteristic of prefamine Ireland, was the outcome of a peculiar combination of fatalism and calculation.[48] For Horace Plunkett, the son of an Anglo-Irish landlord and the first vice-president of the Department of Agriculture and Technical Instruction, emigration was neither inevitable nor economically rational, and it could not be explained by the Act of Union. He interpreted the propensity to emigrate as evidence of a failing in the Irish national character, which resulted in a "lack of appreciation of the comforts of home"—a phrase that anticipates de Valera's strictures against emigration during the 1950s. Plunkett accounts for this attitude, for which he provides no supporting evidence, by noting that the Irish are not long removed from a nomadic life and, furthermore, that the penal laws acted "as a disintegrant of the home and the family"[49]—an argument that bears an uncanny similarity to statements about the impact of slavery on the family life of the Black population of the United States.

Plunkett's assertion is at variance with the emigrant letters cited by Kerby Miller and David Fitzpatrick, which provide voluminous evidence of nostalgia for home. Indeed Miller emphasizes, perhaps to excess, the ties binding Irish Catholic emigrants—especially Irish male Catholic emigrants—to home, and he suggests that these ties made it more difficult for them to adjust to life in the United States.[50] Moreover, one of the key features of Irish emigration is the role of the family: far from reflecting the disintegration of family life, in many instances the decision to emigrate should be seen as part of a family survival strategy.[51]

Plunkett's most famous contribution to the analysis of Irish population concerns the influence of the Catholic clergy over the courtship and sex lives of the Irish people:

> In some parishes the Sunday cyclist will observe the strange phenomenon of a normally light-hearted peasantry marshalled in male and female groups along the road, eyeing one another in dull wonderment across the forbidden space through the long summer day. No Irish men are more sincerely desirous of staying the tide of emigration than the Roman Catholic clergy, and while, wisely as I think, they do not dream of a wealthy Ireland, they earnestly work for the physical and material as well as the spiritual well-being of their flocks. And yet no man can get into the confidence of the emigrating classes without being told by them that the exodus is largely due to a feeling that the clergy are, no doubt from an excellent motive, taking innocent joy from the social side of the home life.[52]

This account shows scant knowledge of the mores of most rural communities at the beginning of the twentieth century. At the time, most young people, especially in rural areas, tended to socialize with their own sex. Plunkett sees the kill-joy attitude of the Catholic clergy as an encouragement to emigration. He believed that they exercised undue influence over Irish society; his initial criticism was prompted by the view that the Catholic church had failed to give sufficient support to the co-operative movement. He also claimed that Catholicism had retarded Irish economic development, hence the link between the Catholic clergy, emigration, and his belief that emigration was explained by cultural factors.[53] While Plunkett has been widely cited, similar views can also be found in conservative Protestant newspapers during the late nineteenth century. Schrier notes that "the more extreme among them were so swayed by their religious intolerance that they saw in the emigration only a flight from the 'tyranny of priests' and the 'endless exactions' of the Catholic church."[54]

The turn of the century brought a flurry of books that discussed the excessive influence of the Catholic clergy over their flock.[55] Their publication reflected the ongoing battle for the hearts and minds of the Irish masses between representatives of the Anglo-Irish ascendancy—including Plunkett and some of his friends in the cooperative movement—who were unwilling to concede their long-standing positions of influence in Irish society, and the Catholic church, the organization that the Anglo-Irish regarded as the greatest threat to their continuing influence. Most of these works suggested that the mass of the Irish people were incapable of making up their own minds about politics or about marriage and emigration. A similar argument was made during the early decades of the nineteenth century to justify denying Catholics the right to vote or sit in Parliament, and many contemporary accounts of prefamine Ireland had suggested that the Catholic clergy were responsible for universal and early marriages.[56] When marriages became later and fewer, responsibility was again laid at their door.

Historians have tended to dismiss claims that the Catholic church was the driving force behind the rise in celibacy during the late nineteenth century, preferring K. H. Connell's argument that the church was simply reflecting the economic dictates of postfamine Ireland, and especially the farming class.[57] In fact there is little direct evidence to substantiate the view that the Catholic church was promoting a more puritanical lifestyle during the late nineteenth century, with the possible exception of the incident where a priest objected to the Gaelic League holding mixed classes.[58] Most of the quotations that are liberally trotted out by Connell and others relate to the years after 1920, when there is substantial evidence of the Catholic church's opposition to dances, courting couples at the cinema, and other forms of modern permissiveness. But there is a real danger in applying this argument to an earlier period unless it is supported by specific evidence. Connell uses material from the Irish Folklore Commission, but this cannot be dated precisely; all that can be said with certainty is that it was collected after 1935.[59] Yet even if Plunkett's assertion is questionable, it remains important, since he foreshadowed an important element in the later debate over population by drawing attention to cultural factors and, specifically, to the lack of a social life in rural Ireland.

Another motif that crops up in the discussion on emigration, and one that was much more favorable toward the Catholic church, was the concept of emigrants as missionaries and travelers. In 1897

Cardinal Gibbons, the Catholic archbishop of Baltimore, noted that the Irish race was "possessed beyond all others with the spirit of the world wanderer. The earliest utterances of their history bear witness that they were seafaring adventurous people; and since their conversion to Christianity there can be no doubt that this spirit has been heightened and consecrated by religious ardour for the propagation of Christianity. Willingly and unwillingly, wittingly and unwittingly, they have been a people of missionaries longer than any other race."[60] "Ireland's spiritual empire" was a theme much favored by Irish political leaders after 1922, since it implied that emigration brought substantial benefits to the nation by giving Ireland an international influence that was disproportionate to its small size. Yet it is probably significant that the above quotation comes from an American clergyman. Schrier noted that it proved difficult to find evidence of the views of the Catholic clergy on emigration. He suggests that while they "probably" regretted emigration, "for the most part they did not actively and openly oppose it."[61]

Irish Population after 1920: Continuity and Change

The remainder of this book is concerned with the debate over the population problems of independent Ireland from the 1920s until the early 1970s. Although the following chapters do not ignore trends in fertility, emigration, or marriages, the primary concern is at one remove from the statistical data.[62] My major interest is in how demographic trends were interpreted or misinterpreted. This is primarily a study of opinions—of the politics (widely defined) of Irish demography, the perceptions of Irish population and Irish society, the policies or lack of policies respecting population matters, and the motivations that lay behind them. Ultimately, it is a study of Irish mentalités and attitudes toward economic and social development. There are obvious continuities with the period from the famine until the 1920s, and some critical differences. The issues remained the same: emigration, rural decline, and few and late marriages, although the details varied. Many of the explanations and claims that were advanced in pre-independence Ireland were repeated in the years after 1922. The major difference concerns the role of the state and the Catholic church.

Before 1922 Irish nationalists could blame depopulation on government policies, knowing that the government in question was in London. Once Ireland became independent, it became more difficult to blame Britain for the failure to reverse the decline in the population. If responsibility rested with politicians, the responsible politicians were now Irish politicians. Moreover, given the widespread nationalist belief in Britain's responsibility for economic and population decline, there was a major onus on Irish governments to reverse these trends. The Catholic church and Catholic social teaching exercised a major influence on Irish opinion and government policies after independence—and they were especially important in matters relating to the family, marriage and fertility, emigration, and the relative merits of urban and rural society. After independence the Irish state aspired not simply to reversing the fall in population but also to reversing the fall in the rural population and the decline in the numbers living on the land. The state also wished for more and earlier marriages, but without any diminution in the large size of Irish families. By the late 1950s the continuing, indeed escalating, rate of population decline seemed tantamount to terminal decline, the "slow failure"[63] of the independent Irish state.

In chapter 2, I argue that the more ambitious objective of reversing rural depopulation ultimately served to make the goal of reversing the decline in the total population unattainable; the most effective means of securing a stable or rising population was to give Irishmen and women the choice of moving from the land to settle in Irish cities and towns, rather than American and English cities and towns, but this option was commonly rejected as almost an equal evil to emigration. A similar argument applies in chapter 3, which examines Irish marriage and the family: the goal of reversing the decline in marriages was ultimately frustrated by large Irish families, which postponed the transfer of land to the next generation and forced many men and women to delay marriage in order to support aging parents or young siblings. Yet the possibility that smaller families might provide a solution to Ireland's marriage crisis, and might also reduce the need to emigrate, was not acknowledged. There were also fears that increased prosperity and a more urbanized society would bring about a fall in family size. With respect to marriage, fertility, and the urban-rural balance, nationalist ideology and Catholic social teaching combined to reinforce a belief that economic development would only worsen Ireland's population crisis.

Chapters 2 and 3 cover the period from the 1920s until the early 1960s; the next three chapters have a narrower chronological span. The major demographic issues of the 1920s and 1930s were the apparent fall in marriage and birthrates and rural decline; emigration did not become a critical issue for the government until the years of the Second World War,[64] when the Irish government was forced to decide whether to cooperate with Britain in smoothing wartime transfer of workers or uphold its principled opposition to emigration. Chapter 4 examines the government's response to emigration, up to and including the report of the Commission on Emigration. Appointed in 1948, the commission was the only systematic attempt by an Irish government to examine Irish population patterns. The report and the evidence that it assembled, cited throughout the book, are a mine of information about Ireland in the years immediately following the end of World War II. Yet when it reported in 1954, the commission was already out of date, because the annual rate of net emigration had begun to rise very sharply. The years 1954–61, when emigration rose to a level last experienced during the 1880s and appeared to threaten the very survival of the state, form the subject matter of chapter 5. The crisis of confidence of the late 1950s, which was precipitated by population decline and chronic economic difficulties, ultimately led to a major reform of Irish economic policies, and the 1960s are generally seen as inaugurating a new phase in Irish economic and demographic history. In chapter 6, I suggest that this is partly correct: the decade brought the reversal of emigration, an acceptance that industrial development was not incompatible with Irish society, and marked changes in marriage and fertility. But the near stagnation in total employment was an augury of the problems to come in subsequent years, and the traditional goal of maintaining the population on the land had been replaced by an equally difficult ideal: that industrial jobs should be scattered throughout the country and not concentrated in the major cities. In chapter 7 the focus shifts outside Ireland to the emigrants and how they were viewed and treated by the state and the church. Any discussion of emigrant welfare was seriously constrained by the relationship between church and state and by the primacy of moral issues, such as illegitimate births and church attendance. Successive Irish governments failed to provide assistance and support for Irish emigrants, although they were more than happy to use these networks to promote tourism or advance causes such as the antipartition campaign.

2

Saving Rural Ireland

1920–1960

In no country have the peasantry exhibited a stronger or more passionate attachment to the land than in that country from which such myriads have gone and are still going forth. And yet the strange fact, indeed the serious evil is that, notwithstanding the vast majority of those who emigrate from Ireland to America have been exclusively engaged in the cultivation of the soil—as farmer, farm-servants, or out-door labourers—so many of this class remain in cities and towns, for which they are not best suited.

John Francis Maguire, *The Irish in America*

Ireland is essentially an agricultural country. The ancient Irish established no cities: with fierce independence they clung to the land. At odds with this ancient tradition is the pronounced drift in recent decades into the towns and cities. Despite the repeated pleas of statesmen and prelates the young continue to flee incontinently from the farms, seeking an escape from its alleged monotony and boredom to the bright lights of the city.

Patrick Noonan, "Why Few Irish Marry"

Somewhat akin to emigration from her shores is the flight of her people from the land into the cities, especially Dublin. It is well known that it is the country districts which constitute the chief wellsprings of population. Cities are notorious for consuming their populations; unless constantly supplied with fresh recruits from the rural areas, they would decline and ultimately disappear.

John A. O'Brien, *The Vanishing Irish*

The overwhelming majority of the "vanishing Irish" vanished from the countryside, and for this reason most studies of the Irish population since the famine have concentrated on rural Ireland.[1] Yet most emigrants from Ireland settled in cities and towns in Britain and the United States, taking jobs in factories, on construction sites, or as service workers in hospitals, hotels, and private homes. [2] Irish emigrants have formed part of the vast outflow from the country to cities and towns, from farming to manufacturing and service employment, that has characterized the economies of the developed world for the past two hundred years. The main difference between Ireland and other countries is not the flight from the land but the fact that a majority of migrants from rural Ireland settled in foreign rather than Irish cities. In 1937 the economist James Meenan pointed out that the population of Northern Ireland was increasing, whereas the population of the Irish Free State was falling, because Northern Ireland was a more urban economy.[3] By the early 1950s it had been established that the men and women living in Irish cities and towns married at an earlier age than their country cousins. There were fewer bachelors in the cities, but a higher proportion of single women because of the imbalance between the sexes;[4] in 1946 there were 1,170 women per 1,000 men in Irish cities and towns. Although urban couples had smaller families, the urban birthrate was above the national average.

On this evidence it would appear that the most obvious means of reversing Ireland's falling population was to encourage the creation of more jobs in manufacturing and service industries, leading to a higher urban population. But the cultural nationalism that was a major force behind the movement for independence believed that Ireland's destiny was to be a rural, agrarian society. One of the directive principles of social policy in the 1937 Constitution, "intended for the guidance of the Oireachtas" and to be applied in the making of law, was "that there may be established on the land in economic security as many families as in the circumstances shall be practicable."[5] In 1954 the majority report of the Commission on Emigration expressed the opinion that the agricultural population could be maintained at its present level, and it did not rule out the possibility that it might rise.[6] If the urban population *had* to rise, the growth should be directed toward smaller towns and away from Dublin. Indeed, Dublin was often seen as contributing to rural depopulation. Other European countries have also lamented the decline in the rural population, especially since World War II—what Braudel described as "this great upheaval"[7]—but in no other country did it assume such national importance. Well into the 1960s, and indeed later, many Irish people passionately believed that it would be possible to reverse Ireland's chronic pattern of population decline if only the government and the Irish people were sufficiently committed to supporting the family farm and the associated rural lifestyle. Such wishful thinking implied that Ireland could defy the demographic and economic trends that applied in other developed countries. In the event, this was not so. Worse still, efforts to achieve the unrealizable objective of a stable or rising *rural* population made it more difficult to reverse the decline in population, and countless men and women may have been denied the choice to marry and raise a family in Ireland as a consequence of this misguided goal.

This chapter examines the views that were expressed about rural and urban Ireland in the period up to the 1960s and the extent to which the belief that Ireland's manifest destiny was to be a rural agrarian society influenced government policies. It also investigates the gulf between images of rural life and its reality and the extent to which underlying changes in Irish society—which were partly facilitated by measures designed to preserve rural Ireland—may have actually accelerated the drift from the countryside.

Ireland was by no means unique in its belief that the rural population had superior characteristics to those living in cities and large towns. This is also true of the United States. "La France profonde"—the true France—is not to be found in Paris but in some remote rural area. Even England, the cradle of the industrial revolution, has continued to attach enormous significance to the culture and traditions associated with the land and with rural life,[8] though many of these "traditions" may be relatively recent constructs. During the 1930s a British "back to the land" movement gained some support as a possible solution to mass unemployment.[9] Rural life was valorized and cities were correspondingly denigrated by the various right-wing governments that emerged in Europe during the 1920s and 1930s. In

1939 Fascist Italy introduced a law that prevented migrants from moving to a town with a population of more than 25,000, which was not repealed until 1961, although it had been widely ignored.[10] In this, as in many other instances, Irish attitudes were often a more liberal version of those found in right-wing Catholic states. The Christian Democrat parties that came to the fore in many western European countries after World War II continued to champion the values of rural society and small farmers, and their views were responsible for the commitment, given by the European Economic Community (EEC) to preserve the family farm, that resulted in the Common Agricultural Policy. In his speech formally tabling Ireland's application for EEC membership in Brussels in January 1962, Seán Lemass specifically mentioned the EEC's commitment to maintain the family farm.[11]

The belief that farming and the countryside were essential elements of Irishness was strengthened by the tendency to define Irishness with reference to Britain. Mathew Arnold claimed that the Celts were "undisciplinable, anarchical and turbulent of nature," the opposite to the Anglo-Saxons.[12] Many of the formative leaders of the Gaelic revival believed that Ireland was destined to be a rural peasant society, in contrast to an urban and industrial England. The identification of Ireland with the land was strengthened by images of a prefamine Ireland that supported over eight million people, the majority on the land, and by the central role played by the Land War in creating a cohesive movement for self-government. Conquest and colonization were associated with the confiscation of Irish land and the settlement of intruders from England and Scotland; correspondingly, the restoration of an independent Ireland was inextricably linked with restoring the land to native ownership. The fact that nineteenth-century industrial development and urban expansion were concentrated in the unionist stronghold of northeast Ulster reinforced the belief that nationalist Ireland was rural and agrarian.

Because the Gaeltacht—the area where Irish was spoken as an everyday language—was in the overwhelmingly rural west of Ireland, the language revival movement reinforced the linkage between Irishness and rural life, going so far as to suggest that the true Ireland lay west of the river Shannon. Most of the Irish language prose writings produced during the late nineteenth and early twentieth centuries described the lives of rural peasants or fishermen. According to Tom Garvin, the Irish nationalist elite at the beginning of the twentieth century was "non-agrarian and middle class, highly educated and socially mobile, but with very recent rural social origins." Consequently, they tended to view Dublin as "the symbol not only of the arrogant and unforgivably brilliant achievements of eighteenth-century Anglo-Ireland but also of the readiness of the native Irish, in their debased urban and proletarian condition, to accept Anglo-American vulgarity and corruption while ignoring the cultural riches of the Irish past and of rural society."[13] Daniel Corkery, the writer and professor of English at University College Cork, claimed that to reach "the Hidden Ireland of the Gaels" involved "leaving the cities and towns behind, [to] venture among the bogs and hills, far into the mountains even."[14] Corkery was writing about the eighteenth century, but this book, published in 1924, reflected the cultural sensibilities of the new state.

This image of an Irish nationalism, whose roots were in the countryside, was further enhanced during the years of the war of independence when the urban middle class—"all the bank clerks, Government officials and tennis players in the land whose spiritual home is in the Strand"[15]—were derided for their lack of republican spirit. Yet support for the war of independence does not reflect a simple urban/rural divide. In county Cork, a county that was particularly turbulent during the Anglo-Irish war, townsmen, particularly artisans, shop assistants and clerks, contributed heavily to the ranks of the Volunteers, while farmers and farmers' sons working on the land were underrepresented and farm laborers even more so. Nevertheless, according to Peter Hart, in Cork Volunteer circles "urban spinelessness and shoneenism was usually contrasted with the natural purity and patriotism of the common people of the countryside. . . . Town life was Anglicized and degraded, its nationalism 'shallow and rootless.'"[16] Many working-class Dubliners took part in the war of independence, but as this reality did not conform to national stereotypes, the role of Dublin and Cork city dwellers has tended to be played down in the simplistic version of the struggle for independence.

The Dark Side of City Life

One of the key factors in the valorization of Irish rural life was the tendency to highlight the grimmer aspects of life in the city. This may well have been a reaction to the fact that Ireland outside north-east Ulster fared badly during the industrial revolution. In the 1860s the editor of the *Cork Examiner,* John Francis Maguire, claimed that Irish emigrants in American cities were much more vulnerable to economic depression and to seasonal unemployment than they would have been had they settled on the land. He contrasted the "fresh, breezy plain or hill-side" that Irish emigrants had left with the "stifling heat of summer in a tenement house" in New York and the disease and wasted energy that typified New York tenement life.[17] This privileging of rural lifestyles drew heavily on a pessimistic version of the early industrial revolution that contrasted the stunted growth and wasted limbs of the industrial workers and their children with the sturdy offspring of peasants.[18] The reference books assembled by the Commission on Vocational Organisation (1939–43) included *The Village Labourer, The Town Labourer,* and *The Skilled Labourer* by the English writers John and Barbara Hammond,[19] prominent exponents of the pessimistic version of the industrial revolution. The Hammonds would have confirmed the commission's belief that "Agriculture . . . provides . . . that greatest asset of the State, a healthy and vigorous population."[20]

In 1954 the Irish-American clergyman John O'Brien claimed that Irish cities and towns had to be replenished regularly with healthy immigrants from the countryside if they were not to lose population. By the 1950s this was incorrect; indeed, even in Dublin—a singularly unhealthy city—the birthrate had consistently exceeded the death rate since the 1880s.[21] Nevertheless, until the late 1940s Dubliners had a lower life expectancy than the national average. In 1941 a baby boy born in Connacht, the most rural province, had a life expectancy almost ten years greater than a boy born in Dublin; for girls the gap was almost seven years.[22] Research into the incidence of tuberculosis confirmed the impression that cities were unhealthy places, because it revealed that Ireland's failure to match the decline in mortality from the disease that was underway in other European countries during the 1930s was due to increased migration to urban areas and the exposure of rural migrants to infection.[23] The higher incidence of infant and child mortality in Dublin was a consequence of poverty and overcrowded housing. Many Dublin mothers were apparently unable to breast-feed their babies because they were malnourished, although breast-feeding would have reduced the high incidence of gastroenteritis, a major cause of death.[24] By the 1940s the ill health and poor nutrition in Dublin working-class families had exposed the inadequacies of the Irish social services. The solution lay either in higher wages and more regular employment or, failing this, in more generous welfare services, for example, a national food policy similar to that operating in the United Kingdom during World War II or additional beds in children's hospitals and a network of child welfare clinics.[25] Yet there is no indication that the government Commission on Population (later known as the Commission on Emigration) established in 1948 showed any interest in the health and welfare of the Dublin working class. The 1951 crisis over the Mother and Child Scheme may well have deterred them from examining comparative urban and rural morbidity and mortality.

In the early 1940s the formidable Catholic archbishop of Dublin, John Charles McQuaid, established a network of social and welfare services throughout the city with financial assistance from Dublin Corporation, but on the whole the Catholic church preferred to denounce the evils of city life rather than alleviate its shortcomings.[26] The lack of interest shown by Catholic clergy in possible solutions for urban poverty contrasts with the steady stream of essays that they produced on the problems of rural Ireland and possible solutions.[27] Ireland's rural character was often cited as an argument against the need to expand state welfare services. In 1909 Dr. Denis Kelly, the bishop of Ross and one of the Irish representatives on the Royal Commission on the Poor Law, claimed that there was no need to introduce a system of unemployment insurance in Ireland for this reason.[28] Undue attention to the health and housing problems of the urban working class might generate pressures for more state intervention.

Catholic social teaching was of the opinion that rural life was manifestly superior to life in the city, and it held to this belief long after the adverse health risks had disappeared. Ultimately the Catholic case in

favor of rural life rested on moral and social arguments, not on physical well-being, although it was happy to cite the latter in support of
its stance. The Catholic church was highly critical of industrial capitalism; in his 1933 Lenten pastoral, Daniel Mageean, bishop of Down
and Connor, told his diocese that capitalism had banished Christianity from the heart of men.[29] The Catholic writer, G. K. Chesterton,
who was a staple feature of Irish secondary school readers during
the first half of the twentieth century, went so far as to assert that
capitalism had destroyed the family in the modern world.[30] Pope
Leo XIII suggested that the ideal socioeconomic system was based
around family farms or other family-run businesses. Reverend Edward Cahill, S.J., a regular correspondent of Eamon de Valera, wrote
in his 1932 book *The Framework of a Christian State* (the most comprehensive guide to Catholic social teaching published in Ireland)
that the rural population was "the real mainstay of the nation." Rural
families offered stability, because only in the country was the family
"attached to a particular locality and a hereditary home"; consequently, a rural population whose interests and traditions were "inti-
mately associated with the very soil of their country form[ed] the
core and strength of a nation." Cahill believed that true patriotism
was found in the rural population, and for this reason it was essential
to stop the decline in their numbers.[31]

In the years immediately after the end of World War II, the Vatican and the Catholic church throughout Europe became increasingly
concerned about rural depopulation. Pope Pius XII told an international conference on rural life in Rome in 1951 that "when the rural
population becomes weakened by the loss of its vital elements, the
soil itself loses its natural productivity and the whole social economy
of the nation becomes plunged into the gravest crisis." He blamed the
decline in the rural population on the predominant place that was
assigned to the interests of industrial capitalism.[32] The Irish embassy
to the Holy See forwarded a copy of this section of the pope's speech
to Dublin. The declaration of principles issued by the Union Internationale d'Études Sociales at Malines began by noting that "country
life makes a deep impression on a man's character and develops in
him precious moral and social values." Such values were fostered by
life on the farm, which accorded personal dignity and independence.

But the Malines declaration claimed that all sections of the rural community were privileged because of the long traditions and stability associated with rural life—the close contact with nature and the fact that life on the land was free from "the whims, the illusions, the artificial and feverish allurements of the cities." The Catholic church believed that because the family lived and worked together on the farm, it was easier to raise and educate children in the countryside, and consequently families were larger. City children were an economic liability, and urban culture promoted materialism and individualism, which were inherently damaging to family life.[33] In 1964 James Fergus, the bishop of Achonry, wrote to Seán Lemass on behalf of the Catholic bishops in the west to express their support for small farmers. The western bishops claimed that the people living on small western farms were "in a special way representative of the nation inasmuch as they have clung longer than people in other parts of the country to the traditions which are characteristic of the Irish way of life and of Irish culture including the native language. . . . [T]heir homes have always been nurseries of religious vocations, thus contributing to the building up of Ireland's spiritual empire."[34]

This statement might suggest that the Irish Catholic church had a rather low opinion of its city congregations. Yet there is no evidence that religious practice in Dublin, Cork, or Limerick was less fervent than in rural Ireland. Indeed a higher proportion of town and city dwellers enrolled in confraternities and voluntary religious organizations, such as the Society of Saint Vincent de Paul and the Legion of Mary. The American sociologist and Catholic priest Alexander Humphreys, S.J., carried out fieldwork among Dublin families between 1949 and 1951 to establish whether family solidarity—which he regarded as an important feature of Irish farming households—was damaged by urbanization. In the introduction to the book, based on his 1953 Harvard doctoral dissertation, he remarked that as the nation's capital and the one major metropolis in the state, Dublin was more exposed to outside ideas and values than any other part of Ireland. The most important of these outside influences was "rationalistic secularism which has been associated with the modernization of Dublin itself." The form of secularism that had impacted most strongly on Dublin was "the individualistic variety," which derived from nineteenth-century liberalism. Humphreys believed that these influences resulted in a decline in interfamilial solidarity and that the conflict between group interests (including family interests) and individualism was much more pronounced in Dublin than in other parts of Ireland.[35] Although Humphreys showed that Dublin families retained a strong commitment to Catholicism and to their family, these findings failed to dispel his concerns, because in his opinion "urbanisation has upset the internal balance of the nuclear family, lessened the scope of its traditional functions, weakened interfamilial solidarity and increased dependence on outside agencies," which "impaired the life of the primary group"—the family.[36] Humphreys claimed that even devout Catholics were unable to avoid the baleful effects of urban life.

The preferred solution of Catholic churchmen for the problems of urban life was to protest that Dublin was too large and urge that the population be kept in the countryside, perhaps even moved there. Industries should be brought to the country, or at least to small towns, so that factory workers could continue to live in the countryside, in privately owned homes with a few acres of land attached. If factory workers lived on the land, and the size of factories was contained, the church believed that it would be possible to "offset the danger of prolitarianisation."[37] Many political leaders concurred. In 1938 de Valera told Dáil Éireann that "I do believe that it will be a serious loss to this country if we are not able to stop the change from country life to city life or to check the tendency that there is to go from the country into the towns. Personally I believe that country life is far better. I believe that there are advantages pertaining to country life which are not realised by a number of people who leave the country and go to the towns. . . . [I]n the long run, country life is better for our people and a nation is a better and a strong nation if it is based on country life rather than on city life and city conditions."[38]

Settling the Maximum Numbers on the Land

National cultural values and Catholic social teaching combined to reinforce the message that the ideal Irish economy should be based around the family farm. The socioeconomic policy pursued during the first decade after independence was predicated on the assumption that the economy would be dominated by farming, with manufacturing and service industries catering to agriculture's needs. Although the 1920s brought little prosperity to the new state, the worldwide economic depression at the end of that decade was a source of consolation to those opposed to an urban industrial economy, because the sharp rise in unemployment seemed to emphasize both the insecure nature of industrial capitalism and the superior quality of rural life. When W. T. Cosgrave, the president of the executive council (head of government) made a live broadcast to the United States to mark Saint Patrick's Day 1931, he told his audience that Ireland had emerged relatively unscathed from the worldwide recession. His remarks attracted considerable interest in the United States, and not only from the Irish community—they were even reported in the *New York Times*.[39]

Ironically, Cosgrave's government lost office in 1932 in part because they were unable to offer a persuasive solution to the economic crisis at the time, a crisis that was aggravated by the collapse in emigration. Cosgrave's successor Eamon de Valera, the founder and leader of the Fianna Fáil party, was much more forthright in his rejection of the international capitalist economy. When Fianna Fáil was founded in 1926, its manifesto included a commitment to settle the maximum numbers on the land. When they took office in 1932 the party anticipated that a program of agricultural self-sufficiency would create additional jobs in farming and an expansion in the number of small farms. Tax concessions, in the form of agricultural rates relief, were given on farms employing male workers—including family members.[40] Industrial policy—also based around self-sufficiency—encouraged firms to locate outside the major cities. One prospective industrial developer was told that "the farther he went from Dublin, the greater attraction would he lend to his proposal," and the implicit ideal seems to have been one or perhaps two factories per town, but no more.[41] Programs of unemployment assistance, relief works, and subsidies for local authority and private housing also tended to favor rural households rather than city dwellers.[42]

The Irish Land Commission was the agency with the most explicit responsibility for promoting a rise in the rural population. Until the mid 1920s it was primarily concerned with completing the transfer of land ownership from landlord to the occupying tenant farmers. In 1903 another government agency established by the British authorities, the Congested Districts Board, began to purchase tracts of grazing land in western counties, subdividing them into small farms that were allocated to smallholders. But the quantity of land available was never sufficient to satisfy the demand, and frustration at the slow pace of land redistribution increased when the scheme was halted during the 1914–18 war. The first Dáil went to considerable efforts to placate land hunger—if only to diffuse the threat of social revolution. Land courts were established to determine priorities for land redistribution, and a National Land Bank financed the creation of thirty-five co-operative land societies, but they all collapsed within a few years.[43] In 1923 the government of the Irish Free State abolished the Congested Districts Board and transferred all responsibility for land reform to the Land Commission, which concentrated on acquiring land that could either be subdivided into smaller farms or used to augment neighboring holdings. During the 1930s the commission began to move farmers from congested areas in Kerry and Mayo in order to free up land for redivision.

Land distribution remained a matter of immense importance in rural Ireland. Many of the surviving letters from constituents in the papers of Limerick Teachta Dála (TD) Donnchadh Ó Briain relate to the Land Commission, and rural TDs tabled innumerable parliamentary questions on this topic.[44] In 1934, to diffuse backbench dissatisfaction at the slow pace of land redistribution, the Fianna Fáil parliamentary party instructed TDs to keep in close contact with local Land Commission inspectors and to inform them of the names of estates whose owners were willing to sell, the names of ranches that should be taken over, and the names of deserving tenants who should be assigned new holdings. The government also gave a commitment to create 4,000 additional farms.[45] But the Land Commission failed to meet this and every other target. Between 1931 and 1949 the number of agricultural holdings fell by more than 17,000. During these years the Land Commission took over 2,700 farms, which were subdivided into 12,000 holdings, each averaging twenty-one acres.[46] Frustration with the slow pace of land redistribution and the continuing decline in the rural population were factors behind the formation in 1938 of Clann na Talmhan, a party that drew support from small farmers, mainly in the west of Ireland.

Ireland—An Exception to the European-wide Decline in Agriculture?

By 1945 there were 9,000 fewer men engaged in farming than in 1939, despite the strong demand for rural workers during World War II when a program of compulsory tillage was introduced.[47] When the war ended, the future prospects for agriculture appeared bright. Food was scarce throughout Europe and the dollar shortage made it desirable to import food from other European producers rather than from the United States. The American government's Marshall Aid program for Ireland was predicated on the assumption that an expansion in agricultural output would provide the engine for economic growth.[48] In the event, European agriculture made a rapid recovery and food surpluses began to materialize by the early 1950s. The number of farmers and farm laborers in western Europe fell sharply during the 1950s as rising productivity reduced the real cost of agricultural produce on world markets and new methods of mass production destroyed traditional small farm enterprises such as pigs, poultry, and eggs. Irish farmers had to compete with producers from continental Europe and the Commonwealth for a declining share of the British market, the largest market in Europe for imported produce. But Britain's demand for imported produce was shrinking because Britain was encouraging its farmers to produce more food by offering them guaranteed prices that were substantially higher than those paid for imported produce. By the mid 1950s, store cattle was the only Irish agricultural commodity that could be exported without a subsidy; yet cattle raising provided very little employment and gave a decent livelihood only to farmers with large holdings.[49]

In the decade or so following the end of the Second World War, two conflicting interpretations were advanced for the decline in the Irish agricultural workforce. On the one hand, the Irish experience was presented as part of a European-wide process—no country was immune from the forces bringing about a fall in agricultural employment and certainly not a small country that exported a substantial share of agricultural output. In an addendum to the report of the Commission on Emigration, statisticians Roy Geary and M. D. McCarthy noted that since the end of World War II the numbers employed in agriculture in Ireland had been falling at a rate similar to other European countries.[50] Perhaps more surprisingly, in 1947 Eamon de Valera told Dáil Éireann that "the idea of talking about a flight from the land as if it were something extraordinary is wrong. It is happening in every country." Given the "ordinary fertility" of farming families (six children), he claimed that at least half would have to find jobs outside farming either in Irish factories or as emigrants.[51] But cautionary statements of this nature did not prevent many Irish people from believing that the decline in the farming population could be arrested if the government made a greater commitment to restructuring land holdings, investing in agriculture, and providing support for small farms, and de Valera was not consistent in his views.

This belief was buttressed by statistics showing that Ireland had one of the lowest ratios of agricultural workers to land in Europe, and that in the hundred years since the famine, the decline in the population outside Dublin city and county was almost uniform throughout Ireland, which suggested that it was not determined by the quality of the land.[52] Reverend Patrick Noonan, a Holy Ghost priest who spent most of his career in Africa and whose credentials for issuing pronouncements on Irish agriculture rested on the fact that he had been born on a farm in county Limerick, believed that rural Ireland could support three times the existing population in comfort and prosperity.[53] In 1946 Aodh de Blacam, a columnist in the *Irish Press*, urged the Fianna Fáil national executive, of which he was a member, to adopt an aggressive policy in defence of rural Ireland. He claimed that a doubling of the rural population was a realistic objective, and to bring this about, he demanded a ban on emigration (particularly the emigration of young women), a ban on women being employed in factories, and a ban on commercially sponsored programs on the state broadcasting company, Radio Éireann, because he believed that they were responsible "for the propagation of debased and commercialised food habits."[54] When the Fianna Fáil national executive deferred a decision on de Blacam's motion, he absented himself from future meetings, resigning some months later to join Clann na Poblachta. Founded in 1946, Clann na Poblachta offered a combination of republicanism and radical economic policies reminiscent of the early Fianna Fáil party. The party's economic policy drew heavily on the third minority report of the 1938 Banking Commission, written by P. J. O'Loghlen, which echoed nineteenth-century nationalists in calling for a state-funded program to create jobs by developing land and mineral resources, to be financed by printing bank notes backed by the same natural resources. A specific goal was to maximize the rural population.[55]

The list of demands that de Blacam presented to the Fianna Fáil national executive indicates that he believed cultural factors rather than economics were the primary cause of rural depopulation. De Blacam and other like-minded people believed that the failure to regenerate rural Ireland indicated a failure of national will. In 1931 veterinary surgeon Joseph Hanly emphasized that "we do not yet understand the intense necessity for vigorous association between nationality and material advancement; between the language and the Shannon scheme; between the grazing ranches and Tara and Clonmacnoise. Pagan and materialistic writers have, again and again, either by direct challenge or by implication, advanced the formula that national material success, without the spirit, is attainable and is supreme; that national economic success can be achieved without nationality or that nationality can be developed when economic prosperity is attained. Nationality, it is urged, will follow when material wants are satisfied."

Hanly believed that the solution must come from within, and that it must reflect national goals. Any attempt to follow the Danish model of agricultural development—which was often cited as a role model for Ireland—would be "as spiritless and nationally distractive as attempting to follow the American example in dancing, or the English example in games."[56] Such rhetoric drew on ideas advanced by the first Sinn Féin party and those that shared its philosophy,[57] and the emphasis on cultural and spiritual values tied in closely with Catholic social teaching.

Hanly and de Blacam were among the speakers at the 1946 Muintir na Tíre Rural Week, when the theme was rural depopulation.[58] A group of those who had attended the conference met subsequently at the Cistercian monastery at Mellifont, where they established a body known as the Mellifont Conference on Depopulation and Council of National Action. They claimed that the problem of rural depopulation was "not directly economic, or even basically economic at all in the broadest sense." Consequently, their action plan offered a combination of cultural protectionism and policies of Catholic social teaching. These included breaking the link between the Irish currency and sterling (so realizing Ireland's external assets, with the money being used to develop national resources);[59] taking measures to shield Ireland from modern consumerism; reinforcing parental authority; prohibiting foreigners from acquiring land; and adopting harsh attitudes toward the changing role of women in the modern world. Undercurrents of xenophobia, even racism, crop up in some statements from the most committed defenders of rural Ireland. Reverend Patrick Noonan claimed that "unless immediate and drastic measures are taken, the Irish race will either disappear altogether or continue to survive only as an enervated minority in a planted country." Ireland was "already . . . the land of promise" for "many adventurous and tax-fleeing foreigners who eagerly purchase the lands and property vacated by the emigrants. . . . Great numbers of aliens . . . whose love of Ireland is on a par with their love of God" had settled in Ireland, buying up some of the best land.[60]

Civil servants and academics came under attack for failing to espouse the cause of rural repopulation. Galway playwright M. J. Molloy claimed that "the Depopulation enthusiasts are organised, entrenched in the various Departments. . . . [E]very kind of argument is used, statistics are doctored," to support the case for depopulation.[61] Chris Curtin and Tony Varley, writing about Clann na Talmhan, have remarked that "the tendency was to set the downtrodden countryside against the privileges enjoyed by remote and uncaring urban-based political, administrative, business and other elites."[62] Yet Joe Lee claims that "the disproportionate influence of the urban milieu that has been detected in many new states did not prevail in Ireland, for the simple fact that Ireland was already a highly politicised society."[63]

Rural Ireland was well represented among the political elite, and many of the senior civil servants were from rural backgrounds.[64]

At the heart of this issue was a fundamental disagreement over the future of Irish agriculture. Should it concentrate on grassland enterprises, where Ireland had a comparative advantage, or on promoting tillage? The first was seen as a recipe for further depopulation and a policy that favored large farms, whereas tillage was seen as ensuring the survival of smaller farms and a means of creating additional rural jobs. However, the experience of the war years suggested otherwise, and tillage was not a realistic option for many small farms in western areas.[65] The 1945 committee on Post-Emergency Agriculture split six to two on this issue. The majority, four university professors, the head of the agricultural co-operative association, Henry Kennedy, and Robert Barton, chairman of the Agricultural Credit Company, saw no future in creating small tillage farms and suggested that the emphasis should be placed on raising the productivity of grassland enterprises and achieving a higher agricultural output. They believed that this would create additional jobs in manufacturing and service industries, but not directly in farming. The dissenters—Professor E. J. Sheehy of the faculty of agriculture at University College Dublin and J. Mahony, chief inspector of the Department of Agriculture—argued that the postwar agricultural policy should encourage small labor-intensive tillage farms.[66]

Opinions on future agricultural policy were closely linked to policy on land distribution. During the closing years of World War II, several leading members of de Valera's government, including Minister for Lands Seán Moylan, Seán T. O'Kelly, tánaiste and minister for Finance, and Minister for Industry and Commerce Seán Lemass, queried the benefits of land distribution, suggesting that the priority should be to raise agricultural production. But this suggestion was rejected by the land commissioners and by Minister for Agriculture James Ryan. De Valera publicly reaffirmed his government's commitment to the existing policy of the Land Commission, which prioritized the "social over the narrow economic aim."[67] However, in 1947 de Valera conceded that there was only a limited amount of land available for redistribution: "the cream of the land" had already been disposed of; he suggested that the remaining land available to the

Land Commission should be used to increase the size of uneconomic holdings, not to create additional holdings.[68] The evidence given to the Commission on Emigration in 1948 by senior officials in the Land Commission suggests that they did not believe that land redistribution offered a long-term solution to the problems facing rural Ireland. One official remarked that "the land that we acquire will never solve the problem."[69] Richard Dunphy attributes the slow pace of land redistribution to the stalling tactics of the Department of Finance, but while Finance tried to curb the Land Commission's budget, money was not the sole factor.[70]

The Land Commission was in an impossible position. To stem protests and provide local deputies with the maximum amount of political benefit, land that became available for redistribution was generally subdivided among the maximum possible number of qualifying farmers. As a result, the additional acreage made little impact on a farmer's standard of living. Moreover, land was allocated to efficient and inefficient farmers alike. Land redistribution was widely favored, provided that the property to be distributed belonged to an Anglo-Irish landlord or some outsider, who could safely be labeled a grazier, and not to an indolent or incompetent farmer or an elderly bachelor with no close relatives. Seán Lemass and the minister for Agriculture James Ryan clashed on this point in 1945, with Lemass advocating measures to wrest land from inept farmers and Ryan arguing that they should not be disturbed.[71] Ryan prevailed. But poor prices for agricultural produce and rising expectations among small farmers meant that holdings judged capable of supporting a family in the 1920s were too small by the 1950s. In 1948 the Galway playwright M. J. Molloy criticized the fact that the twenty-four acres that Patrick Hogan had regarded as the minimum viable size for a farm had risen to forty acres, which meant that fewer families could be settled. Molloy overstated his case; thirty-three acres (or twenty old Irish acres) was the figure set by the Land Commission as the minimum viable size for a farm,[72] but it should probably have been higher.

In 1949 the first inter-party government, which included both Clann na Talmhan and Clann na Poblachta, announced an ambitious scheme to drain and reclaim four million acres of land, which became known as the Land Project. The proposal recalled the recommendations in the minority report of the Banking Commission, though the money was provided by Marshall Aid, not by printing banknotes. The Land Project appears to have been seen as a more realistic way of increasing the supply of land, and until the 1970s, both the Inter-Party and Fianna Fáil governments continued to provide millions of pounds for this purpose.[73]

With limited prospects of providing more land, ministers for Agriculture tried to persuade farmers that it was possible to earn an adequate livelihood on twenty-five to thirty acres. James Dillon, minister for Agriculture in the inter-party governments of 1948–51 and 1951–54, believed that small farms could prosper if they concentrated on pigs and poultry—he threatened to drown England in eggs—but his vision ignored the reality that animal feeds were expensive in Ireland and that poultry and pigs were increasingly being raised in large factory-type units. Fianna Fáil ministers reiterated that self-sufficiency in wheat, sugar beets, and animal feed offered the best means of preserving rural jobs provided that tractors and other modern machinery could be kept at bay. In 1947 de Valera suggested that those who lived on the land should be given as much security as possible by giving Irish farmers the greatest share possible of the home market.[74] When Ireland first attended talks at the Organization for European Economic Cooperation (OEEC) in 1950 on the liberalization of trade in agricultural produce, J. J. Nagle, the secretary of the Department of Agriculture, expressed fears that freer trade in agriculture would spell an end to family farms.[75] In 1951, the incoming minister for Agriculture, Tom Walsh, stated that "complete mechanisation can only result in reduced rural employment and that would be a bad thing."[76] Other Fianna Fáil ministers, notably Frank Aiken, believed that horticulture had the potential to create and preserve jobs on small western farms, but these schemes proved to be a spectacular failure.[77]

James Dillon claimed that many of those who lamented the decline of rural Ireland were hypocrites: "I do not see the philosophers who weep over it, pull up their stumps and seize the opportunity of migrating to Mayo, Galway and Clare."[78] Very few of the men (and they were overwhelmingly men) who were most passionate about reversing the depopulation of rural Ireland earned their living from farming, nor did they have to struggle to find a livelihood for their children on the land. Patrick Moran, who gave extensive evidence to the Commission on Emigration, was the medical director of the psychiatric hospital in Ardee and an active member of Muintir na Tíre. Another witness, M. J. Molloy, earned his living writing plays for Dublin's Abbey Theatre. De Blacam was a journalist who made his home in Blackrock, a seaside village in county Louth. And the most extreme assertion of Ireland's rural essentialism, *The Vanishing Irish,* published by Notre Dame University Press, came from Irish America. The book's editor, Reverend John O'Brien, regarded the flight from the land as "somewhat akin to emigration."[79]

The majority report of the Commission on Emigration reflects the tensions that existed between economic forces and Irish desiderata, with regard to Irish agriculture. On the one hand, chapter 8 of the report states that "agricultural development was unlikely to cause any significant increase in the size of the population on the land."[80] Furthermore, the current volume of agricultural output could be produced by two-thirds of the existing agricultural workforce. Nevertheless, elsewhere the commission asserted that "higher output per head is not of itself sufficient to justify the adoption of extensive rather than intensive farming. . . . If the system of agriculture were based on an intensive use of land, we believe that not only could the agricultural population be maintained at its existing size but that it could be increased, though this would require a very large increase in the volume of agricultural output."[81] Where would the additional produce be sold? When the report of the commission was published in 1954, the only commodity that Irish farmers could export without a government subsidy was live cattle—the product that provided the lowest employment and output per acre.

These contradictory quotations indicate that the commission could not agree about future prospects for agricultural employment, and these disagreements are revealed more clearly in the addenda, reservations, and minority reports. An addendum by statisticians Roy Geary and M. D. McCarthy noted that the numbers engaged in farming would probably continue to decline. Economist James Meenan took a slightly different tack in a minority report when he emphasized that the importance of agriculture was not determined by the numbers employed in that sector. He suggested that the goal should not be to raise, or indeed to maintain, agricultural employment but rather to increase agricultural output and exports because this would enable the Irish economy to support a greater number of people in jobs outside farming, a line that was consistent with the 1945 majority report of the Committee on Post-Emergency Agriculture. A second minority report by the bishop of Cork, Dr. Cornelius Lucey, adopted a much more radical stance, recommending that all farms in excess of one hundred acres should be subdivided into holdings of twenty to thirty acres, which would be devoted to intensive dairy farming and to raising pigs and poultry. He claimed that the additional 40,000 holdings would bring about an increase of 150,000 in the agrarian population.[82]

The Commission on Emigration recommended the creation of a land utilization body that would determine how more effective use could be made of the nation's land, including possible measures for long-term leases.[83] No steps were taken to implement this proposal, although resolutions demanding that the Land Commission be more active in acquiring land for redistribution continued to figure both at Ardfheiseanna and in speeches in Dáil Éireann throughout the 1950s.[84] Yet proposals to set a maximum size for farms or to take land from nonproductive farmers flew in the face of Ireland's deeply cherished commitment to land ownership. Although the Catholic church wished to maintain a strong population of small farmers, any suggestion that the state might tamper with property rights was rebutted by references to church teaching on property ownership. Dr. Lucey was in favor of subdividing hundred-acre farms, but in 1951 he attacked a "Dublin-inspired slogan, Ownership or Trust"—a phrase used by an ex-minister (probably Noel Browne) who had suggested that land not being adequately used by the occupying farmer should be transferred to another farmer. Dr Lucey suggested that the appropriate reply "is unequivocally, ownership."[85] Reflecting the primacy of private property, which was enshrined in both Catholic social teaching and the 1937 Constitution, no steps were taken to ensure that farmers whose land was reclaimed through the Land Project, at considerable cost to the Exchequer, maintained the land in good condition. Indeed, the acreage improved under the Land Project was

probably less than the acreage that fell into disuse during the 1950s as
owners emigrated or abandoned all except the pretence of farming.
Such neglect was most pronounced on farms owned by elderly bachelors. Galway playwright M. J. Molloy regarded "the old bachelor" as
"the greatest enemy of Irish agriculture," because he generally abandoned all forms of intensive farming and ended up with a small
number of cattle grazing on neglected fields. [86]

Forestry, Fishing, and Tourism

If farming could not provide sufficient jobs to maintain the rural
population, one option was to develop other forms of rural employment. Although de Valera believed that at least half of the children
raised on farms would have to find jobs in industry, the most committed advocates of rural regeneration tended to be rather selective
about what occupations were acceptable. Forestry and fishing met
their approval, but tourism did not, because of fears that it would
generate artificial expectations about high wages and undermine the
much-admired peasant values of sturdy independence. Many people
shared C. S. (Todd) Andrews's reservations: "I could not rid my
mind of the notion that Ireland's role in tourism lay in the supply of
still more jarveys, gillies, waiters and chambermaids."[87]

Forestry had long been seen as offering a lifeline to rural Ireland,[88]
and it attracted renewed interest in the years following the end of
World War II, probably in reaction to wartime timber shortages. The
Commission on Emigration determined that 50,000 jobs could be
created by planting 1.25 million acres with trees, but most of these
jobs would not materialize for fifty years. Their estimates showed
that 4,000 jobs would be created after ten years and 8,000 jobs after
thirty years, but this took no account of jobs lost by diverting farm
land to forestry.[89] Nevertheless, the Department of the Taoiseach insisted on adding a sentence to the draft report of the Commission on
Emigration stating that "sufficient attention" had not been paid "to
the wider and more fundamental aspects of an adequate afforesta-
tion policy."[90] The commission investigated other panaceas for increasing rural employment, such as inland and sea fisheries and mineral exploration, but these would provide only a fraction of the jobs

that were disappearing in farming. By the late 1940s the progressive mechanization of turf harvesting by the state-owned company Bord na Móna meant that the number of seasonal and full-time turf workers was significantly lower than during the war years.

There was a reluctance to explore other possibilities for supplementing farm incomes. When the United Nations Food and Agricultural Organization announced plans for a 1957 conference on rural life, which would examine the possibilities of off-farm sources of income as a means of raising the living standards of rural households, neither the Department of Local Government nor the Department of Agriculture expressed any interest in attending.[91] Irish official policy has continued to play down the potential of supplementing agricultural incomes by other means; most of the money earmarked for rural development during the 1990s went to provide direct income supports for farmers.[92]

The "Flight of the Girls"

Jobs for women should have been the first priority in any plan for rural survival. In 1841, on the eve of the famine, women accounted for precisely 50 percent of the rural population, but by 1901 there were only 961 women for every 1,000 men. And by 1951 the ratio had fallen to 868, compared with 1,120 women for every 1,000 men in urban areas. The gender imbalance was even more pronounced among younger urban adults, with 1,165 women per 1,000 men among those aged twenty to twenty-nine. Although every farm needed at least one woman to manage the household and carry out some specific women's farm tasks such as poultry keeping, agriculture offered substantially fewer jobs for women, paid or unpaid, than for men. In 1926 there were only 1,248 female farm laborers but 71,774 assisting female relatives (a category that does not include farm wives) and 48,488 female farmers. By 1951 the number of female relatives assisting had fallen to 30,910. Egg money, a traditional source of discretionary income for farm women, was disappearing as large capital-intensive poultry units replaced the traditional methods of raising poultry.

Domestic service was the largest employer of women in Ireland until 1961. Until the late 1970s, Irish industrial policy discouraged industries that employed women, except in Gaeltacht areas where it had long been recognized that women made an essential contribution to family income, and here the emphasis was on craft industries such as knitting. Those who were most vocal about the decline of rural Ireland and the "flight of the girls" often claimed that providing jobs for women in tourism or manufacturing only made things worse. According to M. J. Molloy, by hiring young girls as waitresses the tourist industry "aggravated the worst feature of the whole situation which is the countryside's loss of virtually its entire stock of women of marriageable age."[93] Kerry housewife Marion Green was not alone in blaming the high wages paid for seasonal jobs in tourism for creating false expectations among young women. In the resort of Waterville, according to Green, "a girl of fifteen whom nobody would employ receives 25/-"[94]—roughly twice the going rate for domestic servants. In a similar vein, Aodh de Blacam suggested that far from helping to resolve population difficulties, employing women in rural factories "broke up the pattern of rural life and causes an increase in emigration. . . . I have seen a great number of factories which merely employ girls upon products of a parasitic kind, taking these girls from productive work on the land where they belong."[95] Despite innumerable laments over the shortage of women in rural Ireland, most recommendations for keeping them at home involved coercion: a ban on women working in factories or a ban on emigration. All government schemes to enhance rural incomes were directed toward men, rather than women, and despite repeated claims that lack of electricity and running water deterred women from remaining in rural Ireland, successive governments were slow to promote rural water schemes.[96]

Factory Jobs

The evidence collected by the Commission on Emigration in 1948 showed that where jobs were readily available in local towns, emigration from the surrounding area was significantly below the national average. In Kilkenny, a town with a range of manufacturing industries and numerous jobs in distributive trade and construction, jobs could be found "comparatively easily," and in many instances the wages were adequate to support a wife and two children, so emigration was mainly confined to agricultural laborers.[97] Midland towns such as Mountmellick, Portarlington, Portlaoise, and Newbridge were reported to be thriving thanks to the expansion of Bord na Móna and a number of successful local factories. In a travel goods factory in Portarlington employing eighty women and six men, adult women earned 50s. a week, four times the wage of a living-out domestic servant in Tullow, county Carlow, a town with no factory jobs for women.[98] Newbridge, county Kildare, was described as a flourishing and prosperous town, with 150 men and 100 women employed in the cutlery factory and 242 men and 23 women in the Irish Ropes plant. Intending emigrants were dismissed as "a poor type," who were fit only for casual employment. Female domestics were unobtainable because they had other options.[99] Most towns were conscious of the benefits of local industry. From the 1930s, communities sent regular deputations to Dublin to meet ministers and Dáil deputies or to lobby state organizations such as the Industrial Credit Company and the Industrial Development Authority. Several towns collected funds that were used to persuade an industrialist to locate to their area.[100] When J. P. Beddy, the chairman of the Commission on Emigration, who was also the chairman of the Industrial Development Authority, visited Swinford on behalf of the commission, he reported that the local parish priest "was undoubtedly inclined to paint the worst possible picture hoping to influence the deputation toward the proposal to have a factory established and on more than one occasion the labour exchange manager intervened and gave the impression that the picture was not so bad."[101]

But not all the evidence that the commission collected gave a favorable impression of factory employment. With a population of 17,000 in 1951, Drogheda was one of the success stories of Ireland's industrial drive during the 1920s and 1930s. When the Commission on Emigration visited the town, 1,640 men and 1,297 women were employed in local factories, and the nearby Butlin's holiday camp at Mosney provided hundreds of additional jobs. Yet far from rejoicing in this rare story of success, the commission suggested that the "over-developed" opportunities for jobs in nondomestic work had given rise to "awkward social problems," where women replaced men

as the main breadwinners for the household. They expressed particular concern about families where daughters, either individually or
collectively, earned more than their fathers. As an instance they cited
a household where the father, an unskilled laborer, earned £3 per
week and the combined weekly wages of his three daughters totalled
£11 5s. Commission members concluded that "parental authority was
fast becoming proportionate to the family budget." Not only was parental authority suffering in Drogheda, but "certain morally un-
pleasant results accrue from this"; unnamed sources had alleged to
them that up to half of all working-class marriages were "forced
marriages," in other words, the bride was already pregnant.[102]

Employment in manufacturing industries recovered during the
late 1940s as wartime shortage of materials and machine parts ended,
and provincial towns with local factories benefited accordingly. Despite this, the report of the Commission on Emigration was much
less optimistic about the potential for creating additional jobs in
manufacturing than in agriculture; it expressed the opinion that
manufacturing employment was unlikely to continue to expand as
rapidly in future as between 1946 and 1951. While conceding "that
there is appreciable scope for industrial expansion and development," it went on to examine the difficulties that Irish industry faced
in some detail, especially the poor market prospects.[103] This caution
may have been justified, given the undoubted shortcomings of protected Irish industries, but the report contains no comparable critical
examination of the market prospects for agriculture, and their dis-
missal of the potential for creating jobs in manufacturing can be
seen as further evidence of a deep-seated assumption that agriculture would and should remain the dominant sector in the Irish economy. In 1952 the government introduced a scheme of grant assistance to encourage firms—primarily, though not exclusively, foreign
firms—to establish plants in underdeveloped areas in the west of Ireland. By 1960, however, this program had only created 2,632 jobs[104]—
a drop in the ocean given that the numbers engaged in farming in the
province of Connacht fell by almost 35,000 between 1951 and 1961. In
the same period, employment in industry throughout the state fell
from 282,000 to 252,000.

Dublin: "A Cancerous Growth"

The Commission was much more forthcoming on the question of decentralizing industry. In their opinion, industry was unduly concentrated in Dublin and in the province of Leinster, and in the absence of a firm government policy of encouraging decentralization, "over-concentration in the Dublin area will continue, the town population outside the capital will remain static or will decline as in the past, and the general demographic pattern of the country as a whole will not be changed in the manner best suited to national interests."[105] Their views coincided with those of Eamon de Valera. In a (so-called) fireside address to the Muintir na Tíre summer school, de Valera noted that "for over a century the principal cities of Ireland have continued to grow to dimensions altogether out of proportion to the rural hinterlands that must sustain them and progressive urbanisation has created most difficult national problems for successive governments."[106]

Statistics do not support de Valera's assertion. In 1951 Finland, Norway, and Sweden were the only countries in Europe with a higher proportion of their population living in rural areas,[107] and between 1926 and 1951 the proportion of the population living in rural areas showed only a marginal decline, from 61.1 percent to 59.5 percent. Cork city did not outstrip its 1831 population until 1951, and many provincial towns such as Kells, Thurles, Athy, and Ennis had a smaller population in 1966 than on the eve of the famine. In his fireside address de Valera went on to express the hope that, with proper rural organization, the Irish countryside could accommodate people "who wish to live a full and happy life rather than endure an existence in the cramped confines of cities whether at home or overseas."[108] This statement ignored the reality that many rural households survived in conditions that were as cramped, as miserable, and as impoverished as city tenements, and that the disparity in material standards between country and town was increasingly being cited as an explanation for emigration and the dearth of rural marriages.[109]

Yet despite statements decrying the lack of modern amenities in the countryside, many Irish people continued to regard Irish and

British cities as fundamentally unhealthy places. One witness told
the Commission on Emigration that one-tenth of emigrants died
within a short time of leaving home.[110] Another likened Dublin to
"an octopus, sucking with its tentacles the life blood out of the country."[111] Dr. Patrick Moran, the director of the psychiatric hospital in
Ardee, claimed that Dublin was "a cancerous growth on the nation."
When asked how he proposed to abolish Dublin, Moran replied that
the obvious, though undesirable, method would be an atomic bomb,
but "the only way you can is by persuading the people of Dublin that
they are in a death trap and that it is up to them to disperse." As Roy
Geary pointed out in response to Moran's remarks, the current statistics for births and deaths indicated that the urban population
could adequately perpetuate itself.[112] Nevertheless, in his minority
report to the Commission on Emigration, Dr. Cornelius Lucey, who
was probably present when Geary refuted Moran's views, asserted
that "all down the ages the rural stock in every country has been the
only source of natural population increase—urban populations do
not replace themselves over the generations but dwindle and disappear, unless replenished with a constant stream of young blood from
the countryside." Lucey claimed that the growth of Dublin was unnatural "because it is against the general trend of population." He regarded the growth of Copenhagen as natural, because the total population of Denmark was increasing. Lucey believed that because the
Irish economy was "largely a planned one," and because most planners lived and worked in Dublin, the needs of the capital were given
precedence.[113] Reverend E. J. Coyne, S.J., claimed that the banking
system and the collection of taxes sucked money out of rural Ireland
and spent it in Dublin—a process that he denounced as "altogether
unbalanced, almost a one-way traffic"; he claimed that the higher incomes of provincial towns were "siphoned off to Dublin." Another
member of the commission, Arnold Marsh, objected to the general
tone of two early drafts of the section of the commission's report relating to Dublin because "they seem to accept Dublin's all round
supremacy as in the natural order of things." Marsh noted that "for
solidity of character and maturity of consideration I put the countryman above the city man."[114] Resentment of the capital city was by
no means unique to Ireland. Similar sentiments can be found in

Paris et le Désert Français, a book published shortly after World War II.[115] In the Irish case, the antipathy may well have been greater because Dublin was a foreign city to many Irish people. Contrary to claims that Dublin siphoned off the population of the Irish countryside, comparatively few rural migrants found work there, especially those without education or qualifications. Micheál Ó Cíosóg, a native of Connemara, claimed that for most emigrants from the west of Ireland "Dublin is less known than Boston."[116]

In 1951 Minister for Defence Frank Aiken used the Korean War to press for a major program of decentralization; he claimed that Dublin was in real danger of mass bombing.[117] By this time officials in the Department of Local Government believed that the city was already too large, though their reservations were prompted by increasing traffic congestion, suburban sprawl, and the high cost of providing roads and other services to meet the needs of an expanding population.[118] Their concern reflected the fact that it was extremely difficult to secure funds for capital projects in Dublin and Cork. Contrary to the beliefs of Dr. Lucey and Reverend Coyne, Dublin's demands for roads, housing, water, or employment schemes ranked far below those of rural and provincial Ireland. Proposals to improve the road from Dublin to Bray, the busiest and the most dangerous road in the state, attracted such hostility in the newspapers that road improvements in the greater Dublin area were shelved in the late 1940s—some were only completed fifty years later.[119] Dublin and Cork Corporations were required to raise their own money for housing, water, and sewerage, whereas the capital requirements of other local authorities were met by the Exchequer, and Dublin and Cork Corporations had to postpone issuing stock on several occasions lest it jeopardize the success of a national loan, part of which was earmarked for housing and other capital schemes in smaller local authorities.[120] In the light of these attitudes, it is scarcely surprising that when the Commission on Emigration was established in 1948, officials in the Department of Local Government anticipated that it would recommend measures to restrict the growth of Dublin.[121]

In the event, the views expressed in the majority report were relatively mild. It noted that the population of Dublin was "not unhealthily large, but that the population living in provincial towns and

cities is undesirably small." It recommended that the relationship
between the two should be adjusted, not by reducing the population
of Dublin but by increasing the population of other cities and towns.
It also recommended that positive measures should be taken to accelerate the growth of provincial cities and towns, including the decentralization of government offices and the headquarters of state
organizations and commercial, social, and cultural organizations.[122]
The reference to decentralization was added by the Department of an
Taoiseach before the report was published.[123] In July 1955 the cabinet
approved the transfer to Galway of the children's allowance branch of
the Department of Social Welfare, only to rescind the decision six
weeks later.[124] The Department of Industry and Commerce resisted
any suggestion that it should decentralize its operations, though it
was apparently quite content to send industrialists to remote areas.[125]
But no government offices were transferred to provincial centers
until the 1970s. Regardless of the merits or otherwise of decentralization, it is important to note that there was no expectation that decentralization would have resulted in an increase in total employment;
jobs would simply be transferred from Dublin to a provincial town.
No consideration was given to the possibility that a policy of providing grant assistance only to industries that located in underdeveloped
areas might hinder industrial development and the creation of jobs.
No such restrictions applied to firms wishing to set up plants in
Northern Ireland, and Northern Ireland proved much more successful in attracting new industrial investment during the 1950s.[126]

Rural Ireland: Stability and Change

The rural Ireland of the mid-1950s was not the rural Ireland of the
1920s. One of the attractions of a rural and agrarian society was the
belief that it was synonymous with stability, whereas an urban and
industrial society was associated with change. The most persuasive
image of the unchanging rural Ireland is found in the writings of
two Harvard anthropologists, Conrad Arensberg and Solon T. Kimball. *The Irish Countryman* is the text of a series of lectures that
Arensberg delivered in 1936 based on fieldwork carried out in northwest county Clare in the early 1930s. A fuller account of this research

appeared in 1940 in *Family and Community in Ireland,* coauthored by Arensberg and Kimball. In *The Irish Countryman,* Arensberg set out to "lay bare the rural life of which old custom is a part."[127] The first example that he gives of the power of custom and tradition is "the west room"—a kind of parlor, the best room in the small farm house containing pictures of dead and emigrant family members; "all the 'fine' pieces of furniture, symbolic brass objects brought in by the bride at marriage; the rubrics used when mass was celebrated in the house, in fact all religious objects, crucifixes, and so forth, except the 'blessed lamp' and a 'holy picture' in the kitchen."[128] Arensberg regards the west room as a domestic shrine—to a Christian God and to family ancestors—and a symbol of continuity. When control and ownership of a farm was transferred to an inheriting son, the older couple withdrew to the west room—as if in preparation for death. He suggested that the west room was linked with fairy lore and fairy paths.

Yet the collection of family pictures, furniture, and bric-a-brac that Arensberg described in the "west room" is more reminiscent of parlors in English Victorian households or middle-class Dublin suburbs than of ancient Irish traditions, and the marriage and succession patterns that Arensberg and Kimball examined only evolved after the famine; indeed, there is an extensive debate about whether these county Clare households were typical of rural Ireland. During the hundred years before the great famine the population of Ireland rose from two million to over eight million, and most of the increase took place in the countryside. Population growth on this scale implies dramatic changes in rural settlement patterns; nevertheless, a lot of what has been written about rural Ireland presupposed that its normal status was as a timeless place, with the same families residing in the same places for generations. In prefamine Ireland many small farms were not self-sufficient in labor; they relied on hired workers, particularly when children were too young to work. Children of small farmers and agricultural laborers left home in search of work when the family economy had no need for their services and might not be in a position to feed them.[129] But in twentieth-century Ireland as elsewhere, the myth of a stable prelapsarian rural society exercised a strong influence on people's minds, and on social policy.

Yet rural Ireland was not frozen in time, and many of the changes that were underway in the first half of the twentieth century made it increasingly difficult to sustain the existing population, let alone to reverse the decline. In 1940 Seán Ó Faoláin claimed that "the old patriarchal rural Ireland is slowly beginning to disintegrate."[130] Damien Hannan suggests that the late 1940s were a watershed for the small farming households of the west of Ireland.[131] This is probably correct, though I would argue that the process was more gradual and had already begun before that date.

Money, Distance, and Time

Economics were important. Contrary to the belief of W. T. Cosgrave, the impact of the post-1929 depression was not restricted to industry. Indeed, the 1930s are remembered as a tough decade for Irish farmers, although with Ireland's parochial instincts, their hardships have been blamed on the Economic War,[132] not an international depression. During World War II farm incomes recovered relative to nonfarm incomes, but in the 1950s and the early 1960s income prospects in agriculture were poor, and many farms only achieved a higher income by reducing the numbers of assisting relatives. But trends in income cannot provide the sole explanation for rural decline; technology, communications, new patterns of consumption and leisure, and changing expectations were also important. If the end of the twentieth century brought about "the death of distance," it could be argued that the early years of the same century reinforced the gap between urban and rural Ireland. In 1946 almost 92 percent of urban homes had piped water and 35 percent had a fixed bath, whereas over 91 percent of rural homes relied on a pump or some other unspecified source for water (commonly a tank on the roof that collected rain water) and only 4 percent had a fixed bath. These statistics prompted Seán MacEntee, minister for Local Government, to speak about the need "to make the conditions of life in rural areas, particularly for those who work on the land, less onerous than in some respects they now are, so that our country people may enjoy as many as possible of the advantages which town dwellers expect as a matter of course."[133] By the mid-1940s all towns had electricity, but many country areas did not. When James McGee, the chairman of Louth County Council, asked a number of young people why they were hanging around the streets of Ardee at night, although they lived several miles away, they explained that they came to Ardee "simply because there is light and they could look at each other."[134] In 1947 de Valera noted that it was essential that rural communities were provided, as far as possible, with "some of the amenities of towns and cities," such as electricity, telephones, and better roads and housing.[135]

Rural electrification is regarded as one of the success stories of postwar Ireland, but the process was slow. Electricity did not reach the countryside near Kinvara in county Galway until 1955, and other areas waited as long, or longer.[136] But although the Commission on Emigration urged that piped water and sanitary services be provided "as widely and as speedily as possible" in rural areas, no serious effort was made to extend rural water schemes until the 1960s, perhaps because running water was regarded as primarily a matter for women rather than men.[137]

Car—or more realistically van—ownership was also slow to spread. In 1948 there were only sixty thousand cars on Irish roads. The high cost of tariffs and excise duties that were designed to protect the Irish car assembly industry seriously restricted car ownership. No Irish politician or businessman shared Henry Ford's vision that every farm family should own a car—the Model T was designed as a farmer's car.[138] For many rural households the tractor was the only form of mechanized transport, and it was often used to carry people, however inefficiently.[139] High tariffs also restricted bicycle ownership.

Although bicycles, cars, and motor buses increased mobility in the Irish countryside, the sense of rural isolation may well have become more pronounced. Arensberg and Kimball claimed that one of the questions that the father of the bride asked a prospective father-in-law was whether the house where his daughter would live was "far from the road or on it . . . near a chapel and the school or near town?"[140] Mogey reported that the farmhouses that were being abandoned in county Fermanagh in the 1940s were the most isolated.[141] Galway playwright M. J. Molloy told the Commission on Emigration that the rural area of North Galway and South Mayo was losing "far more than its surplus of men and *its entire stock of girls* through emigration and migration to Irish cities." He claimed that there were two young men living alone on their farms in Meelick "who need wives badly and would not be too particular. . . . [W]ith the girls of the country all infected more or less with emigration mania, no man has any chance of coaxing one unless he happens to have a really good farm of land, and *situated along a main road.*"[142]

This sense of isolation was necessarily most acute on the offshore islands. The interdepartmental committee established in 1947 to report on conditions on the islands noted that the islanders had a relatively high material standard of living; most complaints related to isolation.[143] A memorandum on the Dingle Peninsula and the Blasket Islands, presented to the Commission on Emigration, lamented the fact that there was "no motor boat service for Island women to go to market; no bus for her sister in Dunquin . . . no brightly-lit shop nearer than Tralee."[144] The growing demand for medical services, both in times of illness and to assist at childbirth, meant that rural households became more conscious of distance from a doctor or a hospital. A meeting was held in Ballyduff, county Kerry, in 1950 to protest the failure of the authorities to provide the district with a resident medical officer, a resident midwife, housing, and an adequate supply of pure water.[145] The evacuation of the Blasket Islands in the early 1950s was triggered by the death in 1947 of a young man, Sean Ó Cearna, after a week's illness without access to either a doctor or a priest.[146]

At the beginning of the twentieth century the Blasket Islands were without doctor, priest, brightly lit shops, or regular connection with the mainland, but Tomás Ó Criomhtháin gives no indication that he or his fellow islanders felt any sense of deprivation. Over the next thirty to forty years, however, it appears that the islanders became conscious of the absence of professional medical care and regular spiritual care. Their diet, and rural diets in general, became more reliant on shop goods—tea, flour, sugar, condensed milk, shop-bought bacon—perhaps because many rural families were receiving regular cash payments from state benefits. By the 1930s there was at least one traveling bread van in county Mayo, but shop bread tended to be bought only when a family member traveled to town, perhaps on a fair day.[147]

William Honohan, an official in the Department of Social Welfare, interviewed would-be emigrants at the employment exchange in Clonmel, county Tipperary, in 1948 and summed up his experiences as follows:

> It may be that, in the past, when standards were lower and perhaps opportunities for spending money not so great in certain areas (no cinema, no dance hall, not so much smoking) many now emigrating were satisfied with work in long or short spells from time to time. The modern requirement, however, is a pay-packet of definite dimensions and I think that the Commission might comment on the fact that we are moving away from that time when employers of labor could count on getting men for a couple of days or a couple of weeks at a time and then laying them off. But in this country we have a relatively large group of people who never work for an employer and who never get much more than subsistence. . . . It may be that, in years gone by, such persons have been content to live virtually on a subsistence basis, but the cinema, radio, newspapers and friends are now luring them into the attitude that they should not be satisfied with this but should leave home and get wages to enable them to raise their standards, get married and have homes of their own. Who can blame them?[148]

Honohan's comment highlighted the importance of a regular monetary income to finance modern patterns of consumption and leisure and, more importantly, to enable these men to marry and set up home. While a steady job and regular money wages ranked equally high among the priorities for people living in cities and towns, such aspirations did not threaten a traditional way of life; they did in rural Ireland. Feminist writers have emphasized that an entitlement to money is a form of empowerment or liberation. They tend to assume that all adult men have or had an independent source of income; however, this was not true of many young, or even middle-aged, "relatives assisting" in rural Ireland. A member of the county Leitrim Vocational Education Committee (VEC) told the Commission on Emigration that the fact that people in towns had more money at their disposal was a major source of dissatisfaction among the rural population.[149] Most labor on small farms was carried out by family members who did not receive regular payment. Many hired laborers were farm servants, who were recruited for six months. They tended to be teenagers, and a substantial proportion of their pay came in the form of board and keep. Money payments made at the end of the six months often went to a parent rather than the actual worker. Older farm laborers who did not live in also received part of their payment in kind.[150] When additional labor was required for hay making, harvesting, or threshing, children were taken out of school (the Department of Education adopted a very tolerant attitude to absenteeism in rural areas) and neighbors and relations helped out in return for reciprocal assistance on their own farms.[151]

Most farmers handled cash infrequently—when they sold stock at fairs or disposed of crops after the harvest, or when they received remittances from America. Shop purchases of food, clothing, and household goods were generally made on credit, and the bill was settled, or more probably reduced, once or twice a year. Trips to town seem to have been infrequent: to attend the fair, for major shopping, and for formal meetings such as matchmaking. The pub formed an important element of the trip to town, but otherwise it does not appear to have been a regular feature of rural social life. Everyday social life was rooted in the community, and it did not depend on money. The most common activity was the *cuaird*, evening visits to a house or houses that were recognized gathering places for a certain category of men; old men congregated in one house, younger men met elsewhere.[152] As Arensberg described: "Night after night, their day's work done, our new acquaintances, at least the males among them, walked out upon the roads to this house and that in search of recreation and companionship. Mention of dances, gambles, sings, ceilidhthe, filled our ears, belying the impression of a gray monotony of rural life too easily gathered by town-bred minds. Some of these sportive gatherings were age-old customs like the bonfires at Saint John's Eve; others celebrated crucial events, such as wakes, christenings, weddings. But many others were less occasional and less specialized gatherings; and others again wore a very modern dress: a turkey raffle and a dance round a gramophone."[153]

In 1949 Micheál Ó Cíosóg claimed that the old traditions of story-telling and Irish music were passé and that young people wanted more modern forms of entertainment.[154] Gambles for a turkey or goose gave way to whist drives and bingo; the "dance round a gramophone" was superseded by commercial dance halls, though the *Donegal Democrat* carried advertisements for dances in private houses in the early 1950s.[155] Social life was being commercialized, monetized, and it increasingly involved both men and women. The traditional social life of women in rural Ireland seems to have been very restricted, their outings being limited to more formal occasions such as marriages, wakes, Christmas visiting, or visits to members of their immediate family.[156] By contrast, modern dance halls and the cinema catered for younger people and mixed company, though one parish priest in Clones, county Monaghan, has achieved a place in Irish history because he insisted that men and women sit on separate sides in the cinema (mirroring a practice in many rural churches).[157] Arensberg and Kimball tell us almost nothing about the social lives of women in county Clare, but the Lenten pastorals issued by the Catholic bishops suggest that the dancing craze was well established in Ireland by the 1930s and the cinema was attracting large audiences.[158] In their concern to record what was unique in Ireland, Arensberg and Kimball did not comment on either of these phenomena. Cinemas and commercial dances involved an admission charge and probably transport—a bicycle or hackney car—to a nearby town or farther afield.

By the late 1930s there were widespread demands for village or parish halls to be provided in order to redress the drift from the countryside. The halls were envisaged as all-purpose community centers—as meeting places for public health clinics, local committees, and parish councils, as subbranches of the public library, or as venues for amateur dramatics, dances, and cinema shows. The 1941 Local Government Act gave the government powers to provide grants toward the cost of erecting village halls, and in December 1942 the Cabinet asked the Department of Local Government to prepare a scheme, but no grants were introduced at this time, probably because of wartime shortages. Grants were eventually provided in 1953.[159] By then the recreational needs of young people were increasingly being met by summer carnivals—held in marquees, which were often fund-raising activities organized by the Catholic church—and by commercial ballrooms. With motor cars becoming more readily available, distance lent enchantment and anonymity; the Limerick Rural Survey revealed that many young people preferred to travel long distances to a dance, where they would be unknown and immune from local gossip.[160]

This capsule account of changes in rural sociability indicates the impact of the spread of money into rural Ireland and the widening gap between those with a regular entitlement to money and those without. Access to money generated new patterns of consumption, including changes in diet and social behavior. Once people became accustomed to shop-bought clothes, in place of clothes made at home or by the local dressmaker, their need for money became correspondingly greater. There is more than a little truth in Aodh de Blacam's claim that commercially sponsored radio programs promoting "debased and commercialised food habits," were a factor in rural depopulation.[161]

Wage-earning employment introduced hitherto unknown concepts to the Irish countryside, such as overtime, weekly half holidays, holidays with pay, and workers' rights. Emigrants returning from Britain for summer holidays bragged about high weekly wages and regular overtime, while their dress, makeup (in the case of women), and high spending patterns testified to the benefits that money could bring.

Ironically, government measures to assist rural households, such as unemployment assistance, the 1936 Agricultural Wages Act, and the decentralization of industry, were among the most potent factors in spreading a money economy. As Arensberg and Kimball noted: "To build the factories is to send into the country districts the very forces of urbanism, such as wage payment, individual recompense, and a job rather than a part in group life, which wean the farm boys and girls away from a familistic [sic] self-subsistence."[162]

The old age pension, introduced in 1908, provided the first regular cash payments to many rural households, and the weekly trip to the post office to collect the money created a new awareness of distance and proximity. Unemployment assistance, a cash payment for those with no means or with insufficient means, was introduced in 1934. Almost a quarter million people applied for unemployment assistance during the first year. By the late 1930s approximately 78,000 people were receiving this benefit; 70 percent of these had some means.[163] In 1935 Roy Geary noted that a "most competent observer" in Connemara had reported that "the whole outlook on emigration had been altered partly by the pessimistic letter with ever decreasing remittances from the United States and partly by the Unemployment Assistance Act whereby large numbers of small farmers' relatives, the great class from which emigrants were drawn in the past, came into benefit. Now, to city wage-earners the amounts received may seem small—possibly the average for males over 18 in this agricultural class does not exceed 5/- per week. It should be borne in mind, however, that such amounts received are for expenditure over and above a standard of living which, if low, at least includes food."[164]

On the Blasket Islands, one native recalled the rumors that every unemployed person would get money for sitting on their backside— "tháinig ráfla amach go bhfáigheadh nach aon duine a bhí díomhaoin airgead, suite ar a dthóin,"—and the amazement when the rumors proved to be true.[165] Increasing numbers of rural men were employed on government relief works during the 1930s, and between 1940 and 1947 local authorities employed 30,000–40,000 men to harvest turf for several weeks every summer—the majority recruited in western and midland counties.

Although de Valera informed the Fianna Fáil parliamentary party in 1933 that if doles were to be given it would be far "more advantageous and less deteriorating to give dole to women rather than to men,"[166] women were almost totally excluded from unemployment assistance. Most relief works were only open to men, although a small number of women were employed on wartime turf schemes, where they were paid less than the daily rate for hiring a donkey.[167] By the early 1950s the traditional source of women's cash income—poultry and eggs—was disappearing, and at a time when money and material possessions were assuming greater importance. Rosemary Harris, commenting on one farming family in Northern Ireland, noted that the farmer gave his wife no housekeeping money: "Indeed it seemed not to have occurred to anyone that he was under any obligation to

give her any cash, for in their experience farmers never did give
housekeeping money to their wives."[168]

Geary's informant claimed that unemployment assistance had
eliminated restlessness among young people,[169] but in the longer
term it is probable that these payments gave rise to changes in attitude and lifestyle. The traditional farming season had a natural
rhythm, with periods of very hard work and other times, such as the
weeks after Christmas, when farm tasks were few.[170] But farmers and
rural laborers increasingly thought in terms of a more regular working cycle, with a standard working week, regular free days, and payment for overtime, and they looked to the state to provide them with
work or benefit during slack times in the farming calendar. In 1949
when the Emergency had ended and life was returning to "normal,"
the government came under considerable pressure to provide additional jobs on local authority road schemes, despite the fact that
employment was running at 29,000, or 10,000 above the prewar figure. One official noted that there had been "a change in the psychological outlook of the rural population. During the Emergency large
numbers of the farming community were called on to assist County
Councils in the turf production campaign. In many cases, these
people formerly self-employed, developed the habit of compressing
their own work into a smaller time space and of spending the remainder of their working hours with County Councils. With the cessation
of turf production, they were left unemployed in a sense, and thrown
back on their resources, and they now consider that they should be
employed on road works."[171]

Clock-watching and the concept of an average working week or a
weekly half day did not form part of traditional farming life; the
only exception was the special nature of Sunday, when no unnecessary work was carried out. The 1936 Agricultural Wages Act, which
set rates of pay and working conditions for full-time agricultural
laborers, brought important changes in rural attitudes toward time
and leisure, particularly in areas such as county Limerick, where substantial numbers of farm laborers worked side by side with family
labor. Some dairy farmers protested that "cows cannot be milked 14
times in 54 hours to get the best results." Others demanded the breeding of "a week-end cow." In 1947 de Valera noted that farm laborers

were no longer agreeable to milking cows on Sunday, "because they want to go off to a game; they see other people off every Sunday, and they do not see why they should not be off every Sunday."[172] Faced with the requirement to give laborers a weekly half holiday, dairy farmers tended to place greater demands on family labor; but it would be naïve to assume that farmers' sons and brothers did not hanker for the right to time off work. The 1936 Agricultural Wages Act still rankled in county Limerick more than twenty years later, when the Limerick Rural Survey commented that "the too rapid introduction of an urban code of employment had contributed to the breakdown of personal relations between farmer and labourer."[173]

While farmers' opposition to the Agricultural Wages Act can be read as a reflection of class antipathy and resentment at being forced to pay higher wages to laborers, the legislation also impacted farmers who did not employ laborers, because the agricultural laboring wage provided a benchmark for comparison with their own annual earnings. In the early 1940s Professor Michael Murphy of the Dairy Science Faculty at University College Cork determined that most farmers in west Cork were not earning the equivalent of the statutory agricultural wage. Dr. Bob O'Connor came to a similar conclusion when he examined farm accounts in county Roscommon some years later.[174] While this had important implications for all small farmers, its significance was even greater for a son who assisted on the farm, since he now had some indication of his notional weekly wage. Assisting relatives accounted for almost 40 percent of agricultural workers in 1926, but only one-quarter in 1961, whereas there was only a marginal decline in the proportion who were agricultural laborers, from 20.7 percent to 19 percent.

During the war, competition from turf schemes forced some farmers to offer more than the statutory agricultural wage in an effort to retain workers, but wages were not the only factor influencing the choice of work. From 1942 the wage set for turf workers was slightly greater than the statutory wage for farm laborers, and turf workers had a shorter working week (forty-eight hours compared with fifty-four for agricultural laborers) to compensate for the time lost traveling to the bogs. They were also entitled to national insurance stamps, whereas farm workers were not. In 1944 a farmer from

Ballincollig, county Cork, reported that two of his three laborers had left to work on a turf scheme in Kildare, although he had offered them 4s. a week more than the statutory minimum wage. They were attracted away by the possibility of piecework and the prospect of more free time. The third laborer left shortly afterward despite being offered 6s. more than the statutory wage. In 1945 Louth County Committee of Agriculture reported that road workers who voluntarily broke their employment to work with a farmer automatically lost their entitlement to one week's holiday with pay.[175] Agricultural laborers were not included in statutory social insurance schemes until 1952; this meant that they had no automatic entitlement to unemployment insurance, sickness benefit, or accident insurance, and many did not receive the statutory agricultural wages.[176]

By the late 1940s the industrial/urban concepts of a regular weekly income had become a major consideration for Irishmen and women, regardless of where they lived or worked. Aodh de Blacam, an unrelenting critic of industrial society, suggested that the factories that opened in rural areas and small towns during the 1930s "broke up the pattern of rural life and caused an increase in emigration" because they gave workers a taste for regular pay packets. Others blamed army service during the Second World War for making young men dependent on a regular money income. Dónal Mac Amhlaigh was one of many who emigrated shortly after being demobilized from the army.[177] A member of the county Leitrim Vocational Education Committee claimed that young men were reluctant to take up farming because they believed that "no matter how hard or how long they work farming shows no profit."[178] But in postwar Ireland the demand seems to have been not just for employment, but for regular employment. De Blacam denied that factory work offered greater security. In the case of Dundalk factory workers, he believed that "the short time in the boot factories . . . is behind the unsettlement of the workers—they show no confidence that they have settled lasting employment"; industrial development "had failed to produce what we need most, security."[179] But most workers disagreed. Reporting on a visit to Loughrea, Dr. Cornelius Lucey—another relentless critic of urban society—noted that the men that he encountered were less concerned with the size of a wage packet than with constant employment and security, but they had little prospect of achieving this because of the absence of local industry. Hardly any of the men interviewed in Longford by members of the Commission on Emigration believed that they had any hope of securing "constant, adequately paid work" in the area, and they were not prepared to settle for casual work. In Kilkelly, county Mayo, where there were up to eight hundred men on the live register, there were claims that Bord na Móna was finding it impossible to hire sufficient seasonal workers because only permanent employment was attractive. Another member of the Commission on Emigration, William Honohan, remarked that "there is a possible danger in new local industries implanting a desire for regular and large wage packets in those to whom such ideas would not otherwise occur, and, if such employment can only be given seasonally or spasmodically, there is an immediate urge to be off in centres where it can be counted on regularly."[180]

The desire for permanent, and ideally pensionable, employment can be viewed as an interesting amalgam of the values of rural Ireland with those of a more developed economy. The quest for security was a driving force in rural Ireland after the famine, prompting campaigns for tenant right and peasant proprietorship, an end to the practice of subdividing holdings, and a reliance on dowries to ensure prudent marriages. This search for security is evident in farmers' demands for guaranteed payments for produce—demands that grew louder after World War II, culminating in the extensive range of price and income guarantees provided by the European Community's Common Agricultural Policy. But the "promised land" of the Common Agricultural Policy did not materialize until the 1970s. The uncertain markets for agricultural produce from the 1920s until Ireland joined the European Economic Community in 1973 meant that even middling and large farmers experienced substantial fluctuations in income. Security was increasingly sought in the form of permanent jobs, a regular weekly or monthly pay packet, and the prospect of career advancement. This search for security prompted many farmers' sons and daughters to become national teachers, guards (policemen), or civil servants. Robert Cresswell noted that by the

mid-1950s there were a growing number of alternatives to emigration for men and women who did not remain in agriculture, but
most of these alternatives were dependent on education.

Education

Education was one of the most problematic issues for rural Ireland.
Postprimary schooling was a requirement for most jobs in the civil
service, in practice if not in theory,[181] and for the gardaí or other
white collar jobs. Several witnesses to the Commission on Emigration demanded better facilities for secondary schooling in western
areas.[182] In Swinford, county Mayo, the community was determined
to secure a secondary school, and local householders were committed to raising the necessary capital to provide premises, whereas they
were neither willing nor able to raise sufficient capital to establish a
factory.[183] But any extension of second-level schooling threatened to
undermine traditional rural Ireland. A leaving certificate reduced the
prospect of emigrating, but few young men or women with leaving
certificates took up careers in farming. A survey by the Department
of Education of fifty secondary schools scattered throughout the
country showed that although few holders of leaving certificates
emigrated, only 5 of the 129 women surveyed were in farming or
at home, and only 10 of the 192 men had entered farming or were
working at home. Twenty-two women were attending university,
16 entered postsecondary courses in education (presumably teacher-
training colleges), 30 entered religious orders, 7 joined the civil service, 15 became nurses, and 14 were described as unemployed. Of the
192 boys surveyed, 46 were attending university, 17 were in other educational courses, 69 had joined religious orders, and 12 had joined
the civil service. Twenty-two were in business, 3 had joined the army,
1 was a bank clerk, 1 a blacksmith, and 10 were described as unemployed.[184] This survey may present a somewhat distorted picture, because the students in question sat their leaving certificates in 1939
and the career details were compiled in 1940. Few people emigrated
during the early months of World War II, and the long-term picture
may have been rather different. Among the pupils of Saint Mary's
Convent of Mercy in Swinford who left school between 1944 and

1948, the largest number, 28, entered religious life. Other career choices included teacher training, 18; university on scholarship, 4; university at own expense, 9; nursing at home and abroad, 18; clerical officers in the civil service, 18; writing assistants in the civil service, 12; assistant teachers in English convents, 19; banking in Ireland and England, 3; medicine, 3; national health insurance positions, 6; pharmacy in Ireland, 8; and secondary teachers in England or Ireland, 6. The career pattern of women who left secondary schools in rural Limerick in 1959 was not dramatically different: the largest number, 242, were destined for "other training" (presumably teacher training or perhaps a commercial class); 29 entered religious life; 92 joined the civil service; 80 became nurses; 35 attended university; and just 6 returned to the family farm.[185]

According to Stanley Lyon, the high standard of education, particularly in convent schools, tended to make girls dissatisfied with conditions in their homes, although Lyon was thinking in terms of their dissatisfaction with the low material standards found in "poorer localities, with few-roomed houses and large families." His views corroborated an earlier statement by a Land Commission inspector that farmers' daughters who had attended secondary school would not contemplate becoming farmers' wives, even with domestic servants to help with the chores.[186]

Many provincial towns lacked secondary schools, so only children whose parents could afford to pay boarding school fees were assured of a secondary education. T. Ó Raiftearaigh, then a senior official in the Department of Education and a future secretary of the department, told the Commission on Emigration that many secondary schools were seriously overcrowded and some had waiting lists.[187] There were few scholarships, often less than five in a county, and these tended to go to pupils who attended the larger primary schools in provincial towns that could offer more concentrated teaching. Secondary schools were private institutions, whereas vocational schools were operated by the local authorities. The commission established in 1926 to report on vocational education insisted that in country areas "it is of vital importance that continuation education—should have a strong rural bias," and that education beyond the age of sixteen "should appertain more to rural than to urban conditions,"[188] and this view prevailed for many years. Dr. O'Sullivan, the official responsible for vocational education in the Department of Education, told the Commission on Emigration that "we [presumably the Department of Education] are definitely opposed to the teaching of commercial subjects" outside urban areas and county boroughs. In the late 1940s only 10 percent of students attending vocational schools in Galway took commercial subjects; in counties Clare and Roscommon the proportion was less than 20 percent, and these students lived in towns.[189]

Statistics compiled by Seán Ó Dochairtaigh, chief executive officer of Galway Vocational Educational Committee showed that the overwhelming majority of students who attended day classes between 1935 and 1948 were working as shop assistants, clerks, cooks, domestic servants, or in industrial employment.[190] On the other hand, half of all pupils who attended vocational schools in county Roscommon between 1936 and 1944 returned to family farms, at least on a temporary basis. Dr. O'Sullivan claimed that few past pupils of vocational schools emigrated, and then only in exceptional circumstances, such as girls who went as trainee nurses. The majority were hired by local employers; in some areas the demand for workers exceeded the numbers available.[191] Other witnesses claimed that in many vocational schools no students remained at the end of the two-year program, because they had already been hired by employers.[192] But this may have been an atypical cohort; this evidence was collected in the late 1940s, when the restoration of supplies and spare parts resulted in a building boom and rising industrial employment.

Those who pressed for an expansion of postprimary schooling in rural Ireland did not necessarily agree about the appropriate curriculum. While many argued that it should be limited to classes in agriculture for boys and cookery and other domestic skills for girls, more pragmatic (and more realistic) voices favored commercial and academic subjects. M. J. Molloy, a supporter of a cookery and farming curriculum, claimed that "as Irish education is absolutely anti-rural, the more of it there is, the worse the position will be."[193] Father Thomas Counihan, S.J., demanded that "at least one decent agricultural and manual training centre" be provided in each county. He also favored a new curriculum for girls that would award diplomas in domestic service and training in household management. He believed that vocational schools "should be almost entirely concerned with agriculture, horticulture and silviculture."[194] Aodh de Blacam complained that a school reader published in the late 1930s targeted at rural Ireland "was not taken up as widely as we would wish, owing to the absence of a rural bias in the Department of Education."[195]

However, most rural parents and their children were only interested in courses that offered career opportunities away from the farm. Dr. O'Sullivan conceded that rural vocational schools and the Department of Education were under considerable pressure from parents who believed a commercial education would make it easier for their children to find jobs, and he quoted a letter from a priest in a small town in county Offaly who referred to "a constant demand for a commercial course" and wondered "if it is wise to resist this demand any longer." The unnamed priest suggested that a commercial course "would be a great help to the enrollment, and even if the course was not of practical importance in all cases, it would, at least, bring the children to the school. They would even be introduced to the atmosphere of the schools, have the advantage of living at home, get a continuation course in national school subjects and get sound knowledge of domestic subjects." O'Sullivan reported that "notwithstanding its appeal the course was not given," because introducing a commercial course would mean "diverting funds and energy from subjects which are much more important," such as rural science. He affirmed that "the whole aim . . . the idea of our schools is to train people to stay on the land," despite the evidence that this was only an option for a minority of rural teenagers.[196]

There was a real danger that even the students who took classes in farming or cookery would frustrate the intentions of the state and the church by failing to settle on the land. Scholarships to agricultural colleges awarded by county committees of agriculture were in demand, not because they would help the successful candidates to become better farmers, but because they offered an escape route from farming. Most of the men who attended agricultural colleges found jobs related to agriculture, administering Department of Agriculture schemes for farm buildings, lime, or land drainage. Many of the women worked in the poultry and dairy industries, but not on farms.[197] Classes on cookery and model housekeeping might encourage rural women to demand electric or gas cookers and running water—although in the late 1940s Leitrim Vocational Education Committee organized classes in Mohill on how to cook on an open fire.[198] Worse still, an emphasis on domestic skills might persuade rural women that they were housewives first, rather than farm wives, a subtle distinction that meant that a woman gave a higher priority to housekeeping than to farm chores, to the extent that she might aspire to create a replica of the modern suburban home in the Irish countryside and might refuse to nurse sick animals in her tidy kitchen. When Rosemary Harris investigated farming households in Northern Ireland during the early 1950s, she drew a distinction between wives who concentrated on housekeeping and those who saw their primary role as helping out on the farm. Henri Mendras drew a similar distinction in his account of rural France in the 1960s. He suggested that younger farm wives had adopted the values of urban and suburban housewives; they saw themselves primarily as housewives, they were house-proud, and they believed that their primary task was domestic housekeeping, whereas older wives devoted much more of their time to the field or farm animals. Harris remarked that women living on poorer farms had to devote more time to "yard work" than women on more prosperous farms.[199]

The report of the Commission on Emigration noted that no other subject elicited such diverse views as education. The report recommended that domestic economy classes for girls should be provided in the senior classes in national school—although how that could be done in the one- and two-teacher schools that were found in most rural parishes at the time, many dating from the nineteenth century and lacking running water, must remain a mystery. They did not recommend that boys should be instructed in agricultural science, although they expressed the opinion that it was "desirable to avoid fostering an urban mentality"; they also urged that emigration and rural depopulation should be a consideration in determining educational policy.[200]

The diverse views contained in the evidence to the Commission on Emigration were replicated in the Fianna Fáil national executive. In

September 1955, when the party was in opposition, they established a subcommittee to examine provisions for education in response to a motion moved by Dr. Noel Browne (of Mother and Child fame) and Eoin Ryan. In 1956 the national executive voted to raise the school-leaving age to fifteen (this had been one of the party's commitments at the 1948 general election). They also approved a resolution instructing all vocational education committees to devise a scheme to provide full-time vocational education in each area as well as resolutions to abolish fees for the first two years of vocational education courses, provide transport for pupils from outlying areas to enable them to attend vocational schools, expand local authority scholarships for secondary and university education, and remove the requirement to matriculate in Latin, Greek, or a modern continental language to enable pupils who attended vocational schools to enter degree courses in science, engineering, agriculture, and dairy science. These resolutions reflected a wish to expand educational opportunities and job prospects for rural children, yet other resolutions demanded that the textbooks used in national schools contain "a bias towards rural life" and that children be encouraged to appreciate the importance of farming to the nation[201]—reflecting the contradictory attitudes that existed concerning rural Ireland and the tensions between preserving the past and preparing for the future. Similar contradictions emerge from the 1962 Interdepartmental Committee on Small Western Farms, which acknowledged that as there was no prospect that farming would provide full employment for the population of these areas "in the immediate future," there was an urgent need to provide a broad-based education for all pupils. However, the education should have "a rural bias" and domestic training for girls was "important"—it might help to promote the tourist industry and girls should also be instructed in knitting, doll making, and other hand and eye skills.[202]

Where rural Ireland was concerned, education was a Janus-like figure. On the one hand there were fears that the countryside would die if young people were not given better opportunities for education, but on the other hand extending second-level education, almost irrespective of the syllabus, threatened to accelerate the exodus from the countryside.

Young and Old: Intergenerational Relations

Arensberg and Kimball claimed that Ireland was in some respects an old person's country. Old people got the best seats by the fire, first place in line for confessions at country "stations" (religious gatherings in rural homes), "the better cup of tea . . . the glass of whiskey . . . the pipeful of tobacco," and they were listened to with respect at a cuaird.[203] A father, or indeed a widowed mother, commonly retained overall control of farm work, at least until he or she signed over control of the farm. Although the main farm tasks might be carried out by a son, this did not entitle him to a regular money income or to make decisions about farming practice.[204] In 1943 Reverend T. H. McFall, a Church of Ireland clergyman from Fiddown, county Waterford, remarked that "very few appreciate the hold which many farming parents keep on their grown up children. I know of more than one instance where young men of 25 years still go to their father (or in one instance their mother) to ask for the price of a smoke or the cost of a ticket to a dance or cinema."[205] Arensberg and Kimball note that "even at forty-five and fifty, if the old couple have not yet made over the farm, the countryman remains a 'boy' in respect to farm work and in the rural vocabulary." They go on to cite, though without giving the exact reference, a statement by a Dáil deputy in 1933 where he refers to "'boys' of forty-five and older with no prospects other than to wait for their fathers' farm."[206]

The growing number of young men or women with weekly wages that freed them from the need to beg for spending money from a parent reinforced the dependent status of "assisting relatives," although many parents laid claim to the weekly pay packet of their sons and daughters. Officials in the Gaeltacht Services section of the Department of Lands alleged that many young women abandoned jobs in local toy factories or as contract knitters and emigrated to England because as long as they remained at home their mothers appropriated all the earnings. "Away what they earn is their own."[207] Arensberg and Kimball describe older farmers who were given work on Land Commission holdings that was carried out by their sons; many of the "old fellows" walked several miles to collect the wages that their sons had earned.[208] Yet while many parents appear to have regarded their children's wage packets as theirs to apportion, sons or daughters with an independent income acquired some independence vis-à-vis their parents. In 1940 Seán MacEntee, then minister for Industry and Commerce, complained that the practice of paying unemployment assistance to single men, who had formerly depended on their parents for clothes and pocket money, had reduced parental authority. He suggested that dole payments for single men be paid to the father unless he was known to be lacking in industry and sobriety, in which case it should be paid to the mother.[209]

Education and rural organizations presented further threats to the patriarchal traditions of rural Ireland. McNabb claimed that most Limerick farmers did not hold agricultural education in high esteem, believing that traditional methods were better than those learned either in agricultural college or from agricultural advisors. He continued: "It is important to understand that the farmer's attitude is not just one of indifference. He is positively opposed to agricultural education. What is involved is not education as such, but the farmer's own status. He is the teacher and transmitter of a craft. By virtue of his understanding of that craft he is head of the family as an economic unit. To admit new methods which he himself does not understand and which are introduced by his son is to resign his position of authority."[210]

While organizations like Muintir na Tíre and Macra na Feirme[211] enhanced the status of farming and rural lives by emphasizing their positive values and promoting a livelier rural social life, in expanding the horizons of their members and raising their expectations, they may well have acted as destabilizing forces. Robert Cresswell suggested that while Muintir na Tíre set out to restore life to the parish and other rural organizations, and attempted to make everyday rural life more satisfying, there was a real risk that it might aggravate the problems that it sought to rectify. In other words, the reforms and attitudes that these rural organizations encouraged entailed a greater monetization of rural society, which in turn magnified the differences between rich and poor, weakening community solidarity and ensuring that the poorer holdings were not only uneconomic but also no longer socially sustainable.[212] McNabb noted that while these organizations were established with the goal of saving traditional society, in practice their objectives were inimical to that end. Macra na Feirme's encouragement of modern farming methods and a more business-like approach to farming constituted a direct attack on the traditional outlook of older fathers.[213] In Muintir na Tíre or Macra na Feirme, young men became accustomed to discussing the drawbacks of their lives, "and implicitly or explicitly, all these discussions are a direct attack on the role of the father. The father is presented as someone ignorant, old-fashioned and self-opinionated to a degree which prevents progress and causes unhappiness."[214] Henri Mendras commented on the growing independence that membership of comparable rural organizations gave to young people on French farms. Technical changes, such as the introduction of tractors, or modern farming methods also increased the influence of farmers' sons at the expense of their fathers.[215]

Arensberg and Kimball called their book *Family and Community in Ireland,* but at no point do they consider that the two might come into conflict. Instead, they see both institutions as inextricably linked. They claimed that the rural community cannot be described apart from the rural family.[216] But Reverend T. H. McFall suggested that the dependent status of adult sons and daughters in farming households was "detrimental to the sense of citizenship and backbone which we do need to foster in the country."[217] Citizenship is not a topic that has been discussed at any great length in Ireland, but there is an extensive and lively literature concerning the extent that familism in Italy has inhibited the development of civil society.[218] Cresswell and McNabb believed that rural organizations undermined traditional family structures because they helped young people to work together as a group, which weakened family links and social control. A young man who became a skilled public speaker as a result of joining Macra na Feirme or Muintir na Tíre might realize that life on twenty-five stoney acres would be a waste of his talents, while trips to Dublin and to more prosperous rural communities would automatically raise his material expectations. Muintir na Tíre played a major role in persuading householders to participate in the rural electrification program and the Irish Countrywomen's Association (ICA) promoted the merits of running water.[219] But by instructing rural women in cookery and the value of hot water on tap, the ICA increased the risk that these women would no longer be prepared to live without such amenities, and they may have exposed the contradictions between becoming an ideal housewife and helping on the farm. The intrusion of modern notions of housekeeping also threatened to exacerbate tensions between the young bride and her mother-in-law, particularly in households where they shared a kitchen.

Conclusion: The Crisis of the 1950s

Social and economic history does not fit into the rigid periodization that applies to political or military events, but this chapter ends, however imprecisely, around the late 1950s. By then a lot of intellectual effort and money had been devoted to saving rural Ireland, in the belief that this was the way to end emigration and population decline. But I would argue that however well-meant, these efforts were misplaced. Although successive governments were berated for failing to create the idealized rural Ireland of de Blacam, Lucey, and their peers, most senior politicians appear to have shared their ideals. Moreover, that idealized rural Ireland subscribed to a cardboard image that took little account of reality. In a 1950 speech to Muintir na Tíre Rural Week, Taoiseach John A. Costello lamented the lack of stability in Irish rural society. He believed that since the famine, emigration and internal migration to Irish cities had "destroyed the foundations of rural community life," and despite almost thirty years of self-government, "it cannot be said that a stable form of rural organisation has been evolved to take the place of the order which was destroyed over a century ago."[220] Costello saw rural Ireland as unstable and believed that this was an unnatural condition, but he and many other Irish politicians were seeking to restore and to preserve a rural society that had never existed. There is no indication that rural society was stable before the famine: all evidence points to the contrary, and the assumption that it could somehow be stabilized in the 1950s was equally unrealistic. On the basis of their research in the 1930s, Arensberg and Kimball believed that Irish rural society was stable and resistant to change. "The matter of demographical conditions—continuous emigration, decline of population, delay of marriage, and rise of bachelorhood—is a persistent and recalcitrant phenomenon.

It seems to resist every change and every attack. No one knows why."[221] But change was underway, even in the 1930s; by the 1950s it was evident that the structures Arensberg and Kimball saw as contributing to the stability of rural Ireland and farm families were in danger of bringing about its collapse, and that a society based on tradition, respect, and deference for elders, one that gave priority to upholding a family's status rather than to increasing its income or spending power, was under pressure from forces such as education, rural organizations, and a modern consumer society. The men and women who lived in rural Ireland aspired to the benefits and trappings of modern life—money, material amenities, and leisure time. If these could be achieved while living on the farm, they would remain; if not, they would look elsewhere. I would argue that however well-meaning the intention, the efforts to preserve rural Ireland— through transfer payments, decentralized industry, and other means—actually served to undermine the traditional rural social order. More importantly, the obsession with reversing the decline in the rural population was ultimately misguided. The objective should have been to reverse the decline in the total population, yet by concentrating on rural Ireland and seeing rural and urban Ireland as opposites, government policies probably contributed to the overall decline in population. The decline in the numbers employed in agriculture, manufacturing, industry, and services during the 1950s suggested that the entire state was in danger of collapse, and that sacrificing economic growth to a mythical and unchanging rural society was a luxury that Ireland could no longer afford.

3

Marriages, Births, and Fertility

The Irish Family

> I do not believe that we can be a happy and prosperous na-
> tion until there are far more early marriages made possible
> by altered economic circumstances
>
> Reverend T. H. McFall to Eamon de Valera, 1943

According to Tim Guinnane a discussion of Irish marriage patterns as they evolved after the famine, "forms a common
starting point for exceptionalist views of Irish history."[1] In
1935 Roy Geary summarized the position as follows: "With the lowest
marriage rate in the world and one of the higher fertility rates (births
per marriage) the Saorstát[2] achieves a more or less average birth
rate." Geary believed that the low marriage rate and high marital fertility were related phenomena.[3] In 1968 Brendan Walsh suggested
that the low rate of marriage was designed to offset high marital fertility in order to keep the natural increase in population in check.
Irish writers, politicians, churchmen, and even public officials wrote
and spoke at length about the reluctance of Irishmen and women to
marry, but few were prepared to confront the fact that large families
may have been a major cause of this—that preventing marriage was
a means of reducing the rate of population increase, and that higher

marriage and birthrates would entail either a decline in the standard of living or higher emigration.

The proportion of Irish adults who were married fell during the second half of the nineteenth century. The decline in marriages began in the more prosperous eastern areas but then spread to all parts of Ireland. In 1871 the highest proportion of married persons of any given age was in Connacht, but by 1911 that province had the lowest rate of marriage. No data was published before 1922 on marriage rates by occupation or social class, but research carried out separately by Guinnane and Fitzpatrick, using samples of the 1901 and 1911 census schedules, suggests that at the beginning of the twentieth century small farmers were more likely to marry than larger farmers.[4] The first comprehensive data on marriage rates by farm size was not collected until 1926, and by then the patterns detected by Guinnane and Fitzpatrick were apparently changing, because the proportion of farmers who were single in 1926 fell as farm size increased (in other words, larger farmers were more likely than small farmers to marry). This pattern was consistent in all four provinces, although small farmers in Leinster and Munster were more likely to remain single than their counterparts in the poorer counties of the west and northwest.[5] In 1926 small farms in Connacht had a much higher number of resident sons, who were potential heirs, than comparable farms in Munster or Leinster. The positive association between marriage and farm size became more pronounced after 1946, and by 1971 the marriage rate for farmers with more than one hundred acres was double that of farmers with less than fifteen acres, and almost double the rate for those with fifteen to thirty acres.[6]

Although farmers and farmers' sons were commonly identified as the largest category of late-marrying males and permanent bachelors, the 1926 census reported that the low marriage rate could not be explained by the high proportion of men in agricultural occupations: for every given occupation the proportion of single men in Ireland was substantially higher than in England and Wales. The son of an English farmer aged twenty to thirty-four, working with his father on the family farm, was four times more likely to be married than his Irish counterpart; the proportion of male teachers aged twenty-five to thirty-four in England and Wales who were married was twice that in Ireland.[7] Nevertheless, the 1936 census suggested that a major explanation for the low Irish marriage rate was the large percentage of males in rural areas classified as "assisting relatives" (sons and brothers of farmers), who were normally not in a position to marry.[8]

Arensberg and Kimball and the Irish Family

The first comprehensive account of Irish marriage and inheritance patterns was given by Arensberg and Kimball. They described Irish rural marriage practices as "unique among civilized peoples."[9] Marriage was a fundamental rite of passage, not just for bride and groom but for the entire family. "The nearly universal form of marriage in the Irish countryside unites transfer of economic control, land ownership, reformation of family ties, advance in family and community status, and entrance into adult procreative sex life. It is a central focus of rural life, a universal turning point in individual histories."[10]

Irish families were large—in 1926 a farming couple married for twenty or more years had an average of six children—but the large families condemned a high proportion of the rural population to a single and celibate life and to an inferior status in the family and the community, because for a man or woman to attain full stature in rural Ireland he or she had to marry. Arensberg and Kimball claimed that a farmer's son could only embark on marriage if or when his father or widowed mother assigned him ownership of the family farm; the marriage of an adult daughter who was living on the farm depended on her finding a spouse whose status, family background, and general character met parental expectations and on her being provided with an appropriate dowry. In Arenberg and Kimball's account, one son inherited the farm, one daughter would marry into an adjoining farm, but "the rest must travel"—either as emigrants or to a life outside farming, though some provision was generally made for noninheriting siblings. Marriages were negotiated through a process of matchmaking and dowries that was designed to preserve or enhance a family's status, and the sanctions of church and society combined to control premarital and extramarital sex.

How accurate is this description of rural households in post-famine Ireland? The growing number of case studies in historical demography have shown that most generalizations need to be qualified; the response by humankind to any circumstance can vary widely.[11] At some future date we will probably have a much clearer picture of regional and local variations in Irish rural marriage patterns.[12] Opinion is divided on Arensberg and Kimball's work[13] and research has shown that inheritance and marriage did not coincide quite as neatly as they suggest.[14] What they have provided is a description of household structures in county Clare in the 1930s: other times and other places probably presented variations on the practices that they described. However, the very limited discussion of emigration serves to confirm the accuracy of their research. The index to the second edition of *Family and Community in Ireland* contains only five references to emigration. Arensberg and Kimball give detailed descriptions of the cuaird, matchmaking, and other rites of passage, so it seems improbable that they would not have included a description of an "American wake" if these had been a regular feature at the time. But emigration plummeted after the Wall Street crash in 1929.

Arensberg and Kimball suggest that the marriage of the heir concerned the entire family because it involved the transfer of the family farm, which might present difficulties for family members who were still living at home. Those who had already left home were presumably less affected. Noninheriting siblings commonly relied on the dowry brought by an incoming bride to provide them with capital or a dowry, so if the designated heir failed to find a suitable bride, they would be stranded in the family home, preventing the formation of a new generation. Yet many Irish farm households consisted of "incomplete families" (spinster and bachelor siblings, for example), and the 1901 and 1911 census schedules examined by Fitzpatrick and Guinnane suggest that such families were more common on larger holdings. Noninheriting offspring on smaller western farms were readier to emigrate, perhaps because it was less of a sacrifice to relinquish a claim to a share of twenty acres than it was for those who had been raised on larger farms, and emigration almost certainly offered them a higher standard of living. But for noninheriting offspring of large farmers, particularly the women, emigration was a less attractive option, since the majority of female emigrants became domestic servants. By the 1930s, however, nursing was attracting emigrant women from more prosperous households, and clerical jobs in the civil service, however menial, offered an attractive alternative to life as an unmarried sibling on the family farm.[15] Similar considerations would also apply to sons from larger farms.

While David Fitzpatrick's research appeared to indicate that a substantial proportion of family farms were on the point of collapse in 1911 because they lacked an obvious heir, most of these farms survived. There were two essential requirements for survival: male and female labor to run the farm and the household, and an heir, preferably male. But these requirements could be supplied by siblings and by designating a nephew as heir.[16] Birdwell-Pheasant has investigated rural inheritance patterns in Ballyduff, north county Kerry, from the beginning of the twentieth century until the mid-1980s, and she concluded that the nonmarriage of an heir did not present major difficulties, because another relative was generally available to take over the farm. Almost 85 percent of unmarried farmers in Ballyduff succeeded in keeping the farm within the family in the next generation.[17] Tim Guinnane and Joanna Bourke, who were writing about the period from the famine to 1914, have suggested that many single people in rural Ireland found satisfactory substitutes for marriage, such as an unmarried sister to keep house.[18] But Arensberg and Kimball claimed that country people regarded such households as "makeshifts, subjects for commiseration."[19] If the goal was to keep the land within the family, these marriage substitutes and inheritance strategies may well have functioned effectively, but Bourke and Guinnane's interpretation runs the danger of bending over backwards to rationalize arrangements that may have been regarded as unsatisfactory compromises. We should not forget Connell's claim that marriage and children offered a major source of comfort for the peasantry of Ireland before the famine.[20] Arensberg and Kimball's comments are more consistent with Connell's point of view, particularly given the central role that they ascribe to marriage in rural society.[21]

As the proportion of the population who were married fell during the late nineteenth century, the age of marriage rose. But most statements concerning age of marriage rely on anecdote rather than statistics, and they tend to exaggerate the late age of marriage and the gap between the ages of husband and wife. In 1925–26 the mean age of marriage for men was 34.9 years, 5.8 years later than in England and Wales; for women the mean age was 29.1, compared with 26.5 for England and Wales. By 1946 the gap had narrowed substantially for both men and women: the mean age of marriage for Irish men had fallen to 33.1, compared with 29.7 in England and Wales; for women the figures were 28.0 for Ireland and 26.6 for England and Wales.[22]

In an unpublished memorandum written in the early 1950s, Roy Geary suggested that "late marriage is now looked upon as the normal thing in life, or at any rate an inescapable accompaniment of the Irish way of life." Consequently, "very few of them have any sense of frustration in being unmarried at an age when other nationalities are almost grandparents."[23] Geary's remarks have some validity. The traditional social life of the Irish countryside centered on groups of men, whose marital status was largely irrelevant; the social life of women was equally restricted, regardless of whether they were single or married. But social behavior was changing, and by the early 1950s early and almost universal marriages had become the norm throughout western Europe and the United States. Irish men and women were probably aware of this through cinema, other media, and the direct experience of emigration. The late age of marriage, especially for men, appears to have attracted more comment during the 1950s, at a time when it was falling, which might indicate that it was no longer seen as "the natural thing." Ironically, there are significantly fewer comments about the late age of marriage among women; there would appear to have been a general assumption that if men married at an earlier age, the age of marriage for women would automatically decline.

The aspect of Arensberg and Kimball's account that has attracted most attention is their description of the stem family, where two couples, and perhaps the children of the younger couple, shared a single house. For a bride it generally involved cohabiting with her parents-in-law, if one or both were alive. Arensberg and Kimball suggest that rural society accepted the social conventions associated with marriage and inheritance, and that the relationship between father and inheriting son was a harmonious one, in contrast to the relationship between mother-in-law and daughter-in-law. "The

theme of strife between mother- and daughter-in-law is one dear to
the hearts of the countrymen."[24] Nevertheless, they do not suggest
that an incoming bride's reluctance to share a home and a kitchen
with her mother-in-law was a factor in the decline of rural marriages
or that older farmers and their wives were reluctant to cede control to
the younger generation.

According to Arensberg, the "more numerous in a county the
numbers of small holdings, roughly, the later marriage takes place,
and the greater number of bachelors, particularly males, of all ages,
there are."[25] Those without land, and those living on backward holdings, were condemned to extinction. He claimed that marriage regis-
trations from 1864 showed an established pattern in county Clare of
brides migrating from poorer farms in the west to larger farms in the
east of the district, with parents paying higher dowries in order to
advance the material and social standing of their daughters. But despite this evidence of a decline in marriages on poorer farms, Arensberg and Kimball believed that "the problems of population decline
in rural Ireland are results not of poverty but of prosperity."[26] Social
standing was increasingly viewed in economic terms, and families
were setting marriage goals that reflected this: "The instances of failure to find wives and husbands, the instances of courtships opposed
by parental and other pressures, the instances of elopements ending
in emigration, the instances of families of brothers and sisters who
stuck together celibate into old age, are far oftener examples of the
force of failure to find a mate of acceptable status than of other
cause." They believed that the problem of delayed marriages was
reaching "some sort of crisis," but a solution was "beyond the reach
of ordinary measures" because the lack of marriages was not caused
by poverty but by the need to maintain a family's relative standing in
the community.[27]

These quotations come from *Family and Community in Ireland*.
In September 1939, Ernest Hooton, chairman of the Department of
Anthropology at Harvard, wrote to de Valera, offering to send him a
proof copy of this forthcoming book and requesting that he might
write an introduction if it met with his approval. Harvard had gone
to considerable lengths to secure government support for their Irish
research program. In the summer of 1932 de Valera had given a letter

indicating his support to W. Lloyd Warner, the Harvard professor who set up the program, and at a later stage the Harvard team invited him to visit their archaeological excavations at Lagore. A memorandum prepared by the Department of an Taoiseach in September 1939 remarked that *The Irish Countryman* "contains much insight into the force of life determining rural society in western Ireland," but the Harvard archaeological mission "outshone them all," because it attracted strong interest from the public.

In his 1932 letter of support for the proposed social anthropology study in county Clare, de Valera noted that, "as I understand it, it will be a scientific study of the socio-economic life of the Irish people and a research into the ancient Irish and in no way will it be political but only interested in the objective truth through careful collection of facts."[28] While the investigation of rural society and family structures was not "political" in the narrow meaning of the term, it was potentially controversial. In January 1940 de Valera took pages 226–31 of the proofs of *Family and Community in Ireland* to read—perhaps because these pages had been drawn to his attention—but instead he handed them to Joseph Walshe, secretary of the Department of External Affairs. Some days later a telegram was sent to Dumas Malone of Harvard University Press under de Valera's name stating that "readers to whom I have submitted book unanimously report adversely. Feel that publication particularly of Chapter 11 will cause considerable misunderstanding and resentment. Strongly advise reconsideration of publication." It appears that the text was altered to take account of these objections, because when senior civil servant Seán Moynihan compared a copy of the published work with the page proofs some years later, he noted that the "most objectionable parts of chapter 11" did not appear in the book. Unfortunately, he then destroyed the proofs,[29] which means that it is not possible to determine what gave cause for offence. Chapter 11, which was titled "Familism and Sex," gives the most comprehensive analysis of rural marriage, the late age of marriage, and the contemporary crisis over marriage in rural Ireland at the time. However, the statement by Arensberg and Kimball that a solution to the crisis in rural marriages was "beyond the reach of ordinary measures," that it was not within the power of an Irish government to resolve the crisis in rural marriages, because a process of social and economic change was transforming the structures of a community that had been built upon a familistic base, raised some key issues for Irish society and the Irish state.[30]

The 1940 telegram to Harvard University Press appears to have terminated all contact between the Department of an Taoiseach and the Harvard academics. Arensberg and Kimball were not cited in official documents relating to Irish demography or rural Irish society, either published or private, and there is no evidence that their work had any impact on government thinking.

Ireland and the European Population Crisis of the 1930s

By the 1930s Ireland was not alone in its concern over future population trends, although in Europe the focus was on the falling birthrate, not the marriage rate. Robert Kuczynski, a German-born statistician at Washington's Brookings Institute, was one of the first to sound the alarm in 1929.[31] Six of the ten projections for the future population of the United States given in a report commissioned by President Herbert Hoover indicated that the American population would begin to decline before 1980. By the mid 1930s a majority of countries in northern and western Europe anticipated that their populations would decline in the near future. During the early 1930s, deaths exceeded births in several provinces in northern and central Italy and in parts of Germany. The British birthrate was only marginally above 50 percent of the 1890s level. In 1933 Enid Charles estimated that Britain was producing only 75 percent of the number of female children needed to maintain a stable population.[32] Some of the concern over a falling birthrate was prompted by the military implications, and the belief that a smaller population would result in a loss in national influence, especially if the population of rival countries continued to rise. In 1929 Kuczynski claimed that "the Anglo-Saxons, the Germans, the Scandinavians, and the French will very likely retrogress in the course of this century; and since the Slavs and some other races will continue to grow, the proportion of the Teutonic and the French race will diminish even more quickly than their absolute numbers. It is hard to see how this process might effectively be stopped. But it will be accelerated if the birth-restriction movement should continue to be most successful among those nations which no longer reproduce themselves."[33]

In Ireland the crude birthrate and the birthrate per 1,000 women aged fifteen to forty-four had fallen by approximately one-quarter since 1871, a rate of decline much lower than in other countries in western European, and Ireland was unique because most of the reduction was attributed to a fall in the marriage rate, not in family size. Only France had a lower birthrate than Ireland in the decade 1900–1909, but by the mid-1930s the Irish birthrate was higher than Germany, England and Wales, and most northern European states, and Irish marital fertility was one of the highest, if not the highest, in Europe. In 1935 Roy Geary calculated that the population of the Irish Free State in 1996 would range from 3.3 to 3.6 million—300,000 to 600,000 higher than the current figure—assuming zero emigration and no change in birth and death rates.[34] While the projected increase was regarded as disappointing—particularly given the assumption of zero net emigration—the figures suggested that if Ireland's population continued to decline, the cause would be emigration, not a low birthrate.

Plummeting birthrates and fears of a decline in the overall population prompted a wave of books and research papers on demographic trends. In 1936 Oxford University Press published three books on this topic,[35] and the International Institute of Statistics commissioned an international study to determine the factors influencing the changes in the birthrate. The countries selected for investigation were the United States, Czechoslovakia, Germany, France, Austria, Italy, and Ireland, with Stanley Lyon, the director of the government statistical service, as the Irish participant.[36] Unfortunately, this study was abandoned following the outbreak of World War II.

A. M. Carr-Saunders, author of a study of contemporary demography published by the Royal Institute for International Affairs and Oxford University Press in 1936, identified Ireland as an exception to the European-wide fall in births, because in Ireland a lower birthrate had been achieved by reducing the marriage rate, which "implies great self-restraint and much personal sacrifice, and is therefore in sharp contrast with the birth-control mechanism, which, while attaining the same end, permits the enjoyment of married companionship and home life." He suggested that an improvement in the Irish economy would bring a rise in the birthrate:

> The case of Ireland is anomalous in that, alone among countries within the sphere of European civilization the small family system was adopted in response to a threatening economic situation and has been maintained primarily to prevent the recurrence of an economic disaster. Elsewhere the motive has been in the main to obtain freedom from burdens, which it is desired to escape, whatever the economic situation of the country or of the family may be. . . . Ireland would seem to be the only country of which we could predict with certainty that opportunities for further expansion would be followed by a growth of population. . . . If another Ireland was raised up from the Atlantic, we might expect to see the Irish birth-rate rise and the vacant land peopled. There is little reason to suppose that, if another England was raised up out of the North Sea, we should see a rise in the English birth-rate.[37]

In common with others who were writing about population trends during the 1930s, Carr-Saunders believed that the falling birthrate was a direct consequence of readier access to information on birth control. According to Carr-Saunders's analysis: (1) There is a correspondence between the date when birth-control propaganda became intensive and the date when the birthrate began to decline in most countries. It is reasonable to assume that birth-control practices were stimulated by the consumption of birth-control literature. (2) In almost every country the decline began in the upper economic class and spread downward in such a fashion that there has come into being a marked negative correlation between social status and fertility.[38]

Information on birth control and access to contraceptive devices became much more widely available in the years immediately following the end of the 1914–18 war, mainly due to the publication of Marie Stopes's book *Married Love* in 1918. Stopes was an outstanding publicist, who campaigned to make contraceptives respectable, especially for married couples. Although contraceptives had been available for some time, they were primarily regarded as a means of avoiding venereal disease, and their use was associated with prostitutes, not the marriage bed. During the 1920s many respectable newspapers and magazines began to carry advertisements offering advice manuals or mail-order sales of contraceptive devices. The British medical profession and the Church of England remained bitterly divided between opponents and proponents of contraception, but in 1930 the Lambeth Conference—the official assembly of the Church of England—reversed its previous opposition and endorsed birth control in limited circumstances and "in the light of . . . Christian principles," a decision that left the Catholic church as the most prominent opponent of birth control.[39]

Carr-Saunders's analysis of the factors bringing about the spread of contraception reinforced his opinion that Ireland would not follow the general trend toward smaller families. He believed that the speed at which information about contraception and new methods of contraception was adopted in a particular country was determined by the proportion of the population living in urban areas and by religious practice. Fertility was generally higher among rural families; where it was possible to compare the fertility of different religious groups, Catholics, who were taught by their church not to use birth control, had a much higher fertility than Protestants.[40] As to why couples wanted smaller families, he suggested the importance of changing attitudes toward contraception, "the unceasing propaganda in its favour," particularly the association between contraception and the movement for women's rights. Other factors that encouraged smaller families included the introduction of legislation that destroyed the value of child labor, such as compulsory schooling and the factory acts,[41] the pursuit of leisure in modern society, and "the effort to rise in the social scale [which] may well be frustrated by a large family."[42]

As a predominantly rural and Catholic country where very few married women worked outside the home (and the state actively discouraged them from doing so), it was highly improbable that Ireland would adopt the "small-family system." Child labor remained important to family farms and family businesses, and the state adopted an acquiescent attitude toward children who absented themselves from school for seasonal work on the farm. It is often suggested that Ireland was cut off from the major intellectual currents in Europe during the 1920s and 1930s; however, Irish churchmen, academics, senior public servants, and some politicians appear to have been very aware of the international debate over a falling birthrate, and there were widespread fears that Ireland would not be immune to this trend.[43] Halliday Sutherland, a Scottish medical doctor and convert to Catholicism who had been one of the leading opponents in Britain of Marie Stopes's birth-control campaign (in 1923 she took a highly publicized libel action against him that went all the way to the House of Lords),[44] was invited to Ireland to give public lectures on the problem of population in 1935 and again in 1936.[45] In December 1936, *Studies*, a periodical produced by the Irish Jesuit community, published an essay by George O'Brien that discussed recent books on population by Carr-Saunders and Glass as well as preliminary results of the 1936 census and Roy Geary's Irish population projections.[46] In March 1937, Professor John Busteed of University College Cork read a paper to the Statistical and Social Inquiry Society on "The Problem of Population," which opened with the statement that "the problem of population is going to be of growing importance to the white races in the coming decades," and he did not exempt Ireland.

Busteed feared that Irish society was too complacent that births would continue to exceed deaths.[47] His concerns were probably a reaction to the preliminary findings of the 1936 census, showing a significant decline in births: although the population had fallen by 3,572 since the last census in 1926, the number under twenty-one years of age had fallen by 69,000.[48] Enrollment in national schools (state primary schools) fell in 1931 and 1932 (perhaps as a result of the establishment of vocational schools), and although it recovered in 1933, all counties recorded falling enrollment in 1934 and 1935.[49] The declining number of primary school pupils was one of the factors behind the 1933 ban on the employment of women teachers after marriage.[50] When de Valera received the preliminary report of the 1936 census he asked government statisticians whether the numbers of children by age were consistent with recent enrollment trends in infant classes.

Censorship and Contraception

Fears that Ireland was not immune from the European trend toward smaller families did not begin in 1936. Although many scholars who have written about the 1929 Censorship of Publications Act have highlighted the banning of many modern novels under the act, its main purpose was to restrict access to information about contraception. When the Catholic Truth Society of Ireland (CTSI), one of the groups who lobbied for the legislation, gave evidence to the Committee on Evil Literature in 1926, their principal demand was that "neo-Malthusian birth control" be made illegal. They urged a ban on all printed matter that advocated birth control or published birth-control propaganda and a prohibition on the sale of birth-control appliances or drugs. The CTSI was convinced that there was a "clear association between the advocacy of birth-control and the publication of obscene literature." Denying people access to modern literature, they argued, was an unfortunate but necessary consequence of the need to prevent the spread of contraception.[51] Indeed a key element in the moral crusade of the 1920s against "flappers," dance halls, and the cinema was the belief that they all served to promote a more receptive attitude toward contraception.

The concerns expressed by the CTSI and other Catholic groups were by no means unfounded, because over one hundred letters from Ireland, written between 1918 and 1940, survive in the Marie Stopes archives. The majority were written by middle-class or upper-class men. Cormac Ó Gráda has described them as "surely a useful guide to the extent that the postal service provided a voice to some of those living far from the early family planning clinics, that it guaranteed confidentiality, and that it was inexpensive."[52]

The 1929 Censorship of Publications Act made it much more difficult for Irish couples to secure information or contraceptive devices. Section 16 made it a crime to print, publish, sell, or distribute "any book or periodical publication which advocates or might reasonably be supposed to advocate the unnatural prevention of conception."[53] Many of the publications submitted to the Censorship Board were periodicals and manuals offering advice about sex and contraception. The April 1930 edition of *Cage Birds and Bird World*—a magazine filled with articles such as "My Method of Rearing Canaries," came to the board's attention because of a back-page advertisement for Le Brasseur Surgical Company in Birmingham offering free copies of several books, including *A Letter to Working Mothers* by Marie Stopes, *Family Limitation* by Margaret Sanger, and *Advice to*

Married Women (illustrated) by Dr. St. Clair Maurice, plus a list of sex books and an illustrated catalogue of birth-control appliances. *The Ladder,* a magazine for racing tipsters, was also reported to the Censorship Board, not for its poor record on the race track but for an advertisement for *Woman and Marriage* by Dr. Richard Harley. The advertisement included a quotation by the archbishop of Canterbury, Dr. Cosmo Lang: "I would rather have all the risks which come from free discussion than the greater risks which we run by a conspiracy of silence. We want to liberate the sex impulse which is part of the heritage of humanity." In March 1931, the CTSI drew the board's attention to a supplement to the February 6 issue of *Poultry World* containing several advertisements for birth-control appliances.[54] In December of the same year Frank O'Reilly, president of the CTSI, wrote to S. A. Roche, secretary of the Department of Justice, urging a ban of the *Sunday Times* newspaper, because O'Reilly claimed that a recent edition had carried an article advocating birth control. In his reply, Roche pointed out that, as it could not be claimed that the *Sunday Times* has usually or frequently advocated birth control, a complaint to the Censorship Board would not be justified. The only legal redress was to prosecute the distributors and retailers, but Roche believed that it would be "unduly harsh" to initiate legal action, and moreover, it would probably fail on the grounds that it would be unreasonable to expect distributors and retailers to check the entire contents of every newspaper or periodical that they sold. However, a letter would be sent to the publishers of *The Sunday Times,* and Roche believed that there would not be "a repetition of the offence."[55] The Censorship Board did not take legal action against periodicals or newspapers that were prepared to give an assurance not to publish such material in future. By 1930 several British periodicals were omitting advertisements for books or birth-control devices in order to safeguard sales in Ireland; however, a three-month ban was imposed on three Sunday newspapers, including the best-selling *News of the World.*[56]

Despite clear evidence that the Censorship Act was proving effective, the Catholic church did not relax its concern. According to David Fitzpatrick, the 1931 Lenten pastorals "provide vivid evidence of contemporary moral panic. Of the twenty-six episcopal pastorals, twelve reaffirmed the sanctity of marriage or inadmissibility of divorce; eleven deplored the insidious effects of the press, wireless, or evil literature; eight inveighed against the cinema or theatre; six warned of the dangers of dancing; four alluded delicately to contraception, abortion or infanticide; three condemned company-keeping; while irregular unions and immodesty in female dress each provoked two admonitions."[57] This "contemporary moral panic" reflects a failure on the part of the Catholic hierarchy to reverse what it saw as the moral decline that occurred in Ireland during the years of World War I and the wars of independence and the civil war, when there was a rising incidence of extramarital pregnancy and venereal disease.[58] The 1931 Lenten pastorals also reflect a growing concern within the Catholic church about the spread of birth control following the decision by the Lambeth Conference. In December 1931 Pope Pius XI issued an encyclical, *Casti Connubi*, on Christian marriage, which emphasized that states should provide a legal code that would protect marriage—including measures to protect chastity and to prevent divorce, contraception, and women working outside the home.[59] One writer has suggested that this encyclical, the strongest statement by the papacy on contraception since the time of Sixtus V (1585–90) was intended "to dissipate all doubts" on this matter. Catholic parents were urged "to bear offspring for the Church of Christ, to procreate saints and servants of God, that the people adhering to the worship of God and our Saviour should daily increase."[60] Priests were urged to enforce papal teaching in the confessional.[61]

The early 1930s marked a high point in the Catholic church's campaign against contraception.[62] In his 1931 Lenten pastoral, the archbishop of Tuam, Dr. Gilmartin, asserted the right of Catholic patients to be treated by doctors who upheld Catholic teaching on "childbirth and kindred subjects."[63] In 1932 Dr. Stafford Johnson, master of the Guild of Saints Cosmas and Damian, a group representing Catholic doctors, enlisted the support of the Department of External Affairs to secure the removal of a reference to contraception from a League of Nations manual on maternal and child health.[64] The fears reflected in the Lenten pastorals were addressed to some degree by the incoming Fianna Fáil government. The 1933 budget imposed severe import duties on imported newspapers and periodicals, which meant that Irish readers were less likely to be tempted by dangerous periodicals such as *Poultry World*. Imports of British newspapers and periodicals fell sharply, and a number of Irish publications, which did not carry dangerous advertisements or articles, emerged to fill the gap.[65]

In 1931 the Carrigan Committee, which was appointed to consider possible amendments to the Criminal Law Amendment Acts of 1880 and 1885, recommended "that the sale of contraceptives should be prohibited except in exceptional circumstances"; an addendum by Reverend John Hannon, S.J., indicated that "exceptional circumstances" was only meant to prevent the banning of drugs that might be essential for other purposes—it was not intended to open up a loophole permitting the limited sale of contraceptives. However, an all-party committee of TDs chaired by the minister for Justice, James Geoghegan, determined that a complete ban on contraceptives might be unduly severe. In the light of their comments, a Criminal Law Amendment Bill was prepared that provided for a ban on the sale, distribution, and import for sale or distribution of contraceptive appliances but permitted qualified medical practitioners to supply contraceptives to their patients and to import them under license from the minister for Local Government and Public Health. However, these provisions were removed by the cabinet. A note written by an official in the Department of Justice to the minister, following the cabinet's decision, commented that "the question of contraceptives seems to have given a very considerable amount of trouble." Section 17 of the 1935 Criminal Law Amendment Act prohibited the sale and import of contraceptives, but not without opposition being voiced in both the Dáil and the Seanad.[66] In Dublin's National Maternity Hospital, established as a Catholic alternative to the Rotunda and Coombe Hospitals, which were regarded as Protestant or nondenominational establishments, the 1930s brought a sustained attack on Protestant acceptance of contraception and a more ostentatious display of the hospital's Catholic credentials with crucifixes on the walls.[67] But according to Earner-Byrne, "even the Church of Ireland shied away from direct statements in favour of birth control." The board of the Coombe Hospital denounced a statement by one Protestant clergyman defending the use of birth control in "hard cases."[68]

The cordon sanitaire against contraception created by the 1935 Criminal Law Amendment Act was threatened by the findings of two medical scientists, Ogino and Knaus (one Japanese, the other Austrian), that it was possible to prevent conception by abstaining from sex during part of a women's menstrual cycle. This discovery attracted widespread publicity in the United States during 1932[69] and sparked a major debate among Catholic moral theologians over the morality of this method of birth control. The Catholic church gave the Ogino-Knaus method, or the "safe period," very qualified approval. In 1934 in response to a query, the *Irish Ecclesiastical Record*, an official publication of the Catholic hierarchy, expressed the opinion that very few married couples would have sufficient cause to justify using the safe period, and for this reason instruction on its use should only be given to individual couples, it should not be disseminated through popular pamphlets. If the practice of the safe period became widespread, the anonymous author feared that it would be as "socially calamitous as the intrinsically immoral practice of birth-control."[70] In his 1937 paper "The Problem of Population," Busteed expressed confidence that the measures in place in Ireland would prevent any significant spread of contraceptives and abortifacients, but he feared that fertility might be threatened by the recent discovery of "the safe period." If it proved effective in preventing conception, Busteed anticipated that the information would spread rapidly, opening up the possibility of "a drastic reduction" in the Irish birthrate and a decline in the size of Irish families similar to what was happening elsewhere. He claimed that information about the safe period had been spreading quietly throughout the Irish middle class for the past two years.[71]

Busteed, a committed member of the Catholic Action movement,[72] noted that there was nothing immoral about the safe period; nevertheless, he was concerned that this method of family planning could not be prevented by the existing legislative code or by church teaching. In 1942 the Censorship Board banned Halliday Sutherland's *Laws of Life*, a book that contained diagrams showing how to calculate the time of ovulation. The banning of this book, despite the fact that it carried a *permissu superiorum* from the archbishop of Westminster indicating that the book was not inaccurate in its references to Catholic doctrine,[73] is one of the most notorious chapters in the history of the Irish Censorship Board. In 1942 Seanad Éireann banned *Laws of Life* and two other books, Kate O'Brien's novel *Land of Spices* and *The Tailor and Ansty* by Eric Cross.[74] Sir John Keane, who proposed the motion criticizing these decisions, noted that *Laws of Life* had been banned only because it contained information about the safe period. In reply, the minister for Justice Gerald Boland expressed his full support for the board's decision, because if the book were in general circulation, in his opinion it "would do untold damage." Boland dismissed the argument that the book should not have been banned because it carried a *permissu superiorum* from the archdiocese of Westminster. He claimed that conditions were different in England and that birth control was freely advocated there; the decision to ban the book was justified because the advocacy of birth control was not permitted in Ireland.[75] *Laws of Life* was first published in 1935 by the leading Catholic publisher Sheed and Ward, but it was not banned until 1941, by which time it had gone through several editions. Although Sutherland provided detailed diagrams of the female reproductive organs and charts, showing how to calculate the time of ovulation, he reiterated the teaching of the Catholic church that the safe period should only be used for grave reasons, and as the text on the dust jacket notes, "without any appeal to ethics he proves the failure of contraception, and shows that in so far as it is successful, this practice has been against the welfare of the nation." Sutherland claimed some years later that the banning of *Laws of Life* was not prompted by the chapter on the safe period but "because I had written in the cold language of physiology an account of the functions of sex. . . . In Eire too many people, including clerics, regard ignorance as synonymous with innocence." He noted that in 1944 he had published a larger book, *Control of Life*, which devoted two chapters to the safe period, and that this book, which received the imprimatur of the Westminster Diocesan Board of Censorship, was not banned in Ireland.[76] However, it is possible that *Control of Life* escaped a ban because of government embarrassment over banning the *Laws of Life*. The controversy would have attracted even greater interest if it had been known that Seán Mac-Entee, then minister for Industry and Commerce, had circulated excerpts from *Laws of Life* among his cabinet colleagues some months earlier to support his claim that paying children's allowances would not result in increased births.[77]

Irish Fertility 1900–1940

By the 1930s it was generally believed that the knowledge and practice of birth control had reached middle-class and professional households first and had then spread to lower socioeconomic groups. This theory emerged from an examination of fertility data in the 1911 population census for England and Wales, which appeared to show a systematic relationship between fertility and socioeconomic status, with the highest fertility found in unskilled laborers and the lowest in professional households.[78]

Although the 1911 Irish census collected identical data on fertility, it was classified not by occupation but by geographical area. Fertility in Dublin and Belfast was slightly below the national average. Irish couples married for twenty to twenty-four years had given birth to an average of 5.87 live children; for Belfast the figure was 5.73, and for Dublin city and suburbs, 5.60.[79] Recent research using the 1911 census forms for Pembroke township, then an independent local authority to the south of Dublin city, suggests that on average Catholic couples had 3.78 children, compared with 2.78 for non-Catholic couples. This disparity applied irrespective of the duration of marriage; among couples married for twenty to twenty-nine years, Catholics had an average of 6.63 children, compared with 5.15 for non-Catholic couples. Catholic couples were also less likely to remain childless. Class differences may explain part of the higher fertility of Catholic couples; 89 percent of Pembroke laborers were Catholic but Catholics only accounted for 32 percent of those in professional occupations. And in Pembroke, as in England and Wales, professional couples had the smallest families: 3.76 children for those married twenty to twenty-nine years compared with 9.47 for semiskilled and 7.64 for laboring couples.[80] These findings confirm earlier research by Ó Gráda, which established that by 1911 many Irish couples, even in rural areas, were practicing some form of family planning. He concluded that the leaders in family limitation appear to have been larger farmers, those in nonagricultural occupations, and Protestants.[81]

The publication of the 1936 census figures showing a fall in births over the previous ten years prompted the cabinet to seek further information on comparative birthrates in urban and rural areas as well as occupational fertility. A memorandum issued to the cabinet in June 1939 reported that the fall in the number of young children between 1926 and 1936 reflected declining fertility of married women in the reproductive age; the decline was much greater among rural women, and although fertility in rural households was approximately 25 percent higher than in towns and cities, the rates were converging. However, because no question on fertility was included in the 1936 census—suggesting that there was no great interest in the topic when the forms were being devised—the analysis relied on reworking data from the 1926 census and examining the parental occupations of all babies whose births were registered between October 1937 and September 1938.

However imperfect, the statistics suggested that high marital fertility was strongly associated with low socioeconomic status. Of the 56,266 infants born between October 1937 and September 1938, almost one-third were the children of laborers, who were described as "the poorest section of the community," although statisticians suggested that some fathers falsely reported their occupations as laborers in order to qualify for welfare benefits.[82] Fertility data from the 1926 census confirmed the impression that poor households had the largest families: "the more well to do the occupation the less [sic] children there are of the marriage, particularly in the earlier years of married life." Farming families had the highest fertility. Catholic couples married for five to nine years had 36 percent more children than non-Catholic couples; for marriages lasting fifteen to nineteen years the difference was 46 percent.[83] However, this unpublished report sidestepped the possible influence of religion on marital fertility by suggesting that lower fertility among Protestants might reflect fertility differences based on class, not religion.[84]

The Relationship between Fertility and Economic Conditions

Although the declining birthrate in western Europe during the interwar years appeared to coincide with an economic recession, the precise relationship between economic conditions and marriage and fertility was unclear. Carr-Saunders claimed that Ireland was the only country where an improvement in economic circumstances would bring about a rise in the number of births, because he believed that Ireland's low marriage rate reflected a lack of economic opportunities, but many Irish experts did not share his optimism. George O'Brien dismissed Carr-Saunders's claim as "very improbable, in view of the increasing urbanization of the Irish Free State and the rising standard of living,"[85] but O'Brien's assumption that Ireland was experiencing "increasing urbanization" and a "rising standard of living" in the 1930s is open to question. In 1935 Geary suggested that there was an inverse relationship between the marriage rate and marital fertility: countries with the highest rate of marriage had the smallest families. He detected a similar pattern in Ireland where Dublin had the highest marriage rate and the smallest families, whereas the reverse applied in Connacht.[86] Seán MacEntee, the minister for Finance, dismissed the idea that Ireland's population decline was a consequence of poor economic conditions: "We are too ready to accept the suggestion that the decline in our population particularly during the last twenty or thirty years, has been entirely due to the economic circumstances which have prevailed here. The fact is that over that period there has been a very considerable improvement in our economic circumstances so that there must be other active factors affecting adversely our population trend, and it would be useful to endeavour to ascertain what these are."

MacEntee was responding to the 1936 Swedish Royal Commission on Population, which concluded that there was little hope of a higher birthrate unless citizens were guaranteed better social conditions and greater security. He pointed out that the decline in family size in Sweden was most pronounced among the middle class, which appeared to indicate that it was unrelated to economic circumstances.[87] As the minister who would have to find money for improved social services and measures to boost family incomes, it was in his interest to deny that population growth could be influenced in this manner.

During the 1930s many European countries responded to concern over a declining population by introducing measures that were designed to boost births and marriages. These ranged from serious financial incentives to encourage marriage and parenthood to the comical (the hundred-lire annual bachelor tax levied by the Italian state was less than the dog tax) and the coercive (a prohibition on contraception or abortion and restrictions on married women working outside the home). Nazi Germany introduced marriage loans that were progressively remitted with the birth of each child, and both Mussolini and Hitler introduced measures honoring mothers of large families—in Italy the ceremony was held on 24 December; in Germany on the birthday of Hitler's mother. In 1937 the parish priest of Bantry, Canon O'Leary, suggested that the government should award marriage bounties to young men living on holdings of £5 valuation or less (in other words, very small farms). There were only twelve marriages in Bantry parish during 1935 and fourteen in 1936, and he believed that marriage bounties would encourage young men to marry, and this in turn would reduce the number of young women who emigrated.[88] Robert Flynn, an Irish-American whose personalized notepaper carried the slogan "Remember—Go to Church this Week," urged de Valera to provide marriage bounties, because earlier marriages would inevitably result in a higher birthrate: "The raging fires of young love are much more productive than the flickering flames of advancing age. The earlier start in creating a family will tend to increase the ultimate size of each family."[89]

Yet the impact of such measures is debatable. Preventing married women from working outside the home or denying access to contraception and abortion appears to have had little impact on the birthrate, and although the German marriage rate recovered after 1933, this probably owed more to improved economic conditions than to marriage loans.[90] In 1940, having reviewed a range of pronatalist measures throughout Europe, David Glass concluded that the trend in fertility "appears unrelated to measurable economic or social phenomena." He claimed that the various measures were "introduced blindly" in the absence of any precise knowledge about the factors that influenced the decline in fertility.[91] Glass was extremely skeptical about the ability of governments to reverse the decline in population.[92]

Family Allowances

By the late 1930s, however, family allowances were widely seen as an effective means of reversing the falling birthrate. In the immediate aftermath of the 1914–18 war, some French employers introduced welfare funds that provided additional benefits for workers with young families. Most were motivated by Catholic social teaching on the family wage. Statistics on family size in participating firms appeared to indicate that the allowances had resulted in larger families.[93] By the mid-1930s campaigns for family allowances in various European countries had attracted the support of a diverse range of interest groups that included feminists, advocates of Catholic social teaching, and workers' representatives.[94] The 1931 papal encyclical *Quadragesimo Anno* urged that the state should create conditions that would enable every head of a family to earn "as much as according to his station in life is necessary for himself, his wife and the rearing of his children."[95] Between 1937 and 1939, legislation providing for some form of family allowances was introduced in Italy, Spain, Hungary, Chile, New Zealand, and the Australian state of New South Wales, and existing state-supported schemes in Belgium and France were substantially extended.[96]

In Ireland the pronatalist justification for family allowances appeared limited, given the high fertility of Irish marriages. When the minister for Industry and Commerce, Seán Lemass, introduced legislation in 1943 providing for children's allowances, he emphasized that its purpose was to alleviate poverty in large families; he did not anticipate that it would have an impact on births or marriages.[97] Yet although family allowances were regarded very much as a means of relieving poverty, their introduction generated some very heated exchanges concerning the relationship between economic conditions and marriages and births as well as the benefits of an increased population, although most of this debate was conducted on unpublished government files, not in Dáil Éireann or in print. There is an extensive secondary literature on the introduction of children's allowances in Ireland; the following pages concentrate on the views of cabinet ministers and senior officials, not on the legislation.[98]

The first Irish politician to champion the case for children's allowances was Fine Gael deputy James Dillon. In 1939 he suggested that the state pay an allowance of 5s. a week in respect of every child after the fourth child in families with a weekly income of less than £2. He estimated that a maximum of sixty thousand children would qualify.

Dillon spoke with knowledge and sympathy about the financial difficulties for families with five and more children.[99] His proposal may have attracted the attention of Eamon de Valera, because the latter discussed the matter some weeks later with his advisor on economic matters, University College Cork (UCC) economics professor Timothy Smiddy. On 26 May 1939, Smiddy presented de Valera with a report on the feasibility of paying a weekly or monthly allowance to heads of families with a weekly wage of less than £3 10s. (more than double the weekly wage of agricultural laborers) and to farmers with a net annual income of less than £38. Smiddy calculated that it would cost approximately £9.5 million annually to pay a family allowance of "say 15/- (75p) per week" to 75 percent of married men in industry and distributive trades—approximately 100,000 men—and to 50 percent of married farmers with holdings under fifteen acres and 50 percent of agricultural laborers.[100] Although the high cost appeared to rule out the introduction of children's allowances, the idea did not disappear, because shortly after this the minister for Defence submitted a memorandum to government, proposing that they should be paid to farm laborers and small farmers, and the Department of Local Government and Public Health was asked to examine the matter.[101]

They reported that paying family allowances to urban and rural wage earners (in other words, categories covered by the existing contributory social insurance schemes) would help alleviate poverty resulting from marriage and parenthood and would encourage earlier marriages. A similar case could be made for paying allowances to self-employed workers "of small means," who were not covered by existing social insurance provisions. However, they were of the opinion that marriage and parenthood were less of a burden on farmers than on other sections of the community, because food and accommodation were cheaper and more readily available and children could help out on the farm. The Department of Local Government and Public Health envisaged that a scheme of family allowances would be financed through social insurance contributions, which may explain their reluctance to include farmers, but it would have been politically impossible to have done this, given the growing concerns over rural marriages. Perhaps this explains why a cabinet committee, chaired by the minister for Local Government, reviewed this report and recommended two separate schemes: a contributory scheme for those covered by social insurance and a noncontributory scheme, subject to a means test, for the remainder of the population.[102]

In June 1940 the minister for Finance, Seán T. O'Kelly, submitted a memorandum that was probably drafted by J. J. McElligott, secretary of the department. It began by expressing surprise that the subcommittee had given no indication of the aims behind the proposed introduction of children's allowances; it suspected that "anxiety as to the trend of population, the decline in the marriage rate, and in fertility, particularly in rural areas, are the propelling forces in putting forward a Family Allowance scheme." If that was so, it suggested that the case for encouraging a higher population "needs to be substantiated, and, in any event, family endowment is not a sure or sufficient means of attaining this end." It questioned the presupposition that "wealth and abundance of enjoyment is greater in a larger than in a smaller population"; the experience in other countries suggested the impact of children's allowances on the birthrate was unproven, partly because the allowances were never sufficient to offset the cost of raising and educating a child. Furthermore, the reasons for late marriages and falling fertility were not entirely economic:

> Once the bare minimum necessary for existence has been reached, every improvement in the standard of living has been followed by a decrease, not an increase in the birth rate. The decline in fertility appears to be due to a complex of psychological, physiological and economic causes. There is a tendency for parents to try to do better for their children; there is a desire to preserve their own comfort and to conform to fashion; and a small family appears to be best adapted in many ways to the modern organisation of society. The age at marriage also becomes higher. This may be due to causes of the following kind in addition to or instead of actual economic inability to marry; the prolongation of the educative period, the greater opportunities now available for interests outside the family home, the relaxation of the rigidity of parental discipline, the desire to start married life on a standard which will not involve much sacrifice, general habit and the influence of parental advice. It would seem likely that, at least in the rural districts in Éire, the chief reason for the late marriage age is generally economic; but the fall in the birth rate may to some extent be a reflection of an improved standard of living among

these farmers who do marry, as it is not due to an increased average age of their wives. *It is improbable that family allowances would increase the birth rate of members of the lowest economic class as they "do not regulate the size of their families by economic considerations."*[103]

This statement displays scant knowledge of Ireland in the early 1940s. The reference to the "prolongation of the educative period" when the overwhelming majority of children attended only primary schools suggests that it was written from the perspective of the urban middle class, and this is confirmed by the statement in the final sentence that there was no necessity to encourage a higher birthrate among the lowest economic class "as they 'do not regulate the size of their families by economic considerations.'"[104]

Seán MacEntee, now minister for Industry and Commerce, had already dismissed claims that birth and marriage rates would respond to economic inducements. "As one may bring a horse to the water and fail to make him drink, so, too, the State may penalize bachelorhood and make the matrimonial state by comparison financially attractive, because matrimony is not at root a matter of money. Indeed such serious investigations into the population problem as have been undertaken so far rather tend to disprove the contention that the financial factor is the predominating one. All sorts of physiological and psychological factors enter into this problem, and however the financial aspect of it may be stressed, the fact remains that in quite a large proportion of cases reluctance to marry is based on other than monetary grounds."

He objected to the fact that single people would be forced to pay higher taxes to finance children's allowances, suggesting that higher taxes would encourage single people to emigrate, adding a quasi-eugenic argument that those who marry were those "who are best fitted naturally to marry. . . . So that in order to drive the unfit into matrimony we are to drive the strongest, the most enterprising, the best educated of our young earners out of the country. It is hard to see how a proposal which would have this effect would help us to solve the population problem." As an alternative to financial incentives, he suggested that the state should enhance the status and privileges of parenthood. "This generation inherited a sound social organisation of immemorial ancestry, deeply rooted in the traditions of our race, based upon the patriarchal principle that honour, respect and obedience were due to the heads of the household, because these shouldered great responsibilities. We have relieved the parents of a large measure of their household responsibilities—rightly so in many cases—but we have also shorn them of many of their public privileges. Today the married man and his wife carrying the whole burden of their families have no more voice in the direction of public affairs than the flapper or the whipper-snapper of twenty-one." To reinvest the married state with "some of its former dignity," he recommended that the electorate of the Seanad should consist of married men and women with family responsibilities, and that unemployment benefits for single men (no single women qualified) should be paid to their parents.[105]

The Department of Finance condemned the growing intrusion of the state into family life in phrases that faithfully reproduced the social teaching of the Catholic church.[106] Far from protecting the family, it alleged that the proposal to redistribute incomes from the single and childless to families with dependent children was motivated by "the extreme objective urged by some schools of thought that the mother and young family are the responsibility of the whole community and must be provided by the State," a point of view that "eventually leads to the nationalisation of mother and offspring and the break-up of the ordinary ideas of family ties and responsibilities." MacEntee was even more apocalyptic. "If the State subsidises parents to have children, it will be but a step to regulate the number of children, then to lay down who shall be permitted to have children and who shall not, how the subsidized children are to be brought up, to what purposes they are to devote their lives, what physical and mental characteristics are to be encouraged by subsidized breeding, who shall be bred to labor and who to govern, etc., etc., until we shall have traversed the whole ground between the initiation of a State System of Family Allowances and the Servile State." (This was a favorite term in Catholic social teaching.)[107]

This outburst may have been a reaction against the population policies being pursued by Nazi Germany. MacEntee made a more explicit reference to Germany in a later memorandum when he noted that "the population problem has been approached in a frankly physical and materialistic way. . . . Men are wanted for the all-conquering German army and the bearing of children, whether in or out of wedlock, is glorified accordingly." There was no military argument in Ireland in favor of a larger population; unemployment was high and many young people were not gainfully occupied. Instead of cash payments, he recommended that large families should be given food vouchers, vitamin supplements, larger houses, and cheaper apartments. The money saved by not paying family allowances would be more usefully employed providing educational facilities, school meals, and a better medical service.

A third, and even longer, report (forty-five pages against twenty-two for the previous installment) from MacEntee, dated 12 September 1940, drew on books by Alexander Gray and D. V. Glass.[108] MacEntee obviously relished some of the more exotic examples cited in Glass's book, which was primarily concerned with population policies and demographic trends over the past twenty years. On this occasion, cabinet colleagues were treated to accounts of the population policies of the Emperor Trajan and Frederick the Great, family practices among the Japanese samurai, and summaries of family policies in postwar Germany, Italy, and France. Although Glass claimed that there was insufficient data to permit him to assess the effectiveness of these earlier attempts to encourage population growth,[109] MacEntee had no such qualms. He claimed that pronatalist measures had not proved successful in the past; indeed that they "have only been revived in modern times when the memories of past failures have been forgotten."[110]

It is highly improbable that any other government in Europe was debating matters such as this in October 1940; however, it is very difficult to determine the effect of these memoranda on government policy. On 22 October the cabinet referred the report of the ministerial subcommittee to an interdepartmental committee of civil servants. Initially they were asked to report on the desirability or otherwise of introducing a system of family allowance and the incidental social and economic consequences, with particular reference to the encouragement of marriage, size of families, emigration, and the movement of population from rural to urban areas. But the terms of reference were later amended, removing all references to births, marriages, and emigration.

Despite these changes in the terms of reference, the report submitted to cabinet in October 1942 *did* consider the impact of family allowances on population. It concluded that the late age of marriage and the decline in fertility were not due solely to economic causes; in general, once the bare minimum necessary for existence had been achieved, any improvement in living standards was followed by a falling birthrate. The evidence that children's allowances would promote a higher birthrate was inconclusive. And even if it could be proven that they were effective, there was no justification for using family allowances for this purpose, because Irish birth and marriage rates were sufficiently high to ensure a rise in population. Emigration was "the primary problem." The interdepartmental committee remarked that whether or not a higher rate of natural increase would be desirable was a controversial topic, but one that would remain "largely academic until a solution is found for the problem of emigration."[111] The committee noted that in Britain the campaign for family allowances was associated with demands for equal pay for women and the recognition of the dignity and status of motherhood, implying that such considerations did not arise in Ireland.[112] However, they also suggested that Irish interest in children's allowances was prompted by the 1936 census, which showed a fall in the number of children.

According to the interdepartmental committee, the only justification for children's allowances was to relieve hardship, given that wages did not take family circumstances into consideration. Family allowances provided "a means of reducing the incidence of hardship due to child dependency, not of ensuring that no family will ever feel the pinch of want."[113]

In January 1942, before the interdepartmental committee had reported, MacEntee presented his cabinet colleagues with excerpts from Halliday Sutherland's book, *Laws of Life*. These were carefully chosen in order to demonstrate that "the reproduction of the species is controlled by vast and complex forces of which we know little,"[114] and that poverty and hardship rather than affluence resulted in a higher birthrate. Among the passages in Sutherland's book circulated by MacEntee were references to: the rapid increase in the Israelite population during their captivity in Egypt; statements by Malthus and other social and physical scientists "that under conditions of hardship the birthrate tends to rise, and that in circumstances of ease the birthrate tends to fall"; the findings of the 1911 census for England and Wales that there was an inverse relationship between fertility and social status; and more chillingly, the views of John Brownlee, a former director of statistics at the Medical Research Council and author of *The Declining Population*, that "the saving of infant life in the more comfortable tenements compensates to but a slight extent for the lower fertility." Sutherland claimed that British fertility data indicated that "as far back as reliable figures can be obtained, the poor have always had more children than the rich, and under conditions of hardship the birthrate has *always* been higher than in circumstances of ease."[115] The fall in fertility since 1851 was due to improved social conditions and what Brownlee described as "race physiology,"[116] a term that he did not define. Halliday Sutherland also claimed that populations grew more rapidly in rural areas than in cities.[117] When MacEntee circulated this document, most politicians in Europe were preoccupied with war and national survival. In Ireland government files dating from the 1920s were being pulped and recycled because of an acute paper shortage, but hundreds of sheets of paper (and typists' time) was devoted to producing this eccentric memorandum.

MacEntee's final tutorial on demography for his cabinet colleagues was delivered in February 1946. On this occasion the text was an article in the English Catholic periodical *The Tablet*.[118] The writer dismissed several popular explanations for "the revolt against parenthood," such as fear of war, insecurity, poverty, and unemployment and suggested that the falling birthrate was a consequence of the "Acquisitive Society," the urge to "keep up with the Joneses," and the growing demand for leisure activities such as the cinema, dances, libraries, dog races, adult education lectures, and summer schools, that could only be enjoyed by adults who were unencumbered with children. He claimed that there was a positive correlation between wealth and education and an inverse relationship between wealth and the birthrate, and he mused whether by introducing the 1944 Education Act, British MPs were "unwittingly . . . hammering another nail in the coffin of the race." MacEntee underlined the following section in the memorandum that he circulated to cabinet colleagues: "Before further remedies are suggested, it will be well to ask if in fact they are remedies at all. All the various social and legislative proposals for increasing the birthrate from domestic helps to family allowances and differential rents, are directed in fact to the production or to the extension of just these social conditions which, in the last two generations, have been accompanied by a decline in the birthrate. Social security is not, it seems the way to the sizeable family; and the bias against babies will not be beaten by Beveridge."[119]

The thrust of this article and of the excerpts taken from Halliday Sutherland is obvious. Any increase in economic prosperity results in a lower birthrate; the extension of social services and educational opportunities would have a similar damaging effect. The only way to maintain Irish fertility at its existing level was to keep the population poor, ignorant, and away from cities. Prosperity would only bring about the dreaded "acquisitive society." MacEntee has been dubbed "a political black-thorn," and it would be unwise to assume that other members of de Valera's cabinet shared his views,[120] nevertheless these memoranda give some indication of the pitfalls facing any Irish government that attempted to devise measures to promote population growth.

If we strip away the antistatist philosophy and the overheated rhetoric that underpin MacEntee's memoranda, his argument that social policies were unlikely to bring about a higher birthrate is broadly correct. Most scholars believe that the pronatalist measures introduced during the 1930s and afterward had little impact on births, although they resulted in a greater interest in the quality of children's lives and more determined efforts to promote maternal and child health and welfare. It has been suggested that the increasing emphasis placed on the importance of motherhood during these years persuaded many women that they should limit the number of children in order to give them a better quality of life.[121]

This did not happen in Ireland. Although there is evidence of a growing interest in health and welfare services for mothers and children during the early 1940s,[122] Irish mothers were not subjected to an aggressive campaign valorizing motherhood, unlike their counterparts in Germany, Italy, or France, and they were less likely to have been bombarded with messages about hygiene, vitamins, and infant feeding than mothers in Britain. A passing comment by Helen Murtagh, a Birmingham city councillor and a member of that city's public health committee, is instructive. In 1942 she told Archbishop McQuaid that the facilities for single mothers and their babies in Dublin's Regina Coeli hostel compared very unfavorably with those in England, "all because the Ministry of Health pays again and again to build future citizens."[123] The 1942 Beveridge Report stated that "in the next thirty years housewives as mothers have vital work to do in ensuring the adequate continuance of the British race and of British ideals in the world."[124] There was little evidence of a corresponding interest in Ireland.

In 1941 Theo McWeeney, a medical inspector in the Department of Local Government and Public Health, presented the interdepartmental committee on children's allowances with statistics giving the minimum cost of a basic diet for households of various sizes, but no serious consideration appears to have been given otherwise to the cost of raising a large family.[125] Yet the 1936 report of the Commission of Inquiry into the Reformatory and Industrial Schools noted that most children were admitted to industrial schools not because they displayed "criminal tendencies" but because of poverty. In 1934, 88 percent of admissions were because of poverty or neglect;[126] many of these were probably children in large families. The National Nutrition Survey, conducted in the years 1946–48, showed that in Dublin "among the poorer and larger families, a high proportion of the meals consisted simply of 'bread and spread'"; the proportion of such meals declined in smaller and more prosperous families.[127] An associated clinical study revealed that seventeen-year-old Dublin boys and girls who were members of large families had lower weights than their peers, and a sample of school children drawn from various towns indicated "a definite tendency for the heights and weights to decrease as the family size increases." While noting that the sample was small and might be subject to sampling variations, the report nevertheless concluded that "it seems very probable that there is, in town areas, a variation in height and weight with family size."[128] At this time the only groups in receipt of child allowances were the recipients of unemployment benefits, unemployment assistance, and widows' pensions as well as army personnel and some (male) civil servants.

The publication of the 1942 Beveridge Report and the subsequent introduction of a welfare state in Britain prompted a debate in Ireland on the role of the state. The prevailing view among those who addressed this question was that there should be strict limits to state involvement in family life,[129] although apparently this did not preclude the state from denying couples access to information on contraception. In 1943 Seán MacEntee claimed that if the state assumed responsibility for providing subsistence for men and their families, this would inevitably lead to more authoritarian measures, with the state directing men to jobs: *If a man cannot earn a livelihood in one district or in one occupation, he will have to be directed to a new district. I see no escape from this.*[130] But a weekly payment of 2s. 6d. for the third and subsequent child, as provided under the 1944 Children's Allowance Act, could hardly be described as state-provided subsistence for children. According to Cousins, the Irish provisions for children's allowances "saw the family as an area within which the state should not interfere."[131] Respecting the norm of the male breadwinner and Catholic social teaching, the allowances were paid to the father.[132] James Dillon, the politician who first proposed a government scheme of family allowances, claimed that "the beauty of this Bill is that it bolts and bars the door against the bureaucrat. It strengthens the citadel of the family against the government." He welcomed the legislation as marking "the recognition in our community, that there should be no penalty for exercising a Christian man's right to marry and raise a family, in so far as the community can help it."[133]

The Dower House

Proposals for family allowances figure prominently in debates concerning population and the family in most European countries. Ireland's unique contribution to this discourse was the dower house, a concept that appears to have originated in the brain (or perhaps the heart) of Eamon de Valera. The underlying premise was simple: providing a second home on the family farm would enable the inheriting son to marry and establish a family without disturbing his parents or siblings, and therefore he could marry at an earlier age. The second house, somewhat larger than a laborer's cottage (note the social gradations), would provide a home for the heir, his wife, and family. In return for working on the family farm, he would receive a weekly wage; his "young wife" would raise poultry and pigs on the one-acre allotment attached to the second house. At some unspecified future date the older farmer and his wife would transfer the farm to this son, and he and his family would move into the original farmhouse. The older couple would retire to the second house, and they would receive a "stipend" from their son. De Valera claimed that he first expounded this idea at a party convention in Cork, "and I was laughed at," but this occasion seems to be lost to history. He repeated the proposal in a speech at an inaugural meeting of the University College Dublin Agricultural Society in December 1943.[134]

The report accompanying the fifth volume of the 1936 census suggested that the large percentage of males in rural areas, who were "assisting relatives," and consequently not in a position to marry, was a major factor in the low rural marriage rate.[135] De Valera believed that dower houses would help to solve this problem. When he expounded his plans in December 1943, the legislation providing for children's allowances was making its way through Dáil Éireann. Although Seán Lemass did not anticipate that the children's allowances would have any impact on births or marriages, many deputies expressed the hope that they would promote a national regeneration, reducing the flight from the land and encouraging marriage. W. T. Cosgrave contrasted the provisions in the Beveridge Report, which would, in his opinion, result in a marriage and baby boom in the United Kingdom, with the limited benefits provided under the Children's Allowances Bill. Others criticized the bill for failing to give special treatment to rural families; several deputies demanded that children's allowances be extended to the first child in farming families.[136]

Arensberg and Kimball claimed that when a son brought his wife to live on the family farm, his parents moved to "the west room," or the best room in the house. In 1936 the majority of farmhouses consisted of three or four rooms, which meant that it was physically impossible for a man to marry until his noninheriting siblings had departed. The collapse of emigration in the early 1930s made it more difficult to disperse noninheriting siblings than in the past. The ratio of potential farm heirs (coresident sons or sons-in-law) to farmers was higher in 1936 than in 1926.[137] There has been an extensive debate about whether the stem family was as prominent a feature of rural Ireland as Arensberg and Kimball have suggested.[138] De Valera's plan for dower houses indicates that he believed that it was, and none of the civil servants who considered this proposal disputed the validity of the stem family concept. If they had believed otherwise, there is little doubt that they would have said so, if only to buttress the case against dower houses, because they were very hostile to the proposal.

Pauric Travers claimed that de Valera believed that the late age of rural marriage was a factor in female emigration, and he saw dower houses as a means of persuading more young women to marry into small farms.[139] Dower houses might promote earlier marriages among inheriting farmers' sons, but they offered no comfort to noninheriting sons, and consequently they were unlikely to result in a substantial increase in rural marriages, unless it was assumed that facilitating earlier marriages would reduce the number of farmers who never married. The proposal was also unlikely to result in a higher birthrate, unless it was presumed that if farmers married at an earlier age, the age of their brides would also fall; at the time the age gap between husband and wife in Ireland was much greater than in the United Kingdom. The proposal to erect dower houses also assumed that the major barrier to rural marriage was the lack of household space, or perhaps two women competing for control of one kitchen. The matter proved much more complex.

Although Michael Garry of Kiladysart, county Clare, a farmer whose children were of marriageable age, believed that dower houses would "do away with a lot of the friction and family quarrels which crop up when the young couple step in under the family roof with the old," the all-male committee of civil servants who considered the proposal were convinced that they would create new sources of conflict. Many years later de Valera described the plan as "a pet scheme of mine that I never got anybody to agree with." His prospects of securing support were not enhanced by the fact that the committee failed to establish the existence of dower houses in Denmark or Sweden, two countries where farming communities did not experience the Irish problem of late marriages.[140]

The committee claimed that erecting dower houses would be tantamount to conferring official blessing on the subdivision of holdings. Officials from the Land Commission claimed that "even now" there was a tendency for farmers in the west of Ireland, whose holdings were "barely economic" to subdivide them in order to provide for a married son or daughter. (The extent of subdivision at this time is unclear, but references crop up so frequently in memoranda from the Land Commission that they should not be dismissed without good reason.)

However, the main reason why the committee refused to endorse de Valera's proposal was their belief that the late marriage age of Irish farmers was caused by family size, not a shortage of accommodation. They claimed that farmers tended to retain control of the holding until the youngest child was economically independent, by which time the oldest son, who was the expected heir, might well be in his late thirties. Holdings were rarely transferred until the father or widowed mother qualified for the old age pension at the age of seventy, because the annuities and other prerequisites available to the older couple under a standard marriage agreement were generally insufficient to ensure an independent living. Ownership of the farm enabled a parent to control the family budget and so protect the position of younger dependent children.

The views expressed by the dower house committee suggest that farming parents were not altogether confident that a married son could be trusted to provide for his younger siblings. In some parts of Europe, such as Austria, a son who inherited the family farm was required to make financial payments to his siblings, but in Ireland the parents provided for noninheriting siblings and the heir was not saddled with debt, but the Irish arrangement may have delayed his marriage and the transfer of land. Another key to a successful transition from the older to the younger generation was the dispersal of nonheirs. At the beginning of the twentieth century, small farmers in the west of Ireland were much more successful in achieving this than larger farmers in Leinster or east Munster.[141] In 1946 farmers with holdings valued at £50 or more married on average 2.2 years later than the average for farmers,[142] perhaps because noninheriting siblings on large farms were more likely to attend secondary school or college and remained dependent on their parents until a later age than the children of small farmers.

In its response to de Valera's speech about dower houses, the *Farmers' Gazette* noted that the process of marriage, succession, and the transfer of the family farm was governed by "natural economic conditions." The dower house committee claimed that many farms could not support a second household, particularly if there was a large number of dependent children; moreover, the financial arrangements between the two households would be "a fruitful source of friction." The cost of providing furniture, utensils, fuel, and lighting for two households was an important consideration, and there is independent evidence that many Irish farms were incapable of paying an adult son even the modest sum specified for an agricultural laborer.[143] De Valera suggested that dower houses should only be provided on large and moderately large farms, and the director of the Statistics Office, Stanley Lyon, was asked to determine the number of farms in excess of fifty acres with a resident adult son who could take over the family farm. One land commission inspector suggested that dower houses should only be provided on farms with at least eighty acres,[144] but it would have proved politically impossible to restrict any scheme to larger holdings.

Arensberg and Kimball claimed that the 1936 statistics showing a low marriage rate, high marital fertility, and a low female/male ratio in the adult population testified to "the continued existence of the familistic order . . . as well as the continuance of its struggle to fit into modern life."[145] This struggle was encapsulated in the proposal for dower houses. One Land Commission inspector informed the committee that "a dower-house is a 'hedgehog' problem [covered in prickles]. Family affairs and circumstances are usually so complicated, varied and difficult that it would be almost impossible (short of writing a book on the subject) to cover all the cases." If a young couple settled in a separate house, the committee believed that they would become "alienated" from the older parents and from family members, who resided in the family home. The remaining children might refuse to leave the family home, and parents might be tempted to will the farm to a son who shared their home and provided them with regular care and attention, rather than to one who was living in a separate house.[146]

One official claimed that the scheme could only work if "a rigid law of succession" ensured that the holding would be transferred to the occupant of the second house; otherwise a bride's parents would be reluctant to hand over a dowry.[147] But farm succession was not clear-cut. It was not regulated by law, or by custom. Large families and the lack of alternative jobs meant that at the beginning of the twentieth century the cards were heavily stacked in favor of parents. Having examined a sample of 1911 census forms, Liam Kennedy concluded that primogeniture applied on less than half of farms, and despite the fall in family size, eldest sons accounted for only half of farm heirs after World War II.[148] De Valera's proposal had enormous implications for intergenerational authority and for familistic values. An eldest son who settled in a dower house could not be confident of inheriting the farm unless he had a legal contract, but this would require a parent to relinquish control of the farm at an earlier date than the norm, and apart from the financial consequences, this would entail a premature loss of authority for the older generation. When the committee deliberated these matters in 1943–44, most farmers were in a position to pick and choose between heirs, but as the ratio of heirs to farmers fell during the 1950s and 1960s, the balance of power shifted from father to son.[149]

Caitríona Clear has suggested that the decision to establish a committee to investigate the provision of dower houses "indicates an official acceptance of the ideal of one couple, one family home."[150] The idea of providing separate houses for newlywed farming couples recognized the importance of marital privacy and a domestic life centered on married couples, in place of older practices. Rosemary Harris noted that in the poorer, mountainy areas that she studied in the early 1950s, men were more likely to visit neighbors in the evening: "Neighbouring men might come in and sit down without knocking let alone without invitation," whereas prosperous farm families were more likely to spend the evening "together and alone."[151] But although de Valera may have acknowledged that modern married couples wanted a companionate marriage,[152] the members of the

dower-house committee were of the opinion that, except in very rare
cases, the two families would prefer to live under the same roof. "The
proposal that the old couple should after a hard and industrious life,
leave their comfortable home and be isolated in their declining years
in a dower-house is however, one that is not likely to find favour with
the farming community." One land commission inspector claimed
that elderly couples usually lived "on terms of love and friendship
with their daughters in law." This unromantic man dismissed de
Valera's proposal as a scheme to provide a "love nest for the newlyweds so that they could spend a protracted honeymoon billing and
cooing until such time as they realised that they had also to earn their
living." He believed that any tensions that might exist between the
two couples were generally eased by the old age pension, although the
women might squabble "around the cooking-hearth."[153] Old age
pensions may have been a significant source of monetary income for
small farming households, but it assumed less importance as modern
couples came to place greater value on marital privacy, companionship, and independence.

Although the interdepartmental committee gave de Valera's proposal a firm thumbs-down, in 1953 he instructed a group of Fianna
Fáil deputies that included Eamon Ó Cíosáin, who had chaired the
earlier committee, to reconsider the matter, "as it can be said that
they would approach the subject with more enthusiasm and less in-
hibitions than would a committee of civil servants." The politicians
were initially sympathetic to the proposal, but their enthusiasm
waned as they became aware of the drawbacks that were highlighted
in the earlier report. Despite this second rebuff, de Valera did not
abandon his "pet plan." On discovering that the average age of Irish
male farmers was fifty-five, compared with forty-six in France, he
asked the Irish embassy in Paris to supply information about farm
succession and dower houses in France. Ambassador Con Cremin reported that French farms did not provide dower houses, but inheriting sons did not generally defer marriage until their father retired; it
was common for a farmer's son and his wife to reside in the family
farmhouse while the father remained in control of the farm, and the
older farmer continued to reside in the family farmhouse after he
had transferred control to his son. But in France unlike Ireland, all

children had an equal right to inheritance. Cremin investigated the matter further with the director-general of the French National Institute of Statistics. He reported that the average age of marriage among French male farmers was only marginally higher than the national average—27.3 against 26.7 years—and farmers' wives were slightly younger than the national average—23.5 against 23.7 years, respectively. Cremin suggested that one reason for the absence of a rural marriage problem in France might be that "the deliberate limitation of families is not uncommon," plus the fact that the qualifying age for old age pensions was sixty-five years compared with seventy in Ireland. Land tenancy was also more common. But when Cremin met the president and secretary of the National Federation of Farmers' Syndicates, they reported that when a farmer relinquished control of the farm to a son, he was commonly treated "little better than a farm labourer."[154]

The French experience suggests that large families were a major factor in the late age of marriage in rural Ireland. Large families, the absence of any regulation governing succession, and the lack of alternative occupations gave parents considerable control over land inheritance and consequently over marriage. The findings of the Limerick Rural Survey indicate that this position lasted until at least the early 1960s. McNabb reported that "a woman [whom he had taped, apparently during the course of a communal discussion] had full support of her neighbors when she said, 'I don't see why he [the inheriting son] should resent helping to educate the other members of the family, so that they can get a good position outside the farm. They are as much entitled to a share as he is, and he is getting the biggest share. It would be very foolish of him to marry before they are provided for.'"

McNabb claimed that many farmers' sons were unable to marry, even after the deaths of their parents, because other siblings remained on the farm. "These could be moved, but until recently family loyalty was strong, and a man would rather forego marriage than turn out his own kin." He noted that some younger parents were endeavoring to interest the youngest son in taking over the farm and working actively "to push the older members of the family out," so that the youngest son would inherit a vacant house at a stage when his parents would welcome retirement.[155] McNabb makes no reference to erecting second houses on farms, although farm income in county Limerick was above the national average.

While separate houses for young couples may have been an important consideration, the key issue was access to land. The nature of the Irish land market, the sanctified status of owner occupancy, and the importance attached to keeping land within the family meant that it was almost impossible for young people to acquire land other than by inheritance. Most land vacated through emigration was let as conacre (eleven-month leases), and farms owned by bachelor farmers tended to remain in family ownership.[156] In France land was readily available for leasing, and it was much easier for young farmers to establish separate households. During the 1950s the rural organization Macra na Feirme pressed the government to introduce a scheme to make land available to young farmers, but the proposal was stillborn, in part because of the hostile attitude of the Department of Agriculture.[157]

The plan to erect dower houses was predicated on the belief that institutional barriers were the major obstacles to early marriage among farmers. Providing a second house offered a less contentious means of reconciling intergenerational tensions than accelerating the transfer of land from father to son. But while we should acknowledge that Irish civil servants had a tendency to resist new ideas, there were strong arguments against de Valera's "pet plan." Many family farms were too poor to support two households. The higher status attached to older people meant that their wishes attracted considerable sympathy and were even accorded greater standing than those of a younger married couple. Providing a second house could not be divorced from the issue of farm succession, and no Irish government was prepared to intervene in this thorny issue. But the critical factor was probably the large size of farming families.

Large families and the high dependency rate also prevented marriage by nonfarmers, although the impact was less acute. In 1926 one-third of single women aged twenty to twenty-four, 48 percent of those aged thirty-five to forty-four, and a majority of those aged forty-five and over were not in gainful employment, and 71,000 children, almost 8 percent of the total, were supported by somebody other than a parent.[158] More than one-third of married men in the Irish Free State had 3 or more dependent children, almost double the proportion in England and Wales (18.6 percent). In Northern Ireland the level of dependency was slightly lower and the peak occurred between forty-five and forty-nine years; in the Irish Free State dependency peaked for married men aged forty-five. The low proportion of young people in work added to the burden of dependency. In 1926, 28 percent of sixteen- and seventeen-year-old boys in the Irish Free State were not in gainful employment, more than three times the proportion in Scotland (8 percent) or England and Wales (9 percent) and substantially higher than Northern Ireland (17 percent). Although the problem was most pronounced in rural areas, over 40 percent of sixteen- and seventeen-year-old boys and over 60 percent of sixteen- and seventeen-year-old girls in Cork, Waterford, and Limerick had no gainful employment; the corresponding figures for Belfast were 17 and 21 percent, figures comparable to English and Scottish cities. By the age of twenty, most men had either found work or emigrated, but many single women remained without gainful employment. The report that accompanied these statistics noted that "taken in conjunction with our abnormally large number of widows and orphans and the strength of family ties in this country they afford reasons for the very late age to which marriage is postponed here; we have an unusually large proportion of young men and women who have to support younger brothers and sisters who cannot find employment, and aged widowed mothers, and accordingly marriages are postponed to a later age than in other countries."[159]

The industrialization drive launched by the Fianna Fáil government in 1932 resulted in a significant rise in the number of young men and women in industrial employment. Nevertheless, in 1936 over 18 percent of boys and girls between the ages of fourteen and twenty were classified as unoccupied, although by 1946 this had declined to 11 percent.[160] In 1951, however, the report of the Commission on Youth Unemployment expressed concern at the large number of young people who were neither in school nor in employment.[161]

Many young men and women who did find jobs, whether in Ireland or abroad, found themselves supporting younger siblings, a widowed mother, or an incapacitated father. The strength of these obligations suggests that the familistic culture extended beyond the family farm.[162] Some men and women, who were saddled with the upkeep of parents or siblings, never married, and others were forced to postpone marriage until these responsibilities disappeared or were assumed by another family member. But the late age of marriage, plus large families, often meant that the process was replicated in the next generation. There was a greater probability that a father would die or suffer long-term illness or incapacity while his children were still young, forcing an older son or daughter to become the family breadwinner. In 1926, 79,331 children, 8.5 percent of the total, lived in one-parent families. A means-tested widows' pension was introduced in 1935, but this provided only a minimal standard of living; most widows were not entitled to a pension from their husbands' employers or from social insurance. But widows were not the only parents who required financial support from their children. Many small farmers, laborers, small shopkeepers, and petty tradesmen did not earn enough to support a family of four or five children. Although the demands placed on older siblings were not unique to Ireland, in Britain improved welfare payments and smaller families meant that they became less onerous, especially after 1945; this did not happen in Ireland.

Marriage, Fertility, and the Commission on Emigration

De Valera's obsession with dower houses suggests that he was concerned about trends in rural marriages and births, but if the memoranda relating to dower houses and children's allowances addressed the question of Irish marriage and birth patterns, they did so in an oblique manner. In theory, a commission on population would confront these issues directly, but when the commission was eventually appointed in 1948, it failed to examine Irish fertility and marital patterns, despite the fact that these were specific in its terms of reference.

The establishment of a commission on population was first mooted in March 1937 when Seán MacEntee suggested that it would be useful to identify the factors that were responsible for the decline in the Irish population; he dismissed claims that it was entirely due to economic circumstances.[163] There is no indication that the cabinet considered this suggestion; however, in 1939 they referred a report on the 1936 census to the minister for Local Government and Public Health, with a request that he should advise them whether or not to appoint a commission on population.[164] Commissions on population were fashionable in the 1930s—a response to plummeting birth-rates. The Swedish Royal Commission on Population reported in 1937, and in February 1939 the French government appointed a population committee—by the following July their report had resulted in the introduction of a Code de la Famille.[165] Such a prompt response was sadly lacking in Ireland. In Britain eugenics groups campaigned for a Royal Commission on Population, but it was not appointed until 1944.[166] It took even longer to establish an Irish commission.

In November 1939, after several reminders, the minister for Local Government and Public Health, Patrick Ruttledge, advised the cabinet not to establish a committee on population, because his department did not believe that Ireland's low marriage rate was susceptible to a solution. Officials cautioned that if the marriage rate returned to the 1841 or 1861 levels—44 percent of men aged thirty-five to forty-four were single in 1936, double the proportion in 1861 and three times the 1841 figure—this would present "still graver problems" for the Irish Land Commission in its efforts to relieve rural congestion. As for the decline in fertility, this was "mainly a psychological problem" that would prove difficult to investigate.

The message from the Department of Local Government and Public Health was clear: the government should let the matter rest; the problem was insoluble; a higher marriage rate would only make matters worse. Despite this strong recommendation, the cabinet continued to press the department to draw up terms of reference. In April 1940, after many reminders, they provided an encyclopedic list of topics to be examined: vital statistics; falling fertility; the composition and social conditions of the population; the effect of state-subsidized social services on the maintenance and welfare of the population; the existence of adequate housing at affordable rents for persons of marriageable age; general social policy; future trends in agriculture and industry and their effect on the maintenance and welfare of the population; and educational facilities. There is one conspicuous omission: emigration.[167]

Although the commission on population was listed for consideration at a cabinet meeting on 23 April 1940, the item was postponed on several occasions until 7 May, when it was withdrawn until further notice. April and May 1940 brought the end of the "phoney war." Germany invaded the Low Countries, and Winston Churchill became British prime minister, so perhaps it is not surprising that the government lost interest in a commission on population. In December 1947, however, de Valera's government decided to establish a commission on population, but the formal appointment did not take place until April 1948, and by then Fianna Fáil was out of office, replaced by the first Inter-Party government.

The terms of reference were almost identical to those of the 1944 British Royal Commission on Population:[168]

> to investigate the causes and consequences of the present level and trend in population; to examine in particular the social and economic effects of birth, death, migration and marriage rates at present, and their probable course in the near future; to consider what measures if any, should be taken in the national interest to influence the future trend in population; generally to consider the desirability of formulating a national population policy. (Commission on Emigration)

> to examine the facts relating to the present population trends in Britain; to investigate the causes of these trends and to consider their probable consequences; to consider what measures, if any, should be taken in the national interest to influence the future trend of population and to make recommendations. (Royal Commission on Population).

Although the proposal to establish an Irish commission on population was initially prompted by concerns over birth and marriage rates, and these topics are specifically mentioned in the terms of reference (whereas emigration is not), the commission treated these as minor matters. When the report finally appeared in 1954, it was styled *The Commission on Emigration and Other Population Problems.*

Births, marriages, and deaths were relegated to the category of "Other."

Responsibility for assembling the evidence relating to marriage (and, apparently, fertility) was assigned to Reverend Cornelius Lucey, the Catholic bishop of Cork. He claimed that those who gave evidence to the commission were primarily concerned about emigration; "references to the marriage problem are as a rule incidental to the main interest."[169] This was a rather disingenuous statement. Although some witnesses supplied unsolicited testimonies, the commission collected extensive written and oral evidence on inland and sea fisheries, forestry, and education, and members visited rural labor exchanges, Irish emigrants in Britain, and factories and hospitals that employed large numbers of Irish workers. Yet the only evidence collected concerning pregnancy and childbirth was in relation to unmarried Irish women who gave birth in Britain. There is no indication that interviews were sought with obstetricians, the masters of the Dublin maternity hospitals, midwives, the Department of Health, clergymen, or anybody who might have provided insights into marriage, fertility, and family in Ireland. The chapters on marriage and fertility are almost entirely based on published statistics, and even these sources were used to a limited degree. Although one commission member, Stanley Lyon, had published several articles on Dublin births in the 1940s using the Notification of Birth returns,[170] these are not cited in the published report (they did, however, feature in a draft written by Roy Geary). These omissions are in marked contrast with the British Royal Commission on Population, which examined the "fall in family size," "voluntary and involuntary causes of family limitation," "the spread of family limitation," and "the probable trends of marriage in future."[171]

The failure to conduct a more comprehensive investigation of marriage and fertility is unlikely to have been accidental. An unpublished memorandum written by three members of the commission—the Dublin pediatrician and author Dr. W. R. F. Collis, Church of Ireland clergyman and TCD philosopher, the Reverend A. A. Luce, and the headmaster of Drogheda Grammar School Arnold Marsh—noted that "the Commission heard no evidence medical or educational on the subject [large families] though at least one member asked for it. As a commission we are wholly in the dark about contraceptives, and as long as we remain in the dark about them we ought not to speak of them."[172] In a published personal reservation to the majority report, Luce stated that when he was appointed, he considered it "a public duty" to collect information on contraceptives, and he had requested that information and evidence on the matter should be placed before the commission, but none was forthcoming.[173] It is difficult not to conclude that the commission deliberately failed to consider any topics that might cause disquiet to the Catholic church.

The majority report suggested that Irish marriage patterns were a consequence of economic and institutional factors. The "deterioration" in Irish marriages was set in motion by the famine; it was a predominantly rural problem, whose causes could be found in the economic and social structures of rural Ireland: low agricultural productivity and income, lack of employment due to underdevelopment, the desire for a higher standard of living, the late age at which farmers inherited land, uncertainty over inheritance, and the ban on the employment of married women in teaching and the public service. Economic conditions were responsible for the "undue caution" or "reluctance" to marry shown by many Irish men. The commission claimed that there was a wide disparity between the age of marriage in urban and rural areas, although they presented no supporting data, and they reiterated the finding of the 1926 census that the differential marriage rates between England and Wales and Ireland could not be explained by occupations.[174]

Although family size had fallen between 1911 and 1946 by approximately 20 percent for all marriages regardless of duration, they did not believe that there was any immediate cause for alarm. In 1946 Irish couples who had been married for thirty to thirty-four years (married 1912–16) had an average of 4.94 children, compared with 6.77 for couples with marriages of similar duration in 1911 (married 1877–81). But in 1946, Irish couples with marriages of twenty years duration had twice as many children as their counterparts in Britain, 4.39 against 2.16. The differences in fertility by social class identified in 1926 persisted: higher professional households had the smallest families, and the largest families were found in the families of farmers, semiskilled and agricultural workers, and general laborers.[175]

Family size was a very sensitive topic. Chapter 5 of the commission report, "Births, Fertility and Family Size," faithfully reiterated Catholic social teaching: the downward trend in family size was "unwelcome and every effort should be made to arrest it"; the burden of a large dependent family generally only existed for a short period; they had received no evidence to support the view that the large family size that prevailed in Ireland "makes for a general condition of poverty"; it would be "unreasonable to assume that our family pattern imposes an undue strain on mothers in general"; there was no support for the belief that "apart from the increased risk associated with more frequent child-bearing," large families had a deleterious effect on the general health of mothers; the number of families with a very large number of dependent children (ten or more) was "relatively few."[176]

None of these statements was supported by empirical evidence; indeed, data presented in table 75 showed that in 1946, 38 percent of Irish children lived in families with five or more dependent children.[177] No effort was made to update the data provided by Dr. McWeeney in 1941 showing the cost of living for various sizes of household. Indeed, McWeeney's data was not cited, nor was the National Nutrition Survey. No information was collected from mothers, almoners, or social workers attached to maternity hospitals, nor from the Dublin Catholic Social Service Council about the difficulties of coping with large families, and no obstetricians gave evidence about the medical risks of multiple pregnancies. A 1953 study of "grand multipara"—women who had undergone seven or more deliveries—conducted by Dr. J. K. Feeney of the Coombe Hospital showed that they were more than twice as likely to miscarry or suffer hypertension than mothers with fewer previous births. Dr. Feeney noted that as large families were more common among the poor, many of these women had to contend with inadequate domestic arrangements, but the commission did not consider this report.[178]

In paragraph 166 the commission broached the theory that large families were a cause of Ireland's low marriage rate, only to reject it:

There is fairly widespread belief that our poor marriage background is partly attributable to the fact that, since the great majority of the people of Ireland are Catholics, marriage is to them an indissoluble contract and family limitation by contraception is against the moral law. It is said that the indissolubility of marriage and, in the absence of contraception, the fear of large families deter many from marriage altogether and others until a relatively advanced age. No convincing evidence has been put before us in support of this view. As Table 49 has shown, the marriage rates in other Catholic countries are markedly higher than in ours. Moreover the marriage rate in the Six Counties—where only about one-third of the population is Catholic is also exceptionally low.[179]

Chapter 9 of the report, "Population Policy," also reiterated Catholic social teaching: "The primary purpose of marriage, in the natural order of things, is the birth and bringing up of children. The principle which rightly guides the normal Christian married couple in this matter is to have as many children as they can reasonably hope to bring up properly, assuming the practice of Christian virtues in their lives and the readiness to make certain sacrifices." Married couples were free to plan or space their families "if their decisions are based on morally good motives and their actions and methods of control do not violate the moral principles of the natural law," but the commission denounced the practice of family planning designed to produce one, two, or no children, "from purely selfish or purely materialistic motives."[180] The commission evaded the question of the relationship between religion and marital fertility. The subject occupies one paragraph of nine lines plus a footnote that suggest, in keeping with the interpretation given in the 1926 census, that the smaller Protestant families may reflect social class rather than religion.[181]

The published version, from which the above quotations are taken, underwent several rewrites in an effort to meet the objections expressed by Arnold Marsh and Drs. Collis and Luce. The original version probably quoted the injunction in the Gospel to "increase and multiply"—a phrase that figures prominently in the 1931 papal encyclical *Casti Connubi*.[182] Marsh acknowledged that "the most Rev. Dr. Lucy [*sic*] has gone some way to meet us in the hope that by so doing we should be unanimous," but "his careful phrasing and moderation, tend to obscure some fundamental differences in outlook." Marsh claimed that chapter 9 "speaks with 2–3 voices; but the first voice speaks loudest and longest"—presumably the voice of Dr. Lucey.[183] William Honohan, a member of the commission who was released from his position in the Department of Social Welfare for six months in an effort to speed up publication, redrafted Lucey's version, but according to another member of the commission, Richard Orpen, Honohan reduced the report to "a bag of bones with no flesh."[184] The final version was probably written by commission chairman J. P. Beddy.[185]

We can get some indication of the disagreements over this section by examining the reservations and minority reports that were published. Marsh and Collis criticized the emphasis that the majority report placed "on the idea that large families are *per se* good, that the decline in family size is *per se* bad, and that a very numerous family is better in the sight of God and good men than a people numerous enough but not too numerous to secure for themselves conditions of good, healthy happy living conditions."[186] In a separate reservation, Reverend Dr. Luce referred specifically to paragraph 166 (see above). He claimed that the right inference from this paragraph is "that the Quiverful families of Victorian days are not, in general, possible or desirable today." He believed that Irish people were deterred from marrying by "the unselfish and justifiable fear of large, *unhappy* families in reduced circumstances that offer no chance of betterment for parents or for their children. . . . Remove it, and earlier marriages, more marriages, and more families of moderate size would follow. The grudging and negative reference to family planning (para. 458) ought to have been replaced, in my opinion, by a full and positive statement, in touch with modern conditions, stressing the *quality* of human life, frankly accepting family planning as a primary duty of responsible Christian parenthood, and offering practical and detailed advice."[187]

Marsh, Luce, and Collis were members of the Protestant minority; however, Alexis Fitzgerald, a Catholic, also dissented from the views expressed in the majority report about large families. Lee has suggested that the reservations expressed by Fitzgerald, an economist and son-in-law to Taoiseach John A. Costello, "deserves careful consideration from students of the mentality of the professional classes." Fitzgerald regarded the low marriage rate as a more serious matter than emigration, and he expressed the wish "to have seen in the Report a franker recognition that changed economic and social conditions have made inevitable smaller families if the children are to realise in life the excellencies of which they are capable."[188]

Although the majority report reflected Catholic teaching, it proved too bland for Dr. Cornelius Lucey. His minority report reinstated the phrase that "the first injunction on the human race, is: 'Increase and Multiply, and fill the earth.'" Most of this report was taken up with expounding a scheme to increase the number of small farms, because Dr. Lucey believed that preserving small farms was the only means of ensuring a population increase. He railed against the downward trend in family size and insisted that every effort should be made to arrest and reverse it. Echoing some of MacEntee's earlier memoranda, he claimed that any assumption that economic security would promote large families was "positively misleading"; the rich tended to have small families, whereas the poor, "who had no fear of losing their social or economic status," had large families. Economic development would accelerate the fall in family size unless it proved possible to promote "a less materialistic outlook among our people."[189] The other two Catholic clergy who were members of the commission offered a degree of support to Dr. Lucey. Reverend Coyne recorded his support for "that portion of the Minority Report of Dr. Lucey in which population principles are set out," and an addendum by Reverend T. Counihan mentioned "the danger in this country lest we imbibe the modern society vice of family limitation."[190]

The most interesting contribution on family size was by Roy Geary, who would appear to have written draft chapters on this topic that were severely pruned in the final version. Geary did not submit an addendum or reservation on the matter, except in connection with the fall in the Protestant population. In the unpublished draft Geary noted that "two important demographic abnormalities" had to be explained: the high fertility of married women and the very low marriage rate and late age of marriage. Contraception was now widely accepted outside Moslem and Catholic countries. People wanted smaller families to give them better opportunities in life and because, "with the growing freedom permitted to them," women viewed excessive childbearing as a burden. Geary asked whether the low Irish marriage rate and late age of marriage was "a necessary evil and the only alternative in the long run to contraception?"[191] Answering his own question, he inferred that "the fundamental reason for the low marriage rate may well be the high fertility rate." He cited Lyon's data showing that only 15 percent of first children born in Dublin were born to couples who had been married for more than two years, compared with 38 percent in England and Wales, and suggested that this difference could not have arisen by chance. In England couples could marry before they were capable of providing for children, but not in Ireland. He believed that some Irish women chose to remain single in order to avoid "what they might consider the drudgery of marriage—frequent and many conceptions."

Geary began his account of marriage and fertility with the famine, an event that he believed had left the Irish people fully aware of the dangers of overpopulation, resulting in "an excessive care for the future, for security at almost any price." The memory of the famine, and the quest for higher living standards, resulted in emigration, the abandonment of the Irish language, and a falling birthrate.

> This care for the future made it imperative to prevent another rapid population increase, and as the practice of contraception conflicts with religious ideas, they adopted the method of total continence and large numbers of men refused to marry. Gradually the practice of abstaining from marriage for many years or for life has developed among the Irish until today it has quite as strong a hold on Ireland as contraception has on other countries. The reasons for this abstention seem to be the same as that for contraception, namely the desire of the people as a whole to maintain a high standard of living and to check rapid population increase. In Ireland therefore, while large numbers of men and women are compelled to celibacy, those that marry have nearly as many children as formerly, while in other countries the average family became smaller but the same numbers married.

The Irish solution had not brought about a stable population: if emigration ceased and fertility remained unchanged, the population could only be stabilized by a further fall in the marriage rate. Geary tried to account for the smaller families in other Catholic countries such as Spain, Portugal, and Italy, and to do so, he resorted to the unsubstantiated, and probably unsustainable, assertion that "modern influences" were stronger than in Ireland, contraceptives were more widely used, and infant mortality was higher.[192]

Geary believed that the high proportion of Irish men and women who remained unmarried should not be looked upon with equanimity; if a fall in family size was accompanied by an increase in the marriage rate so that total fertility remained constant, it would be a good thing. "Surely many families of four children will give greater contentment and happiness to a community than a few families of twelve children." The most important variable was not family size but average female fertility: if the latter remained at a satisfactory level, a drop in the fertility of married women need occasion no alarm. He anticipated a further drop in family size, but he believed that it was unlikely to fall to "disastrous levels" if the only form of family planning being practiced was natural birth control, "as the physiological disadvantages of such methods will remain sufficient to counteract such a happening." Geary's draft also included sections on the adverse consequences of late marriages and large families; evidence showing that child mortality increased with family size or maternal age; a paragraph claiming that the large number of widows was "conducive to celibacy in the next generation," because widows often relied on their children for support, and this problem was accentuated by large families; and a paragraph about the large, though declining, number of orphans. The published report does not mention widows; the only reference to orphans is a brief statement that the commission did not consider it necessary to make any recommendations on the matter.[193]

A comparison between the treatment of marriage and fertility in Geary's draft and the published report, together with the reservations and addenda from Marsh, Collis, Luce, and Fitzgerald, suggests that marital fertility may well have been the most contentious topic that the commission confronted, or failed to confront. Any discussion of maternity and fertility conjured up the ghost of the 1951 Mother and Child crisis, where the fear that mothers might be given advice about family planning was a factor, though by no means the only factor, in the opposition of the Catholic church. Members would also have been aware that the Irish Censorship Board had banned the report of the Royal Commission on Population on the grounds that it "advocated the unnatural prevention of conception or the procurement of abortions or miscarriages." The ban was imposed on 14 October 1949, coincidentally the day that the Kinsey Report was banned. Although it was revoked in January 1950 following widespread criticism, even in the *Irish Press*,[194] the event would have served as a warning of the dangers involved in discussing family size or contraception.

The Catholic church was not represented on the Royal Commission on Population, and its report was denounced by the Catholic authorities. Reverend Cathal Daly, a future cardinal and archbishop of Armagh, noted that for the Royal Commission, "moral and religious considerations are largely irrelevant." He was concerned at the evidence showing a decline in the size of British Catholic families, although this was happening at a slower rate than the general population, and the fertility of Catholic families there replicated the occupational differences of the wider population. He claimed that British Catholic families were not replacing themselves.[195]

With the fertility of Catholic families declining on the far side of the Irish Sea, there was a pressing need for the Commission on Emigration to affirm the positive virtues of large families. Irish Catholic clergy would also have been determined to prevent any discussion of birth control. A Scottish priest, who reviewed the report of the Royal Commission on Population for the Maynooth publication *Christus Rex,* highlighted the statement that until recently coitus interruptus, which required no mechanical appliances, was the most widely used form of birth control.[196] Irish Catholic priests remained hostile to the safe period. Cathal Daly claimed that the term was "coloured with a stain of the world's hedonism" and that Catholic teaching provided no justification for advocating it without qualification as a policy for family limitation.[197] Yet in 1951, the year when this statement was published, Pope Pius XII referred to the safe period "as a method open to all Christian couples" in a speech to midwives, and he repeated the message one month later.[198] There is no indication that the Irish Catholic bishops publicized this change in papal teaching, or that books explaining the safe period were widely available in Ireland during the 1950s, but a doctor and several priests informed American Jesuit priest and sociologist Alexander Humphreys that

Table 1. Average Number of Children Born per Hundred Women with Marriages of Twenty to Twenty-Four Years Duration

Census Year	Year of Marriage	Children Born per 100 Women
1911*	1887–91	596
1946**	1922–26	449
1961**	1937–41	416
1971**	1947–51	424
1981**	1957–61	407

* All Ireland

** Republic of Ireland

birth control by abstinence and the safe period were widely practiced by middle-class and lower-middle-class couples in Dublin.[199]

Scholars who have researched the history of fertility decline believe that attitudes toward children or desired family size as well as the wish to control fertility are more important than access to contraceptive devices in bringing about a significant fall in fertility. Most of the modern fall in fertility predates the availability of reliable methods of contraception.[200] A frank discussion by the Commission on Emigration of the disadvantages of large families and the methods of contraception available might have contributed to changing Irish attitudes. Research on marital fertility in Pembroke in 1911 has shown that Catholics living on predominantly Protestant streets had smaller families than those with Catholic neighbors.[201]

Census data indicates that completed family size fell in the early years of the twentieth century, but the rate of decline then slowed and may have been partly reversed among couples who married in the late 1940s, though the fall in family size resumed among couples who married in the 1950s. In Dublin city, 19.95 percent of births in 1945 were the sixth or higher parity, compared with 16.4 percent in 1955. Social class continued to have a significant impact on marital fertility. Twenty-eight percent of children born to unskilled laborers in Dublin in 1955 were the sixth or subsequent child, compared with 6.2 percent of the children of higher professionals. While the later age of marriage is a factor in the lower fertility of professional and middle-class couples, many of these families were undoubtedly using some form of family limitation.[202]

Sexual Puritanism and Irish Bachelors: The Vanishing Irish

Two seminal works on Irish population appeared in 1954: the *Report of the Commission on Emigration and Other Population Problems* and a collection of essays called *The Vanishing Irish*, edited by an Irish-American priest, John O' Brien. The views expressed in *The Vanishing Irish* were closer to those of Dr. Lucey than to the majority report of the Commission on Emigration. The opening essay by the editor quoted the divine injunction to "increase and multiply and fill the earth."[203] O'Brien claimed that Ireland was "teetering perilously on the brink of near extinction." This was an enigma to him because "Ireland has been traditionally a nation of large families." This is a puzzling statement, because by international standards Ireland remained a country of large families in 1954. For O'Brien, the "unusually high fecundity rate" of Irish women was the one bright spot in a "somber black" picture; he expressed the hope that a higher marriage rate and earlier marriages would boost the birthrate and increase "the nation's margin of safety," and thus prevent a fall in population due to emigration. He asserted that Irish emigrants to the United States continued the "nonmarrying tradition," a claim that, if true, would refute economic explanations for Ireland's low marriage rate.[204] Other contributors placed responsibility for the lack of marriages and the high rate of female emigration[205] (it was widely believed that women emigrated in search of husbands) on "the strangest species of male on the face of the earth today, the Irish bachelor." O'Brien described them as, "men who spent their evenings in pubs, engrossed in cards, drinking and endless chatter about horse racing."[206] Arland Ussher, a writer and critic who had campaigned against censorship in the 1920s, claimed that the Irish reluctance to marry was caused by repressed attitudes toward sex that were fostered by the Jansenist views of "the parish clergy and the missioners, for whom "company keeping" is a stable subject of denunciation." He described the attitude of Irishmen to women as that "of a very primitive, peasant community"; Jansenism was also to blame for this.[207] According to Seán O'Faoláin, writer and former editor of *The Bell*, among Irish men, "sexual desire was sublimated by religion, exhausted by sport, drugged by drink or deflected by either an innate or an inculcated Puritanism."[208]

It was common for rural societies to enforce a code of behavior for young people, which was delicately balanced between ensuring that men and women found suitable marriage partners and preventing them from embarking on relationships that were unlikely to end in a socially approved marriage. In northern Portugal, although the absence of a dowry and the postponement of any property transfers until a parent's death meant that the family played a much less significant part in the choice of marriage partners than in rural Ireland, sociability between young men and women was geared toward engagement and marriage. Couples seen together on a regular basis entered into a *namoro* or quasi engagement, which effectively precluded them from close contact with other partners. A young woman whose *namoro* failed to marry her found it difficult to secure another husband.[209] In rural Ireland Arensberg and Kimball noted that "pastimes of the young people in which the usual segregation of the sexes is breached point toward matchmaking and country marriage."[210] Expanding on this, they explained that "Although premarital virginity and complete abstinence from any kind of sexual activity is the ideal for the young, local custom emphasizes marriage all the while. Local dances and other festivities are the chief times of meeting and play for the young men and women of the rural communities. The customs and conventions that surround them are constant reminders of marriage and its hopes and privileges. Yet as soon as any intimacy of acquaintanceship builds up between a particular pair, they are matched together in local gossip. They are forced to take a position which is only a single step from betrothal."[211]

From the 1920s the Catholic church issued a stream of Lenten pastorals and Catholic Truth Society of Ireland pamphlets denouncing sexual license, and these messages were reinforced by missionary priests. The state played its part by introducing legislation restricting the craze for dancing and other occasions of temptation. But the volume of denunciation and its stridency might suggest that this message was not being heard. Arensberg and Kimball quote "a countryman" who says that "every year we have a talk from the priest about the dances. He says the dances are all right but it is the going home that is bad. There is always a laugh when he says that. Then some of the parents get worried and they won't let their daughters go to a dance for a month or so, and they forget about it after that.[212]

Patrick Kavanagh's quasi-autobiographical novel *Tarry Flynn*
suggests that the strictures of mission priests against sexual misconduct encouraged greater interest in sex among the male population
of Inniskeen, county Monaghan.[213] Arensberg and Kimball detected
two "ambivalent" attitudes toward sexuality: a rigid code of conduct,
which led to a censorious attitude regarding sexual misconduct, particularly in relation to women, and "very hearty sometimes ribald attitudes which make their appearance in banter, jibe, and repartee
even between speakers of different sex." They go so far as to suggest
that the reported spread of a puritanical attitude toward sexual matters may be the outcome of "the spread of education and the opening of the countryside to urban influence."[214] If their account is accurate, county Clare in the 1930s had more in common with other
rural societies than is generally believed. This interpretation is also
consistent with the picture of rural life presented in *Tarry Flynn* and
Eric Cross's Rabelesian book, *The Tailor and Ansty,* which was banned
in 1942. Efforts by the Catholic church to curb the dancing craze appear to have been singularly unsuccessful, judging by the innumerable advertisements for dances that appeared in every local newspaper. The church did succeed in preventing dances on Saturday
nights, however, in case young people might be too tired to attend
mass on Sunday morning, and dances were generally suspended during the penitential season of Lent. By the 1950s the church's anti-
dancing message was becoming rather ambiguous, because priests
often relied on revenue from dances in local halls or summer carnivals to finance new churches and school repairs.[215]

The Commission on Emigration expressed some sympathy for
the argument that opposition to "the social mingling of young
people . . . because of the moral risks involved" made it more difficult
to find possible marriage partners, especially in rural Ireland. But
economic explanations again came to the fore; they suggested that the
restricted social lives of rural Ireland reflected the fact that economic
circumstances were not favorable to marriage: better economic conditions would "lead to a freer social mingling of young people."[216]

The fact that the commission gave some consideration to this
argument as well as the discussion about sexual puritanism and
Jansenism in *The Vanishing Irish* suggests that this was a much less
sensitive issue than high marital fertility. Did puritanical attitudes

inhibit some men and women from marrying? The question cannot be answered in the absence of an Irish Kinsey Report. Sexual frigidity was not a uniquely Irish problem, so there is little doubt that some people either did not marry or failed to have sexual relations for this reason, but it would be impossible to determine if this had a significant impact on the marriage rate. Stanley Lyon's data on Dublin births during the 1940s indicate that in the years 1943–45 almost 7 percent of first births were to women who were married for less than six months, and 44–47 percent of first babies were born to mothers who had been married for less than one year.[217] These statistics suggest that sexual frigidity was not a significant problem, at least for those who married.

There remains the wider question about the quality of Irish marriages and the degree to which social pressures—the dowry, finding a marriage partner from a farm of a specified size, or a preoccupation with family status—led some men and women to shun marriage entirely. Twentieth-century Irish novels, short stories, and memoirs offer a depressing array of joyless, loveless marriages or instances where love and marriage were frustrated by social or family pressures, though not all the joyless marriages or frustrated spinsters were Catholic, and not all lived in rural Ireland.[218] Marriages devoid of love and the frequent occurrence of young brides and elderly husbands are often regarded as the inevitable outcome of matchmaking, dowries, and postponed marriages. But the age gap between husbands and wives has been exaggerated; in 1946, the age difference was less than five years in half of all marriages, and more than three-quarters of couples had an age difference of less than ten years.[219] Arensberg and Kimball note that matchmaking—which was primarily governed by economic considerations and family status—did not rule out "some kind of sexual attraction. . . . Matchmaking was, in fact, far from presenting a scene of 'loveless' marriages. The match is a convention like any other. For those who are trained in it, it provides occasion for arousing sexual interest and marital aspirations in young couples in the manner of 'falling in love' in communities where courtship is more immediately a matter of personal ambition."[220]

By the middle of the twentieth century, the economic and familial considerations that governed Irish rural marriages, and many nonrural marriages, were regarded as incompatible with modern romantic love and marriage as depicted by Hollywood or the widely read novels published by Mills and Boon. According to Seán Ó Faoláin, Irishmen were seeking "not love, not romance, not passion, not beauty, not companionship, not charm, not wit, not intelligence— but simply the plain homespun qualities of housekeeper and mother," plus a dowry.[221] Whereas Irishmen continued to view marriage in a practical and material light, it was widely believed that women demanded love, romance, and companionship. If so (and there is no means of proving or disproving such an argument retrospectively), it suggests that Irish women adopted "modern" attitudes toward marriage at a more rapid pace than men.

Nobody has yet documented the decline of matchmaking by geography, social class, or timing. Arensberg and Kimball suggest that matches were the norm among farmers and shopkeepers in county Clare in the early 1930s, though in some instances matchmaking occurred after a couple had already met and formed an emotional attachment. This was the practice outlined by Robert Cresswell in Kinvara in the late 1950s; if a match could not be arranged, the couple often married regardless, but they had to emigrate.[222] Several witnesses to the Commission on Emigration in 1948 and 1949 complained that farmers continued to insist on a wife with a dowry.[223] Father Counihan and Stanley Lyon noted that many of the people they met in Swinford, county Mayo, mentioned dowries, and both men were in "no doubt but that it played a very definite part in the marrying of the young women at home." But Galway playwright M. J. Molloy, who urged the state to provide dowries in order to encourage marriage, conceded that fewer farmers were providing dowries, because many young women were now earning "good livings" as nurses or in industry. He claimed that current practices in rural county Galway were a mixture of the city "love match" and rural matchmaking.[224] The maladroit and unromantic behavior of Irish males depicted by Irish writers may reflect the uneasy transition from matchmaking to modern courtship.

One of the most interesting aspects of *The Vanishing Irish* is the extent of the criticism directed at older people for preventing their sons and daughters (but especially their sons) from marrying; "the maternal dog in the manger"[225] was condemned for encouraging an unnaturally close attachment on the part of her son or sons, as were parents who refused to transfer control of a farm, or those who offered "unreasonable opposition" to the marriage of a daughter or son. *The Vanishing Irish* quoted a Lenten pastoral by Dr. James McNamee, the bishop of Ardagh and Clonmacnoise, where he referred to "unreasonable opposition" by parents to their children's marriage, "an obstinate refusal to make such domestic arrangements and settlements as would enable them to marry and found a family."[226] Such criticism contrasts with the views expressed in the early 1940s by the interdepartmental committee on dower houses, where the wishes and rights of the older generation and the obligations of the parent-child relationship took precedence over those of the young married couple.

The changed attitude may reflect an emerging but fragile youth culture in postwar Ireland; alternatively, the belief that rural marriages were in crisis may have prompted the Catholic clergy to adopt a more sympathetic attitude toward the parents of the future.[227] Arensberg and Kimball noted that Ireland was an old person's country.[228] By the 1950s the balance was altering. Why? Several explanations come to mind. Mass emigration meant that Irish farmers were less likely to be in a position to pick and choose between potential heirs, and this lessened their ability to determine inheritance and made it easier for the remaining heir or heiress to assert their demands. Second, however obliquely, the postwar youth culture that was manifesting itself in the United States and the more urbanized parts of western Europe was beginning to seep into Ireland, and this was happening at least partially under the auspices of the Catholic church, who were following the example of the French and Italian churches in promoting Catholic youth groups.

Conclusion

The Irish marriage patterns that were described by the Commission on Emigration and *The Vanishing Irish* were already a matter of history when these books were published. Brendan Walsh has noted that Ireland "not only participated in the European marriage boom of the immediate postwar years but also began to close the gap between itself and the rest of Europe."[229] In 1945–46 only 41 percent of grooms were aged less than thirty years; by 1965 the proportion had risen to 66 percent.[230] The proportion of women aged twenty-five to twenty-nine who were single fell by two-thirds, from 57.5 percent to 37.8 percent.[231] The move toward earlier marriages was more pronounced among men than among women, so the age gap between couples fell. In 1965 the mean age of marriage for men was 29.4, 2.3 year earlier than in 1957; women married 1.6 years earlier, at 26.1 years.[232] These changes were well underway by the mid 1950s, but they were not noticed, perhaps because the image of middle-aged newlyweds or young brides and elderly grooms was more in keeping with the sense of crisis and gloom that pervaded Ireland during that grim decade or perhaps simply because of the lack of statistics on age of marriage.[233] The narrowing age gap should have resulted in more companionate marriages and greater equality between couples, making it easier to negotiate some form of family planning.[234] The rate of natural increase rose during the 1940s and early 1950s; it fell slightly in the mid 1950s, probably in reaction to the poor state of the Irish economy, but by 1961 the population was growing at a rate of 68 percent per generation, compared with 20 percent per generation in 1936. Albania and Iceland were the only countries in Europe with a higher rate of natural increase.[235]

Although Irish marriage and fertility patterns in the 1950s were out of line with elsewhere, "the vanishing Irish" were disappearing through emigration and not because of a lack of marriages or births. Indeed, the increase in the number of young people entering the labor force in the 1950s compared with the 1930s is a factor in the higher rate of emigration. The rise in the marriage rate, earlier marriages, and the decline in the numbers of women in paid employment during the 1960s suggest that many young Irish people shared the church's belief in the importance of marriage and family but were unable to attain it until economic growth and the despised urban industrial economy made it possible.

4

The Irish State and
Its Emigrants

1922–1954

It may be taken as axiomatic that no Saorstát Government
will allow emigration to assume dimensions which will lead
to a permanent lowering of the present population.
R. C. Geary, "The Future Population of Saorstát Éireann."

Emigration prompted a variety of responses in independent Ireland. Politicians, churchmen, and some citizens gloried in
Ireland's large expatriate community, which gave the new
state a degree of international recognition that was utterly disproportionate to its size,[1] although the greatest affection was often re-
served for second- or third-generation expatriates. It provided a
safety valve for both the state and Irish society, facilitating the per-
petuation of large families and nonpartible land inheritance in a
country that was incapable of providing sufficient nonfarming jobs
for its children; it enabled Ireland to cling to the myth that it could
remain a predominantly rural society; and by reducing the numbers
claiming unemployment assistance and other social welfare payments, it saved considerable sums for the Irish Exchequer. Although
the overwhelming majority left for economic reasons, emigration
also provided an escape for misfits—veteran republicans who could

not adjust to the new state, disillusioned writers and intellectuals, pregnant single women, couples embarking on marriages without parental approval, or those who felt stifled by an introspective Ireland. By doing so, it helped to preserve the image of an idealized Ireland. Although every Irish government claimed that ending emigration was a major objective, the possibility that it might be curtailed by a recession in Britain or by British government restrictions gave rise to fears, not rejoicing. In 1948 Seán MacBride, then minister for External Affairs, noted that Britain's economic future would "preclude her from providing an outlet for Ireland's surplus population indefinitely" and that Ireland would be forced in the near future to absorb her own natural population increase.[2]

But if emigration was a safety valve, it could also threaten the status quo, depriving Irish middle-class families of cheap servants, luring young men and women away from the uncertain status of "relatives assisting" with the promise of a bulging wallet and a lively social life in London or Coventry. By bringing young women and men (but particularly women) into contact with "pagan" culture, emigration was often seen as challenging the values of a traditional Catholic Ireland. It exposed the shortcomings of life in independent Ireland, breaking through the cultural and economic protectionism that enveloped the state after independence. But the mental or intellectual self-sufficiency of Irish society meant that emigration was rarely seen in a comparative context, as part of a wider transition from rural to urban economies. The mass emigration of the mid-1950s eventually prompted a rethinking of Irish economic policy, although it is also possible that without the safety valve of emigration, this might have happened at an earlier date.

Emigration attracted relatively little attention during the first two decades of independent Ireland. The Saorstát Éireann *Irish Free State Official Handbook*, published in 1932, does not mention emigration or population.[3] The report on the 1936 census suggested that, allowing for the abnormal migration during the years 1911–26—Irishmen enlisting in the 1914–18 war, the departure of British troops and their dependents, and the emigration of former members of the Royal Irish Constabulary after independence—the rate of emigration had shown an unbroken decline since the 1880s.[4] When Eamon de Valera asked whether the 1936 census figures indicated a rise or a fall in emigration, he was informed that they indicated "a diminution."[5] This equanimity about emigration was not justified. Although the number of overseas emigrants fell to less than one thousand a year in the early 1930s, this was due to the severe depression in the United States, not to improved circumstances in Ireland. Gerry Hughes has calculated that throughout the 1930s, more people left Ireland than entered the country in every year except 1932, when unemployment in the United Kingdom was at its peak, and 1939–40, when the outbreak of war precipitated return migration to neutral Ireland, possibly to evade conscription.

By 1936 emigration had regained the pre-1929 level,[6] and opposition deputies were citing this as evidence of the failure of Fianna Fáil policies. When Roy Geary presented a paper in 1935 on the future population of Ireland, he suggested that emigration was not a matter of immediate concern, but in a report on the final volumes of the 1936 census, written in 1939, he indicated that emigration posed the major threat to a stable population; if emigration persisted at the current rate, the population would continue to fall.[7]

Emigration to Britain: Continuity and Change

The 1930s initiated a new phase in Irish emigration and the emergence of patterns that would remain dominant during the mass emigration of the 1950s and beyond. After 1930 the overwhelming majority of emigrants went to Britain not to the United States. The transition from the United States to Britain as the primary destination began during the 1920s. Unrestricted access to the United States for Irish (and indeed all) emigrants ended in the early 1920s, when the United States introduced national quotas. The 1924 Johnson-Reed Act gave the Irish Free State a quota of 28,567, which was subsequently reduced to 17,853 beginning in 1929. Although the reduced quota prompted widespread protests in the United States,[8] there is no evidence that the Irish government made representations on this matter. Walshaw's figures suggest that 18,000 Irish people emigrated to Britain in 1924; during the first half of that year it was almost impossible for Irish people to secure emigrant visas for the United

States. In 1926, when Ireland "practically exhausted" its American immigrant quota, net emigration to Britain was in excess of 11,000. In other years during the 1920s, when the American immigration quota was not under such pressure, the number of emigrants to Britain was substantially lower.[9] Medical tests were tightened in 1917, and it appears that many Irish immigrants were deported on medical grounds; by the late 1920s, would-be immigrants were being rejected on the basis that they were "likely to become a public charge." When American unemployment rates soared after 1929, some Irish emigrants decided to return to Ireland. Matt O'Brien claims that "the return of thousands of economic refugees from the American Depression discouraged many prospective emigrants, embodying the human cost of failure in the United States."[10] Although the American economy recovered during the 1940s, wartime travel restrictions prevented emigration. By the time that normal trans-Atlantic travel had resumed in the late 1940s, immigrant networks had weakened considerably. Ireland filled less than half of its annual immigrant quota of 17,853 throughout the 1950s, except in 1957 and 1958.[11] By 1951 there were more people of Irish birth living in Britain than in the United States—reversing a century-long trend.[12] In 1958 the Irish consulate in New York estimated that there were twice as many people of Irish birth in Britain as in the United States.[13]

Most Irish emigrants who went to Britain after 1930 settled in London, the south of England, and the Midlands, areas where construction workers, female servants, and factory workers were in demand. Traditional destinations such as Scotland, Lancashire, and the northeast were in recession, and unemployment in these regions remained well in excess of the national average even after the end of World War II. Although the destination of Irish emigrants altered, in other respects there was continuity. Nineteenth-century emigrants to Britain and the United States were extremely mobile; many worked as railway and canal navvies. Although Irish emigrants came from diverse backgrounds, the largest concentrations of emigrant men in the twentieth century were found on construction schemes— motorways, wartime aerodromes, or large factories such as the Ford plant at Dagenham—where the workers were almost entirely Irish, with Irish foremen and supervisors. These sites were often in remote locations; the men lived in labor camps, isolated from the indigenous population, moving on to the next site when the work had finished.[14] During the nineteenth century, the largest group of Irish women emigrants became domestic servants, and domestic service or other service jobs such as ward maid, waitress, and chambermaid provided the first jobs for most Irish women who came to England after 1920. Irish women also changed jobs quite frequently; many women hired as domestic servants in private houses soon moved to jobs that gave them greater personal freedom.[15]

Irish emigrants to the United States before 1914 had one of the lowest rates of return emigration in Europe,[16] but "those staying in Britain left their options open."[17] The 1901 and 1911 census enumeration forms for Dublin city record many working-class households with English-born children or an English-born wife, indicating that many workers, especially those in construction, moved between Britain and Ireland in response to changing economic circumstances.[18] In 1926 an Irish civil servant commented that "there is migration between the Free State and Great Britain, but that is not with a view to permanent settlement. The migrants return to this country when employment is not available in Great Britain. The majority of the people who emigrate from this country go to the United States."[19]

The distinction between permanent emigration to the United States and short-term migration to Britain was overstated. Many emigrants settled permanently in Britain, but a substantial number returned to Ireland either to settle or for holidays.[20] Return visits for Christmas and during the summer became common after World War II; most workers were entitled to at least two weeks' annual paid holidays, and cross-channel sea and rail fares were relatively cheap. This meant that emigrants kept in closer contact with family and friends than those who left before 1920; some married men left wives and families in Ireland, returning at Christmas and in the summer.[21] The first generation of Irish emigrants to the United States to make regular visits home were those who left during the 1980s and 1990s.

This two-way traffic meant that twentieth-century emigration had a more direct impact on Ireland than the earlier wave of emigration. It was widely believed that emigrants who returned on holidays with flashy clothes (especially the women), bulging wallets, and stories of high wages and regular overtime lured others to England.[22] Fears were often expressed that Irish emigrants—particularly female emigrants—would be assimilated into British society,[23] a prospect that appears to have aroused much greater hostility than the prospect of Irish emigrants becoming part of the United States "melting pot." There are obvious reasons for the different attitudes. Britain was the former occupying power and, according to many Irish nationalists, the source of all undesirable cultural and moral influences. Britain, or strictly speaking England, offered less scope for a hybrid identity than the United States. Irish-America was a well-recognized identity badge, whereas Anglo-Irish carried very different connotations.

Emigration to Britain challenged the Fianna Fáil government's ideal of economic self-sufficiency, confirming the continuing close ties between the British and the Irish economies.[24] In 1968 the Irish Department of Labor claimed that the tradition of short-term emigration to Britain made it more attractive for Irish workers, especially skilled workers, to join a British trade union, which would ensure that their qualifications were recognized in Britain.[25] The close association between the British and the Irish labor markets, particularly in industries such as construction, exerted upward pressure on Irish wage rates. Emigration made workers aware of the welfare benefits available in Britain and Irish shortcomings in this regard; the Irish authorities were all too conscious of this.[26]

Irish emigrants formed an important source of labor for the British economy when Ireland was part of the United Kingdom, and Britain appears to have been keen to retain the links between the two labor markets after 1922, despite the rise in British unemployment. In 1926 a British interdepartmental committee recommended that social insurance schemes should be standardized throughout the Empire, with reciprocal arrangements enabling migrants with contributions in one country to draw benefit in another, but the Irish authorities replied that the Irish Free State was "not really interested in the matter at all," because they regarded the proposal as encouraging emigration and immigration.[27] Until 1935 the *National Clearing House Gazette,* the official British Ministry of Labor list of all job vacancies that could not be filled by the local labor exchanges, was sent to Irish employment exchanges; the practice was discontinued because there were few unfilled vacancies in Britain that would prove attractive to Irish workers, but the British Ministry of Labor continued to send a copy to the Department of Industry and Commerce.[28] Given the high rate of unemployment in Britain during the 1920s and 1930s, it is not surprising that there were reports of hostility toward Irish workers or that the British authorities explored the possibility of introducing work permits to control the number of Irish immigrants working in the United Kingdom.[29] But they remained in demand as seasonal farm laborers, domestic servants, and for heavy construction work—jobs that did not attract unemployed British workers. In 1938 a British interdepartmental committee recommended that no restrictions be imposed on Irish immigrants, because they did not constitute a serious charge on public funds, they were particularly well suited to unskilled, heavy navvying jobs, and they did not deprive unemployed Englishmen or women of work.[30]

Irish Labor in Wartime Britain

Emigration began to feature on the Irish cabinet agenda for the first time during the Second World War. Approximately 50,000 Irish men and women served in the British forces,[31] and thousands more took civilian jobs in key wartime industries. Wartime labor shortages forced many British employers to overcome their reluctance to hire Irish workers, and this extended the range of occupations open to postwar emigrants. In the early years of the war, most Irish workers were found in the construction industry, but by 1943–44 they had spread into other occupations.[32] In Ireland the government had to decide whether to facilitate emigration by cooperating with the British authorities or to maintain its official hostility. "The policy of our Government, as I interpret it from public announcements which I have seen in the Press from time to time, is to discourage emigration and to concentrate on the creation of activities here which will reduce as far as possible the tendency to find employment in other countries."[33]

This position, first enunciated by Cumann na nGaedheal during the 1920s, was continued under Fianna Fáil. Both governments rejected all overtures to participate in Empire Resettlement Schemes;

during the 1920s the state of Ontario was dissuaded from advertising an assisted emigration scheme targeted at "capable Irish girls" and prospective farmers, and the Cunard and White Star lines from advertising for potential emigrants. In 1937 de Valera informed the Dáil that the government's aim was "not to provide facilities for the emigration of our people to the States of the Commonwealth or elsewhere" but to "concentrate on utilising the resources of this country and so providing conditions of life here that our people will not have to emigrate, but will be able to find a livelihood in their own country."[34]

After the outbreak of war in 1939 it became progressively more difficult to sustain this position. From September 1939 Irish people traveling to Britain were required to produce an identity card, so the Department of External Affairs began to issue travel permit cards; applications were made at local garda stations. When a German invasion of Britain seemed imminent in the summer of 1940, Britain imposed further restrictions on travel between Britain and Ireland; all travelers had to apply at the British permit office in Dublin either for a visitor's visa or a work visa.[35] Recruitment agents for British construction companies were reported to be visiting towns in the west of Ireland, offering wages and bonuses that far exceeded local rates.[36] Ireland was attracting British employers at this time because Ministry of Labor regulations prevented them from advertising for workers in Britain or hiring them without the ministry's consent.[37] In the summer of 1940 Lemass warned that if imports to Ireland dried up, unemployment would climb to 261,000, perhaps even to 400,000. The odds of this happening shortened considerably in January 1941 when Churchill imposed severe restrictions on the volume of imports reaching Ireland in an effort to persuade de Valera to abandon neutrality. Many Irish factories closed or went on short time because of shortages of fuel and raw materials. Construction sites came to a halt, and a growing number of workers began to apply to the British Ministry of Labor liaison officer in Dublin or their local employment exchange for jobs in Britain. By March 1941 Irish employment exchanges had over 1,500 unsolicited applications for jobs in Britain on file, and it was decided not to accept further applications without government approval. Meanwhile, the Dublin Typographical Association had asked the Department of Industry and Commerce to assist them in finding jobs in Britain for unemployed printing workers, and the Amalgamated Transport and General Workers Union had contacted its parent union, the British Transport and General Workers Union, with a similar purpose.[38] Some Irish employers were complaining that advertisements promising high wages and steady employment in Britain were "creating a measure of dissatisfaction with wage conditions at home." On 28 March 1941 the Department of External Affairs presented the government with proposals for joint arrangements between the British Ministry of Labor and the Department of Industry and Commerce to regulate emigration to Britain.[39]

In theory, the Irish government had two options. It could implement a major scheme of public works to employ the displaced workers, as Lemass recommended, or it could facilitate emigration. In practice the shortages of fuel and supplies that had brought about the increase in unemployment made it impossible to carry out a substantial program of relief works.[40]

Travel permit cards made it possible for the Irish authorities to control emigration, and Britain could use work visas to select the workers that it needed. According to a report compiled by the Department of Social Welfare in 1948, the arrangements reached with the British authorities in 1941 were designed to safeguard the interests of Irish employers and ensure a sufficient supply of labor for farming and turf production, although to achieve this, Irish employment exchanges were effectively transformed into offshore branches of the British Ministry of Labor and National Service. All applications for jobs originating in Ireland would be processed through the Irish employment exchanges. The Department of Industry and Commerce—which was responsible for the exchanges—would forward applications to the British ministry, which would notify interested employers. Offers of jobs would be forwarded to Industry and Commerce, and the Irish employment exchanges would issue approved emigrants with a card, entitling them to a British working visa. The British Ministry of Labor paid the travel costs of workers emigrating under this scheme.[41] From August 1941, when this arrangement came into effect, everybody who was recruiting workers for British employers had to operate under the control of the British Ministry of Labor liaison officer in Dublin.[42] The arrangement was not put into effect until Britain gave an undertaking that workers who emigrated under this program would not be liable for conscription.[43] Recruitment advertisements for jobs in Britain were banned under the 1942 Emergency Powers Order number 241.[44]

These travel restrictions breached a long-standing tradition of freedom to emigrate. The Irish authorities were determined to ensure that emigration did not threaten Ireland's continued neutrality by leaving the country short of troops and agricultural and turf workers. Initially they decided that no permits would be issued to applicants from rural areas or from towns with a population of less than 5,000, but this proposal took no account of areas with a long tradition of seasonal migration, and the government had to agree that no embargo would be placed on seasonal emigrants. Intending emigrants living in small towns or rural areas with no tradition of seasonal migration had to obtain a permit from the local garda station, testifying that they had not been engaged in turf or agricultural work. Permits were denied to any worker for whom employment was available in Ireland and everybody under twenty-two years, though this provision was waived in exceptional circumstances—if a family was dependent on emigrants' remittances, for example, or for those going to Britain as trainee nurses or seminarians. The age limit may have been introduced to protect enlistment in the army and the army reserve, but it came to be seen as a form of moral protection for women. Travel permits were issued only to workers with a confirmed offer of work from the British liaison office. The Department of Industry and Commerce expressed the opinion that it would be preferable for Irish workers to emigrate to Britain than to Northern Ireland, because there was considerable ill feeling against them in Northern Ireland.[45]

The wartime cooperation between the British and Irish authorities prompted protests from a wide variety of interest groups. Some, like farmers and those responsible for turf production, were motivated purely by self-interest, whereas the Catholic church and former members of the Irish Republican Army (IRA) couched their objections in moral or nationalist rhetoric. Michael Kilroy, a veteran of the war of independence in county Mayo, who was the Westport District leader of the Local Defence Force, complained to de Valera that the British travel permits amounted to "conscription in disguise."[46] The Mayo county surveyor, Seán Flanagan, a future Fianna Fáil minister and TD, went far beyond the normal remit of an official employed by a local authority when he issued a "pastoral letter" calling for a ban on emigration so that turf would be saved, with instructions that it should be read in all churches in the county.[47]

It is impossible to determine how much credibility should be given to the allegations of labor shortages that proliferated during the Emergency, because such claims were inextricably linked with issues of social control and nationalist or anti-British sentiment. The increased demand for rural workers gave employers less freedom to pick and choose, or to hire and fire, than in the past, and they were under much greater pressure to meet laborers' demands over wages and working conditions. Many farmers reported acute shortages of agricultural laborers, although the registers at the local labor exchange listed men who claimed to have experience of agricultural work. Reports of a shortage of turf workers are fraught with similar contradictions.[48] Allegations that gardaí adopted a lax attitude to the ban on former turf and agricultural workers emigrating, signing permits for men who should have been rejected, were probably correct, and the ban on emigration by those under twenty-two years of age was widely breached. One large farmer in Westmeath informed the gardaí that two brothers who worked as agricultural laborers on his farm were planning to emigrate, and he became extremely irate when one succeeded in getting away.[49]

The cabinet was divided on the matter. In 1941 the minister who was most sympathetic to facilitating emigration was Seán MacEntee, then minister for Industry and Commerce, whose views might have been determined by departmental considerations. If emigration was prohibited, the Department of Industry and Commerce would have come under pressure to provide for the increasing number of unemployed workers. But MacEntee's attitude did not change when he became minister for Local Government and Public Health in August 1941, despite the fact that he was now responsible for wartime turf production. When the Irish authorities were considering introducing further restrictions on travel to Northern Ireland in 1943—many would-be emigrants who had been refused visas were crossing the

border en route to Britain—MacEntee announced that he was opposed to "further restrictions being placed on the natural right of
persons to sell their labour where it will give maximum return," and
he repeatedly queried the more hysterical complaints about shortages of turf workers. He claimed, with some justification, that government regulations were discouraging men from taking jobs in turf
or agriculture because they were aware that they would be denied the
right to emigrate at a future date and that the threat of a future clampdown on emigration deterred seasonal migrants from returning to
Ireland.[50]

F. H. Boland, a senior official in the Department of External Affairs, also cautioned against imposing additional restrictions on emigration. In 1942 Boland warned that Britain was "very anxious" to
recruit Irish workers; if Ireland restricted emigration, Britain might
retaliate by reducing the quantities of raw materials that it supplied
to Ireland.[51] Although the strongest opposition to emigration came
from officials in the Department of Agriculture—echoing protests
from farmers—Agriculture preferred to exert pressure on Industry
and Commerce, leaving Seán Lemass, who had returned to his old
post as minister for Industry and Commerce in August 1941, to fight
the case for tighter restrictions.[52] Lemass was much less willing to facilitate emigration than MacEntee, which begs the question whether
the decision to move MacEntee from Industry and Commerce to
Local Government and Public Health in August 1941 was influenced
by his stance on emigration. In June 1942, before his return to Industry and Commerce, Lemass had put forward proposals to establish a
Department of Labor, with powers similar to the British Ministry for
Labor and National Service. If Lemass's plan had been accepted, no
worker registered as working in agriculture, turf, or several other industries would have been permitted to emigrate or change jobs within
Ireland without official permission, although in compensation the
state would undertake to provide work throughout the year for those
who were liable to seasonal spells of unemployment.[53] These proposals were not accepted by the government, but in 1944, in response to
further pressure from the Department of Agriculture, the Irish authorities took advantage of Britain's clampdown on travel between
Britain and Ireland (part of the security precautions in the run-up to

the D-Day landings) to tighten the restrictions on emigration. A blanket prohibition on emigration was extended to all residents of towns with a population of 5,000 or less, and exemptions in hardship cases were ended because officials argued that they could not be enforced. Some civil servants wished to extend the emigration ban to all towns with a population of less than ten thousand. However, these new regulations proved so draconian that they were removed in November 1944.[54]

Wartime emigration was of considerable benefit to the Irish Exchequer: it removed the threat of mass unemployment, reduced the cost of unemployment assistance and other benefits, and improved the balance of payments, though this was a less important consideration because of an unaccustomed payments surplus.[55] Some officials and ministers acknowledged these benefits in private. In 1941, while attempting to persuade the cabinet to approve formal cooperation with the British Ministry of Labor, the Department of Industry and Commerce suggested that "the placing of Irish unemployed workers in employment in Great Britain would provide a very welcome mitigation of difficulties at home."[56] Some months later F. H. Boland noted that J. J. McElligott, the secretary of the Department of Finance, regarded wartime emigration as "a safety valve against revolution"; McElligott also believed that the inflow of an estimated £100,000–£150,000 a week in emigrants' remittances had done much to relieve distress and boost the economy.[57] Connolly notes that the men who emigrated during the war were noticeably older than previous emigrants, which might suggest that more were married men with families. Frank McCourt has described how wartime remittances transformed the lives of many of his neighbors in the back lanes of Limerick city, but not the permanently doomed McCourts.[58] A series in *The Bell* on "Other People's Incomes" records what "a big blow" it was to Mr. K., an unemployed Dublin laborer with a wife and six children "when he was refused a British work permit because of his sight."[59]

But the safety valve could be reversed, and there were fears that large numbers of emigrants would return to Ireland when the war ended.[60] In 1942 Boland claimed that "if there is one thing more certain than another, it is that immediately the "ceasefire" order is given, the whole aim and purpose of the British authorities will be to rush all these workers back to the country as quickly as they can." He predicted that within weeks of the war coming to an end, more than 100,000 unemployed men "who will no doubt, have imbibed a good deal of 'leftism' in Britain" would be " 'dumped' in Ireland."[61] Such fears were a factor behind the government's plans for a program of postwar investment in housing, roads, rural electrification, and other outlays on infrastructure.[62] But the ending of World War II was not followed by mass unemployment in Britain; there was no mass return migration, and indeed, emigration continued, very much on Britain's terms.[63]

Emigration and the Postwar British and Irish Economies

In 1946 a cabinet working party estimated that Britain would need an additional 1–1.5 million workers in the next decade. Wartime casualties and the fall in the birthrate during the 1920s and 1930s meant that the number of men and women aged between twenty and forty-four in Britain was declining annually by 100,000.[64] The *Report of the Royal Commission on Population* published in 1949 calculated that Britain would need 140,000 young adult immigrants every year for the next ten years to compensate for the fall in the number of Britons entering the labor force. It also suggested that "the tendency towards a fall in the working age groups may make it difficult to recruit an adequate supply of native labor for industries that are comparatively unattractive. . . . We saw the beginning of this process in Great Britain before the war in the field of domestic service; and since the war difficulties in securing workers for domestic service, mining, agriculture and a few other occupations have led to the measures which the Government have taken to recruit workers by immigration." The royal commission believed that "Eire is likely to be a continuing source of emigrants to Great Britain; between the years 1933 –37— years when employment prospects in Great Britain were improving— net immigration here from Eire was probably about 16,000 a year, and there are possibilities that this rate could be increased."[65]

Britain removed all wartime controls on female employment on 1 July 1946, which meant that employers could hire women without having to seek approval from the Ministry of Labor, but male employment remained subject to controls. In June 1946, when it became obvious that Britain was about to ease wartime labor restrictions, the Department of Industry and Commerce asked the cabinet to determine whether all intending emigrants should still be required to obtain travel permits; what steps should be taken to prevent or to regulate British employers and their agents recruiting workers in Ireland; and, if it was decided to retain controls on emigration, whether they should seek the cooperation of the British authorities in enforcing the controls. On 28 June 1946 the government decided to lift wartime controls over emigrant women when British controls ended two days later, but travel permits were retained, and "in accordance with normal peacetime practices," applicants for travel permits who were less than twenty-one years of age would require parental consent. The ban imposed in 1942 on recruitment advertisements for jobs in Britain was lifted; however, Industry and Commerce was instructed to examine the possibility of regulating employment agencies who were recruiting workers for Britain.[66]

From 1 July 1946, women with valid travel permits could travel to Britain in search of work using a visitor visa. Ministry of Labor controls meant that it was much more difficult for men to find work if they did not have a work visa; in order to obtain one they had to apply to an Irish employment exchange, where they were required to prove that no job was available to them in Ireland and that they were not precluded from emigrating because they had formerly worked in farming or turf. The 1947 British Control of Engagement Order, which applied to women aged eighteen to forty and men aged eighteen to fifty, stipulated that all workers, except those in professional or managerial positions, should be engaged through the local office of the Ministry of Labor, but many domestic jobs continued to be filled through less formal channels. Some British employers appear to have written directly to Irish workers offering jobs, and others found jobs in Britain through family or neighbors. But many male emigrants were recruited through the Irish employment exchanges, where they were interviewed by a representative of the British Ministry of Labor's Irish liaison office, apparently in the presence of an Irish official. In their report on a visit to the Cork labor exchange in August 1948, Reverend Cornelius Lucey and Professor M. D. McCarthy claimed that certain branch officials "place every difficulty in the way of intending emigrants, even those not covered by restrictions." The British liaison officers selected workers on the basis of physical fitness, intelligence, educational standards, the type of worker, and the numbers required to meet Britain's needs. Six out of the fifty-five prospective emigrants interviewed in Cork city were rejected for being unable to read, either because of bad eyesight or illiteracy.[67] In 1948 a representative of the British liaison office was paying weekly visits to the Tralee employment exchange. In Wexford, where there were fewer prospective emigrants, visits took place at three-week intervals; liaison officer Mrs. O'Mara interviewed approximately twenty-four or twenty-five at each visit.[68] British officials also interviewed applicants for student nurse places in the United Kingdom.

Demobilized British soldiers got the pick of the available jobs; nonnationals were directed toward the less desirable occupations. During 1946 and 1947, in a desperate effort to recruit coal miners, the British authorities refused to grant permits to Irishmen who had definite job offers from other employers. In July 1947 with all jobs in Britain except coal mining closed to Irish male emigrants, the newly created Department of Social Welfare (which had taken over responsibility for employment exchanges from the Department of Industry and Commerce) suggested that the Irish authorities refuse to cooperate in future with the British Ministry of Labor in recruiting Irish workers, but Industry and Commerce feared that Britain might retaliate by reducing Ireland's allocation of coal. The cabinet decided that Britain should be permitted to recruit coal miners in return for guaranteeing Ireland an increased supply of coal, but this attempt to trade workers for coal collapsed when it was learned that coal supplies were being allocated through the European coal organization: any increased allocation of British coal would automatically mean a reduction in the amount provided from other sources. Nevertheless, Ireland's tough stance was not entirely ineffective; in September 1947 Britain relaxed the insistence that work permits be given only to coalface workers, and some men were permitted to take jobs on building sites.[69]

In 1948 Britain established an interdepartmental working party to examine the feasibility of recruiting labor in the British colonies, and 180,000 foreign workers, the majority of them Poles, Ukrainians and German ex-prisoners of war, were offered jobs in industries with acute labor shortages such as coal mining, although many of them declined.[70] If Britain needed immigrant workers, Irish immigrants were probably the first choice: they were white, English speaking, and there was a long tradition of emigration from Ireland. If Britain was in recession, British officials believed that the majority would return to Ireland.[71] Despite the undoubted existence of anti-Irish sentiment in Britain, E. P. Thompson's comment on nineteenth-century Irish emigrants is equally true of the twentieth century: "It is not the friction but the relative ease with which the Irish were absorbed into the working class community which is remarkable."[72] The Royal Commission on Population expressed fears that large numbers of immigrants would present "serious problems of assimilation," but several unpublished memoranda written by British civil servants during the 1950s referred to Irish emigrants as "assimilable" or "in no sense difficult to assimilate."[73]

The importance that Britain attached to Irish immigration is evident in the 1948 British Nationality Act. While formally acknowledging for the first time that Irish citizens were not British subjects, the act granted Irish citizens the same rights as British citizens in matters such as employment and freedom of entry, and this was done in clauses that were specific to Ireland and distinct from the clauses relating to other Commonwealth countries.[74] When the British Nationality Act received the royal assent, Ireland was still a member of the Commonwealth, at least in name, but within weeks John A. Costello, taoiseach in the first Inter-Party government, had announced that Ireland would declare a republic and leave the Commonwealth. Britain responded by threatening to restrict the rights of Irish residents in Britain, a threat that attracted some support from politicians and sections of the press. However, one senior British official acknowledged privately that treating Ireland as a foreign nation would present greater difficulties for Britain than for Ireland. In the event, the British authorities decided not to change the status of Irish residents in Britain, partly because any alteration would have resulted in protests from Commonwealth governments,[75] but also because it was in Britain's interests to facilitate the free movement of Irish workers to the United Kingdom.

Britain's strategy in the bilateral negotiations that resulted in a new trade agreement in the summer of 1948 was likewise influenced by the wish to encourage migration from Ireland. During the course of talks in London in the autumn of 1947, de Valera suggested that both governments should attempt to bring about "a dovetailing of the two economies," which was a far cry from the self-sufficiency program that he had introduced in 1932. Instead of rebuilding war-damaged plants in Britain, he suggested that British firms should be encouraged to move to Ireland, where they could occupy vacant premises and readily find workers. But one official in the Board of Trade noted that it would be "better to bring the Irish labour to Lancashire than to take Lancashire industries to Eire." Other British civil servants pointed out that "Irish ideas of 'dovetailing', 'integration' etc. are likely to run counter to our own. We should like Eire to revert to a source of foodstuffs particularly cattle products" and presumably, though he does not say this, a source of unskilled and semi-skilled labor.[76] On 18 June 1948, when the trade agreement was in the final stages of negotiation, an internal British civil service memorandum suggested that unemployed Irish workers take jobs in British industries that were undermanned, "which seems to be one of the most practical and mutually beneficial forms of co-operation between the two countries."[77] Shortly after this, N. E. Archer of the Commonwealth Relations office informed a colleague that he had raised with Lord Rugby (formerly Sir John Maffey), the British minister in Ireland, the possibility of holding discussions with the Irish government, with a view to "doing everything possible to facilitate the mobility of Eire citizens to this country to work in our building industry." Archer referred to the long and painful history of Irish emigration and the fact that the Catholic church was strongly opposed to emigration. "Hence no Eire government can afford to give overt encouragement even to the temporary movement of Eire labour to this country. The most an Eire government can do is to remove obstacles but even such action is liable to be defied in some areas by various forms of local obstruction."[78]

Emigration and Irish Politics in the Aftermath of World War II

Archer's comments were perceptive. By the late 1940s the high rate of emigration was increasingly cited as evidence that the economic policies pursued by Fianna Fáil since 1932 had failed. Opposition deputies raised the matter whenever an opportunity presented itself, but discussion was by no means restricted to Leinster House. One of the unintended consequences of wartime travel permits was that they provided the first detailed statistics of emigrants to the United Kingdom by age and gender.[79] The revelation that almost two-thirds of travel permits issued in 1946 were awarded to women, and that one-third of these women were in their teens, prompted widespread expressions of outrage. "The flight of the girls" was blamed for the alleged collapse of rural marriages and for robbing Ireland of future wives and mothers. There were also claims that it created a servant shortage that deterred nonemigrating women from marriage. In October 1947 the Catholic hierarchy wrote to de Valera expressing concern about the 1947 Health Act (especially the Mother and Child Scheme) and about emigration. They specifically requested that restrictions be placed on emigrants who were under eighteen years of age and on the activities of British employment agencies.[80]

When de Valera consulted the minister for Social Welfare, James Ryan, the latter outlined three options: passing legislation that would require intending emigrants to obtain an emigrant permit from the Irish authorities; requiring all Irish visitors to the United Kingdom to deposit a substantial sum that would be refunded on their return (some emigrants were reputedly using visitors' visas); or lifting all restrictions on travel to the United Kingdom. From 1 January 1948 Irish persons entering Britain would no longer require a visa, although they would need some form of official identification, such as a travel permit or passport. Ryan pointed out that many Irish people already held travel permits—170,000 had been issued since 1939—and they were valid for five years. He suggested that the government establish a commission with wide terms of reference to examine the effect of emigration on present and future population trends, particularly in view of the population changes that were anticipated in Britain.[81]

This memorandum was on the cabinet agenda but was with-drawn until further notice on 16 December 1947. The Dáil had been dissolved on the previous day, and a general election was called for 4 February 1948.[82] However, on 16 December de Valera asked the De-partment of Social Welfare to examine allegations that individuals or foreign businesses were encouraging young men and women to emi-grate. He also asked for a comprehensive statement of the "functions and utility from the point of view of this country" of the British Ministry of Labor's Irish liaison office and whether or not it was de-sirable that the office should continue when visas were abolished. The Department of Social Welfare reported that, although some ad-vertisements for jobs in Britain had appeared in Irish newspapers in recent months, any immediate return to the free-for-all that existed before 1942 was highly unlikely, given that the Ministry of Labor con-trolled the filling of all job vacancies in the United Kingdom. Only three recruitment advertisements for men had appeared in Irish newspapers over the previous three months, and these were for do-mestic and institutional jobs. However, the decontrolling of female employment in Britain in July 1946 meant that employers could ad-vertise for women workers without going through the Ministry of Labor. The advertising columns of the *Irish Independent* for the three months ending on 31 December 1947 contained 286 advertisements seeking nurses, probationers, and student nurses—almost 4 per issue—30 advertisements for female industrial workers or bus con-ductresses, and 23 advertisements seeking domestic staff for institu-tions. There were only 3 advertisements targeted at men, and these sought domestic staff for institutions. Only two agencies advertised for domestic staff (mainly for institutions) and both were Irish: Bro-phy's of Earl Street in Dublin and Taaffe's of Ardee. British agents were reported to be recruiting workers in provincial towns as far apart as Gorey and Ballybofey, but they were either interviewing applicants for trainee nursing places or hiring factory workers for large compa-nies that offered extensive benefits including hostel accommodation, staff canteens, and welfare officers. The only dubious recruitment practices reported involved a former member of Donegal County Council who was promising jobs in Birmingham on payment of a 5s. fee.[83] De Valera was obviously preoccupied with emigration at this time. A comment on a file dated 30 December noted that the Department of External Affairs had prepared a series of questions and answers about emigration for the taoiseach "before he goes away because I think he wants to take it with him."[84]

Emigration featured in the 1948 general election, but it was not the dominant issue: partition, an Irish republic, the dangers of coalition government, and the cost of living were also hotly debated. Every party promised improved health and social welfare services, more investment in housing, hospitals, and other public services, and measures to promote increased output and employment in agriculture and industry. It was implied, and sometimes more explicitly stated, that this additional spending would bring an end to emigration. *Our Country,* a political documentary commissioned by Clann na Poblachta, featured bleak scenes of poverty and deprivation in the city and the countryside and shots of emigrants and rural depopulation.[85] Clann na Poblachta picked up on the anti-emigration mood that was being fostered by the Mellifont Group, whose members included Aodh de Blacam, a disaffected former member of the Fianna Fáil National Executive and the Clann's candidate in Louth. De Blacam had resigned from Fianna Fáil because he was impatient at their failure to adopt radical policies on emigration and rural Ireland.[86] Seán MacBride, leader of Clann na Poblachta, made several speeches accusing de Valera's government of using the employment exchanges to encourage and facilitate emigration to Britain. On one occasion he claimed that the Department of Social Welfare was "aiding foreign agents to recruit young boy and girl emigrants at £1 a head."[87] But the poet Patrick Kavanagh, writing about the campaign in counties Monaghan and Louth, claimed that the Clann's critical attitude toward emigration to England "does not go down well in a county of small farmers with large families where so many have gone to England and done well for themselves."[88]

De Valera refuted accusations that his government should be held responsible for the high rate of emigration. He claimed that wartime emigration was due to exceptional circumstances such as the shortage of supplies, and he promised to "remedy" the lack of employment once wartime difficulties ended.[89] Fine Gael gave a commitment to provide employment at fair wages and under good conditions "for every youth and girl"; a party election advertisement made the rather dubious claim that "before they left office in 1932 Fine Gael had ended emigration. They can end emigration again."

The outcome of the election was a coalition government, comprising all parties in Dáil Éireann, other than Fianna Fáil, plus six independent deputies.[90] The government made a determined effort to create employment by a program of investment in agriculture and public capital projects such as housing and hospitals. "Keynes came to Kinnegad" and to many other parts of Ireland in the form of housing schemes, land drainage, new hospitals, power stations, and rural electrification; the investment drive was a conscious attempt to create jobs and bring an end to emigration.[91] Ireland's high rate of emigration was cited to bolster the case for obtaining Marshall Aid. Seán MacBride, the minister for External Affairs, noted that Britain's economic future would "preclude her from providing an outlet for Ireland's surplus population indefinitely," and that Ireland would be forced in the near future to absorb her own natural population increase.[92] In 1950 the Departments of Local Government and Health produced a glossy brochure with the title *Ireland Is Building*, which was designed to persuade Irish construction workers in England to return home. Copies were distributed in Britain through Irish organizations, and it was advertised on posters displayed at churches and Irish dance halls and on a weekly program for emigrants broadcast by Radio Éireann. The brochure was liberally illustrated with pictures of new housing developments, power stations, factories, and hospitals, all designed to suggest that there would be plenty of jobs available in the coming years. The text and photo captions linked images of a modern Ireland with historical references. Turf-burning power stations were "the new Round Towers of Ireland"; the airmail stamp on letters to emigrants from their family in Ireland depicted the Angel Victor flying to Saint Patrick in exile, "with many letters; calling him back to Ireland." Returning emigrants were assured of steady employment, higher wages, and lower tax rates than in Britain, and a better quality of life. Food (which was still subject to severe rationing in Britain) and drink were "pure and wholesome";"the amenities of life" were "more attractive than anywhere else," especially to the emigrant who was described as "ill-fed and ill-housed in uncongenial places."[93]

It is impossible to determine how many male emigrants read this brochure and decided to return to Ireland. Despite the widespread concern about female emigrants, they were not mentioned, perhaps because it was widely believed that women emigrated in search of husbands not jobs. Between 1948 and 1951 the numbers insured in Ireland under the Unemployment Insurance Acts rose by 39,000 (30,000 men and 9,000 women). In 1951 Roy Geary informed the summer school at University College Dublin that 36,000 emigrants had returned to Ireland during the previous year.[94] The postwar investment program was financed by Marshall Aid counterpart funds, by running down the external assets that had accumulated during the war, and by government borrowings. In the short term it was effective. The economy grew—though the ending of wartime shortages of fuel and raw materials was also a factor. The 1951 census recorded the first increase in population since the famine. But a sharp increase in the balance of payments deficit following the outbreak of the Korean War prompted a deflationary budget in 1952, which coincided with the ending of Marshall Aid. Consequently, Ireland's short burst of economic growth came to a halt.[95] The ensuing stagnant economy of the 1950s ensured a steady flow of emigrants at a time when Britain was becoming increasingly reliant on immigrant workers.

Between 1950 and 1973 unemployment in Britain averaged 2.8 percent. The decline in the number of young British-born people entering the labor market was only partly offset by the rising number of women in paid employment. The "Golden Age of Economic Growth" that lasted until the oil crisis in 1973 saw large numbers of workers from less developed agricultural economies such as southern Italy, Portugal, Greece, and Yugoslavia taking industrial and service jobs in Germany, Belgium, the Netherlands, and Northern Italy.[96] Irish emigration to Britain (or strictly speaking England) was part of this wider pattern.

The Commission on Emigration

On 24 February 1948, less than three weeks after taking office, the first Inter-Party government determined that the minister for Social Welfare and leader of the Labor Party, William Norton, should establish a commission to examine the problems of emigration, rural depopulation, and related matters and make recommendations about how they should be tackled. On 10 March Norton presented the cabinet with draft terms of reference: "To investigate the causes and consequences of the present trend of population in Ireland with particular reference to problems of emigration and depopulation; to consider what measures should be taken to influence the trend of population in the future; and to make recommendations accordingly."

Although the cabinet approved the draft terms of reference, it authorized the minister to amend them in light of suggestions made in the course of the discussion; unfortunately, the minute gives no indication about the nature of this discussion.[97] Rather surprisingly, the terms of reference that were eventually adopted (see p. 171, chapter 3) made no direct reference to emigration or rural depopulation; however, the preponderance of the evidence and the contents of the report indicate that the commission was primarily concerned with emigration and rural depopulation, and it soon became known as the Commission on Emigration.

Why did the Inter-Party government decide to establish this commission? As I discussed in the previous chapter, the idea was first proposed in 1939 but was dropped the following year; it did not resurface until December 1947, when then Minister for Social Welfare James Ryan proposed establishing a commission. Norton reminded de Valera of this during a 1953 debate on a motion of no confidence.[98] The commission may have been established to placate the Catholic hierarchy and Clann na Poblachta, one of the government parties that had campaigned on the issue of emigration. On 16 February the new taoiseach, John A. Costello, replied to the letter that the hierarchy had dispatched in October 1947 expressing concern over the 1947 health act and emigration. With regard to the health act, he reassured the hierarchy that the government "both in their legislative proposals and in administration have constantly in mind, not only the state's functions as guardians of the common good, but also the respect which is due to the fundamental and family rights." On the question of emigration, he reported that the government was deeply concerned about the numbers of young men and women leaving the country for employment abroad, in many cases without having experienced any real difficulty in finding suitable employment at home; the numbers of young women emigrating was a cause of "particular anxiety." It was the government's policy to develop Ireland's natural resources to the maximum extent and encourage increased output in agriculture and industry in order to create jobs. Costello's reply also addressed two specific issues that the hierarchy had raised: controls on advertisements for jobs overseas and restricting emigration. On the former he gave a commitment that the government would consider imposing restrictions if it were proved that these advertisements were a major cause of emigration, but there was no evidence that this was so. On the question of restricting the freedom to emigrate, he affirmed that "the denial to individuals of the opportunity to seek a livelihood or a career abroad, would in the Government's view be the retraction of a fundamental human right which would only be justified in circumstances of great national emergency."[99] There is a draft copy of this letter on unheaded notepaper and without a signature in McQuaid's papers, suggesting that it was shown to him for his approval before it was sent.[100] The commission may have been established as a "safety valve" for a government that was under pressure from the Catholic church and some of its supporters to restrict the right to emigrate.

Although it was established in April 1948, the commission did not report until 1954. A substantial section of the report was taken up with an historical account of Irish demographic trends. Perhaps this is appropriate, since the report was probably out of date before it was published and it fails to capture the sense of crisis over emigration that gripped Ireland during the mid-1950s. Most of the evidence was collected during 1948 and 1949, at a time when the prospects for the Irish economy appeared promising. When the commission was established, the minister for Social Welfare gave instructions that it make the fullest use of available data and hold no large-scale statistical inquiries, so that the report would be available at the earliest possible date. But the commission soon indicated that they were "aware that important demographic changes had taken place since 1946," and they requested that a population census be taken in 1951. The report of the commission claimed that the results of the 1951 census and of a special inquiry for 1949 –50 that represented Ireland's contribution to a world census of agriculture required them to reexamine "many aspects of the problems with which we were concerned."[101] But in 1949 and 1950, world agriculture was heavily distorted by the aftermath of World War II and did not present an accurate indication of later trends. The 1951 census, which recorded the first population increase in the Irish Republic since the famine, proved to be an equally inaccurate guide to the future. Between 1946 and 1951, 1,365 women emigrated for every 1,000 men, but by 1954, a majority of emigrants were men, and net emigration between 1946 and 1951 was substantially lower than between 1951 and 1961.

It is particularly regrettable that the commission did not publish transcripts or summaries of the evidence, which included interviews with emigrants, would-be emigrants, British employers, welfare officers, and Catholic clergy who were in regular contact with Irish emigrants as well as submissions and evidence submitted by various self-appointed experts. There is a striking contrast between the overblown rhetoric of some of these submissions, with their adulation of the quality of life in Ireland, and the case histories of intending emigrants.

The nature of the evidence, and its source, raises the question of an implicit gender bias in the commission's work. Most firsthand evidence collected in Ireland about the motives for emigrating came from men. Intending male emigrants were easily found through the employment exchanges, where they were being interviewed by the liaison officer of the British Ministry of Labor. The commission claimed that it was impossible to conduct similar interviews with women emigrants, because they did not have to present themselves at Irish employment exchanges before emigrating. But trainee nurses were interviewed by the British Ministry of Labor liaison staff, and all travelers to Britain were required to obtain travel identity cards, which were issued by the Garda Síochána, so it should have been possible to identify intending women emigrants and to arrange interviews. They did interview a small number of returned women emigrants in Dublin, but most of the evidence concerning women and their motives for emigrating was presented by other witnesses, such as the Galway playwright M. J. Molloy and Miss Marion Green of Castle Cove, Killarney. On the other hand, most of the evidence collected in Britain about the lives of emigrants and their problems concerned women. The contrasting sources may account for the differing interpretations given to the motives of male and female emigrants.

The case histories of would-be male emigrants present compelling evidence that emigration was prompted by economic need.[102] Those interviewed in Ballina and Sligo included a twenty-one-year-old married man with a one-year-old son who was living in a small house on his parent's twenty-five-acre farm. He appeared to have married without parental consent as he was not the eldest son, and it was unlikely that he would inherit the farm; irrespective of this, the farm in question could not support two households. He was deemed to be a "special release case," who was exempted from the regulations preventing men engaged in agriculture from emigrating unless they lived in areas with a tradition of seasonal migration. A forty-five-year-old hackney driver from Ballysodare, a married man with two children, had lost his contract with the post office and could not survive on the remaining earnings. A farmer aged fifty years, who had been a migratory laborer for more than twenty years, sought seasonal work with the British Sugar Corporation. Another farmer, aged thirty-eight, lived with his mother, wife, and children on nine acres of middling land and ten acres of bog and rushes. During the war he had supplemented his income by working on the bogs; this income was no longer available, so he had to go to England.[103] All the men in Cork who accepted jobs as miners were aged over thirty, which suggested that they were determined, even desperate, to find work.[104]

A survey of 490 men and women who emigrated from Athlone between 1945 and 1948, carried out by a local group, revealed that one-quarter of the men had left wives and children in Ireland; the overwhelming majority would return if they could find employment. Many emigrated when they were demobilized from the army; others were tradesmen who had been working intermittently in England since the falloff in construction work in the early years of the Emergency. Most of the Athlone men who were under forty years of age wished to return to Ireland, though younger men and women would only return if they were assured of long-term employment at higher wages and better conditions, and men who were married with families in England were deemed unlikely to return.[105] Many prospective emigrants had been thrown out of dead-end jobs in Ireland on reaching the age of eighteen or twenty. In Cork, two young men complained that a local engineering firm hired school leavers at low rates of pay, only to discharge them when they became eligible for full adult rates.[106]

The pressure to support parents and/or siblings emerges as a key factor for many would-be emigrants. One young man aged twenty interviewed in Ballina had to support a widowed mother and an invalid brother, assisted by another brother who had a job in the town. He claimed that the only work available in Ballina was casual employment training dogs. Another eighteen-year-old who worked as a casual laborer at the local golf links was supporting his elderly parents.[107] The majority of men, both single and married, were supporting dependents: wives and children or parents and siblings. The evidence presented in these interviews suggests that the burden of large families was a major factor in decisions to emigrate.

The prospect of higher wages and the possibilities of earning overtime and gaining promotion were also factors in the decision to leave Ireland. One young laborer in the building trade claimed that Ireland offered him no avenue for promotion, whereas laborers in England were often upgraded. Another wished to train as a mechanic, and he claimed that this would not be possible in his hometown of Wexford, because apprenticeships were invariably given to townspeople.[108] A Leitrim barman, who earned £1 a week plus his keep for a fifty-six-hour week, was moving to a similar job in Shrewsbury for a wage of £4 plus his keep.[109]

This evidence would have occasioned few surprises to anyone with a knowledge of rural and provincial Ireland. One witness quoted an article in the *Clare Champion* on 12 June 1948: "If the members of the commission happened to attend Wednesday's meeting of Clare county council they would have got a striking illustration of the main cause—unemployment. They would witness the piteous spectacle of able-bodied and willing workers begging for work."[110] The testimonies of would-be emigrants are sombre; they are concerned with wages, working conditions, family pressures, and job insecurity. Economic need appears to have left little scope for sentiment. Honohan notes of intending emigrants in Clonmel that "none appeared to be concerned sentimentally about leaving the country."[111]

Yet at the time many people in Ireland believed that emigrants were lured by false promises of high wages and a better standard of living or by the wish for a more glamorous life in an English city. And if Ireland was suffering from a high level of unemployment, this was not caused by economic factors; it was an indication of some fundamental spiritual or cultural malaise. M. J. Molloy referred to England's "Extermination through Emigration Campaign"; he regarded the current wave of emigration as yet another episode in the long centuries of British malevolence toward Ireland.[112]

The members of the Mellifont Conference and Council of National Action (a group of right-wing Catholic activists) were emphatic that the causes of emigration were "not directly economic, or even basically economic at all in the broadest sense." They regarded emigration as a reflection of multiple flaws in Irish society. Its causes included: tradition; faulty rather than bad education; fashion; frustration among young people; a faulty political, social, and economic system; unemployment resulting from poor organization; inferior financial standards prevailing in Ireland relative to those in Britain; bad social conditions; bad organization of society resulting in black marketeering, profiteering, selfish accumulation of wealth, and wanton extravagance; false standards of values at home compared with corresponding prospects and values abroad; seductive emigration agencies; the neutral or unnatural atmosphere and outlook in universities and higher schools; a deficiency of moral courage in public representatives; the absence of any code of national direction; the unrestricted license among nationals and nonnationals to pursue, with impunity, un-Irish activities and speak against the common good; and, finally, the practically unrestricted immigration of undesirable aliens and their ability to purchase Irish property without restriction. The solution to emigration was to foster a spirit of Christian patriotism and replace a government based on party politics with a government of national unity, whose policies would reflect Christian teaching.[113]

Aodh de Blacam, a member of the Commission on Emigration who died in January 1951 before the report was completed—
otherwise he would undoubtedly have submitted a minority report
or reservations—claimed that economic explanations for emigration
were inspired by Marxist ideas and should be rejected by anyone who
believed in the Christian tradition:

> For, if men were moved only by material factors, our country would
> have a rapidly growing population instead of being the one white
> country in which population has declined in modern times. We have
> the most fertile soil west of the Ukraine; our country stands beside
> the inter-continental trade-routes; our people are strong and intelli-
> gent and possess distinguished schools and universities. But it has
> only half as many people as it did in the days before drainage . . . the
> produce from our soil is dwindling . . . we have not used the oppor-
> tunities in our natural inheritance and, since this is contrary to eco-
> nomic reason the cause must be non-economic. It is spiritual, men-
> tal; it is simply a continuance in the mid-twentieth century of that
> racial despair which smote our people after the horror-years of the
> Famine; a failure of national hope. No normal people flies from its
> native soil if there is reasonable hope of survival. No normal family
> is content to be broken up and scattered into far lands. No normal
> man or woman, able to make a living at home, prefers a living abroad
> for the sake of an increase in salary. What is a hundred pound's in-
> crement when balanced against separation from one's kindred, one's
> old class-fellows, one's home-town and nation, the rearing of one's
> children in their rightful spiritual environment? The flight from Ire-
> land, now that we have control of its resources and our personal fu-
> ture, is abnormal, morbid and one might say absurd.[114]

De Blacam's solution was to create "an anti-emigration spirit; a spirit
of re-colonisation."[115] He was not prepared to acknowledge that
"normal" men might be forced to emigrate because they were unable
to find work. If they were without work, this was because of the "air
of proletarianism . . . deracinated labour, always in the market";
which meant that they were no longer willing to work on the land.[116]

Many witnesses claimed that young people were emigrating
because of the "drabness of country life," but these statements
invariably came from witnesses who were not directly affected by

emigration, such as the Monaghan county librarian, who believed that activities organized by the library service, such as the study of local history and local exhibitions, would discourage emigration.[117] But reflecting on his visit to counties Sligo and Leitrim, Roy Geary noted that it was his "impression that there were no complaints about 'the dullness of rural life' so dear to the social scientists among intending and returned emigrants."[118] Delaney concludes that "this is a case where the perceptions of parents, clerics and teachers were imposed on the calculations of migrants."[119]

Given the weight of evidence showing that most men emigrated because they could not find work or because the jobs on offer were either insecure or badly paid, it is not surprising that the commission determined that the primary cause of emigration was economic, though it added that the decision to emigrate was prompted by "the interplay of a number of motives." It suggested that most individuals were influenced by a combination of "push" factors—"the failure of conditions at home to provide an adequate basis for livelihood, and by 'pull'—the force of attraction, whether economic or social, which other countries exert." Push factors predominated among emigrants from the western seaboard, and they exerted a greater influence on men than on women. Many of the supplementary causes of emigration that it listed—the desire for improved material conditions, dissatisfaction with life on the land, the attraction of urban life, lack of water, electricity, transport, and educational and social amenities—could be regarded as consequences of economic circumstances. So, too, could "tradition and example"—emigrants remittances, prosperous returning emigrants and emigrant letters.[120] It is noteworthy that the minority report submitted by Dr. Lucey accepted this section without change.

Women Emigrants

The commission believed that women were motivated less by economic factors than by a wish to secure an improvement in personal status and opportunities for marriage. But this assessment is called into question because they failed to interview women emigrants about their reasons for emigrating.

Yet the limited evidence that they collected relating to the circumstances of Irish female emigrants suggests that the factors prompting them to emigrate were not radically different from those that influenced men. Women also experienced lack of employment, low wages, and insecure and unattractive working conditions, and many women provided financial support for parents and siblings. A survey carried out by members of the Irish Countrywomen's Association noted that "those that left the land did so through want of suitable employment."[121] Evidence from provincial centers suggested that the scale of female emigration was influenced by the local employment market, as was the case with men. In Tullow, county Carlow, a town that offered minimal job opportunities for women other than domestic service at wages as low as 12s. 6d. a week, emigration was high.[122] A majority of the women emigrants contacted by the Athlone survey group claimed that they were attracted by higher wages and better working conditions, although some had emigrated because they were unemployed.[123] Irish women employed by the Birmingham-based General Electric Company received a weekly bonus of 10s. after six weeks. Initially the company made arrangements to deposit this bonus at its Dublin office, where workers would collect it when they were home on holidays, but General Electric abandoned this arrangement because the office was being visited by parents demanding their daughters' earnings. When the end of the postwar boom reduced the amount of overtime being worked, the manager of the plant expressed fears that many Irish female workers were "quite hard up" because they were under an obligation to send regular remittances to their parents, despite the fall in their incomes.[124] The personnel manager at a textile mill in Oldham claimed that nearly all the Irish women employed at the mill sent money home; however, none of the women interviewed by Stanley Lyon in a hostel in Chorley (Lancashire) did so. On the basis of his interviews with a number of Dublin women who had returned home from England, Lyon came to the conclusion that in the absence of "complicating factors" such as unemployment or a boyfriend in England, most of the women would prefer to work in Dublin and would willingly accept lower wages than in England, but he qualified this assessment by noting that the sample was small. Some women had returned home because they were lonely or homesick; at least one returned to care for a sick father.[125] Some women may have emigrated to evade familial obligations, as did some men. Officials in the Gaeltacht Sources Section of the Department of Lands alleged that many young women in Gaeltacht areas abandoned jobs in local toy factories or jobs as contract knitters in order to emigrate, because as long as they remained at home their mothers appropriated all the earnings. "Away what they earn is their own."[126] However, interviews conducted by Sharon Lambert with forty women who emigrated to Lancashire between the 1920s and 1960s confirm the importance of economic factors and family obligations. Lambert notes that "economic reasons were most often cited as the impetus for emigration, especially amongst women from poorer rural backgrounds." The economic circumstances of the emigrant's family, and her birth order, were also important; remittances from several of the women interviewed enabled younger siblings to attend secondary school.[127]

Yet when the Commission on Emigration was taking oral evidence from the Irish Housewives' Association, Roy Geary interjected that "it is probably true that large numbers of men are forced through unemployment and poverty to emigrate. In the case of women, emigration is largely just the result of a desire for a change or to make more money."[128] Although the commission dismissed many of the wilder statements that witnesses made about emigrant women, it concluded that for women "the purely economic cause is not always so dominant." However, it would appear that they interpreted the term "purely economic" in a very restricted sense. There is probably some merit in the commission's claim that "pull" forces exercised a stronger influence over women emigrants than over men. Employment opportunities for women in Ireland were even more limited than those available to men, so the attractions of Britain were correspondingly greater. The disparity in wages and working conditions between England and Ireland appears to have been particularly pronounced in female occupations, such as domestic service and nursing. In the late 1940s nearly half of all women employed in the manufacturing industry in Ireland earned less than £2 per week, which was 10s. less than the going rate for indoor domestic servants in Britain.[129] Between October 1945 and March 1946, when women still required permits from the British Ministry of Labor, 30 percent of emigrant women were taking up positions as trainee or qualified nurses (mostly trainees); most of the remainder were domestic servants.[130] In 1948 girls working in Denny's bacon factory in Tralee were reportedly emigrating to England and taking jobs as domestic servants "to better themselves."[131]

John McElhinney, who collected evidence on behalf of the commission in county Galway noted that "girls in industrial occupations with good wages and good hours and conditions have not emigrated to any large extent." Rather, emigration attracted domestic servants, "underpaid shop assistants in small shops," and unemployed and casual workers. The working conditions of domestic servants were not regulated in Ireland, while in Britain servants were guaranteed a forty-eight-hour, five-and-a-half-day week. McElhinney, who spoke to seven girls who were leaving Galway for domestic jobs in hospitals and canteens in London, commented that "these girls have very hard things to say about Irish employers of domestic workers, long hours of duty, bad food, and above all, lack of respect. They are treated as inferior human beings who have very few rights. . . . In all cases friends or sisters had written from England or talked during the holidays of wages of £3 indoors."[132] When Stanley Lyon tried to summarize the interviews that he conducted with eleven returned women emigrants in a Dublin employment exchange, the first point that he noted was that they disliked domestic service because of prewar memories, "real or imaginary," of long hours and very small wages— as little as 5s. a week for those who lived with families in Ireland.[133] An official of the Department of External Affairs noted that in England servants had "more personal freedom, shorter working hours and better living quarters" than in Ireland, because "scarcity has already raised the social status of maids and has put them in a position of considerable independence of their employer."[134]

These statements are in marked contrast to the views that Aodh de Blacam expressed to members of the Irish Housewives' Association:

> Would you like to see any girl you know, a daughter or a sister, go into domestic service in a decent typical Irish home where she would be treated as a member of the family, and living in exactly the same conditions and with the same material and spiritual circumstances as the family, or would you like to see that girl going to England where she will be treated (to use a vulgar expression) "like a dog"?

Would you like to see any girl in whom you had any interest going into a Jewman's house in the English slums? That is where the girls are going, while they would be well treated in Ireland. In England, the "Irish scivvy" [*sic*] is spoken of. That is how they regard the domestic servants while in Ireland they are treated as one of the family. Any woman that has lived in the country towns of Ireland will bear me out; if a girl goes to work in one of our Irish country homes she is treated as one of the family and nobody can hope for more.[135]

Emigration offered even greater benefits for trainee nurses. Many Irish nursing schools charged a training fee, ranging from 10 guineas in Mercer's Hospital to £100 in Jervis Street, though fees had recently been abolished in Sir Patrick Dun's and Baggot Street Hospitals due to a shortage of applicants. The demand for training places was most acute in Catholic hospitals. In England, however, training fees were not charged, and the trainees received a wage. Furthermore, educational qualifications were lower, particularly for the lower-grade categories of nurses such as State Enrolled Nurses, and if probationers failed their examinations they could find work as assistant nurses, a grade that did not exist in Ireland.[136] Some English hospitals demanded a certificate stating that the applicant had attended a secondary school, and it was reputed that some girls spent a brief period at secondary school—perhaps only a few months—in order to meet this requirement, though many entrants to nursing in England were past pupils of vocational schools.[137] It is highly improbable that any Irish general nursing school would have admitted a trainee who had attended a vocational school. The marked difference in entry requirements and pay reflected the acute shortage of nurses in Britain. The matron of one London hospital told Stanley Lyon that they would take as many trainee nurses from Ireland as they could get; only two hundred of the hospital's five hundred beds were in use because of a shortage of staff.[138] In contrast, there was an oversupply of qualified nurses in Ireland and career opportunities were poor.[139]

Explaining Irish Emigration: The Commission on Emigration and *The Vanishing Irish*

When it came to discussing the consequences of emigration, the commission reiterated the importance of economics, noting that emigration meant the removal from Ireland of "a proportion of its potentially productive manpower."[140] Emigration was "a reflection of the failure of the economy to provide the rising standards of living, which are increasingly being sought, particularly in rural areas,"[141] and it reduced "the need for drastic action" to develop the economy.[142] The majority of emigrants improved their material circumstances by leaving, and their departure enabled those who remained in Ireland to maintain or increase their standard of living. Emigrants' remittances helped to bring about "greater equality in the distribution of wealth."[143] Having noted that there was no indication that emigration had resulted in a labor shortage,[144] and having adopted an agnostic position on the question of whether emigration had brought about higher wages,[145] they concluded that it was impossible to determine whether an emigrant was an economic loss or gain to the community.[146]

With regard to noneconomic factors, the commission again suggested that the evidence was mixed. Emigration had given Ireland an international significance that was disproportionate to the size of the home population and it had promoted "the cause of Christianity in many countries," but there was an enormous emotional cost attached to the separation of families and the failure to retain a larger population within Ireland. The current high level of emigration "weakens national pride and confidence which of itself retards the efforts required for national progress."[147]

Ultimately the commission came back to economics: the solution would be found in developing the economy and in raising living standards. And there was a greater need to raise rural living standards than urban living standards, a statement that reflects a degree of confusion between the twin issues of emigration and rural depopulation. Appeals to sentiment as a means of preventing emigration were dismissed as "likely to meet with little response" unless people were offered a reasonable standard of life in Ireland, and they rejected calls to ban or restrict emigration—an inescapable decision given the emphasis on economic factors. However, as a sop to the anti-emigration lobby it suggested that some safeguard was needed against misleading advertisements for jobs overseas, and they recommended the establishment of a bureau to cater for Irish emigrants in Britain.[148]

The carefully balanced comments on the causes and consequences of emigration reflect the determination to arrive at an agreed-upon report, which was a tall order given a membership of twenty-two men and two women from diverse backgrounds. Reverend Cornelius Lucey, the bishop of Cork, submitted a thirty-two-page minority report, but he did not dissent from any paragraph in the majority report concerning the causes and consequences of emigration. However, an addendum by Roy Geary and M. D. McCarthy, with which Reverend Coyne wished to be associated, stated that "in our opinion, certain important parts [of the report of the commission] reflect in their phrasing the reconciliation of different points of view and, as a natural result, are somewhat indefinite." Geary and McCarthy opened their discussion of emigration with the sweeping statement that "the Irish have always been a great migratory people," before going on to suggest that since the 1880s there had been little evidence of any relationship between the volume of emigration and the state of the Irish economy. The fall in the rural population bore no relationship to the decline in tillage; all four provinces (including the Six Counties) had experienced a similar rate of population decline since the 1840s, despite having radically different economic circumstances. They claimed that "emigration cannot in any sense be regarded as a marginal or residual problem. It has grown up to be largely a separate and distinct part of the Irish social and economic system. To state that emigration is due to a lack of economic development at home is true only in the sense of being a truism." Emigration would cease if people were prepared to accept a lower standard of living, but such a decision could only be made by the Irish people individually and collectively. The primary cause of emigration since the famine was "a change in the Irish mental attitude occasioned by that catastrophe," because up to the famine the rural population had consistently increased despite having a low standard of living. After the famine people migrated to places that offered the highest wages. Their addendum highlighted the contradictions in Irish attitudes toward emigration: "The great majority of the people disapprove of emigration, though this disapproval certainly does not attach itself to the individual who decides to emigrate even when he could find employment at home. It is very likely that this disapproval is instinctive even

though an attempt is usually made to justify it on social and economic grounds." A forced cessation of emigration would result in
heavy unemployment, lower wages, and a lower standard of living;
they did not believe that people would be willing to make the necessary sacrifices to end emigration. They dismissed as meaningless any
effort to determine whether emigration was good or bad. "Emigration is a fact and the problem facing the country is the reduction of
its magnitude and the mitigation of its undesirable effects." They
further suggested that "the national outlook, the too low level of national productivity, the stationary population, the low marriage rate
and the too high emigration rate are all facets of the some problem.
All will be solved together or they will not be solved at all."[149]

According to John Spencer, Roy Geary liked to think of Ireland
as a "mother" country; he believed that emigration had given Ireland
an influence on world affairs disproportionate to her size.[150] Another
member of the commission, Alexis FitzGerald, extolled the fact that
Irish emigrants had a significant role in the history of the church
(presumably the Catholic church). FitzGerald believed that it was
more important to "preserve and improve the quality of Irish life
and thereby the purity of that message which our people have com-
municated to the world than it is to reduce the numbers of Irish
emigrants." He denied that "a high rate of emigration was necessarily
a sign of national decline or that policy should be over-anxiously
framed to reduce it"; emigration brought positive benefits: it released
social tensions "and makes possible a stability of manners and customs which would otherwise be the subject of radical change." He saw
the low marriage rate as Ireland's major demographic weakness.[151]

It may be worth pausing to consider how a young man or woman
in their late teens or early twenties, leaving home to work as a
builder's laborer or a domestic servant, would have responded to Fitz-
Gerald's remarks. I suspect that they would have had greater sympathy with the views of writer and labor activist Peadar O'Donnell, who
was also a member of the commission. O'Donnell reiterated that for
the majority of emigrants the decision to emigrate was prompted by
"the scarcity of reasonably secure unemployment for men." A minority of well-educated emigrants left because they were attracted by opportunities elsewhere, but he did not believe this was a major cause

of "the mass emigration which is the national problem."[152] This places O'Donnell very firmly in the "push" camp, whereas the minority report of James Meenan, another economist, came down firmly in favor of "pull" forces.

Meenan pointed out that Ireland was "situated between two of the great labor markets of the world, North America and Great Britain"; because they spoke English it was much easier for Irish people to emigrate than for citizens of other European countries. Irish parents and children weighed up their prospects abroad and at home; their concept of an acceptable standard of living was mainly derived from overseas. Emigration reduced the pressures on the Irish government to provide an acceptable standard of living for its citizens; in countries where workers were less likely to emigrate a number of governments had introduced "vigorous policies of economic development." Meenan agreed with Geary and McCarthy that emigration could be ended if people were prepared to accept a lower standard of living; Timothy Smiddy had made this point in a 1940 memorandum to de Valera.[153]

Meenan attempted to distinguish between emigration and population decline, arguing that because Irish emigration was an emigration of individuals, not families, it did not necessarily result in a fall in the rural population because it provided the conditions for a new generation to emerge. He was careful to indicate that he was not trying to prove that emigration was a good thing or that it was a problem that defied all remedies, but he emphasized that it would be more difficult to end emigration from Ireland than from an underdeveloped country. Given Ireland's location, the fact that "its political and economic boundaries do not coincide," and the demand for labor from countries with lower fertility and higher standards of living, he believed that it would be phenomenal if there were not emigration. "No useful purpose is served by regarding emigration as a reproach to national pride or as a sign of the failure of self-government. The fact that it still continues is no reason for talking ourselves into whatever may be the economic equivalent of an inferiority complex." In his opinion it would be more helpful to concentrate on devising policies that would create circumstances where emigration no longer resulted in a declining population.[154]

Geary and McCarthy were undoubtedly correct in describing the majority report as "somewhat indefinite," but the addenda, reservations, and minority reports only added to the confusion. Many of the statements by so-called experts do not withstand scrutiny: emigration was rising sharply before the famine, which suggests that even then people were not content with their standard of living; the apparent uniformity in population decline throughout Ireland since the famine presupposed that emigration had ceased, whereas the population loss was decidedly greater in western areas during the 1950s. Meenan seriously underestimated the importance of emigration from non-English speaking countries, but this is consistent with the complete lack of interest that the commission showed in contemporary migration and emigration in western Europe.

The failure to carry out a comprehensive study of British and Irish comparative wages was another major omission. The commission claimed that there was no substantial competition between industrial wages in Ireland and in Britain, or between agricultural wages in the two countries; it concluded that the effect of emigration on wage levels "is not easily determined," although a shortage of domestic servants had brought "some improvement" in the terms and conditions offered to servants in Ireland.[155] It also conceded that outside the larger towns, the wages of general laborers, shop assistants, and messengers "seem very low" compared with the wages offered to unskilled workers in Britain, and that "the rather wide difference" between the earnings of unskilled workers in Ireland and Britain had been a major incentive to emigration.[156] Geary and McCarthy expressed reservations about the statement that there was little competition for labor between Ireland and Britain; they claimed that emigration has raised nonagricultural, and probably agricultural, wage rates in Ireland, but they repudiated the suggestion that nonagricultural wage rates in Ireland were lower than in the United Kingdom, although they acknowledged that the earnings of United Kingdom building workers were higher than in Ireland because of overtime and more regular employment.[157] This confusion over relative wages and earnings in Britain and Ireland fueled claims that emigration was prompted by noneconomic and irrational motives. In August 1951, Eamon de Valera claimed that "the saddest part of all" was that work was available at home in conditions that were "infinitely better" from the point of view of health and morals; in many occupations the wages on offer were higher in Ireland than in England.[158]

In the same month, William Honohan attempted to deflate expectations about the outcome of the report of the Commission on Emigration. He informed a colleague in the civil service, Patrick Lynch, that

> Its value *in my opinion* is largely in the keen analysis and interpretation, which it will provide, rather than in its practical recommendations. It may also be of some value to secure a common viewpoint (from a diverse group of citizens) on a subject which has, up to now, been rather controversial. So far there has been no definite cleavage among members although there are some sharp differences of opinion. Discussion has shown that many of these differences are of emphasis and approach rather than of substance and are capable of being removed by painstaking drafting. Although others may not be amenable to such treatment, there is no indication yet that there will be any minority reports. There will, of course, be disagreements, reservations and addenda on many points.[159]

The prediction that the commission would produce few practical recommendations proved all too accurate. The report made twenty recommendations and a considerably longer list of suggestions—the distinction is theirs not mine—but, with the possible exception of the recommendations that an export corporation and an investment advisory council be established, they were unlikely to have had any significant impact on emigration. Many were designed to provide better demographic statistics: a census at five-year intervals instead of the previous ten and changes in the system of registering births, occupational mortality statistics, and the certification of deaths. The commission recommended that it should be a matter of national policy to improve the Irish demographic position, but this was an aspiration, and they did not suggest how it might be achieved.[160] Recommendations that educational policy "should have due regard to the desirability of counteracting emigration and rural depopulation," or that tax relief be offered for employing domestic servants, may have been included to placate some vocal witnesses. But as a blueprint for future policy, the commission offered very little except the message that higher investment was an essential precondition for economic development. Politicians and civil servants were already aware of this. Having stated the obvious, they passed the buck, noting that it was outside their realm to advise on the most effective means of financing large-scale development programs involving heavy capital expenditure.[161]

Honohan's prediction that the report would present "a common viewpoint" was not fulfilled. What emerged was the sense that there was confusion, even complacency, about emigration. In his evidence to the commission, M. J. Molloy asserted that "at present the country is rotten from top to bottom with defeatism."[162] This was probably an exaggeration in 1948 or 1949, but by the mid-1950s when the report was published, emigration was significantly higher, and the search for either a magic solution or a scapegoat was becoming more urgent.

It is highly improbable that the report of the Commission on Emigration could ever have satisfied Molloy, de Blacam, or others who sought a dramatic and simple response to the problem, but the commission's difficulties were undoubtedly compounded by the fact that it was beaten into print by *The Vanishing Irish*, a book that did not shy away from outrage and emotion and did not explain emigration by referring to economic factors and the need for investment. If the *Report of the Commission on Emigration* reflected the views of academics, civil servants, and churchmen, *The Vanishing Irish* has a decided touch of melodrama—which is scarcely surprising given that the contributors included at least one playwright, Paul Vincent Carroll. *The Vanishing Irish* heightened emotional concerns over population decline by declaring that emigration was merely one aspect of Ireland's propensity toward racial suicide; the other symptoms were the flight from the land and the unwillingness of Irish bachelors to marry.[163] Carroll played to the gallery by condemning "synthetic doom prophesied for them [the Irish race] by that chief of humbugs, the statistician." He saw emigration as a symptom of national decay; Carroll described the Irishman as a mystic; materialism had never captured his inner being, although other essays in this volume describe the crass material instincts that underlay Irish marriage practices. Like the Mellifont group Carroll believed that the solution was to replace "corrupt and bombastic political leaders" with social leaders who would educate the people in "essential social principles within a Christian framework"[164]—a quasi-fascist solution.

The Vanishing Irish was published in March 1954, whereas the report of the Commission on Emigration did not appear until July. The timing is important: The Vanishing Irish appeared just before Saint Patrick's Day, when attention naturally turned to the Irish overseas, and shortly before the second An Tóstal—a festival designed to attract Irish emigrants and their descendants, particularly Irish Americans, to visit their ancestral homeland.[165] It was also in print before the general election in May 1954, when Fianna Fáil lost office to a second Inter-Party government that included many members of the cabinet that had established the Commission on Emigration in 1948. The Vanishing Irish provided an interpretation of Irish population decline that was more in tune with the mood of the mid-1950s. The book attracted considerable attention, and some concern, in government circles. Peadar O'Donnell claimed that the government used the Irish News Agency in an attempt to counteract the somewhat exaggerated claims that the Irish people were in danger of vanishing from the face of the earth. But their wish to present a less apocalyptic point of view was handicapped by the fact that the report of the Commission on Emigration was not yet in print—publication had been delayed pending the arrival of Dr. Lucey's minority report.[166] The government gave some consideration to publishing the report without waiting for Dr. Lucey's contribution, but decided against doing this, probably wisely; a stencilled version that included Dr. Lucey's report was released in July.[167]

In May, at the height of the election campaign, several members of the commission took part in a symposium on The Vanishing Irish in Dublin's Gresham Hotel. The proceeds were in aid of the restoration fund at the Jesuit house of studies at Milltown Park; nobody seems to have commented on the irony of holding a discussion on emigration in one of Dublin's top hotels to raise money for a Jesuit retreat house. If this symposium was designed to counteract The Vanishing Irish, it was not a success. The report in The Irish Times was headed "No Need of Guilt Complex About Emigration, Says Dr. Geary."[168] An editorial the following day carried the headline, "Cynical Comfort."[169] Geary told the audience that emigration was neither good nor bad. It was a gigantic fact, and Irish people should make the best of it; the Irish nation should not feel guilty about emigration. James Meenan decried the fact that the Irish approach to emigration was often emotional—yet surely emigration was an emotional issue, at least for those who were directly affected? The Maynooth theologian Dr. P. Cremin, the only speaker who had not served on the commission, claimed that there was no cause for alarm over the declining population, because "for the Irish, emigration is the inevitable characteristic that went back to the very beginning of the Christian past." Cremin believed that emigration was not an unmixed evil since it had given Ireland a spiritual empire, enhanced the country's international prestige, and ensured greater prosperity for those who remained in Ireland.[170]

Statements about Ireland's spiritual nature, or that emigration was neither good nor bad, inevitably led to accusations of indifference toward a major human and social problem. The editorial in *The Irish Times* described the tone of the symposium in the Gresham Hotel as one of "complacency—almost of defeatism" and ended by decrying "the cold, despairing logic implicit in the new 'statistical' evaluation of our country."[171] Yet in many respects, the cold logic of the commission was closer to the spirit of intending emigrants. William Honohan noted that none of the men that he interviewed in his tour of labor exchanges in the southeast "appeared to be concerned sentimentally about leaving the country."[172] Sentiment was a luxury few of them could afford. In the course of the symposium, Peader O'Donnell urged the audience not to become "mawkish about the young people leaving home from Donegal, Connemara and such places. Rather let us consider can these young people live at all in these areas." If Ireland could not use the resources of all its people, O'Donnell suggested that it would be preferable that they should be prepared for emigration.[173] Emigration was a subject that pitted economists and statisticians against the wider public. Some of this confrontation was probably justified, but there is also an element of shooting the messenger who bears bad news. M. J. Molloy expressed a loathing of "the Dublin school of economists and their top-heavy policies of the big ranch farms," though he did not include "Professor Sheehy and the Albert College men" (a reference to the

Faculty of Agriculture at University College Dublin), or "the Cork University Professors" among "the Depopulation enthusiasts."[174] One emigrant complained bitterly to Taoiseach John A. Costello that "Geary's Statistical Questionnaire cards are thrown overboard by those with scorn for those responsible for breaking and separating families." This man had emigrated two years earlier with his wife and nine children; two older children were working away from home, one as "a Black and Tan in Cyprus," four had been fostered out, and three remained with their parents.[175] The commission could have avoided accusations of complacency by including a summary of the evidence given by actual or prospective emigrants, which would have given a human dimension to their study while counteracting much of the sentimentality and emotional rhetoric that was so common at the time.

The most ironic evidence of the commission's apparent lack of impact comes in the form of a letter from the Dean of Ferns to Taoiseach John A. Costello, suggesting that the "time was more than ripe for a Government commission to be set up to examine all aspects of emigration." The letter is dated 2 November 1955, sixteen months after the report was first published. When Costello drew the Dean's attention to the report of the commission, the latter wrote to apologize, adding that "I have already read the minority report of Dr. Lucey . . . and consider it to be pertinent to the whole situation." Although he had only given a cursory glance to the majority report, this had led him to imagine "that it is not at grips with the problem."[176] An even stronger indictment came from Seán Lemass in a speech to the Dublin Chamber of Commerce in October 1960, when he claimed that the report "made very little impact on Irish public opinion when published and was now almost forgotten."[177]

5

The Vanishing Irish

1954–1961

Only two European countries experienced a fall in population during the 1950s: Ireland and East Germany. Their common fate was noted in August 1961 when the preliminary results of the 1961 Irish census were published, just days after the East German government sealed off the crossings between East and West Berlin and began to erect the Berlin Wall to prevent the flow of emigrants to the west. Under the headline "Fleeing Irish and East Germans," the *Belfast Telegraph* reminded readers that the flow of refugees from East Germany, which prompted Walter Ulbricht (the East German leader) to seek Russian help, was less than the number who emigrated from the Irish Republic every year.[1] Adopting a slightly more sympathetic tone, *The Irish Times* commented that "it is agreed that Ireland, apart from East Berlin, has to endure the greatest pressure and attractions to induce people to leave their own country."[2]

Table 2. Survivors: Percentage Alive and Resident in Ireland in 1961

Birth Year	Male	Female
1926–31	55%	58%
1931–36	53%	55%
1936–41	60%	59%

Note: Calculated from population census age tables, 1936, 1946, and 1961. Lee, in *Ireland 1912–1985*, p. 379, stated that "four out of five children born in Ireland between 1931 and 1941 emigrated in the 1950s"; this is incorrect. Lee's source is Fergal Tobin, *The Best of Decades: Ireland in the 1960s* (Dublin, 1984), p. 156.

The population of the Irish Republic fell by 11,399 between 1926 and 1951. Between 1951 and 1956 it fell by 62,329 (2.11 percent). The rate of decline accelerated during the years 1956–1961, resulting in a net population loss of 79,923 (2.76 percent). The fall was wholly due to emigration. During the 1950s the rate of natural increase (births minus deaths) was higher than at any time since the 1880s. The number of young people entering the labor force was also rising, reflecting the fall in infant mortality during the 1930s and the fact that fewer young women remained at home without a job when they left school.[3] But total employment was falling. Between 1951 and 1961, the numbers of occupied men and women (at work and out of work) fell by almost 164,000, or 13 percent. Most of the jobs were lost in agriculture, where employment fell by 120,000. But not only did employment in industry and services fail to compensate for the jobs lost in agriculture, by 1961 they employed 44,000 fewer people than in 1951. Irish agriculture was incapable of generating the balance of payments surplus or the savings necessary to finance a program of capital investment that would bring about economic growth and more jobs in industry and services. Low farm incomes and a declining population reduced demand for the goods produced by Ireland's heavily protected manufacturing industries.

During the 1950s emigration reached levels not seen since the late nineteenth century. Between 1951 and 1956, almost 197,000 (13.6 per 1,000) more people left Ireland than entered the country, considerably higher than the 120,000 (8.2 per 1,000) between 1946 and 1951.[4] Net emigration reached 212,000 (14.8 per 1,000) between 1956 and 1961.

The Emigration Crisis of the Mid-1950s

"Analyst," alias Garret FitzGerald, has suggested that 1954 was the year when emigration began to pose a serious threat to the stability of the population. An estimated 43,000 men and women emigrated in 1954. In an article published in *The Irish Times* in February 1958, he commented that it was "ironical that we now have to struggle to achieve the stability of population on which less than four years ago the Commission on Emigration looked as an intolerable form of stagnation: stability moreover at a level about 65,000 lower than that which the Commission forecast."[5]

Net emigration peaked during the latter half of 1955; it fell somewhat in 1956 before rising to a new peak of 54,000 in 1957.[6] Although emigration began to rise in 1953 and 1954, and the Central Statistics Office had published figures indicating that the population was falling,[7] it would appear that this was not widely noticed at the time. An editorial in *The Irish Times* in June 1954 on the report of the Commission on Emigration, remarked that the decline in the population "seems to have been halted within recent years,"[8] and although emigration was mentioned during the general election campaign in May 1954, it was by no means the dominant issue. When *The Irish Times* asked de Valera during the course of the campaign what should be done to reduce emigration, he gave what was by now a standard reply: the solution was to increase employment by "developing the natural resources of the country, and increasing agricultural and industrial expansion and production." Replying to the same question, John A. Costello spoke about the need for "an expansion of production."[9]

The publication of the 1956 census returns, showing that the population had declined by 2 percent since 1951, gave renewed life to the phrase "the vanishing Irish." The *Roscommon Herald* announced that "the vanishing Irishman is no longer a myth dreamed up by an American Churchman," while an editorial in the *Nationalist and Leinster Times* attacked Roy Geary for dismissing the phrase "vanishing Irish" as "an odious cliché."[10] A Catholic priest who addressed a gathering at Feis an Dúin in Downpatrick, county Down, said that when Dr. J. A. O'Brien wrote his book, *The Vanishing Irish*, "many people accused him of exaggeration. Not many would blame him now."[11] The Catholic hierarchy announced a special day of prayer for emigrants on the first Sunday of October.[12]

Yet the 1956 census refuted many of the assertions in *The Vanishing Irish* concerning late marriages, elderly bachelors, and the shortage of women, and it provided much clearer evidence than the Commission on Emigration about the nature of Ireland's population problem. At 9.2 per 1,000, the rate of natural increase was higher than at any time since 1881–91, and substantially above the 1926–36 figure of 5.5 per 1,000. The proportion of women in the population was higher than at any time since 1901, and the ratio of women to men had improved in all four provinces. More ominously, the 1956 census showed that the decline in population was not confined to rural areas, or to the west of Ireland. The preliminary returns suggested that the population fell in all four provinces (the final figures showed a marginal rise in Leinster). Every town with a population of less than 10,000 recorded a lower population than in 1951, as did central Dublin. The only areas where the population rose were Dublin county, Dun Laoghaire, counties Meath and Louth, and the county boroughs of Waterford and Limerick. A headline in the *Roscommon Herald* noted that "Roscommon Town Was Hardest Hit."[13] In April 1956, when the census was being taken, the *Roscommon Herald* lamented that Boyle, Ballaghadereen, Castlerea, Elphin, Strokestown, and Roscommon were becoming ghost towns.[14] The *Nationalist and Leinster Times* claimed that 50 percent more natives of Borris, county Carlow, were living in England than in the town.[15]

Reviewing the preliminary returns of the 1956 census, Analyst identified some "disturbing" trends. Emigration was no longer confined to rural areas, and although the census did not collect employment data, he estimated that the numbers in employment had fallen by 50,000, or 4 percent, since 1951. The concluding paragraph of his article painted a grim picture.

> The significance of the 1956 Census is that emigration is no longer merely a social problem—an inevitable consequence of a high rate of natural increase in a country already struggling to create sufficient new non-agricultural employment to absorb the labor surplus of a static or declining agricultural sector. Today stagnation in agriculture is accompanied by stagnation in the rest of the economy; and,

in consequence the population is once again declining as it did during the last 75 years of British rule. Such a trend cannot easily be halted, save, perhaps by the fortuitous disappearance of the carrot of full employment in Britain; but it is at least desirable that the unprecedented scale and novel character of this recent emigration should be appreciated. Irish emigration is such an old story that there is a danger that it may no longer command the attention that it now deserves.[16]

The publication of the preliminary census returns coincided with a major economic crisis. A sharp rise in the balance of payments deficit and a serious fall in Ireland's external assets during 1955 meant that by the end of the year the commercial banks were either unable or unwilling to provide the government with sufficient short-term funds. 1956 is remembered as the year of three budgets, all designed to cut private and public spending. In March the minister for Finance, Gerard Sweetman, introduced special import levies on a wide range of "less than essential consumer imports" and restrictions on consumer credit; these levies were extended and increased in the budget proper in May, and higher taxes were imposed on cigarettes and petrol. July brought major spending cuts on housing and roads.[17] The financial crisis meant that the government could not respond to rising unemployment and emigration in the time-honored manner by introducing yet another program of public works.[18] Between 1955 and 1957, fixed investment fell by over 20 percent in real terms, with disastrous consequences for employment in the construction industry. Industrial output fell by almost 4 percent in 1956, and by a further 5 percent the following year. Agriculture fared better, with net output rising by almost 2 points in 1956, and by a further 4.7 points in 1957, but this did not result in any additional jobs. By 1958 national output was 3 percent lower than in 1955, and employment in manufacturing and construction industries was 11 percent below the 1955 level. Britain was also in recession at this time, so the initial impact of the crisis in Ireland was reflected in higher unemployment. By the beginning of 1957 there were almost 95,000 people on the live register.[19] In May 1956 an advertisement for a position as a lorry driver with Monaghan County Council attracted two hundred applications.[20] In July the Dundalk labor exchange reported one of

Table 3. Immigration from the Irish Republic to the United States of America

Year	M	F	Total
1951	1,329	2,410	3,739
1952	1,288	2,508	3,796
1953	1,734	2,918	4,652
1954	2,209	3,023	5,232
1955	2,632	3,343	5,975
1956	2,819	3,664	6,483
1957	4,370	4,744	9,014
1958	4,999	5,384	10,383
1959	3,049	4,322	7,371

Note: Statistics are taken from Patrick Blessing, *The Irish in America*, table 13, p. 308. Blessing's figures for the early 1950s differ from the figures given in the *Commission on Emigration*.

its busiest days ever.[21] On 1 January 1957 the Dublin Trade Union Congress demanded the recall of Dáil Éireann to consider the grave problem of unemployment.[22]

Although Britain was also in recession, with an estimated 150,000 people emigrating *from* Britain in 1956, Irish emigration reached a twentieth-century high in the years 1955 to 1957.[23] For the first time since the 1920s, between one-quarter and one-third of emigrants were traveling to destinations other than Britain. Cheaper emigrant airfares were introduced on Atlantic routes in November 1956, and Garret FitzGerald believed that this was a factor in the increasing numbers emigrating to the United States and Canada. Emigration to the United States peaked in 1958. By then, the American economy was also in recession, while the British economy had not yet recovered. In February 1958 FitzGerald noted that the unfavorable economic conditions in Britain and North America might lead to a reduction in emigration as happened in the early 1930s.[24] An editorial in *The Kerryman* in 1956 claimed that Ireland was facing "perhaps the most serious economic crisis since 1922." The sense of crisis was undoubtedly accentuated by fears that the "safety valve" of emigration to Britain was no longer assured. An editorial in *The Irish Times* in January 1957 noted "how much worse" the situation would be if Britain could no longer maintain full employment.[25] In 1957 *The Kerryman* expressed concern at "this British 'squeeze,' which was affecting Irish people at home and in exile," and at the extent of Ireland's economic dependence on Britain.[26]

The comparative novelty of emigration to the United States, Canada, and other distant destinations meant that it attracted more coverage in local newspapers than emigration to Britain, and this may have led to an exaggerated sense of its scale. In April 1956, one week after the census was taken, the *Roscommon Herald* described how two hundred "young boys and girls," the majority from counties Roscommon and Leitrim, boarded a liner at Cobh on their journey to the United States.[27] Two weeks later a reporter for the same newspaper watched two cars and two station wagons crammed with luggage leave Kilbeggan in county Westmeath carrying twelve young men and women on the first stage of their journey to Edmonton in the Canadian province of Alberta. Under the headline "The New World Has Supplanted Britain in Popularity as the Destination," the Carrick Gossip column reported that twenty young men were planning to emigrate to Canada.[28] Most editions of the *Roscommon Herald* and *The Kerryman* carried advertisements for farming jobs and farmland in Canada. Advertisements in the *Dundalk Democrat* promised interest-free loans to suitable candidates who were interested in emigrating to Canada and guaranteed employment on arrival. In July 1956 a Dundalk travel agent reported that he had received over one hundred inquiries about traveling to Canada, many from railway workers and boot and shoe operatives, who were either out of work or threatened with layoff.[29] Canadian emigration counsellors appear to have visited the Irish Republic to interview prospective emigrants—they had been active in Northern Ireland for many years. An article in one Canadian newspaper, the *Windsor Daily Star,* claimed that the Irish government had relaxed its previously hostile attitude to these activities, although the Department of External Affairs denied this.[30] On 14 September 1957, one week after it was announced that the Great Northern Railway engineering works at Dundalk was to close, Rhodesia Railways placed an advertisement in the *Dundalk Democrat* seeking railway clerks, trainee shunters, and locomotive firemen.[31] Other advertisements sought trainee miners for South Africa.[32] However, England remained the destination for the majority of emigrants, and most job advertisements in local newspapers offered employment in England.

The topics that attracted most attention both at cabinet and in the media were reports of men and women resigning from secure white-collar and public service jobs in order to emigrate and stories of family emigration. In 1958 a total of 1,962 men and women emigrated to Canada to take up employment; 443 were clerical workers and 441 were professional workers, mainly teachers and nurses. They were accompanied by 441 wives, 747 children, and 141 other dependents. Reports that up to 80 national teachers had emigrated to Canada during 1956 appear to have originated with the Irish National Teachers Organization; the minister for Education claimed that only 19 teachers had resigned during that year in order to emigrate. Fifteen went to Canada, the remainder traveled to the United States, France, and Rhodesia. The records of the Department of Posts and Telegraphs showed that in 1954, 60 staff had resigned in order to emigrate; the numbers rose to 98 in 1955, 100 in 1956, and 164 in 1957.[33] Local newspapers regularly reported the departure of men and women who had been employed in their area.[34] An editorial in the *Roscommon Herald* claimed that young gardaí were "throwing up good, secure and pensionable positions" to join police forces in other countries,[35] but no figures were supplied. When the *Garda Review* reported one garda's claim that 120 had resigned from the force since 1952 in order to emigrate, garda headquarters countered with a statement that the emigration of gardaí did not give cause for alarm.[36]

Family emigration also attracted attention. Analyst suggested that the easing of the housing shortage in Britain had made it easier to bring wives and families from Ireland. Men who had lived in England for several years were eligible for local authority housing.[37] Although there are occasional references in local newspapers to entire families emigrating, they tend to be unspecific, and it would appear that the overwhelming majority of emigrants were young and single. Some reports stated that no families had left.[38]

Local newspapers carried stories of talented footballers emigrating, of senior football teams losing several players at the same time, and of the difficulties that this posed for the Gaelic Athletic Association (GAA). In 1957 Boyle Agricultural Show was threatened with closure; five other shows in the county had already collapsed. Emigration was also blamed for falling membership of the Catholic Young Men's Society. Under the heading "Social Dry Rot in Country," the *Dundalk Democrat* reported that several rural organizations in county Louth, which met to analyze the findings of the emigration commission and the farm survey, agreed that the old structure of rural life had broken down.[39] Headlines like "Seven Leave Stradbally," "Emigration Continues to Hit G.A.A. Teams," or "Carrick Gossip—Soccer Star Leaves for America,"[40] are typical of the stories carried by the provincial press during the mid and late 1950s. In provincial Ireland emigration meant the departure of neighbors and friends from the local community.

Emigration attracted much less attention in the national newspapers; the coverage was dominated by speeches and statements from political and religious leaders and letters to the editor, and there is often an underlying sense of distance, even complacency. The report in the *Sunday Independent* on the preliminary findings of the 1956 census carried the headline, "The Dáil may be smaller after the fall in Census," and the accompanying article concentrated on the need to redraw constituency boundaries.[41] The *Sunday Independent* supported the Inter-Party government; Minister for Agriculture James Dillon was a close friend of the editor Hector Legge.[42] As Fianna Fáil was in opposition, the *Sunday Press* should probably have felt that it had greater freedom to comment, but while acknowledging that the fall in population had tragic implications for social welfare and national income, it concluded with the limp statement that "perhaps the most tragic feature of the situation is that there is no agreement in Ireland as to its cause, which is to be found, perhaps in the realms of the metaphysical rather than in the field of economics."[43]

The daily papers focused on economics. The leading article in the *Irish Press* commented that "more urbanised areas have failed to hold their ground." The flight from the land, it stated, was no longer confined to the poorer areas, and employment in industry was failing to compensate for the fall in agricultural employment. The article concluded that "obviously our whole economy, agricultural and industrial, is badly in need of a fresh stimulus."[44] The *Irish Press* published a second editorial on the decline in the population in Gaeltacht areas and a number of letters to the editor, including one from Labhras Ó Nualláin, professor of economics at University College Galway, who recommended that all TDs and senators be sent to Saint Patrick's Purgatory on Lough Derg, the site of a famous penitential pilgrimage, armed with copies of the census and the report of the Commission on Emigration. Fasted and chastened after their pilgrimage, he recommended that they travel to the now-deserted Blasket Islands, where they should study the IBEC report on the export prospects for Irish industry.[45] The *Irish Independent* told its readers that the census returns "cannot fail to intensify the prevailing gloom," a gloom that the remainder of this leading article did little to dispel. It suggested that the prospects for emigrants had been "exceptionally promising" in recent years, and it questioned "how far the effects of capital investment policies, industrialisation and urbanisation and social services can be trusted to produce a thriving community in the face of these figures." The *Irish Independent* ended by expressing the hope that Ireland might rediscover "the primary importance of agriculture as the basis of prosperity . . . and re-shape our policies accordingly."[46] The paper carried an article on emigration from Scotland two days later, which seemed to imply that the Irish experience was not unique.[47] The most emotional response came in the editorial in *The Irish Times*, which suggested that if the trends revealed by the census continued unchecked, "Ireland will die—not in the remote, unpredictable future; quite soon." But the only diagnosis offered for this malaise was this: "What is happening in the Twenty-six Counties is comparable with what has happened so often to small coastal islands: the young people move to the mainland, the old die off, and presently the place is uninhabited." The sentiments expressed, and the phrases—"Twenty-six Counties" and "mainland"—betray the newspaper's unionist background.[48]

Two Northern Ireland papers with unionist sympathies, the *Belfast Telegraph* and the *Newsletter*, provided a much clearer assessment of the economic predicament facing the Dublin government. According to an editorial in the *Belfast Telegraph*, "The reasons for emigration are not hard to find: one has only to look at the state of industry and agriculture in the South, and at the opportunities in other countries." The writer referred to the lethargy and restrictive atmosphere that prevailed, concluding that the problems were "not simply economic. There is a sore need for a revival of spirit."[49] An editorial in the *Newsletter* combined a concise assessment of the state of the economy of the Irish Republic with something approaching an obituary:

> All who have been associated with the development of Eire during the past 34 years must feel sad and disillusioned. When the links with the U.K. were severed, and again when the last fragile tie with the Commonwealth was demolished, they had high hopes of building a prosperous State in which agriculture would flourish, new industries would provide work for an increasing population, the economy would be so buoyant that taxation would be the lowest in Europe, that every boy and girl would be educated without cost to the parents, that adequate provision would be made for the sick and distressed, and that bigotry and tolerance would disappear from the land. Not one of these dreams has come true. Although taxation is on an almost unbearable level, Eire is faced by an economic crisis. Exports are insufficient to pay for imports, farmers have a hard struggle to make ends meet, the number of unemployed has risen to more than 70,000 and the social services and standard of living are far below those obtaining in Northern Ireland. Worst of all, the population, as recorded in the census taken last April, has fallen to 2,894,822—the lowest figure in the history of the 26 counties.[50]

How to End Emigration: The Politicians' Response

Although the preliminary returns were published on 1 June, the Dáil did not discuss the census until 19 June, when Roscommon TD Jack McQuillan tabled a question for the taoiseach. In reply, Costello said that emigration was a long-term problem that required long-term remedies. "It has been, and will continue to be, the Government's policy to 'produce conditions favourable to increased population.' We will vigorously press forward the implementation of our policy of promoting an expanding economy, higher levels of agricultural and industrial production—with an increasing surplus available for disposal at competitive prices abroad—and better living conditions at home."[51] On 25 July Costello told the Dáil that the country was faced with "a trinity of problems, . . . large-scale and persistent emigration, substantial unemployment and a serious deficit in the balance of payments."[52] But the Dáil and the Dublin newspapers appear to have devoted greater attention to the balance of payments deficit and tax increases than to emigration, confirming the fears expressed by Analyst that "Irish emigration is such an old story" that the significance of the 1956 census results would not be fully appreciated.

Although Costello referred to a "disturbing increase" in the annual rate of net emigration, his speech on 25 July suggests that he regarded this as the continuation of a long-term problem; he quoted extensively from the *Report of the Commission on Emigration,* placing particular emphasis on the sections that referred to "effort and sacrifice . . . more and better work . . . a revolution in the attitude of the individual. . . . To solve it, the mind and spirit of the people must change so that they possess the necessary degree of resolution not only to develop the economy fully but also to accept readily the sacrifice and hard work which this would involve." Costello claimed that it was "significant that the commission have so repeatedly emphasized the importance, in dealing with the problem of emigration, of the attitude taken by the community toward that problem. Time and again the commission have drawn attention to the personal, as distinct from the social and economic factors, which influence the decision to emigrate and have emphasized the effort, sacrifice, resolution and determination required of the community if our demographic and economic problems are to be solved."[53]

Given that the government's misguided policy on interest rates was the immediate cause of the balance of payments deficit, and that the measures taken to rectify this had driven the economy into recession, the emphasis that Costello placed on personal factors is questionable, but it served to shift responsibility from the government to the individual. A second aspect of this speech that merits attention is his emphasis on the continuity of policy despite changes of government. He referred to "a long-term policy . . . pursued by successive Governments, . . . continuity in the efforts to develop the natural resources, to raise the general level of production, to create diversified opportunities of employment at home and to improve progressively the living conditions of the people."[54]

De Valera agreed that "the situation does demand the active cooperation of all public representatives"; he expressed the hope that they would all speak with one voice and would tell the people that "we must of necessity live within our means. . . . We on this side of the House will do everything in our power to see that the present crisis is surmounted successfully and quickly. We will do everything in our power to help whatever Government might be in office, and to do it ourselves if we get the responsibility, to try and see that emigration will be stemmed and unemployment lessened." He ended by appealing to the Labor Party, who formed part of the second Inter-Party government, "to help us in our efforts,"[55] an appeal designed to drive home Fianna Fáil's message that coalition governments were incapable of pursuing a common policy. This debate suggests that the government and opposition were in broad agreement on economic policy. De Valera claimed that those who had criticized his government or the current government for "working about in a haphazard manner" were incorrect; both governments had clear objectives and ways to secure them and "that, as far as we have not secured them, these will be the targets and the aims for the immediate future."[56] But he also indicated that the government and the opposition regarded the balance of payments deficit and the difficulty in financing the national loan as more pressing matters than emigration; no leading politician acknowledged that there had been a sharp rise in emigration.

Although Costello and de Valera conceded that economic conditions were the primary cause of emigration, they confused the argument by asserting that emigrants were abandoning a life in Ireland that offered many attractions. Costello claimed that "the young men and women who are leaving Ireland to seek a living abroad are not, as a body, fleeing from intolerable conditions at home: they are seeking what they have come to believe are better economic conditions." He urged that "young men and women should not lightly shake the dust of their homeland from their feet. The plea of economic necessity is, in many cases, one that cannot be sustained. Only too frequently do we hear of men and women leaving good jobs in this country for apparently better ones in England. They should weigh the attractions of higher monetary rewards in other lands against comforts and happiness—real and substantial, if not measurable in money—that are theirs to enjoy at home."[57] De Valera went so far as to suggest that Britain did not offer emigrants a higher standard of living: "If you take the extra costs from the extra remuneration, I wonder very much whether in real terms, when you come down to it, the number of people who have emigrated would not find they were better off materially at home. I should like to give it consideration but I know that if you take and compare the national incomes or something of that sort they would not give you anything like a true picture. In the case of Britain you will have in the national income the lords of manors, industrial magnates, and so on."[58]

Few Irish people would have agreed. An editorial in the *Roscommon Herald* stated that "to keep these 'bona fide' emigrants in Ireland we must offer them something—security, work, a decent standard of living. We must intensify industrialisation and agricultural production." The newspaper demanded to see "in the near future the embryo of an incentive and the nucleus of a plan, which will ultimately convince Irishmen that it is possible to live in comfort by staying in Ireland."[59]

Achieving Economic Growth

By June 1956 all the major political parties were in agreement that higher investment offered the solution to emigration and unemployment. When Costello spoke about "promoting an expanding economy, higher levels of agricultural and industrial production—with an increasing surplus available for disposal at competitive prices abroad—and better living conditions at home," Jack McQuillan retorted that "statements similar to that outlined by the Taoiseach have been made to this House from the year 1948 onwards and that, in spite of that the rate of net emigration has stepped up considerably."[60]

There was no shortage of blueprints for transforming the Irish economy; the difficulty was to find one that was both effective and realistic given the economic constraints and Ireland's political and cultural values. Any plan had to address three key issues: the respective roles of the public and private sectors, whether economic development should be based primarily on agriculture, manufacturing industry, or some balance between the two, and whether it would entail a continuation of economic protectionism or moves toward free trade. These issues could not be determined on purely economic grounds: they went to the heart of Irish culture and Irish identity.

In July 1953 the minister for Industry and Commerce, Seán Lemass, presented the cabinet with proposals to create 30,000–40,000 man-years of employment through a program of public investment. Most of the money was earmarked for infrastructure, a lot of it of dubious economic merit, such as minor roads in the west of Ireland. Lemass claimed that these jobs would boost demand for manufactured goods and bring about an increase in manufacturing employment. Despite the predictable opposition of both the Department of Finance and the Central Bank, the cabinet agreed to establish a National Development Fund of £5 million that would be replenished every year up to that amount; however public expenditure from this fund never came close to reaching the annual target.[61] Two years later at a party meeting in Clery's Ballroom in O'Connell Street when Fianna Fáil was out of office, Lemass unveiled a more ambitious plan to create 100,000 jobs over five years, but on this occasion he recommended that additional state investment should be used to expand productive capacity in manufacturing industry and agriculture, and not on public works and the construction industry.[62] An editorial in *The Irish Times* criticized this proposal because, in the writer's opinion, the plan was unduly dependent on the expansion of manufacturing industry: "The proper course is surely to work for the rehabilitation of agriculture and at least a doubling of its productivity, rather than to concentrate on manufacturing industries which have no root in our own resources." Presenting a remarkably static view of the Irish economy, and ignoring the fact that employment in agriculture was falling and industrial employment was rising in every developed country, the editorial suggested that a united Ireland would be "disastrously overstocked with manufacturing industry." *The Irish Times* regarded manufacturing industry as the preserve of Northern Ireland.[63]

In his 1955 plan, Lemass proposed to overcome any potential shortage of capital or foreign exchange by realizing the overseas

assets held by Irish residents and Irish banks, including the Central
Bank. Fine Gael made a similar proposal in its 1953 *Blueprint for Prosperity*.[64] Fine Gael was in opposition in 1953, as was Fianna Fáil when
Lemass made the Clery's ballroom speech. But such radical proposals
tended to be toned down, if not abandoned, when the same politicians were in office, which meant that the balance of payments remained a serious constraint on most development plans.

The public/private dilemma presented another difficulty in a
country where any extension of state control conjured up images of
"the servile state" and warnings about the need to respect Catholic
social teaching. When Fine Gael, in government, drafted a revised
economic plan in October 1956, they referred to the dangers posed by
"the growing power of the state," placing considerable emphasis on
cooperation with the private sector in order to distance themselves
from Fianna Fail.[65] In contrast, the plan adopted by the United Trade
Union Movement in December 1956, "Planning for Full Employment," relied heavily on state intervention.[66] During the 1957 election
campaign, Lemass was forced to refute allegations that he planned to
implement Stalinist economic planning. McCarthy notes that Clann
na Poblachta, the only party to advocate planning during the 1957
general election, saw its representation fall from three seats to one.[67]

By the mid-1950s most of the indigenous (or pseudo-indigenous)
industries established during the 1930s were moribund and almost
wholly dependent on economic protection for their survival. Furthermore, employment in manufacturing industry was falling, in
contrast to what was happening in most European countries. Fine
Gael was keen to encourage foreign manufacturing plants to invest in
Ireland by repealing the Control of Manufactures Act (which restricted foreign ownership of manufacturing firms), whereas Lemass's 1955 speech made no reference to foreign investment.[68] Fine
Gael's economic plan, *Policy for Production,* proposed to provide tax
incentives to encourage exporting firms to expand in Ireland. However, it also protected existing industry from competition by restricting new industry grants to firms that intended to manufacture products not already being made in Ireland, and it reiterated agriculture's
central role in achieving economic progress.[69]

Yet the provincial press looked increasingly to industry rather than agriculture. The publication of the preliminary results of the National Farm Survey in October 1956 prompted *The Kerryman* to comment that the "statistics reveal that farming is not a very profitable occupation and that in the case of many smaller farms the income of the hired hand is higher than the owners." *The Dundalk Democrat* carried the story under the heading, "Is Farming Worthwhile? Interim Report Raises Doubts."[70] A later story in the same paper noted that Louth was one of the few counties to record an increase in population between 1951 and 1956; this reflected the number of industries in the county, which provided jobs for those living in the towns and the countryside. It suggested that other areas should attempt to achieve a similar balance between industry and agriculture.[71] *The Kerryman* claimed that young people were leaving the land "because their heart is not in it. They have changed: not the land." The solution to unemployment was to establish more factories in the locality.[72] The *Roscommon Herald* suggested that the solution to emigration was either to attract factories to the town or decentralize government offices; the latter had been one of the recommendations in the *Report of the Commission on Emigration.* The first point in a "programme to boost Carlow," launched in April 1956, was "to begin agitation for the establishment of a new industry." Tralee Development Association announced that it was planning a bigger effort to secure factories for the area.[73] But not everybody accepted that industry offered the best solution to emigration, which is not surprising given that unemployed shoe operatives and engineering workers were emigrating from Dundalk. Some farmers believed that agriculture had been handicapped by the need to subsidize industry. Headlines such as "Urban Ireland a Parasite on a Neglected and Undeveloped Rural Economy" and reports of statements at a meeting of the Monaghan County Committee of Agriculture that the country could not continue indefinitely in circumstances where agriculture was supporting industry[74] featured in the same local newspapers that were demanding new factories.

By 1956 prospects for Irish industry were becoming increasingly uncertain as negotiations began on the creation of a European free trade area; by January 1957 proposals had been drawn up for the seventeen member countries of the Organization for European Economic Co-operation to form a customs union. On 23 January the Inter-Party government issued a statement to the effect that regardless of whether Ireland joined this free trade area or remained outside it, its formation would have "significant implications for Ireland's economy requiring fundamental reappraisal of economic plans and policies." The overall tone of the government press statement was negative: unless Ireland was granted special treatment, membership in the proposed free trade area would entail the removal of all protectionist measures, and future Irish governments would be precluded from extending protection.[75] Liam Cosgrave, the minister for External Affairs, referred ominously to the "serious implications" of the proposed free trade area. Most press coverage reflected a similarly gloomy tone: *The Irish Times* reported a speech by Seán Lemass, in which he expressed the opinion that free trade throughout western Europe would automatically assist Irish economic development, under the heading "Free Trade Could Lose Markets in Britain—Mr. Lemass."[76]

Population and Patriotism

John McCarthy has claimed that the publication of the preliminary returns of the 1956 census resulted in "a collapse of public confidence in a State which alone amongst the countries of Western Europe was now seen to have achieved economic stagnation at the very time when its neighbours' economies had been expanding at a record rate in historic terms." He referred to "universal disillusionment with the political system."[77] In December 1956 the Irish Republican Army launched "Operation Harvest," a series of raids on police stations and army barracks in Northern Ireland and border customs posts. When two IRA volunteers, Seán South and Fergal O'Hanlon, were killed during raids in January 1957, their funerals prompted mass demonstrations in the Irish Republic; however, the only direct link between IRA activity and the state of the economy was Clann na Poblachta's decision to table a motion of no confidence in the government, over its failure to deal adequately with partition and the mismanagement of the economy, in retaliation for the government's decision to arrest suspected members of the IRA.[78] Costello asked for a dissolution of the Dáil without waiting for the motion to be debated, and the general election took place on 5 March 1957.

The initial stages of the election campaign appear to have been dominated by partition, the government's handling of the IRA offensive, and the alleged instability of coalition governments. However, economic issues came to the fore during the closing stages of the campaign. According to an article by the (unnamed) political correspondent of *The Irish Times*, "Fianna Fáil and Labour last night declared full employment to be their main aim in the general election contest. Fine Gael and Clann na Poblachta have referred repeatedly to the problem, and it appears to have raced ahead to beat the question of coalition governments or the use of illegal physical force as the question of the election."[79]

The plans for full employment aired by the main political parties differed only in detail. Lemass claimed that a national economic policy was emerging for the first time since the war.[80] All parties were committed to raising investment, and all were somewhat ambiguous on key issues such as free trade versus self-sufficiency and the relative importance of agriculture and industry. Fine Gael promised to provide further financial grants and tax incentives to encourage investment in industry and an expansion in manufacturing exports. They also predicted up to 250 new factories.[81] Eamon de Valera gave a commitment that if Fianna Fáil was returned with an overall majority, "it would enable them to try to continue on the path they had trodden before"—developing agriculture and industries with the goal of becoming "as self-contained as possible."[82]

If de Valera's speech suggested that there would be no major change in Fianna Fáil's economic policy, the proposals outlined by Lemass steered a careful course between continuity and change, no doubt reflecting differences within the party. In the short-run, his proposals promised to create additional jobs by a program of public works and measures to promote self-sufficiency, which would have the additional benefit of reducing the import bill by an estimated £30 million. But Lemass also announced measures similar to those proposed by Fine Gael aimed at increasing industrial and agricultural output and exports. The most significant section of Lemass's speech concerned the standard of living. In order to ensure that there would be sufficient money for investment, he suggested that everybody who was not unemployed should be prepared to see their standard of living reduced by 5 percent—either through voluntary saving or taxation—but he ruled out any permanent reduction in living standards as a possible solution to economic difficulties. "A permanent lowering of living standards in this country is not a practicable course. I doubt if anybody is prepared to consider it. So long as there is freedom for families to move to Britain, which will continue as long as there are full employment conditions in that country, our standards must approximate to British standards, or our population will go. It is the survival of the nation that is involved and not merely our living standards, unless we can achieve by our own efforts a rapid and substantial increase of our resources."[83]

The reference to families moving to Britain suggests that this was a matter of particular concern. In the past, emigration had rarely involved the permanent departure of entire families—indeed, the emigration of a nonheir often facilitated marriage and the reproduction of the next generation.

The outcome of the election was a strong majority for Fianna Fáil; it would appear that the electorate wished to punish the outgoing government. Four Sinn Féin candidates were also elected in 1957, but their success should be seen as a response to Operation Harvest and the deaths of Seán South and Fergal O'Hanlon (O'Hanlon's brother was one of the successful candidates) rather than a loss of confidence in the state. Jack Murphy, an unemployed carpenter and former IRA internee, was elected in Dublin South Central as the candidate of the Unemployed Protest Committee (UPC), an organization dominated by members of the small Irish communist movement.[84] In May Murphy and two other members of the UPC began a hunger strike to protest against unemployment and the removal of food subsidies in the budget, but they called off the hunger strike after four days when the government announced that it was reintroducing controls on the price of bread. During the hunger strike an estimated one thousand unemployed men marched on Dáil Éireann, and four thousand people attended the rally announcing the hunger strike's end.[85] In a speech delivered shortly after the hunger strike had ended, Seán Lemass warned that "there are people who are even now meeting and calculating how to foster discontent for ulterior motives out of our difficulties and to weaken our will to tackle them."[86] His predictions appeared to be borne out when three thousand women, many pushing prams or carrying children in their arms, marched to Dáil Éireann on 22 May before attending a rally at College Green.[87] The UPC also organized marches in Cork and Waterford, but these attracted a small attendance. In August Murphy broke with the communists (apparently following the intervention of the archbishop of Dublin, John Charles McQuaid), resigned his Dáil seat, and emigrated to Canada.[88]

Unlike the unemployed, emigrants had no vote, and they were not in a position to march on Dáil Éireann. However, 1957 did see the formation of the Anti-Emigration Movement, whose goal was to promote cooperation between church, state, employers, trade unions, and others in order to bring an end to emigration. Its policies were very much a rehash of earlier ideas: "buy Irish" campaigns in Ireland (where punitive tariffs meant that there was little alternative) and among the Irish abroad; a campaign to encourage investment in Ireland; a "back to the land movement"; and the establishment of an export distribution center.[89] The chairman was Feidhlidh Ó Broin, an engineer and commercial traveler with an address in Santry. The only other individual identified with the organization was Father Edward Coyne, S.J., who had been a member of the Commission on Emigration. Although it posed no obvious threat to the state, the activities of the Anti-Emigration Movement were closely monitored by gardaí. Jack Murphy attended the early meetings along with other members of the UPC; but according to the gardaí, the meetings in Moran's Hotel in Talbot Street attracted an average attendance of only ten to fifteen, and several journalists who attended the first press conference left after a short period, remarking that their presence was a waste of time.

In September 1958 the gardaí reported that the Anti-Emigration Movement had recruited approximately eight hundred members, all in Dublin city. According to the gardaí, the group had the support of the Irish National Teachers Organisation, the Vocational Teachers, the Irish Countrywomen's Association, and the Unemployed Workers (presumably the UPC). The organizer "resides in a very good class house and is most law-abiding and a strong supporter of the present Government." It would appear that the Anti-Emigration Movement staged only one public demonstration: a protest at a public meeting promoting emigration to South Africa.[90] In May 1959 Ó Broin announced that the committee was considering forming a national council of interested bodies to draft proposals for solving emigration; he had been in contact with Muintir na Tíre, the National Agricultural and Industrial Development Authority (an economic lobby group), the Irish Housewives' Association, and Dr. Moran, the director of the Ardee psychiatric hospital, but nothing materialized, and the organization seems to have disappeared.[91]

The Cork anti-emigration movement—TEAM (The Anti-Emigration Movement)—was a more radical organization. It called on the Irish people to stage a national, nonpolitical uprising to bring an end to unemployment and emigration by creating a true sound national economy. This would be achieved by various measures that had been rehearsed repeatedly since at least the 1930s: repatriating Irish money invested in Britain; creating an independent Irish currency and manipulating foreign exchanges; disowning the national debt; and reforming the fraudulent banking system. TEAM distributed circulars to tenants of Corporation housing in Cork, protesting against the "scandal" of high rents. They distributed another leaflet directed at ratepayers, demanding that the cost of health services become a national charge. And they called on the youth of Ireland to learn the truth about emigration and unemployment. Although TEAM saturated the city with posters, their meetings attracted a small attendance.[92] These groups should be seen as the descendants of earlier bodies such as the Mellifont group and Council of National Action. The major change from the past was that they were concentrated in urban areas, indicating that emigration was no longer regarded as solely a rural phenomenon.

It is not surprising that an unemployed man was elected to Dáil Éireann in 1957, or that some insignificant organizations were formed to oppose emigration. What is more surprising is that the economic crisis gave rise to such muted protest; this would appear to confirm the belief that emigration provided a safety valve for social and political protest. The 1957 budget, introduced by Fianna Fáil's James Ryan, continued the deflationary measures of the Inter-Party government. Despite a decided improvement in the balance of payments deficit, capital levies were retained, public capital spending fell, and unemployment rose to 9.2 percent in a year when emigration reached the highest level in the twentieth century.[93]

There is no indication that the Anti-Emigration Movement or the protest marches by the unemployed exercised any influence on government policy, with the exception of the decision to restore a price subsidy for bread. However, the coincidence of the IRA's border campaign and a major economic crisis, a sharp drop in population, and a record level of emigration prompted some rethinking about patriotism and national objectives. Michael Kilroy, a veteran of the war of independence in Mayo, who had protested against emigration during the Second World War, appealed to young people to stay at home: at worst they would not be asked to make anything like the same sacrifices for the country as the previous generation, and Micawber-like, he believed that if they remained in Ireland "they would surely find something to do."[94] The *Belfast Newsletter's* editorial on the 1956 census referred to the "ineptitude" of successive governments, "who have spent far too much time and energy chasing the will o' the wisp of Irish unity and posing as the representative of a world power instead of devoting all their attention to the country's bread and butter problems."[95] Such views were not restricted to Ulster unionists. Reverend Cornelius Lucey suggested that "the true Irish patriot is not the man whose eyes are fixed on the six lost counties, but the man whose eyes are on the 800,000 Irish men and women lost to the nation by emigration since 1922."[96] Monsignor Temple of New Jersey expressed the opinion that for the young Irishman of today "it might be a nobler service to the motherland to furrow and fodder on an Irish farm or to fire the furnace of an Irish factory than to fight at a ford. There was a need for one generation of Irish youth that would be inspired by heroic resolve to stay at home and break off once and for all the habit of emigrating."[97]

An editorial in *The Kerryman* in 1957 reported that when it asked its readers to rank the urgency that they attached to three major national evils—emigration, partition, and unemployment—"with unfailing regularity our correspondents in towns, villages and rural areas in Kerry and Cork refer to the departure of young men and women to the United States, Britain, Australia and Canada." The editorial continued, "We have become case hardened to it. Nobody is now concerned except the family across whose doorstep a young person has passed, perhaps for the last time."[98]

Politicians in Northern Ireland and the Republic were very conscious of the contrasting fortunes between the two parts of Ireland: in Northern Ireland the population was increasing, likewise the numbers at work.[99] When Seán Lemass addressed an election meeting in the border town of Dundalk he suggested that it was essential that "our national faith" be "justified by practical results in the Twenty-Six Counties before we can carry conviction in the Six Counties—85,000 unemployed and 60,000 emigrants per year are not good arguments for the ending of partition."[100] In March 1957, the secretary of the Department of Finance, T. K. Whitaker, presented the incoming minister, James Ryan, with a memorandum emphasizing that without "a sound and progressive economy" political independence would be "a crumbling façade."[101] In May 1957 Lemass, who was once again the minister for Industry and Commerce, told a Fianna Fáil meeting at Bettystown, county Meath, that "this is a critical fight on which we are entering. It is not just a matter of winning material advantages. The preservation of the freedom which has been so hardly won turns on the outcome of effort which is now being made to put firm economic foundations under it."[102]

The most explicit linkage of emigration, patriotism, and national survival comes in *Economic Development,* the report by T. K. Whitaker published in November 1958:

> After 35 years of native government people are asking whether we can achieve an acceptable degree of economic progress. The common talk amongst parents in the towns, as in rural Ireland, is of their children having to emigrate as soon as their education is completed in order to be sure of a reasonable livelihood. To the children themselves and to many already in employment the jobs available at home look unattractive by comparison with those obtainable in such variety and so readily elsewhere. All this seems to be setting up a vicious circle—of increasing migration, resulting in a small domestic

market depleted of initiative and skill, and a reduced incentive, whether for Irishmen or foreigners, to undertake and organize the productive enterprises which alone can provide increased employment opportunities and higher living standards.[103]

This is a direct response to the mentalité of the mid-1950s, when local newspapers referred to the "general depression and perplexity," "discontent and disillusionment," a "palpable sense of frustration," and "the spirit of dissatisfaction, if not disillusionment with politics."[104]

The publication in 1958 of the government's *Programme for Economic Expansion* and Whitaker's *Economic Development* are generally regarded as the catalysts for a major upturn in the Irish economy. Most importantly, they provided a very necessary psychological boost.[105] By 1958 emigration had fallen from the peak levels of the previous year, although the decline owed more to a recession in North America than to any improvement in the Irish economy; 19 percent of building workers were unemployed, only marginally below the 19.6 percent recorded in 1957.[106] The recession in Britain ended in 1959, and by May Analyst was suggesting that the worst was over. He believed that the high rate of emigration during the past decade might turn out to be a temporary phenomenon rather than the beginning of a free fall in the Irish population. He warned that the Irish people had been unduly complacent in the past. There was now a danger that they would be "misled into an even less warranted pessimism" and might fail to spot a turning point until it was some distance behind.[107] FitzGerald was one of the first to recognize that the tide had turned, but at the time few shared his optimism. It is my impression that more speeches were delivered in 1959 and 1960 about emigration than in 1954 and 1955, when it was significantly higher,[108] but it is not uncommon for people to be more preoccupied with the problems of the past than with those of the present. There was a delay in recognizing the arrival of the Celtic Tiger in the 1990s.

The Age of Lemass

The mood upswing coincided with a major landmark in Irish politics: the election of Eamon de Valera as president of Ireland in June

1959. His successor as taoiseach, Seán Lemass, was keen to broadcast the news that the economy was prospering. All politicians like to publicize good news, but Lemass used the evidence of economic growth to boost national confidence and to generate support for the process of economic change. In October 1960 he told the Dublin Chamber of Commerce that the economy was expanding, although there would be "a long upward climb before we will have attained any platform of security where we can afford to rest." The continuing emigration was "the most disturbing feature" in the current economic picture; it provided "evidence of the dimensions of the national problems still to be solved and of [the] insufficiency of our efforts today to develop a completely attractive way of life for all the elements of the national community and adequate opportunities of employing individual talents in Ireland to earn livelihoods equivalent to those which emigrants hope to find elsewhere."

Lemass asserted that the removal of the economic causes of emigration was "now within our grasp," and that the current rate of industrial progress offered the possibility of full employment "when the back-log has been removed." But action on this front must be supplemented by efforts to change the "traditions, habits and tensions which encourage emigration." Reminding his audience that the *Report of the Commission on Emigration* had suggested that social and psychological factors were "as potent, if not more potent than economic forces" in accounting for emigration, he cited the recently published interim report of the Limerick Rural Survey[109] to justify the assertion that "social reasons predominate over economic ones" as motives for emigration. He also suggested that the numerous emigrants who abandoned jobs or the prospect of a job in Ireland indicated the strength of social and psychological factors. He told his audience that this aspect of emigration had received insufficient attention: "The tendency to present emigration as solely an aspect of our economic development problem may be one reason why more thought has not been given to non-economic factors, and why more comprehensive and successful measures to cope with them have not been developed. It would be more effective to devote greater attention to non-economic factors and measures to overcome them than [to] a futile deploring of the situation or [in] resolutions calling for somebody else to do something about it."[110]

Many aspects of this speech are open to question. A close reading of the *Report of the Commission on Emigration* does not support Lemass's interpretation that social and psychological factors were "as potent, if not more potent than economic forces." Moreover, in 1960 and for many years to come, there were strong economic reasons why emigration persisted. Lemass's claim that a solution to the economic causes of emigration was "now within our grasp" was far-fetched. An unsatisfactory 1960 trade agreement with Britain had left Irish agriculture with uncertain market prospects, and net agricultural income remained below the 1957 level.[111] Employment in the manufacturing industry was rising, but from a very low base and there were too few additional jobs to absorb the workers who were leaving agriculture, let alone the rising numbers of school leavers. Some emigrants abandoned jobs in Ireland, but very few of these jobs were secure or well paid.

Nevertheless, this speech indicated that Lemass was concerned about emigration. In the final section he called for people to "think deeply" about its causes, "not merely as a political catch-cry, or as a measure of our economic expansion needs." He was keen to encourage "more objective thinking . . . without allowing judgments to be swamped by emotionalism," although by deprecating "the unduly glamorous and often false picture of urban life abroad often conveyed by the cinema," Lemass laid himself open to charges of emotionalism. And by directing attention away from the economic causes of emigration, which were regarded as the government's responsibility, toward more nebulous psychological and social factors, he could be accused of shifting the responsibility from the government to others, as former taoisigh de Valera and Costello had done.

The winter of 1960–61 brought a series of resolutions demanding government action to reduce emigration. In November 1960 Dublin Corporation passed a resolution expressing alarm at the extent of emigration and demanding that the government take steps to raise wages and improve social services. Other local authorities took up the cause. On Christmas Eve the *Sligo Champion* carried a report of a debate on emigration by Sligo Corporation, which called for government action. Limerick and Cork Corporations passed similar resolutions, and all Irish local authorities were asked to do likewise.[112] In December 1960 the *Irish Catholic* published British national insurance records showing that 64,494 persons with addresses in the Irish Republic were added to the British national insurance register in 1959, greater than the 58,316 new entrants in 1958; the accompanying report told of a mass exodus of individuals and families from Ireland.[113]

By 1959 Britain was seriously considering restricting immigration, and these statistics were an attempt by the British authorities to discover the true extent of Irish immigration. Pressure to restrict immigration was undoubtedly prompted by the rising number of immigrants from the Indian subcontinent and the West Indies, yet throughout the 1950s the number of immigrants from Ireland was greater than the number from the West Indies, Africa, and the Indian subcontinent combined. In 1958 officials at the Commonwealth Relations Office asked Irish ambassador Hugh McCann how restrictions on immigration would affect Ireland. McCann informed them that they would have "a disastrous impact on an already precarious economy."[114] The prospect that restrictions would be placed on Irish immigration gradually faded, and in September 1961 a senior official at the Commonwealth Relations Office hinted to an official at the Irish embassy that the imminent report of the interdepartmental committee on emigration should cause the Irish authorities "neither alarm nor despondency," and this proved to be the case.[115] The 1962 Commonwealth Immigration Act, which imposed restrictions on Commonwealth citizens immigrating to Britain, did not apply to Irish citizens. During the debate on the bill, several members of Parliament raised the question of limiting immigration from Ireland, but most speakers acknowledged that this would be extremely difficult to implement, not least because of the inability to control travel between Northern Ireland and the Irish Republic. During discussions with officials in the Irish embassy on the Commonwealth Immigration Bill, the undersecretary at the Commonwealth office referred to the long tradition of Irish workers in Britain and suggested that they might even be regarded as an essential part of the British labor force.[116] In order to diffuse demands from Tory backbenchers that restrictions be imposed on Irish immigration, the British government gave a commitment to examine national insurance records in order to determine the scale and composition of immigration from the Republic of Ireland, but having carried out this investigation, the Home

Office was reluctant to publicize the findings because they did not wish to rekindle interest in the matter. Instead, they arranged for a number of MPs to table questions on the matter.[117] This strategy suggests that the Home Office was unwilling to take any action that might prompt demands for restrictions to be placed on immigration from Ireland. By exempting Ireland, Britain managed to set limits to nonwhite emigration while minimizing the risk of a labor shortage.[118] Yet while it did not materalize, this threat to Irish emigration to the United Kingdom served to concentrate Irish minds on the need to reduce or end emigration, and it may well have been a factor in Lemass's efforts to improve Anglo-Irish relations.

The 1961 Census

A population census was taken every ten years from 1841 until 1911, but the pattern was broken in 1921 (when none was taken) because of the disturbed state of Ireland. The first census of the Irish Free State took place in 1926, and thereafter, years ending in the number 6 became the normal census year. The 1951 census was a special one, taken in response to a request from the Commission on Emigration, so the government was not obliged to take a census in 1961, although the Commission on Emigration had recommended that a census be taken every five years. The Department of the Taoiseach was very much in favor of holding a census in 1961 for several reasons. The last comprehensive census taken was in 1946, and in 1951 and 1956 no information on employment, housing, the Irish language, or other socioeconomic questions was collected. Additionally, the considerable variation in net emigration since 1956 made it difficult to estimate the current distribution of population by age or conjugal status, and furthermore, the United Nations had requested that all countries take a census in 1960 or 1961 with a view to compiling an accurate estimate of world population.

With these things in mind, a special census was planned. In August 1959 Lemass asked Tom Linehan, the director of the Central Statistics Office, whether April or May were suitable months for taking a census in view of the fact that migratory workers would be absent; Lemass suggested that it might be held on 1–2 January. This query suggests that the government wished to record the highest possible population, because many emigrants would have been in Ireland for Christmas and New Year. However, Tom Linehan favored the traditional census month of April, cautioning that a January census would show "a pronounced fall" in the numbers engaged in agriculture. Although Niall Blaney, the minister for Local Government, accepted Linehan's argument, he claimed that excluding migratory workers from the census "results in a preponderance of representation going to the eastern side of the country."[119] The constitution stipulated that the total number of deputies should not exceed one per 20,000 and that "so far as it is practicable" the ratio of deputies to population should be uniform throughout the country. A planned revision of constituencies in 1959 that would have given one deputy to 17,758 people in counties Donegal, Mayo, Kerry, and Galway, compared with one to 22,753 in Dublin city, was successfully challenged in the High Court. [120] As minister for Local Government, Blaney was responsible for redrawing constituency boundaries; he was also TD for Donegal Northeast, an area with a long tradition of seasonal migration.

The 1961 census revealed that the population had fallen to an all-time low of 2,818,341, and that the rate of decline was greater between 1956 and 1961 than between 1951 and 1956. Male emigrants outnumbered female by a ratio of almost six to four (58 percent to 42 percent). Every province reported a fall in population, as did every county except Dublin. The population increased in Dublin city and county, in Dun Laoghaire, and in many of the larger towns that were benefiting from industrial expansion. There are a number of puzzling features about the publication of the preliminary returns of the 1961 census. In 1956 and on previous occasions, the preliminary returns were published in June or July when the Dáil was in session, but in 1961 they did not appear until mid-August. Since 1936, the preliminary figures had been the subject of a feature article in the government publication, *Irish Trade Journal and Statistical Bulletin*. In 1956 the *Trade Journal* published a three-page article on the census, but the 1961 census did not even merit a brief mention. Every census report since 1841 contained an introductory essay that highlighted the major trends, but this was missing in 1961. The delay and the lack of commentary may have been caused by administrative difficulties within the Central Statistics Office, or they may reflect a wish to play down the bad news.

The news that the population had fallen to the lowest figure since independence, and that the rate of decline was greater than between 1951 and 1956, threatened to undermine the self-confidence that had been nurtured in recent years, and it gave another lease on life to the Irish Cassandras. References to "the vanishing Irish" were dusted off and recycled. According to the *Nationalist and Leinster Times,* "The Census proves that once more we are indeed the vanishing Irish and that hope for the country is low indeed unless the trend is stopped. The news of the census is the news of a national catastrophe in slow motion."[121]

Lemass and his ministers made the best of the difficult circumstances. In addition to contending with the census returns, a general election was imminent. During the adjournment debate in Dáil Éireann on 2 and 3 August Lemass indicated that the census would reveal that the fall in population "will not be less than 3%." He disclaimed any desire

> to minimise the seriousness of that situation. It will be a powerful additional stimulus to our economic progress when we can arrest that decline and get the population moving upward again. Because of the results, which have been achieved under the Programme of Economic Expansion we can now face that aim with some increase in confidence, some additional belief in our capacity to realise it. The reduction of the net emigration trend this year is substantial enough to be significant in relation to the prospect that our population is becoming stabilised. During the period of twelve months, which ended on May 31, emigration was 65% of the rate during the corresponding period, which ended in May, 1960, and the greater part of that fall took place in the first 5 months of this year. During that 12 months period the rate of emigration was 27% below the average annual figures for the past decade. We know that since the middle of 1959 the numbers occupied in all economic activities, including agriculture, have become stabilised following upon a long period of continuous decline.[122]

This speech, more than two weeks before the census results were published, set the tone for the government's response: the figures were bad, but conditions were improving; a stable population was in sight, but it was essential to continue the program of economic development. On 13 August, less than a week before the census returns were published, in what might be seen as a preemptive strike, the *Sunday Press* (which was controlled by the de Valera family and generally reflected the party line) carried a story with the headline, "Reduction." The article noted that unemployment had fallen to approximately 60,000 and the rate of emigration over the previous twelve months was almost 30 percent below the average for the previous ten years, but nevertheless, "the emigration problem still assumes serious proportions." The census returns would "highlight the need for maintaining and improving the efforts currently being made to redress the balance."[123] When the *Sunday Press* commented on the census two weeks later, it emphasized that emigration remained "our greatest social problem"; however, the annual rate was now 30,000, "'a figure,' said the minister for Finance, 'which is almost matched by the natural increase in population.'" The article ended: "The Programme of Economic Expansion is bearing fruit, it must go on."[124]

The *Sunday Press* was quoting a speech by James Ryan (minister for Finance) to his constituents in county Wexford, which was widely cited in local newspapers. Ryan claimed that the government was not surprised by the fall in population, and he placed the blame firmly on the economic slump during the coalition government's final year in office. The population decline was a reminder, he said, of the need to maintain economic progress. The economy had not yet achieved its full potential, and the country needed "to double its efforts."[125] Ryan claimed that "the Government believed in presenting the Irish people with all the facts—good and not so good—so that there would be the most widespread public understanding of the position." They had decided to take a census in "the present election year" to enable people to assess the merits of the government's policy. "Nobody forced the Government to take a Population Census this year. That was taken by our decision. Nobody could compel us to hurry up the publication of the provisional results."[126]

Despite the record low in the population and the record rate of net emigration between 1956 and 1961, the 1961 census attracted much more limited coverage than the 1956 census. An editorial in the

Roscommon Herald claimed that "the fact that the census returns have occasioned little surprise is, perhaps, the best indication there is for how much we have taken for granted the continued fall in population. . . . [T]here seems to be general acceptance too, that there is nothing that can be done about it."[127] Yet this was precisely the message that Lemass and his ministers were determined should not be drawn. They preferred to employ evidence of continuing emigration to reinforce two messages: industrial development offered the best hope of bringing an end to emigration, and the government must continue its program for economic development. The editorial in the *Sunday Press* noted that:

> The census shows that about four of our cities and about half of our towns increased in population between 1956 and 1961. The urban figures suggest the lines on which the emigration problem must be met. It has, for over 30 years, been the objective of those in power to set up industries in towns near to agricultural populations. These industries were and are intended to absorb the workers who leave the land.
>
> For generations, agriculture all over the world has employed fewer and fewer people. Especially has this been so in recent years, as farming became more and more mechanised. Therefore it becomes vital to our economy to establish more industrial capacity in our smaller towns. The census returns show the good such a policy has already accomplished. In the coming years the policy will have to be extended to the areas worst hit by emigration.[128]

This editorial indicates a major shift in government thinking, because it acknowledged that the numbers employed in agriculture were declining throughout the world and that this would happen in Ireland. Shortly after the census figures were published, Lemass made a speech to Muintir na Tíre Rural Week where he pointed out that "the special aspect of the situation in Ireland is that the movement from rural areas is often to urban centres outside the national territory." Migration from rural Ireland emphasized the urgency and importance of pressing ahead with industrial development; this was the way to stop emigration and increase population.[129]

The government's "spin" on the 1961 census results highlighted the fact that the population had increased in quite a number of towns and cities, and this was widely noted in the provincial press, though often in a negative tone. The *Dundalk Democrat* lamented that "despite all the talk of the flight of the rural people to the towns, this provisional report shows decreased urban populations, in an astonishingly large number of cases."[130] Dundalk was one of the towns to record a fall in population, an inevitable consequence of the closure of several of the town's traditional industries. *The Roscommon Herald* noted that several urban districts, especially Castlerea, had suffered a very sharp fall in population.[131] Under the headline, "What the Census Shows in Carlow, Kildare, Laois," the *Nationalist and Leinster Times* drew a clear connection between urban growth and industrial development:

> In Laois the general pattern is that the smaller centres, which have no industry of any worthwhile significance, have lost heavily. Stradbally is one of the worst-hit centres. Lack of opportunities for young people has forced many of them to leave the country. Our reporter has learned this week that a good percentage of the girls and women who leave get work in Dublin. Many of the young men go to England. . . . In Laois clubs of all types, especially in the sporting sphere, have been seriously depleted. Many stars in the football and hurling world have emigrated. . . . Once again the rural areas have suffered. The flight from the land continues at a rate of almost 1,213 a year. . . . The increase of 5.6% in Carlow is good news for the town. It means that emigration is on the wane and employment on the increase. Carlow boasts of many factories giving full-time and part-time employment. The future looks bright.[132]

The other major theme was the continuing need to transform the economy. A leading article in the *Irish Press* on 18 August noted that the census returns indicated Ireland had reached "the half-way mark" in the process of developing the economy.[133] Lemass outlined the way forward in the adjournment debate on 2–3 August 1961: membership in the European Economic Community; a second program for economic expansion when the original one ended in 1963; and discussions with Irish manufacturers with a view to introducing a free trade area for "six county products."[134] The emphasis was on "change and innovation in every sphere of national activity," a prospect that Lemass described as "stimulating and exciting." The main test of the policies introduced in the years ahead would be whether they succeeded in reducing emigration to a level well below the rate of natural increase; it was also essential to improve the standard of housing, health, social services, and general living conditions in order to make life in Ireland more attractive and counter the "pull of conditions abroad."[135]

Population and Partition

One of the most innovative aspects of Seán Lemass's career as taoiseach is the manner in which he linked Fianna Fáil's long-standing goal of ending partition with economic development and the need to persuade Ulster unionists that independence from Britain was not incompatible with economic success.[136] Although this marked a new direction for the antipartition strategy, the emphasis on economics was consistent with the traditional nationalist belief that hardheaded Ulster unionists were motivated by economic self-interest. In the early twentieth century, many Irish nationalists had deluded themselves into thinking that economic considerations would determine Ulster's response to home rule. Lemass also linked Ireland's application for membership in the EEC with ending partition, arguing that "in the context of membership of the European Economic Community, any economic argument for partition will disappear; north and south will have exactly the same problems and exactly the same opportunities within the wide European market. A united approach to these problems and opportunities would be far more effective and it is in my view the only course that makes sense."[137]

In a speech to a party gathering in May 1961, he spoke about "the present drive for economic development as the completion and justification of the fight for freedom. . . . We believe that there has fallen to the Irish people the responsibility of demonstrating, by our success in economic development that the people of a small nation like ours are always better served in freedom than in subjection."[138] He went on to note that "this economic effort is of special and immediate significance and importance in relation to our aim of reuniting the Irish people and ending partition. . . . We are determined to demonstrate that we can bring about a higher level of achievement and greater economic progress with freedom than could ever have been gained without it."[139] He invited the people of Northern Ireland to observe the contrasting economic conditions in Northern Ireland and the Irish Republic, "between their despondency and our optimism" and to share in a common effort at economic development.[140] In August 1961 the people of Northern Ireland duly observed the contrasting circumstances in the two Irelands, an exercise that did not favor independent Ireland. In an editorial on the day after the publication of the 1961 census the *Newsletter* stated that

> The comment that "partition has been an economic failure" has been put about since the projected entry of the U.K. and Eire into the Common Market, and has aroused Nationalist hopes of adding Northern Ireland to the Republic. That failure lies south of the border, not north, and this is proved by the provisional census figures for the Irish Republic published yesterday. In five years the population of the Republic is down 83,561 or 2.9% whereas the recent Northern Ireland census recorded a rise of 52,000 since the previous census ten years before. Population figures are a pretty fair guide to the economic stability of any territory. When things are good they tend to rise: when a fall is recorded something must be wrong. Something would have gone very wrong indeed in the Republic if it had not had the outlet of Great Britain for its net drain of 43,000 a year who sought emigration. On the figures now published, those who are raising fresh cries for a united Ireland may perhaps pause and think—not excepting the *"New Statesman"* which let itself go with great warmth on the subject just recently.[141]

The *Newsletter* suggested that the census results should persuade people in the Irish Republic to reconsider the merits of EEC membership. The *Belfast Telegraph* referred with disdain to a speech by Lemass (cited above) where he had suggested that the Northern Ireland government should follow the example of the Irish Republic if it wished to solve its unemployment problem.[142] The provincial press in Northern Ireland followed the story closely. *The Impartial Reporter,* published in Enniskillen, quoted letters to *The Irish Times,* suggesting that an iron curtain should be erected around Ireland to prevent emigration.[143] Under the headline "The Irish People: Streaming out of the Country," it claimed that "the Irish people streamed out of the country over a century ago to escape the famine and rackrent landlords. They are streaming out today because they are fed up with a country that gives only a pittance for life with no hope of improvement in one's status."[144] In common with other newspapers in Northern Ireland, the *Impartial Reporter* noted that the rate of population decline was greatest in the three Ulster counties in the Republic of Ireland.

The Northern Ireland coverage of the 1961 census was much more abrasive than in 1956, perhaps in reaction to Lemass's claims of economic success, but also because there was some truth in what he was saying. The economy of Northern Ireland was in crisis. The traditional industries of shipbuilding and textiles were in recession, and unemployment was rising. Net emigration from Northern Ireland increased in 1956 and 1957, in line with trends in the Republic, although the rate was much lower. By the early 1960s emigration was rising in Northern Ireland at a time when it was falling in the Republic. In 1961 and 1962 Northern Ireland and the Republic had identical rates of net emigration.[145]

EEC Membership and the Irish Economy

The implications of the 1961 census results and the future direction of Irish economic policy were threshed out during the general election campaign of September and early October 1961—the last election campaign without television.[146] The debate revealed growing differences between Fianna Fáil and Fine Gael, and to a lesser extent between Fianna Fáil and the Labour Party, over the future direction of economic policy. Lemass reiterated that industrial development, with factories scattered throughout provincial Ireland, offered the solution to emigration, and he outlined an economic strategy based on EEC membership, a second program for economic expansion, and moves toward freer trade. Throughout the campaign Fianna Fáil candidates, including senior party members such as Frank Aiken and Seán MacEntee, spoke at length about the challenge of preparing for membership.[147] The Labour Party was decidedly less enthusiastic about EEC membership because it posed a threat to jobs in protected industries, and it deferred a definite decision on membership until after the election.[148] Fine Gael gave a commitment to lead Ireland into the Common Market, but it continued to insist that agriculture should be the bedrock of Irish economic development; the party's election speeches are littered with statements such as "prosperity must come from the land."[149] Unlike Lemass, Fine Gael leader James Dillon's "thinking continued to be dominated by the centrality of agriculture in economic development, by his general scepticism about the viability of industrial growth, and by his old distrust of excessive state involvement in economic activities." Dillon and other Fine Gael TDs attacked the outgoing government for its neglect of rural Ireland. The party's election advertisement in the provincial press emphasized three issues: a united Ireland, the need to improve arable land and farming, and restoring the Irish language.[150]

The 1961 election campaign attracted limited press coverage, because many other stories were competing for attention: the crisis over Berlin, events in the Congo—the secession of Katanga, the death of Dag Hammarskjöld—and a fatal air crash at Shannon. Nevertheless, some local newspapers appear to have had very clear views about the electoral priorities. In an editorial on 2 September, before the election was called, headed "A Time to Act," the *Nationalist* noted: "The returns of the Census are bound to be an issue in the general election. A country whose population is falling by 43,000 a year is fundamentally in decline. People are the dynamics of a nation, as they dwindle, so must everything else decline. . . . For all the discussion on emigration we are still unable to cure it. . . . Mr. Lemass is convinced that emigration is a social phenomenon with only a slight economic cause. His diagnosis is only half true. Obviously many leave Ireland for social reasons. But when we ask ourselves why, we must inevitably return to the contraction of the economy and the lack of opportunity."[151] Another editorial in the same paper some weeks later examined the election manifestos of all the opposition parties and concluded that only Clann na Poblachta offered policies to solve emigration.[152] This suggests that Fianna Fáil was correct in its decision to emphasize economics. An editorial in *The Kerryman* on 28 October 1961, shortly after Lemass was returned to office with a minority government, commented on Fine Gael's proposals for a much improved health services, which together with improved access to education had been a major element of the party's election campaign. "We consider a health services on the magnitude that Fine Gael envisages should come into operation only when the economy of the country is buoyant enough to support it. We are far from that happy state. Fine Gael, we suggest would do better if it directed its thinkers and planners to the making of opportunities that would provide more work on the land and in industry for the many hands that are now unemployed and under-employed. Emigration and employment should be foremost in the minds of politicians who should make these problems their immediate and urgent concern."[153]

A trawl through the national and local newspapers suggests that the 1961 census was soon consigned to history. Lemass's government overcame a potential pitfall by using it as an occasion to reaffirm the need for economic development, a strategy that directed attention toward the future rather than the past.

6

1961–1971

"A Worthy Homeland for the Irish People"?

Many Irish people remember the 1960s as "the best of decades."[1] Economic growth brought higher living standards—new cars, better-equipped homes, even foreign holidays. Couples married in their early and mid-twenties rather than their late twenties and early thirties; there was a sharp rise in the number of marriages, and during the second half of the decade net emigration was running at just over 10,000, one-fifth of the level of the mid-1950s. The 1966 census recorded the first significant population increase since independence, giving rise to hopes that a century of population decline had ended. In 1971 the population reached 2,978,248—6,256 higher than in 1926.

The 1960s brought a new optimism about the Irish economy; Ireland's modest economic growth even became a matter of national pride. A cover story in *Time* magazine on 12 July 1963, shortly after American President John F. Kennedy's triumphal visit to the home of his ancestors, was headed "New Spirit in the Ould Sod," and the article was illustrated with photographs of modern factories and traffic jams on Dublin streets.[2] Although the target of a 50 percent rise in national income between 1960 and 1970 was not reached, there was a "sense of national economic purpose" that had not been evident in the past.[3]

There was also a greater willingness to embrace modernity and to accept change. In the past the dominant Irish response had been to oppose change—to rail against it, and to try and prevent it—while expressing confidence that a largely unmodernized agriculture and a protected industrial sector could provide a basis for ending emigration. But after 1958, Irish economic policies set out to adapt to the economic forces rather than resist them. The *Second Program for Economic Expansion,* introduced in 1963, assumed that industrial development would drive economic growth, and it predicted a fall in the numbers engaged in agriculture—the first official document to make such an admission.

When Seán Lemass launched the report of the Limerick Rural Survey in November 1964, he made the point that "change is the law of life and while we may not always regard the course of change as beneficial or desirable, it is rarely practical to stop it. Rather must our purpose be to try and direct it into avenues which seem likely to lead to the development of the kind of society we wish in Ireland."[4]

In practice, turning the economy around proved to be a slow and difficult process, and not everybody accepted that change was inevitable, but government ministers were less likely to be accused than in the past of having "acted the ostrich" on matters such as farming in the west of Ireland.[5] Whereas social and economic development had previously been viewed as a threat to key institutions like the Irish family and the family farm, it now appeared to offer a possible solution to chronic social problems such as emigration and lack of marriages. There was a greater, but by no means universal, acceptance that the numbers employed in farming would decline, and that "dissatisfaction with our economic programmes—and its outward manifestation, emigration—will remain," unless the standard of living approximated to that in Britain and western Europe.[6] There was also a greater willingness to acknowledge that rural depopulation was not unique to Ireland. Reverend Jeremiah Newman, editor and coauthor of the *Limerick Rural Survey,* noted that "as the Report on Emigration sees things, it would seem that the problem of rural depopulation is especially peculiar to Ireland"; he pointed out that this was not so.[7] In 1967 statistician M. D. McCarthy highlighted the fact that if the postfamine exodus was excluded, emigration from Ireland fitted into the general European pattern of urbanization.[8] This subtle reinterpretation of Ireland's social and demographic history is symptomatic of a society that was adopting a more positive attitude toward the outside world.

But there was also an emerging sense of two Irelands: a dynamic, urban Ireland, with thriving industries and service jobs located in modern office buildings, whose employees could look forward to regular increases in wages and salaries, and an agricultural, rural Ireland, condemned to a lower standard of living and a declining population. During the 1950s economic stagnation and population decline were national rather than regional phenomena. Dublin was the only county whose population was greater in 1961 than in 1951. Between 1961 and 1966 the population fell in fourteen counties, but by 1971 the decline was confined to the north and the west—every Connacht county except Galway plus counties Cavan, Donegal, Longford, and Kerry (the population of Kerry fell by only thirteen). Prospects for agriculture remained uncertain until Ireland's admission to the EEC was confirmed in December 1969.[9] Agricultural difficulties were most acute on the smaller farms of Connacht and Ulster, areas with few industrial or service jobs and a weak network of towns and cities. Between 1956 and 1961, when the population fell to a postfamine low, half of all towns recorded a rise in population. The 1966 census indicated that the growth in the urban population was correlated with size: towns with a population of 5,000–10,000 grew by 5.6 percent, compared with 4 percent for towns with a population of 1,500–3,000 and 2.2 percent for villages with a population of 200–500.

Helena Sheehan cites two 1960s television plays in Irish—Oileán Tearmainn and An Bullaí—that "gave forceful expression to the seething anger and resentment of country people towards their urbanised countrymen."[10] Gibes about mohair-suited politicians or executives[11] highlighted the widening gap between the modern urban Ireland and rural Ireland. The belief that farmers and western counties were not sharing in the economic prosperity gave rise to new protest movements. In the autumn of 1966 Ireland's largest farming organization, the National Farmers' Association, marched on Dublin and followed this with a sit-in on the steps of Government Buildings. The 1960s also brought Gluaiseacht Chearta Sibhialta na Ghaeltachta (the Gaeltacht Civil Rights Movement), a movement demanding civil rights for Achill, and a Committee for the Defence of the West.[12] The Mayo-born journalist John Healy, a columnist with *The Irish Times* and the *Western People*, claimed that there was an air of helplessness in the west of Ireland over what was happening to the local economy,[13] but I would dispute this. Protests by farmers, Gaeltacht residents, or the "Save the West" campaign reflected a desire to become part of modern Ireland, albeit on their own terms. Farmers sought annual income increases, just like wage and salary earners, bandying statistics for gross national product and growth rates in a manner that would have been unthinkable ten years earlier.[14] The protest marches, sit-ins, and references to civil rights indicate that these interest groups had fully embraced the culture of the 1960s.

One of most obvious characteristics of the earlier debate concerning emigration, late marriages, or rural depopulation is the absence of firm evidence on many of these topics as well as the greater weight that was given to opinion and sentiment, even where evidence could have been found without much difficulty. Sentiment and emotion by no means disappeared from the discussion; however, the 1960s brought a torrent of official reports and scientific studies, in marked contrast with their absence in the past. Many were produced by official bodies that were established to conduct research and provide advice on a range of socioeconomic topics. These organizations were also used to create a climate in favor of change among businessmen, trade unionists, and the wider community. Although the reports drawn up by bodies such as the National Industrial and Economic Council (NIEC) can be criticized for their bland tone, the range of issues that they confront is commendable, and the belief that economic problems should be analyzed and solutions advanced contrasts with the passive fatalism of earlier decades.[15] Reports were often produced in months, rather than years, and up to at least the mid-1960s, it seems that serious efforts were generally made to implement them. This contrasts with the past, when long delays characterized the publication of the *Report of the Commission on Emigration* and the *Report of the Commission on Youth Unemployment* and when any identifiable outcome from their work was absent.[16] The 1960s probably marked the peak in Ireland's faith in the ability of economics and economists to deliver a better standard of living; the much greater success of the late 1990s came at a time when economists and their predictions were viewed with greater skepticism. There was also a significant expansion in sociological research. Patrick McNabb, who carried out the social investigation for the Limerick Rural Study, was first sent to the department of rural sociology at Wageningen (Netherlands) for postgraduate training because of the lack of expertise in Ireland at this time.[17] By the end of the decade, two state-funded research agencies, an Foras Talúntais and the Economic and Social Research Institute, were investigating a range of contemporary issues.[18] However, traditional reticence still applied with regard to fertility: no official report examined what was happening to the birthrate.

Economic Growth: Emigration and Population

The *Programme for Economic Expansion* covering the years 1958–63 contained only one statistical target—an annual growth rate of 2 percent, whereas its successor, the *Second Programme for Economic Expansion (1964–70)*, set detailed targets for most sectors of the economy in a manner worthy of a Stalinist plan. The most important target was to achieve the Organization for Economic Cooperation and Development (OECD) goal of a 50 percent growth in real incomes between 1960 and 1970 for all member states, which would require an annual growth rate of 4.4 percent for the years 1963–70. The Second Program estimated that by 1970, employment would have increased by a figure in the range 26,000–110,000, with annual net emigration for the decade in the range 15,400–23,700. This was the first time that an Irish government set realistic estimates for emigration.[19] By 1968 it was becoming apparent that the growth rate would fall short of the target, and the Second Program was abandoned in favor of a *Third Programme for Economic and Social Development,* covering the years 1969–72. The Third Program projected that employment would rise by 16,000 between 1969 and 1972, with annual emigration averaging 12,000–13,000. It also estimated that the population would be in excess of 3 million by 1972.[20]

By 1969 net emigration was in the region of 5,000—which was commonly regarded as equivalent to "voluntary" emigrants. But net emigration of 5,000 masked a much larger annual outflow, and throughout the 1960s thousands of men and women continued to emigrate because Ireland—or at least their local neighborhood—was incapable of offering them jobs that met their aspirations. The 1967 study by John Jackson of the small west Cork town of Skibbereen and Damien Hannan's study of the migration intentions of Cavan teenagers show that the motives prompting emigration were not dramatically different from earlier decades. Jackson claimed that "a simple economic pull-push model is inadequate to explain the complex variety of factors which enter into decisions to emigrate." He went on to state that, "while it was recognised that [these] economic factors were fundamental to the life of the community the main emphasis of the study was to be placed on sociological characteristics."[21] Yet when he examined the reasons why people emigrated, 34.4 percent were seeking better jobs and 41.6 percent were emigrating because of the lack of jobs.[22] Economic motives also predominated in Hannan's study. Although he concluded that migration, whether within Ireland or abroad, was "primarily due to the frustration of certain aspirations in the community of origin," the aspirations that were commonly frustrated related to employment.[23] Hannan refuted many popular stereotypes regarding emigrants: "Very few had migrated on impulse or without 'serious cause'"; the majority of his respondents would have preferred to remain at home; the majority of those with primary or vocational schooling had tried to find work locally before they left; very few migrated without having arranged transport, accommodation, and jobs.[24] Jackson and Hannan highlighted the importance of informal networks of family or friends in assisting, and perhaps even promoting, emigration, especially for those with limited education.[25]

The 1971 census recorded the population at 2,978,248, which was 94,246 higher than in 1961. More people returned to Ireland in 1971 than emigrated, beginning a period of sustained net immigration.[26] The reversal of emigration in the early 1970s is rather surprising, because the growth in employment during the 1960s fell seriously short of the targets set by the Second and the Third Programs. By 1971 there were only 2,300 more people at work than in 1961 and 40,000 fewer than in 1951. During the 1960s the additional jobs in services and industry just about compensated for the jobs lost in agriculture. The enormous challenge of providing work for all the Irish citizens was spelled out in the 1967 NIEC Report, *Full Employment,* an exercise that was designed to bring about "a fuller appreciation of what needs to be done to achieve full employment in this country" as well as a rising standard of living. The NIEC determined that "unless past trends are radically changed, full employment is unlikely to be achieved in the foreseeable future."[27] To achieve full employment by 1981, it would be necessary to create 135,000 additional jobs over a fifteen-year period, which would entail an annual growth rate of approximately 5.5 percent, almost double the existing rate, and investment on the order of 27 percent of gross national product. The 1981 population was projected to be 3.3 million (18 percent higher than in 1966), with annual net emigration of 5,000—again, a rate that was assumed to be equivalent to "voluntary emigration."[28] The *Full Employment* Report and the 1971 employment statistics indicated that while the 1960s marked an end to more than a century of emigration and population decline, the challenge of providing work and a prosperous lifestyle for those who had returned to Ireland or chose to remain there had not been surmounted.

Fertility and Family Size: The 1960s Revolution

The planners who drew up the Second Program went to considerable efforts to make detailed projections for the future of the woollen and worsted industry as well as other industries, but they failed to consider the impact of a rising marriage rate on the number of women at work, or the probable fall in the number of teenagers in the workforce because of plans to extend access to postprimary schooling.[29]

Their methodology, therefore, assumed that there would be no change by age or gender in the composition of the labor force during the 1960s.[30] In December 1965 the director of the Central Statistics Office, M. D. McCarthy, described the manpower forecasts in the Second Program as "perhaps the least valid of the forecasts made."[31] The 1967 *Report on Full Employment* assumed that the proportion of adult men in the workforce would decline in the period up to the mid-1980s, because of increased opportunities for education and earlier retirement of elderly farmers, and that the proportion of women in the workforce would remain unchanged. According to the report, the increasing number of married women in paid employment would equal the reduction in female participation because of earlier marriages, a higher marriage rate, and the extension of post-primary schooling, but the planners gave no rationale for this suspiciously convenient assumption.[32] *Third Programme Economic and Social Development, 1969–72* also fudged the issue, simply noting that "it cannot be taken for granted, therefore, that the present trends will continue."[33] The most considered projections were given in the OECD report *Investment in Education*, which began by noting that "demographic forecasting is at best hazardous." Their projections for future school enrollment were based on age-specific fertility data for 1961–63; however, the report noted that the estimate of future births might be conservative.[34]

By the mid-1960s it was evident that a revolution was underway in Irish marriage and fertility, although no official document, published or unpublished, appears to have adverted to this. In 1968 the Economic Research Institute published a paper by Brendan Walsh showing that Ireland's "century-and-a-half-old method of population control," which was based on a low rate of marriage and high marital fertility was breaking down.[35] From 1963 there was a steady rise in the number of marriages, and a fall in the age of first marriage. In 1972 Walsh showed that the post-1963 marriage boom did not result in a corresponding rise in the birthrate; indeed the number of births fell during the mid-1960s despite a rise in the number of marriages. The fertility pattern among couples who married after 1960 was clearly very different from the past. Beginning in Dublin, the downward trend in fertility soon spread throughout Ireland. By

1970, almost half of all births (48.6 percent) were first or second babies compared with 39.4 percent in 1958, and the percentage of fifth
or higher-order births fell from 22 to 15 percent. Walsh claimed that
the marriage boom of 1963–65 could be explained by the upturn in
the economy, but the further rise in marriages in the years 1967–69
represented a departure from established patterns; he suggested that
it might have been a response to the decline in marital fertility.[36]

What brought about the change? During the 1960s couples not
only married at an earlier age, but there was also less of an age gap
between husbands and wives, which might have resulted in more
companionate marriages and more negotiation over intimate matters such as family size. Increasing affluence—the nightmare of
many Catholic clergy—may well have been a factor, as couples strove
to buy a car, and equip a new semidetached house with the trappings
of modern living. The increasing emphasis on education as the way
to economic success and security may also have concentrated parental minds on how many children they could provide for.

Above all, contraception, and the difficulties presented by large
families, were being openly discussed in Ireland for the first time,
even by the Catholic church. In 1963 the Jesuit periodical *Studies*
published an article by Reverend Clement Mertens, a leading Belgian
theologian, in which he stated that "birth regulation is one of the
most urgent questions facing the Church today," and he argued that
"there must be boldness to preach a planned parenthood."[37] The
winter 1964 edition of the same journal carried an article on "The
Pill," which reviewed the debate "in the Catholic world."[38] *Studies*
was not read by the average man and woman, but it did reach many
of the Catholic clergy, and the article could be seen as a straw in the
wind. More to the point, a new Irish women's magazine, *Women's
Way,* began to include occasional articles about contraception.[39] In
1966 the Irish-born journalist Peter Lennon noted that "in a very
short time—a matter of less than four years—the ordinary Irish
Catholic without apparent difficulty or distress, has come to accept
the fact that contraception—a practice which he had always been led
to believe was criminal—is, if not yet officially acceptable, at least a
possible solution to a human dilemma."[40]

The contraceptive pill has generally been credited with bringing
about a revolution in Irish fertility. The pill successfully evaded the

1930s prohibition on the sale, importation, and distribution of contraceptives by being classified as a cycle regulator, and until Pope Paul VI issued the 1968 encyclical *Humanae Vitae,* it was widely expected that it would be permitted by the Catholic church. The pill became available at a time when Irish people were becoming more receptive to limiting the size of their families. In 1968 Garret Fitz-Gerald claimed that "the whole of this change may not have been brought about by the pill—there may have been, for example, more widespread use of the rhythm method—but the pill must have played a very large part in this development."[41] The publication of *Humanae Vitae* made the issues of contraception controversial, but it did not end the debate, nor did it reverse the practice. Although the birthrate rose after 1968, reversing the decline of the previous four years, Walsh argues convincingly that the rise was not as a consequence of *Humanae Vitae* but of the soaring marriage rate.[42]

In 1968 FitzGerald emphasized that if the rise in the marriage rate had not been accompanied by falling fertility, the economy would have to expand at an average annual rate of 8–9 percent in order to provide sufficient jobs in the 1990s for all the additional babies being born; the only alternative would be "a massive increase in emigration." Because Irish fertility was declining, he hoped that it would be possible for the economy to provide sufficient jobs for the next generation.[43] Walsh was less optimistic. In his 1968 paper he concluded that unless marital fertility fell as the marriage rate continued to climb, Ireland would achieve a rate of natural increase higher than all countries in the world except a small number of countries in Asia and Central America, and this would make it extremely difficult to provide sufficient jobs. He predicted that emigration would continue.[44] Four years later he cautioned that despite the recent decline in fertility, the Irish population was rising at a much more rapid rate than any other European country, and it was unclear whether the gap would be reduced in the near future. It wasn't.[45]

Agriculture and Rural Ireland

There was very little discussion throughout the 1960s about the implications of the rising population or the increase in the number of births, although these were issues that would have a significant impact on Irish society, both in the short run and in later decades. However, the future of rural and agricultural Ireland was debated at considerable length; indeed no other aspect of socioeconomic change attracted as much attention, an indication yet again that in any discussion of Irish population, rural Ireland continued to occupy center stage.

Once Lemass's government had acknowledged that the numbers in agriculture were destined to fall, it became necessary to revise long-standing commitments regarding agriculture and rural Ireland, otherwise Fianna Fáil would be accused of abandoning the farmers. The *Second Programme for Economic Expansion* subtly revised the traditional goal, by giving a commitment to retain the maximum number of people in agriculture "consistent with social and economic progress," and to create sufficient jobs in tourism and industry to maintain the rural population.[46] Statements by government ministers relating to agriculture referred to increased output, productivity, and farm incomes as well as the need to ensure that farm households have a standard of living comparable to wage and salary earners and not to the total numbers in farming.[47]

There were several good reasons why farm incomes should be kept at least in line with those of the rest of the community. The *Second Programme for Economic Expansion* assumed that employment in agriculture would fall by almost one-quarter between 1960 and 1970, from 390,000 to 303,000 (this turned out to be an underestimate).[48] Some civil servants argued that it was essential to prevent too rapid a decline in farm employment because there was no confidence that there would be sufficient jobs available for former farm workers. In 1962 an official in the Department of Finance remarked that farmers' attitudes "will be fortified by Government policy declarations that the farmers, as well as other sections of the community, should share equitably in increases in the national income." Unless agricultural incomes kept pace with other workers, there would be a rise in the numbers leaving agriculture, and this was something that the government wished to avoid until more jobs became available in industry and services. Any further increase in the numbers leaving agriculture would "be represented as reflecting a cynical attitude by the Government to agriculture." This official believed that it would be in the public interest to improve farm incomes.[49] Political considerations were also important. James Dillon, the leader of Fine Gael, continued to believe that agriculture was the key to the Irish economy,[50] and he drew comparisons between the generous grants and tax concessions for industry and the alleged lack of similar largesse for agriculture.[51] It was important, then, that Fianna Fáil avoid the charge that it was neglecting farming in favor of an industrial and urban Ireland.

In the early 1960s it was widely anticipated that EEC membership would provide the solution to low farm incomes and the needs of Irish agriculture, but this prospect vanished in January 1963 when French president Charles de Gaulle vetoed Britain's application for membership, effectively putting the Irish application on hold. The 1965 Anglo-Irish Trade Agreement, which Lemass secured in the teeth of British indifference, was a second-best effort to provide a secure market for Irish farm produce, even at the cost of factory closures and job losses in some sectors of Irish industry. But the outcome proved less than satisfactory, even for farmers, because during the late 1960s Britain imposed successive restrictions on Irish agricultural imports.[52] Given these difficulties, it is not surprising that farm output and employment failed to meet the targets set in the Second and Third Programs. Nevertheless, by 1968 per capita real incomes were one-third higher than in 1960, although a substantial part of the increase reflected a 17 percent fall in the number of family farm members.[53] Higher prices, mainly because of government price supports, were likewise important. By 1970 price subsidies accounted for almost half of the estimate for the Department of Agriculture, and the agricultural estimate was now larger than any other department. The greatest share of price subsidies went to milk. Dairy farming was increasingly seen as offering the best hope of saving the family farm; it provided a reliable return on small and medium holdings, and farmers who sent milk to the creamery received regular monthly checks, giving them the closest approximation to the security of waged or salaried employment (further evidence that the mores of a modern urban economy were infiltrating rural Ireland).[54]

The moral argument for boosting farm incomes was enormously strengthened by Pope John XXIII's 1961 encyclical, *Mater et Magistra*.

Published seventy years after Leo XIII's encyclical *Rerum Novarum,*
which was a major statement of church teaching on social problems
at the end of the nineteenth century, *Mater et Magistra* provided an
updated version for the 1960s. The section that attracted the greatest
interest in Ireland was headed "The Depressed State of Agriculture,"
which discussed the large-scale migration from farms to cities and
the fact that agriculture had become "a depressed occupation." Paragraph 265 claimed that nearly every country faced the fundamental
problem of the difference in productivity between agriculture and
industry and the need to ensure that agricultural living standards approximated as closely as possible those in industry.[55] *Mater et Magistra* helped to make people aware that rural depopulation was not
unique to Ireland. Lemass quoted the encyclical at some length during a speech to the Muintir na Tíre Rural Week in August 1961. His
biographer, John Horgan, claims that Lemass "instructed his ministers to keep a copy . . . on their desks for guidance." Farm leaders
commonly cited *Mater et Magistra* in support of their demands for
additional state funding. In 1962 the National Farmers' Association
received financial support from the Department of Agriculture to attend a conference in Rome on the encyclical.[56]

Relative living standards between country and town were not
simply a matter of income. *Mater et Magistra* emphasized the importance of running water, adequate transport, and decent housing in
rural communities. The Limerick Rural Survey showed that most
villages lacked amenities such as shops, medical services, and piped
water and sewerage; however, they were better provided with clubs
and social organizations.[57] There were approximately fifty clubs and
societies in Skibbereen, although half the town population, and
three-quarters of those living in the countryside, were not involved
in the formal social life of the town.[58] There was very little said during the 1960s about "the drabness of rural life" or the need for parish
halls. Lack of running water, sewerage, and postprimary schooling,
however, were emerging as critical issues. Piped water was beginning
to reach many rural villages by the early 1960s,[59] and the numerous
stories about water schemes in provincial newspapers suggest that it
ranked with factories and postprimary schools among the top priorities for rural Ireland.[60]

The process of installing running water and bathrooms in farmhouses and isolated rural houses was slow. The Irish Country-women's Association campaigned vigorously on this issue with the support and approval of the Department of Local Government, and one of the most popular Irish television programs, *The Riordans* (a fictional account of life in a farming community) also took up this cause. But part of the cost of running water schemes was met from local taxation, and the male-dominated farming organizations were more concerned about rising taxes than about clean water.[61] This was regrettable. Apart from the obvious health benefits of proper sanitary services, a pilot study of county Galway by Colin Buchanan and Partners showed that rural areas with piped water and sewerage were more likely to retain their population, whereas access to shops, doctors, or social facilities were not significant variables.[62] Government subsidies or their absence appear to have been a key factor in bringing sanitary services to rural Ireland. A survey carried out in west Cork in 1960–61, where only 3 percent of farmers had bathrooms and toilets, though 14 percent had piped water, showed that most farmers who planned to install water in the near future did not intend to take it "past the kitchen sink"; they claimed that they could not afford to do so.[63]

The 1960s brought important changes in rural lives: more cars (though they were still driven by men rather than by women), television, and earlier marriages. Family farm income rose by 52 percent between 1960 and 1968, and income per head increased by 82 percent in current prices. Real incomes grew by one-third.[64] Yet this failed to prevent what Damien Hannan has described as "a massive down-grading of farming as an occupation," both within the wider society and among farmers' children and their parents.[65] Ironically, as farming became less attractive, it became easier for farmers to marry. When McNabb carried out the Limerick Rural Survey, he commented that migration among farmers was probably too low, which aggravated what he described as "bad marriage patterns."[66] The growing willingness of farmers' sons and daughters to leave home, with the blessing of their parents, cleared the way for the remaining son or daughter to marry. The west Cork survey revealed an exceptionally high proportion of farmers who had inherited land before the age of thirty-five, but in practically all cases the heir was a younger son or the only son; the eldest son(s) had left home and other family members had been provided for.[67]

Saving the West

In 1961 Lemass told James Ryan, the minister for Finance, that "in my view the main, if not the only question arising in national economic policy to which we have not yet found a satisfactory answer, is how to deal with the problem of the small (mainly western) farms, and to ensure reasonable standards of income for those who live on them."[68] In April 1961 he announced that he was appointing a committee to examine the prospects for improving living standards on small western farms. In this speech he remarked on the importance of piped water, the need to improve rural housing, and to develop off-farm employment in the countryside and the smaller towns. He also broached the most difficult issue:

> Can the typical Irish small farm with less than good land be made a viable economic unit, by a 1961 definition of that term? It has always been our policy—it is indeed a directive principle of social policy prescribed in the Constitution—to seek to establish as many families as possible in economic security on the land. But the meaning of the term "economic security" changes with the general conditions prevailing in the nation. It cannot mean a bare subsistence level. That is no longer acceptable. It must mean economic security comparable with that which can be gained in other activities, and, as general living standards rise, the standard on the small farms must be capable of rising with them, or this small farm problem will always be with us. This question is if this is possible, and if so, how? If the small farm cannot be made an economic unit in that sense, by bringing about changes in its production pattern and methods, then, notwithstanding the tenacity with which Irish people hold on to the ownership of land, we may expect a trend towards amalgamation into larger holdings, and few families living on the land. We can see something like that happening in other countries. The small farms have however, been such a typical feature of the Irish scene, and such strongholds of the Irish traditions which we value most highly that I do not think that we should accept this change as inevitable until we have examined all other possibilities very thoroughly.[69]

The committee of senior civil servants highlighted a number of factors that accounted for the backward economy in the west of Ireland: young people were reluctant to remain in the area when they could achieve a higher living standard elsewhere; there were few jobs available outside farming, and farm incomes were extremely low because farms were small. One-quarter of farms in Connacht and Ulster had fewer than fifteen acres, but the traditional small farm enterprises of pigs and poultry were no longer profitable, and the gap in output and productivity between farmers in western areas and the national average was widening. Many small farmers in western counties did little more than graze a few store cattle, and the miniscule income that this produced condemned them to a life of poverty. The committee was emphatic that emigration did not solve these problems. Land vacated by emigrants did not pass to expanding farmers; it remained in family ownership and was often leased as conacre for rough grazing. Emigration sapped community initiative. They recommended that development be promoted on multiple fronts—agriculture, tourism, rural industries, fishing, and forestry—and that measures be taken to improve educational services and keep women in rural Ireland.[70]

Their most controversial recommendations concerned land distribution: they recommended that the Land Commission be given the power to acquire land that had been derelict or abandoned for five years; that elderly farmers be encouraged to transfer their land to the Land Commission while retaining their home and their old age pension; that large western farmers be given loans to enable them to move to other parts of Ireland, freeing up land for redistribution; and that the minimum size of holdings created by the Land Commission be raised.[71] In August 1962 Lemass informed the Muintir na Tíre Rural Week that in future, government policy would be based on a minimum size family farm of forty to forty-five acres of good land, which was substantially higher than the average-sized holding in Connacht or Ulster.[72]

This was a very contentious decision; some people regarded it as tantamount to recommending the extinction of the small family farm. Muintir na Tíre counseled "slow and careful action" before embarking on a policy of consolidating small farms, noting that "economics alone does not envisage all aspects of the question. The sociologist and the politician must ask what the total results of such land

reform will be." If "a ruthless implementation" of a policy of creating holdings of forty to forty-five acres led to a drop of one-third in
the farming population "it is hard to see how the politicians any
more than society could be happy. . . . For any administrator to lay a
native Irish Government open to being labelled 'confiscator' or 'ex-
terminator' would be to pay a price which, by its undermining of
confidence in the Government would make the game far from being
worth the candle."[73]

E. A. Attwood, an economist with An Foras Talúntais dismissed
such arguments, suggesting that "the widespread national desire for
a strong rural life could much more adequately be realized if the land
policy of our country is deliberately orientated towards the creation
of farming units viable in relation to a continuing rise in the acceptable standards of living."[74] But Attwood was an economist, a group
that Dr. Lucey, the bishop of Cork, bracketed with industrialists and
"the lineal descendants of the old landlord class" as responsible for
creating "an atmosphere hostile to the small farmer. . . . They keep on
saying that small farming is uneconomic, inefficient and of its very
nature on the way out." [75]

Responsibility for implementing the proposed changes in land
policy rested with the minister for Lands, Mayo TD Michael Moran.
Although he has been described as "belonging to the old school of
agrarian radicals" who "sought to keep alive de Valera's vision of a
traditional peasant society,"[76] Moran appears to have accepted that
creating larger and therefore fewer farms was essential in order to
preserve family farms.[77] A land bill that raised the minimum size for
Land Commission holdings and contained watered-down versions
of other recommendations from the interdepartmental committee
was introduced in July 1963 and became law in 1965.[78]

Moran rejected any suggestion that the proposed bill was designed to bring about the depopulation of the west of Ireland:

> This idea is so very far removed from what we really have in mind that
> it must be repudiated. If we pension off an old bachelor or an unfor-
> tunate cripple or if we pay off some smallholder who has taken up
> permanent employment in Britain we are not engaged in actively re-
> ducing the farming population; we are merely rationalising the posi-
> tion and making it possible for the younger and more active element

of this community to prosper. Any work done in this field is so easily misrepresented that I feel we must be much on guard against any group of people who raise the "depopulation" argument. The fact is that when the bachelor decides not to marry or when the emigrant brings his wife and family over to England the vital move towards "depopulation" is taken—let it be clear to all that in the first instances it is taken by the people themselves.[79]

Resistance to this land bill joined forces with the strong campaign that was already underway throughout the west against the purchase of land by foreigners.[80] Critics suggested that the government was tolerating mass purchases of land by foreigners—or aliens, as they were generally described—while planning to take land away from emigrants or negligent elderly farmers. Although Moran estimated that nonnationals were buying no more than 5,000–6,000 acres in any year, and though he reassured Dáil Éireann that an improved land register meant that "the Land Commission are aware of every square foot of land sold to anybody not an Irish national no matter for what purpose,"[81] these claims persisted.

The most direct challenge to the government's policy came in a 1963 public meeting in Charlestown, county Mayo, which was addressed by Reverend James McDyer, who was already well-known for his work in establishing a vegetable-growing co-operative in Glencolumbkille, county Donegal.[82] The co-operative had been formed with the assistance of General M. J. Costello, managing-director of the state-owned Irish Sugar Company, to supply a subsidiary of the Irish Sugar Company, Erin Foods, which processed dried vegetables.[83] At the Charlestown meeting, Dr. Fergus, the bishop of Achonry, demanded that the government provide grants to enable a network of vegetable-growing co-operatives to be established throughout the west of Ireland. He described this as "an enlightened agricultural policy," an alternative to the government plan to increase farm size, which he decried as "based on the faulty assumption that the mere acreage of a holding is the sole test of economic sufficiency. It also leaves out of account the human factor. There is no guarantee whatsoever that men possessed of holdings of forty acres or more will be more conscious of their social responsibilities than they are at present."[84]

The bishop of Cork, Dr. Cornelius Lucey, had called on small farmers to organize in defence of their way of life.[85] When they failed to do so, it appears that the Catholic church undertook the task on their behalf.[86] *The Irish Times* journalist John Healy, a native of Charlestown, later claimed that their action was prompted by seeing "fewer marriages and fewer christenings, and a growing surplus of rural school benches."[87] Charlestown soon became synonymous with the decline of the west. The support of John Healy, who had an extremely close relationship with Lemass and other members of his government, was important. So, too, was the involvement of the hierarchy. The authority of the Catholic church had not yet been seriously challenged, and the campaign benefited from the popularity of Pope John XXIII and his interest in rural society. Lemass treated the Charlestown group with considerable deference; in the summer of 1963 he listened to their proposal for pilot areas throughout the west, modeled on Father McDyer's efforts in Glencolumbkille, and he asked the committee of civil servants to consider this option.[88] The committee duly met the Charlestown group and they visited Glencolumbkille, but relations remained frigid. The Charlestown group dismissed the interdepartmental committee as "the group of back-room boys," whereas they described themselves as a "bunch of ordinary men."[89] Yet the group that met the interdepartmental committee consisted of four priests and twelve laymen—all townsmen, whose experience of life on a small western farm was, at best, secondhand. As such they can be regarded as the successors of earlier groups such as the Council of National Action. Varley and Curtin have rightly questioned whether the "Save the West" group could claim to be popular or "participative," given that it depended heavily on the Catholic church for its existence.[90]

The second report of the interdepartmental committee, which dealt specifically with pilot areas,[91] was no more palatable to the Charlestown group than the first. Although the committee recommended establishing pilot areas, they were determined that these would be selected by the Central Development Committee—a committee of senior civil servants and county managers—whereas the Charlestown group wanted the selection to be on the basis of "local initiative," with voluntary bodies rather than public servants responsible for overseeing the program.[92] When these demands were rejected, they issued a statement dissociating themselves from the pilot areas scheme.[93] The western bishops came out with a strong statement of support for Canon McDyer and his team:

> The people of the small western farms are in a special way representative of the nation inasmuch as they have clung longer than people in other parts of the country to the traditions which are characteristic of the Irish way of life and of Irish culture including the native language. Even if this can be attributed in large part to an accident of history, it is nevertheless a fact. Moreover, their homes have always been nurseries of religious vocations, thus contributing to the building up of Ireland's spiritual empire. We believe it would be an irreparable loss to the nation and to the Church if they were left to thin themselves out under the merciless operation of economic laws.
>
> We refer in particular to the group known as the Charlestown Committee, which is close to the people and representative of all sections, and which seems to us to have come to grips with the problem in a practical way by its insistence on the need for capital investment in the small farms and in the intensification of production through community development and the establishment of cooperatives.[94]

The Charlestown group launched a series of protest meetings throughout the west in the autumn of 1964, following the publication of volume 2 of the *Second Programme for Economic Expansion,* which estimated that the numbers engaged in farming would fall by over 90,000 between 1960 and 1970. In November 1964 they published a broadsheet, noting: "Government plan for Economic Expansion: 43 per cent increase in the number of cattle. 17 percent fall in the country population which will affect the West to not less than a 30 per cent fall in small farm population. The truth is industry, banking, big business have taken over the State. They speak through the civil servant cadres, who preserve the appearance of democratic government by using ministers as their public relations officers."[95]

Tensions between the government and the Charlestown group, renamed Committee for the Defence of the West, eased considerably in 1965 with the appointment of Charles Haughey as minister for Agriculture. Haughey made a special tour of the west; he established a consultative committee for the west, chaired by Father McDyer, and appointed a western regional officer to the Department of Agriculture based in Athenry, county Galway, which became a center for research and education of the specific problems of western agriculture—the first regional initiative in the department's history. A 1971 report on the pilot areas program by the Department of Agriculture's western regional officer, John Scully, suggested at first sight that the program had been highly successful. Gross margins (a basic measure of net agricultural output) had risen by 40 percent between 1964/65 and 1969/70, which was five times the rate achieved throughout the twelve western counties, and the proportion of farmers classified as viable or potentially viable increased from 23 to 38.5 percent, at very little expense to taxpayers. Nevertheless Scully concluded that the pilot areas program had a limited potential because the majority of farmers had too little land, the land was too infertile, or the farmers were too elderly and too lacking in education to benefit. He reiterated the need to consolidate farms and to raise educational standards.[96]

The reaction to the reports of the interdepartmental committee on small western farms and to proposals to consolidate farms reflect the tensions between efforts to modernize the economy—in this instance farming in the west of Ireland—and the wish to preserve a traditional way of life. Some of the statements by the western bishops, and by Father McDyer, dripped with nostalgia:

> Many of the fires that are still sending up smoke are only tended by the enfeebled hands of an ageing couple whose children have gone elsewhere. It was indeed an eloquent commentary that what pillage, persecution and the battering ram failed to achieve the lure of faraway urban life and the lack of initiative co-operation and patriotism are fast accomplishing. We must bend all our efforts to have the farmer tighten his grip on his own holdings. But what if we allow this grip to loosen, if we stand by and see the people felled? The land and house after house fall to ruins, then there are cultural and demographical issues involved for which no substitute can be found, that the sturdy stand of our forefathers and the furious fight of our patriot dead will have gone for naught and Ireland will be no longer the loveable, friendly, the populous Ireland which has been known for centuries.[97]

Nostalgia is likewise evident in John Healy's 1968 book, *The Death of an Irish Town*, where he writes about Charlestown in the 1960s: "Yet on the surface the town looks well; it looks healthy. A few new people have moved in; the paintwork is fresh and what houses are occupied are kept well. But it is a false vitality for the fresh paint merely throws into relief that shuttered house; the new shop fronts bring the eye to the mortally wounded old businesses." In language that echoes Father McDyer's plan for vegetable-growing co-ops, Healy recalled Charlestown during the 1930s and "farmers with hundreds of bags of potatoes. Outside them were carts of turnips, farmers with cabbage plants in season, and big bundles of sally rods to be sold to the thatcher and the ciseán [basket] maker. Fat women waddled in with wicker baskets of eggs and rolls of butter."[98] I wonder if the fat women and farmers were equally nostalgic about those times? For all his undoubted sympathy with the people of Charlestown and the surrounding countryside, Healy's attitude is that of somebody who was removed from the harshness of life on small farms.

Father McDyer decried the "gathering force of lethargy, of apathy and despair" in rural Ireland,[99] and in 1968 John Healy claimed that "life is at a low ebb in rural Ireland today,"[100] but there is little evidence of apathy or lethargy in the local newspapers, the Dáil debates or government files. Rural and small-town communities lobbied energetically for factories, second-level schools, and water schemes. They understood that survival would involve changes in jobs and lifestyle, and that selling cabbage plants or baskets of eggs at a weekly market, however picturesque the scene, would not provide an acceptable standard of living in 1960s Ireland. I find the comment of Damien Hannan about Cavan teenagers more convincing: "The level of aspirations and expectations of the majority of the cohort has more in keeping with a modern industrial city than one might have expected."[101]

Rural Industry

"We are concerned on this side of the House to keep as many people as we can in rural Ireland. However, it is only right to say that these people should not be asked to stay on the land unless they can make a decent living from it. It is only natural that if we divide up all the land into 45 or 50-acre holdings, there will be fewer people on the land than there are at present, but if we take this Bill in conjunction with the development of rural industry, we can see the possibility of success in keeping the people in rural Ireland."[102]

Rural industry appeared to offer a means to square the circle: a painless reduction in the number of farms and farmworkers and a better standard of living for those remaining in agriculture, without any corresponding fall in the rural population. Scattering factories throughout rural and provincial Ireland had formed part of Fianna Fáil policy since the early 1930s, but the long-standing objective was now dressed in modern clothes, and it was supported by scholarly research. A paper by Rosemary Fennell, an economist with An Foras Talúntais, claimed that "the imbalance of the Western economy stems from lack of industry and almost complete dependence on agriculture, emigrants remittances and relief work, and any attempt to correct this is of great significance." Ministers were presented with copies of this paper along with the report of the interdepartmental committee on small western farms.[103] The numerous, positive references to rural industry in speeches by ministers or government deputies were not simply an attempt to offer a painless solution to the problem of rural decline; they were also designed to create a more positive attitude toward factory work in rural communities. When Damien Hannan interviewed young people in Cavan in 1965 and 1968, the young men rated unskilled and skilled factory jobs higher than most comparable positions, but three-quarters of the young women regarded unskilled factory work as unacceptable. Hannan concluded that if enough factory jobs, attracting a range of skills and offering satisfactory pay, had been available, the great majority of boys and girls with primary or vocational schooling would not have migrated, although the term "factory girls" had negative class connotations.[104]

A study by Kaldor and Lucey showed that rural industry provided jobs, more spending power, a higher population, and improvements in agriculture. Few farmers were employed in local factories; the jobs went to their sons or other relatives, who often continued to work on the farm on a part-time basis; the farmer and his wife commonly had to work harder than before, but factory earnings paid for additional investment and greater use of farm machinery.[105] In the introduction to the book, director of the Economic and Social Research Institute

Michael Fogarty noted that "for intelligent and relatively well-educated young farmers with too little land industrial employment has proved to be the way out, in the sense not only of providing a new source of work and income but of enabling them to farm more effectively and increase their farm output. As farm labor became less readily available, farm work was planned more carefully."[106] There was also a clear benefit from higher incomes: the factory jobs paid £11–£12 a week compared with £2–£6 in alternative occupations in the area, "supposing of course that some kind of local job had been available."[107] In 1967 a special Small Industries Program was introduced, initially in seven western counties; by 1969 it was extended throughout the state. Industries that employed fewer than thirty people were regarded as particularly suited to rural Ireland.[108] The program was run by the county development teams, assisted by the Industrial Development Authority; additional assistance in western areas was provided through a Special Regional Development Fund.[109] But despite a steady growth of small industries, the population of the west continued to fall. Emigration continued, though at a reduced rate, and more young people were taking up jobs in Dublin.

By the 1960s government statements were highlighting two major objectives: promoting economic growth to create sufficient jobs to eliminate involuntary emigration and redirecting a greater share of these jobs to western areas. But the two were not necessarily compatible: in order to end involuntary emigration, it might be necessary to concentrate development in selected areas, while redirecting jobs to western areas might result in continuing emigration.

Physical Planning and a National Spatial Strategy

The satirist Myles na Gopaleen was of the opinion that "the whole country lacks the population that would sustain even the fraction of 'planning' that is proper to the temperament and economy of this country. . . . The problem to be addressed here is simply that of the falling birth-rate."[110] As Myles, alias Brian O'Nolan, was for many years an official in the Department of Local Government, this statement may reflect the views of his fellow civil servants. It is certainly true that there was no need to plan in the 1950s for the new towns or major industrial complexes that were a feature of most European countries at the time. Ireland's only new town was Shannon, which owed its existence to trans-Atlantic air services and the adjoining customs-free zone. The suburban sprawl on the outskirts of Dublin, Cork, and Limerick was on a very modest scale compared with urban development elsewhere. In 1958 the Department of Finance's *Economic Development* suggested that demand for housing and other forms of social investment "are virtually satisfied over wide areas of the state."[111] This was a considerable overstatement. Many houses lacked running water; there were slums in central Dublin; and some important provincial routes were too narrow for bus and lorry traffic.[112] But it reflected the government's wish to transfer investment from infrastructure to more "productive" purposes.

By the early 1960s the upturn in the economy and the marriage boom were leading to complaints of a housing shortage. On the eve of the 1961 general election, Seán Lemass was presented with a memorial from young married couples in Arklow, complaining about the lack of council houses. Families who had surrendered the tenancy of local authority houses in the mid-1950s before emigrating were returning to Ireland. Local authority housing only catered for long-term residents with a proven need; it was not designed to house newcomers to an area. The National Building Agency was established in December 1960 to house skilled workers moving to a new factory in a provincial town and other mobile workers.[113] But its creation cannot disguise the fact that too few houses were being provided to meet the needs of a rising population. In 1963 Ireland built only 2.6 houses per thousand of population; in every other OECD country except Portugal, the figure ranged from 5.6 to 10.7 per thousand.[114] Three tenements collapsed in central Dublin in 1963 killing four people; an emergency survey of city-center housing that was ordered as a result closed nine hundred dwellings, and those left homeless were placed in temporary dwellings.[115] By the end of 1964, according to one expert, "the government found itself with a full-blown housing crisis on its hands."[116] Ten thousand houses were urgently needed in Dublin, and there were serious housing shortages in Waterford, Cork, and Limerick. In an effort to meet this emergency, the National Building Agency commissioned the Ballymun housing scheme—Ireland's first experiment in high-rise, system-built housing—and several large, but more conventional, projects in Dublin, Cork, and Limerick. The scramble to provide sufficient houses continued well into the 1970s, with targets rising as the population continued to rise. But the pressure to provide as many houses as possible, as rapidly as possible, and as cheaply as possible, together with Ireland's lack of experience of major urban developments, meant that shops, schools, health clinics, cinemas, public transport, playing fields, and the other essentials of modern life took second place. However, there is no evidence that the 1960s tower blocks erected elsewhere in Europe fared any better than Ballymun.

It was also becoming apparent that industrial development involved the provision of roads, electricity, water, sewerage, and telephones, and that priorities had to be established for providing these services; the existing ad hoc policy was creating bottlenecks. There was a shortage of developed industrial sites, and ministers and councilors were being lobbied by property owners, who were aware that road access or adequate water supplies could determine the value of their land. The first comprehensive planning legislation was not enacted until 1963; the fact that this coincided with a period of economic development ensured that the awarding of planning permission assumed great significance in local politics.[117]

In 1962 the Committee on Industrial Organization recommended that a limited number of towns should be earmarked as growth centers; they argued that Ireland could achieve a higher rate of growth if economic and physical planning was integrated and investment was concentrated in these centers. At the time, there was a wish to attract larger industries to Ireland, and specifically heavy industries, because it was widely believed that real industrial development meant smelters, steel mills, and chemical plants.[118] As Dublin was regarded as the only suitable location for large industries, others had to be created. In August 1965 the government announced that a number of development centers would be identified when the regional planning surveys, then underway, had been completed. In the meantime, industrial estates would be established in Waterford and Galway. Although the process of selecting development centers was only beginning, the potential difficulties that would ensue were becoming apparent. The government statement reassured the public that the identification of development centers "is not intended to involve the discouragement of industrial development at other locations," that dispersing industry throughout the state had decided social benefits and it would continue to encourage dispersal, and that the planned industrial estates (at the time, development centers and industrial estates were believed to be synonymous) would attract industries that would not otherwise locate in Ireland.[119] Development centers were regarded as a bonus, icing on the industrial development cake. There were other auguries of the political difficulties arising from the policy in a letter to Lemass from Limerick TD and minister for Health, Donogh O'Malley, who expressed fears that the decision to establish industrial estates in Galway and Waterford indicated that Limerick would be neglected. Limerick City Council passed a resolution demanding that Limerick be identified as a development center. Tralee Urban District Council embarked on a similar campaign, and a deputation from Sligo Chamber of Commerce demanded a meeting with Lemass to press their case as well.[120]

Plans for the Dublin and Limerick regions were published in 1967. Nathaniel Lichfield and Associates recommended that development should be concentrated around the Limerick, Shannon, and Ennis area, with a secondary concentration around Nenagh.[121] In the Dublin region, Myles Wright recommended the creation of new towns to the west of the city at Tallaght, Blanchardstown, and Clondalkin, with additional development concentrated at Drogheda, the Naas, Newbridge, and Kilcullen area, and Arklow.[122] These recommendations were not universally welcomed. When Limerick Junior Chamber of Commerce invited him to a meeting to discuss the Limerick Regional Plan, Clare TD and Minister for Labour Patrick Hillery replied that "I do not think, however, that Clare people want to tie our County to the less successful people of Limerick and their various gyrations." Hillery sent a copy of this letter to Lemass, pointing out that he had used Dáil notepaper "to distinguish the Clare TD from the member of the Government." Thurles Urban District Council was also aggrieved by the Lichfield report.[123]

The controversy over development centers came to a head in 1969 with the publication of a report by British planning consultants

Colin Buchanan and Partners setting out a national development strategy. Buchanan believed that the key to ending emigration and creating sufficient jobs was to develop a network of cities and larger towns. The report pointed out that since the 1940s, the counties with the lowest share of population in cities and towns had recorded the highest rates of emigration, whereas counties with a strong urban base had been the most successful in retaining people in rural areas. Buchanan cautioned that current policies would have "only a temporary and limited degree of success in meeting the main objectives of government economic policy."[124] If the present policy of dispersing industries continued, it predicted that in 1986 the population would be 3.36 million (300,000 below the estimate given in the National Industrial and Economic Council Report, *Full Employment*), there would be 14,000 emigrants per annum, and two-thirds of rural counties would have a lower population than at present. Extending the projections to 2001, and again assuming the continuation of present policies, it predicted that emigration would tend to rise, because there would not be sufficient jobs for the expected increase in births.[125]

Buchanan set out a number of options for a spatial strategy: the most extreme would concentrate all development in Dublin. The favored option would focus on Cork, the Limerick-Ennis-Shannon region, and a limited number of regional centers, and development in Dublin would be neither discouraged nor encouraged. This would result in a higher population and greater employment than current policies, and every region except the northwest (Sligo, Donegal, Mayo, Leitrim, Longford, Cavan, and Monaghan) was projected to have a higher population in 1986 than at present.[126] Buchanan believed that the government needed to choose between regional dispersion and maximizing national population and employment. One policy would bring about a higher national population and an end to emigration at the cost of a declining population in the northwest. Continuing the existing policies would result in higher emigration, a smaller total population, but a lesser population decline in the northwest—in other words, there would be less internal migration but more people would emigrate.[127] The penultimate paragraph of the 1967 National Industrial and Economic Council Report, *Full*

Employment can be read as anticipating the Buchanan report: "Full employment may be accepted as a desirable goal but the policies which would work for its attainment may be rejected because they would not at the same time achieve the goals of particular localities, groups or interests. If sectional interests are not to be pressed to the point where national loss outweighs sectional gain, there must be a deeper sense of personal and corporate responsibility, greater reluctance to exert demagogic pressures and less willingness to respond to them."[128]

The Buchanan report was doomed even before it was published. Submitted to the government in September 1968, it was not published until May 1969; the cabinet postponed a discussion of the report for four months—clear evidence that it was politically unpalatable. Although the minister for Local Government, Kevin Boland, expressed strong support for its findings in official memoranda, he was fully aware that there would be political difficulties in securing public support; as part of this process, Local Government recommended carrying out further studies with a view to devising measures that might reduce the projected rate of population loss in the northwest.[129] Opposition within the cabinet was led by the minister for Agriculture, Donegal TD Niall Blaney, and the Mayo TD and minister for Lands, Michael Moran. A memorandum submitted by the minister for Agriculture claimed that the report failed to give sufficient weight to the imbalance between western areas and the rest of the country; it could have "a disheartening effect" on areas not marked out for development. He suggested that all towns earmarked as locations for regional technical colleges should become growth centers.[130] Claims that Buchanan had neglected the west of Ireland crop up even more forcefully in a letter from Michael Moran to the taoiseach on 4 February, the day when the cabinet finally considered the report. Moran referred to the "serious situation" in county Mayo where hundreds of men, recently unemployed because of the completion of the Moy drainage scheme, would be forced to emigrate. And he drew Lynch's attention to the publicity being given to the campaign by Achill islanders for "human rights" as well as their demand that Achill island and county Mayo be declared "disaster areas." As there appeared to be no immediate prospect of going ahead with the government's plan to move the Department of Lands to Castlebar,[131] Moran urged that there should be "an immediate overall assessment of the existing imbalance between the Western areas and the rest of the country, and that a co-ordinated policy plan should be outlined. I think that unless industrial growth centers are located in the center of the areas of highest emigration our national policy does not make any sense."[132]

Over the next three months a subcommittee of ministers tried to reach consensus on the Buchanan report, until eventually the cabinet decided that it should be laid before each house of the Oireachtas.[133] The statement that accompanied the report's release on 19 May 1969 failed to endorse the Buchanan recommendations; it noted that they would be referred for further consideration "in the context of proposals for regional development generally." The government's objective was "to achieve broad-based regional expansion leading to a faster rate of industrial growth and a higher level of employment in industry and services and to keep population dislocation to the minimum consistent with these objectives." It expressed the wish "that the potential of every region should be exploited to the full."[134] The Buchanan report was published on the same day as the *Report on Physical Planning* by the NIEC.[135] The NIEC "fully endorse[d]" the strategy outlined in the Buchanan report, although it emphasized that this endorsement related to the principles, not the details. The NIEC cautioned that "it is important the Buchanan strategy is seen in its proper perspective. It must not be viewed as a strategy for apportioning the economic growth that will in any case occur, and the benefits that will follow from it, in a particular way along the different parts of the country. It is rather a strategy which will accelerate growth to the rate which will make full employment a realisable objective."[136]

Doubtless, the twenty-seven worthy men — the NIEC represented various interest groups, but gender was not a consideration — who signed this report believed that their advice might help to garner support for the Buchanan strategy. If so, they were to be disappointed. Towns selected as growth centers remained smug, and relatively silent; those not on the list protested loudly. Padraic White has highlighted how "the west of Ireland triumvirate of John Healy, Jim Maguire and Ted Nealon [all journalists] . . . generated immense firepower in favour of the west through skilful use of the media."[137] Buchanan received the support of the *Irish Independent,* which asserted that "this is not a policy which neglects the land or rural population." Another predictable supporter, Garret FitzGerald, highlighted Buchanan's claim that the consequences of pursuing current industrial policies would be to "reduce the population of this country seventeen years hence by 140,000 below the level that could be attained by a policy of development growth centres," and "121,000 of this avoidable loss would occur in the western half of the country," but this message did not percolate through to the local newspapers. The *Argus,* which was published in Dundalk, reported nonchalantly that "Buchanan was not news in Dundalk"—there was no great surprise that Dundalk had been selected as a growth center. The leading article in the (Carlow) *Nationalist and Leinster Times* carried the headline "Passed over by Buchanan"; *The Free Press,* "Report Shock for Wexford"; *The Derry Journal,* "Future of the North West a Matter of Anxiety"; *Kilkenny People,* "Kilkenny-Carlow to be 'Left Out'" and "Beware of Buchanan."[138] The claim by one opposition deputy that the plan would "obviously ring the death knell for quite a number of our towns, large and small which are not included in the report as growth centres" was a common response. That the report was produced by "a man sitting in an office in London" provided further ammunition for critics. One TD suggested that "while it [the Buchanan plan] may be said to be economically wise initially by these experts, it is totally unsuited to Irish needs."[139]

A leading article in the *Western People* summarized the government's dilemma: "The Government must have been aware that for every centre like Sligo and Castlebar which welcomed its status in the recommendations there would be dozens of other towns which would hear their death knell in the officialise of the Report. We are told that not all the Buchanan Report will be accepted but indeed why should we take the direction of our own development from outsiders at all? Are towns like Ballina, Claremorris, Westport, Tuam to name but a few—going to accept the crumbs while a selected few take the cake."[140]

Desmond Roche has suggested that "[Niall] Blaney [minister for Local Government 1957–66] would certainly have put up a powerful fight against the fate of the Buchanan Report."[141] Yet the official cabinet records suggest that Local Government, under its minister Kevin Boland, supported the plan and that Blaney, now minister for Agriculture, was one of its opponents. A more pertinent question is whether there would have been a better prospect of implementing Buchanan were Seán Lemass taoiseach? I have seen no evidence that Jack Lynch ever embraced radical or innovative economic policies. The government's failure to support the Buchanan report should not surprise us. In 1968 the same government asked the Irish electorate to endorse a constitutional amendment permitting a lower ratio of population to Dáil deputies in rural constituencies.[142] Introducing the proposed amendment in the Dáil, Jack Lynch noted that "the Government have always taken the view that the special difficulties of persons living in large constituencies in rural areas should be recognised. These people do not have the same ease of access to their Deputies as persons living in the more compact urban constituencies. Moreover, experience has shown that people living in rural areas are more likely to have to seek the help of their Deputies for quite legitimate reasons."[143] Most deputies who spoke in support of this motion referred to the practical difficulties that they experienced representing rural constituencies, compared with urban constituencies, but the "growing urbanization of representation"[144] was also a consideration; likewise fears that a redistribution of seats to urban constituencies would make it more difficult for Fianna Fáil to hold office. The electorate defeated the amendment by a margin of 60:40.[145]

Despite being published shortly before the 1969 general election, the Buchanan report does not appear to have become a major issue in the campaign. Fianna Fáil managed to distance itself from the report. Their campaign concentrated on the social and economic improvements of recent years, promises of more to come, claims that a Fine Gael–Labor coalition would not provide the necessary stability for a prosperous economy, and a large dollop of old-fashioned "red scares" that were directed at Labor's more socialist agenda. On the eve of the election, minister for Industry and Commerce George Colley announced a large number of new factories that were strategically scattered throughout the country.[146]

During an adjournment debate in December 1969, one opposition deputy noted that the government had been "strangely silent" on the topic of Buchanan. There had been no official government pronouncement on the question of industrial centralization and the taoiseach's speech had "carefully avoided any reference to that particular aspect of the situation."[147] By this point, Buchanan was a matter of history. To diffuse tensions over regional planning, in the autumn of 1969 the government created regional development organizations consisting of representatives of regional planning authorities and "other public bodies" who would be responsible for coordinating regional programs, although one expert claimed that they "had no executive functions and little real substance."[148] The real decision-making power rested with the men and women who drafted the regional industrial development plans. The Industrial Development Authority's *Regional Industrial Plans, 1972–77,* were published on the eve of Ireland's referendum on EEC membership. They set an annual target of 7,600 additional manufacturing jobs, a figure that would ensure full employment and an end to involuntary emigration. Although this was substantially greater than the average annual increase of 4,700 jobs achieved over the previous five years,[149] the IDA suggested that it could be achieved without radical changes in the existing regional pattern. The plans envisaged limiting the growth of Dublin to the natural population increase and exploiting the potential of the smaller towns. Maltby and McKenna note that this was "in line with Government policy,"[150] but Padraic White, who was a member of the IDA regional team, has claimed that civil servants were sharply divided between those who favored dispersal and those who supported concentration.[151] Whether these targets were met does not concern us—the post-1973 collapse in international growth rates makes this an academic question—but there is little doubt that they were a political success, not least because they killed off the notion that hard choices might have to be made in order to achieve full employment and bring an end to emigration. However, it might be worth considering whether the rejection of the Buchanan strategy meant that some Irish people were unemployed and growth rates were lower during the 1970s and 1980s than otherwise might have been. One of the most pertinent arguments against Buchanan was made by Damien Hannan: if Cavan was not designated as a growth center, would Cavan workers move freely to Dundalk or Drogheda? He believed that they would not.[152] Evidence from Ireland in the

1990s and today, however, suggests that they would have been willing to commute there.

The outcome of the Buchanan debate is not surprising. Battles over industrial location date back at least to the 1930s, and in any dispute between consolidation and decentralization, the advocates of decentralization have invariably triumphed.[153] The Irish experience confirms the theory of the economist Mancur Olsen that large groups are less capable of acting in their common interest than small groups. In this instance, the large group was the Irish population; the small groups were residents of Kilkenny,[154] Offaly,[155] or anywhere that was not listed as a growth center. Emigrants—the real losers— were probably the group that was least capable of acting in their common interest. According to Padraic White, one of the authors of the IDA regional plans, "Few passions can match regional passions, particularly the west of Ireland brand, about the location of foreign industry within the country." White is a native of county Leitrim; in 1970 he talked himself into a job on the IDA regional planning team, "fired up with fury against the regional strategy of Colin Buchanan and Associates."[156] Olsen also noted that the political benefits from redistribution outweigh the benefits of economic growth.[157] Irish politicians were fully aware of this.

The 1960s brought an end to the demographic patterns that set in after the famine: late marriages, few marriages, high marital fertility, and emigration. By the end of that decade Irish society was faced with new issues: how to provide sufficient jobs for those who were no longer emigrating, now and in the decades to come.

7

"A Ticket to London Is a Ticket to Hell"

Emigrants, Emigrant Welfare, and Images of Ireland

We are a small country. Our material wealth is comparatively insignificant. . . . Though we are a small nation, we wield an influence in the world far in excess of what our mere physical size and the smallness of our population might warrant. We are sometimes accused of acting as if we were a big nation. But, in fact, we are a big nation. Our exiles have gone to practically every part of the world and have created for their motherland a spiritual dominion which more than compensates for her lack of size or material wealth. The Irish at home are only one section of a great race which has spread itself throughout the world, particularly in the great countries of North America and the Pacific area.

John A. Costello, Dáil Éireann, 24 November 1948

Ireland is not alone losing by emigration to Britain her most valuable sons and daughters, her university graduates and professional men, and the enterprising, go-ahead men who find no scope for them at home. She is also exporting her social failures; just as Britain exported her n'er-do-wells and men-on-the run, her shiftless and her black sheep, to her colonies in the nineteenth century, so Ireland sends hers to Britain in the twentieth. She also sends her moral failures—unmarried pregnant girls seeking anonymity in a British hospital, and husbands deserting their families.

A. E. C. W. Spencer, "The Religious Arrangements
for the Integration of Irish Catholic Immigrants
in England and Wales"

Ireland's relationship with the Irish community overseas was, and is, a complex matter. On the one hand, the Irish state and its people took pride in the large number of men and women of Irish birth or descent scattered throughout the world; it was widely believed that they enhanced Ireland's international standing, and they were a valuable source of funds and influence for political causes. Their successes in politics, business, sport, the church, and the arts were lauded, but most particularly their contribution to bringing Catholicism to Britain, the United States, and Australia. In the early 1950s, all the cardinals in English-speaking countries were of Irish birth or Irish ancestry.[1] In a speech introducing the second stage of the Republic of Ireland Bill, taoiseach John A. Costello referred to the Irish nuns and brothers that "have gone forth to England and brought the faith there and are giving no inadequate contribution to the spiritual uplift which is necessary to the atheistic atmosphere of the world today." He mentioned, too, "our teachers . . . lay and religious . . . our doctors and professional men" and, finally, "our working men and our craftsmen and our girls who have gone over to earn a living there."[2] He also cited a speech by Archbishop Cushing of Boston where the latter claimed that Ireland had been chosen to extend the spiritual kingdom of Christ to the ends of the earth: "Like the grace of God, the Irish are everywhere and everywhere they do good." Costello suggested that Ireland was "a big nation," courtesy of the worldwide "spiritual dominion" created by Irish exiles, "which more than compensates for her lack of size or material wealth." He went on to speak about Irishmen bringing religion to the "barbaric tribes of Eastern Europe . . . teaching philosophy in the Court of Charlemagne," Colmcille's mission to "the Pict, the Briton and the Scandinavian."[3] Similar images crop up in the speeches of other political leaders. When Seán Lemass formally presented Ireland's application for EEC membership in Brussels on 18 January 1962, he referred to the contribution made by Irish monks in bringing learning back to Europe during the Dark Ages.[4]

Irish emigrants or their families are unlikely to have been consoled by the knowledge that they were advancing Ireland's spiritual empire. Although the Irish in Britain traveled regularly between the two countries, in other respects the traffic between emigrants and their native land was relentlessly one-way. In addition to boosting national esteem, emigrants supported families who remained in Ireland, and by doing so they reduced the incidence of poverty, they injected valuable money into the economy in the most deprived parts of Ireland, they reduced the burden on Irish charities and taxpayers, and they made a significant contribution to the balance of payments. Until the late 1950s, emigrants' remittances and legacies were the largest source of dollar earnings, far outstripping tourism or merchandise exports, and by the 1940s remittances from Britain probably exceeded those from North America.[5]

Irish America was also a vital source of funds for nationalist movements of both the physical force and the constitutional varieties. Parnell and other leaders of the Irish Parliamentary Party made regular fundraising trips to the United States during the 1880s, and successive generations of political leaders followed in their tracks. During the Anglo-Irish War, Dáil Éireann used the Irish diaspora not just as a source of money but also as an important lobby group, and the fledgling Dáil Ministry of Foreign Affairs relied heavily on these Irish networks. But emigrants got little in return other than messages from the head of government or the head of state to mark Saint Patrick's Day or Christmas.[6] The 1956 Irish Nationality and Citizenship Act was deliberately drafted with a view to enabling the descendants of earlier emigrants to claim citizenship, but most applicants for citizenship by descent were prompted by pragmatic needs, such as the right to work and reside in Britain or in the European Union, not by sentiment.[7]

In the decade following the end of World War II, when Ireland was isolated in international affairs because of its wartime stance on neutrality and a mindset that was dominated by cultural and economic protectionism, the Irish community overseas offered a cheap and comforting substitute for a foreign policy. Meeting visiting Irish Americans or accepting invitations to address Irish groups in Britain and the United States added a touch of glamor to the calendars of government ministers, who had very limited opportunities for international events by today's standards. In February 1946 de Valera entertained four Irish American prelates in Killarney—Francis Spellman of New York, Edward Francis Mooney of Detroit, Samuel Stritch of Chicago, and John T. Glennon of Saint Louis—when they were en route to Rome for their consecration as cardinals. The party included James Farley, who had served as postmaster general in Franklin Roosevelt's cabinet, and Reverend Robert Gannon, the President of Fordham University.[8] By the 1930s Irish ministers were commonly guests of honor at dinners of Irish organizations in Britain; after the Second World War they began to accept similar invitations in the United States. In 1956 John A. Costello became the first head of government to spend Saint Patrick's Day in the United States when he was guest of honor at the annual dinner of the Friendly Sons of Saint Patrick in Philadelphia; he had turned down three previous invitations.[9] The success of the descendants of Irish emigrants and the extent of Ireland's "spiritual empire" appear to have offered some consolation to Irish politicians, particularly during the 1950s when emigration reached a twentieth-century peak. This sentiment probably reached its apogee in 1963 with the visit of American President John F. Kennedy, whose eight great-grandparents had emigrated from Ireland. Whether families who were more directly affected by emigration derived much consolation from Ireland's "spiritual empire" is uncertain.

The Irish tourist industry began to woo the ethnic market in the United States in the early 1950s as part of a wider effort to boost dollar earnings; however, their campaign was targeted more at high-spending Irish Americans, whose ancestors had left Ireland in the distant past, than at the less affluent men and women of Irish birth, who tended to stay with relatives when they visited Ireland. The Irish diaspora was also accorded a key role in the postwar antipartition campaign.[10] But the Irish state provided minimal assistance to its emigrants. In 1954 Paul Keating, the Irish consul general in New York, commented that "we in the Consulate do not do very much for new arrivals. There is at present no effective means of keeping in touch with them, they are not, for example, encouraged and advised to register here so we do not know of their existence. Even if we did we have little to offer them of a cultural or social nature due to our small resources." In a follow-up memorandum some weeks later he added: "As you know generally we are embarrassed by callers who have nothing to recommend them except their Irish citizenship. We cannot afford to entertain them and we have no cultural or other services."[11]

While not dismissing the value of cultural services, "other services" were more important. Keating recounted the story of two elderly sisters, who had been persuaded to emigrate to the United States under false pretences and the promise of jobs, but now wished to return to Ireland. One sister had traveled on a British passport and her return fare was paid by the Saint George Society—a welfare agency for British citizens in the United States that operated under the auspices of the British consulate. Her sister, who held an Irish passport, had to rely on a Polish American priest in the Bronx to fund her return fare. Emigrants who fell on hard times in the United States because of injury or ill health were dependent on fund-raising dances organized by county societies for assistance.[12] The Department of External Affairs did not pay for the repatriation of Irish citizens until the 1960s.

Most reports reaching Ireland about emigrants in the United States boasted of their success. Some Irish in the United States undoubtedly became homeless or destitute; some ended up in prison, and some Irish emigrant women became pregnant out of wedlock, but reports of their difficulties rarely reached Ireland.[13] After 1929 the numbers emigrating to the United States were small; the Irish American community was mature and well established, and the American Catholic church, which was then dominated by Irish American clergy, had an elaborate network of agencies to cater for Irish immigrants. The requirement of a visa, plus the high cost of trans-Atlantic travel ruled out impulsive emigrants; a sixteen-year-old boy or girl who emigrated to the United States would have been sponsored by a relative or friend, whereas many young people arrived in London without money, friends, or contacts. The bleaker aspect of Irish emigration to the United States that inspired writers such as Eugene O'Neill and William Kennedy only became known in Ireland during the new wave of illegal or undocumented Irish during the 1980s.[14]

By contrast, a lot was known about the conditions of Irish emigrants to Britain, despite, or possibly because of, the fact that Britain offered much more extensive state supports than the United States. Social workers employed by English local authorities and church agencies documented the inadequate housing conditions of Irish emigrants and the numbers of Irish women in mother and baby homes, and they relayed this information to politicians and church-men in Ireland. Accounts of drunken men, pregnant single women, and nonattendance at church threatened both the comforting belief that emigrants formed part of "Ireland's spiritual empire," with a mission to reclaim Britain for Rome, and the myth that Irish people were not as others, that they were more spiritual, more noble, and therefore immune to the failings of modern life. Emigrant welfare also raised questions about the boundaries of citizenship and the re-spective responsibilities of state and voluntary services. If Irish emi-grants needed assistance, who should provide it—the British social services, the Irish state, or the Catholic church?

Aid, Encouragement, or Coercion? Government Attitudes toward Emigrants

Nineteenth-century Britain interfered to a minimal degree with mi-gration to or from the United Kingdom. This was consistent with a liberal economic policy, which was based on free trade, mobility of capital, and mobility of labor. In 1840 the British government estab-lished the Colonial Land and Emigration Department to promote and assist emigration to the colonies, but government-subsidized emigration was terminated in 1878 and the department abolished. An Emigrants Information Office was established in 1886 under the Co-lonial Office, but its functions were limited to supplying information to intending emigrants. Britain exercised minimal supervision over emigration societies and those engaged in transporting emigrants.[15] The right to freedom of movement was deeply ingrained in the Irish consciousness; beggars and migrants workers moved freely through-out Ireland and between Britain and Ireland. The Irish Poor Law, un-like the English Poor Law, did not include a law of settlement. Most Irish emigrants during the nineteenth century left on their own ini-tiative; fares were paid by the emigrants, their family, or friends, not by public funds, and this remained the position after 1922. The Irish government rejected offers to participate in assisted emigration schemes to Canada and Australia during the 1920s, and they discour-aged advertisements by states or by shipping lines that were targeted at emigrants. Although de Valera's government cooperated with the

British authorities to facilitate Irish emigration to Britain during
World War II, when Australian minister for Information and Immigration Arthur Calwell visited Ireland in 1947 hoping to implement
an assisted-passage scheme for Irish immigrants to Australia, the
government rejected the proposal without giving it serious consideration. At the time, a one-way fare from London to Australia cost
from £60 to £100.[16] The Sydney Patrick Pearse Branch of Cumann
Naisiúnta na nGaedheal condemned the Australian government's
offer as "wicked and anti-Irish" and they urged the Irish government
"to employ every device in its power to staunch the flow of emigrants
from Ireland." They claimed that Australia's sentiments were "grossly
hibernophobic"; emigrants became "submerged under an alien, hostile and semi-pagan culture and civilization," and they were unlikely
to return to Ireland.[17] The Irish authorities also refused to participate
in an assisted places scheme for non-Commonwealth emigrants,
which was organized in 1959 under the auspices of the Council of
Europe, despite strong lobbying by the Australian hierarchy, who
were keen to increase the number of Irish Catholic immigrants. A
minute signed by Department of External Affairs official Máire Mac-
Entee noted that the minister for External Affairs "sees no good reason for modifying our attitude, . . . having regard to the continued
validity of the objections which have always existed to our being associated with measures to assist emigration from this country."[18]

The Irish government also refused to participate in conferences
or organizations that were designed to secure better conditions for
emigrants. In 1924 Italy invited Ireland to send a representative to a
meeting of the International Conference on Emigration in Rome.
The agenda included proposals to create collaborative groups of employers, workmen's unions, and emigrant aid societies to discuss
problems associated with emigration, but an official in the Department of Industry and Commerce minuted that it was unlikely that
"any useful purpose would be served by attempting the establishment of such bodies."[19] In 1949 the Department of Social Welfare
recommended that Ireland should not sign an International Labor
Organization Convention governing the treatment of migrants and
their employment and welfare rights, because in the minister's opinion, the encouragement of emigration, which ratification of the

Convention might entail, would be "contrary to national policy." The convention was designed to ensure that foreign workers should have equal treatment with natives in matters such as wages, social security taxes, housing, and trade union membership, and that intending emigrants would be adequately informed about conditions in the country of destination and protected against misleading propaganda about emigration. Other provisions covered immigrant travel, assistance with bureaucracy, finding accommodation, and schemes to repatriate emigrants who failed to find work in the new country. The convention specified that the right to recruit migrant workers should be restricted to public employment offices or other approved public bodies, and that private recruitment agencies would be subject to regulation and supervision by the state. Although the Department of External Affairs pointed out that the Council of Europe was encouraging all member states to ratify this convention, the Irish government decided against doing so. An official in the Department of Social Welfare noted that the convention appeared to "envisage a situation involving large-scale migration such as is needed to meet the refugee problem or the substantial surpluses and shortages of workers which exist in certain countries at present, rather than the position in this country where there is no general desire to encourage or facilitate either immigration or emigration."[20] At this time, net emigration from Ireland was between 35,000 and 40,000, and gross emigration was substantially higher.

Britain ratified this convention;[21] consequently, Irish emigrants benefited from its provisions once they left Ireland, but they had no protection against recruitment agencies operating in Ireland. Britain and Ireland ratified a 1953 Council of Europe agreement guaranteeing immigrant workers entitlement to pensions and other social security benefits on the same terms as natives, and in 1961 both countries ratified Article 19 of the Social Charter of the Council of Europe. The latter required the contracting parties to provide protection and assistance for migrant workers and their families, including free services to assist them in receiving accurate information, and to ensure cooperation between the social services in the countries of emigration and immigration.[22] However, it is unclear whether these conventions were enforced.

Ireland's reluctance to sign international conventions and to participate in assisted emigration schemes reflects a refusal to acknowledge the reality of Irish emigration. It is also symptomatic of a failure to see Irish emigration as part of a European or worldwide process, with common causes and common problems. Italy, another country with a significant emigrant population, went to much greater lengths to assist its emigrants. From 1891 the Italian government provided an annual subsidy for the Italian Home in New York City—an institution that included a hospital, relief bureau, immigration bureau, and a school. In 1894 they established an office on Ellis Island to assist newly arrived emigrants in finding employment, and by 1921 the Italian government was providing subsidies to fifty-eight Italian organizations and twenty-seven foreign-based units that assisted immigrants.[23] In the years after World War II, the governments of Italy, Netherlands, Malta, and Spain all provided a measure of assistance for emigrants.[24] The government of Northern Ireland established training schemes during the 1920s to prepare would-be emigrants for life in Australia and Canada.[25] These measures acknowledged the reality of emigration, whereas successive Irish governments combined formal opposition to emigration with a *laissez-faire* attitude toward emigrants and their needs. The fact that most twentieth-century Irish emigrants went to the United Kingdom, where they were accorded welfare and citizenship rights identical to British citizens and an entitlement to social services that were much more generous than in Ireland, made it easier for the Irish government to maintain this stance.

The reluctance of successive Irish governments to assume a role with regard to emigrant welfare was undoubtedly colored by the delicate matter of the respective responsibilities of church and state. Any discussion of emigrant welfare had a tendency to become embroiled in moral questions, such as church attendance, extramarital pregnancies, or marriage to non-Catholics, and for this reason most government ministers and officials preferred to leave matters in the hands of the Catholic church. But the needs of Irish emigrants also generated tensions between the English and the Irish hierarchies; the Irish clergy regarded some of the statements made by English Catholic organizations as a slur on their pastoral care. There was also ambivalence over the question of assimilation. Was it desirable that Irish emigrants become part of the English Catholic community, or should they retain their distinct identity? Few Irish people seem to have been troubled when Irish emigrants to the United States absorbed the cultural values of their adopted country, perhaps because American society provided for the hybrid identity of Irish American. They were much less enthusiastic about emigrants, especially female ones, being assimilated into English society. Anglo-Irish had quite a different meaning than Irish American; England was the ancient enemy, whereas the United States was regarded, sometimes naïvely, as Ireland's friend. A. E. C. W. Spencer, a sociologist who wrote a controversial report on religious practice by Irish emigrants in Britain, noted that emigration to Britain was widely condemned by church and state, but he believed that the "awful warnings about what happens to the Irish in England" were counterproductive: "A few must be deterred by these warnings, but it is evident that the majority are impressed but not deterred. . . . [B]efore he has been here long he discovers that the ordinary English men and women in the street are not Cromwells, Orangemen, Black-and-Tans or bigots; he finds that on the whole they are pleasant and kindly, with a high standard of natural virtue, 'good pagans' whose charity often puts the Catholic to shame." Spencer claimed that the dire warnings of Redemptorist missionaries that "a ticket to London is a ticket to hell," and the anti-emigration rhetoric of government ministers may have caused emigrants to discard any advice given in Ireland.[26]

A disproportionate amount of the material on emigrant welfare concerns women. Whereas men were generally treated as adults who were capable of fending for themselves, it was commonly believed that women needed protection. This concern reflects the great importance that was attached to sexual morality and the need to ensure that Irish women would continue to be suitable mothers for the next generation of Irish Catholic children. Men gradually entered the picture during the 1950s, with reports that many emigrants were no longer practicing their religion. By the 1960s the focus of emigrant welfare broadened to include the homeless, former industrial school pupils, and men who had been discharged from psychiatric hospitals.

The remainder of this chapter examines the response of the Irish state and the Catholic church toward the material, moral, and spiritual needs of Irish emigrants. I begin by investigating two incidents that drew attention toward the living conditions of Irish emigrants in Britain—the fire in a bothy in Kirkintilloch in 1937 that resulted in the death of ten migratory laborers from Achill, and a 1951 speech by de Valera about the living conditions of Irish emigrants in the British Midlands.

Kirkintilloch: "This Unfortunate Aspect of Our Relations with the Neighboring Island"

On 16 September 1937, ten migratory laborers from Achill Island, whose ages ranged from thirteen to twenty-three years, died when fire swept through a shed where they were sleeping in Kirkintilloch, East Lothian. The Mangan family lost three sons, the McLoughlin and Kilbane families each lost two sons. They were part of a team of twenty-six potato diggers, fourteen girls and twelve boys and men, employed by Glasgow potato merchants. Some hours before the fire broke out they were brought by lorry to what should have been their last job at Kirkintilloch. The ten young men were accommodated in a shed that was normally used to store farm equipment; the fourteen girls slept in three small rooms in an adjoining cottage. An Achill islander named Duggan, who had recruited and organized the work team, and his twelve-year-old son, slept in the kitchen of this cottage. It rained heavily on the day of their arrival and no work was possible. Irish officials believed that the fire was caused either by their efforts to dry wet clothes on a hot plate, which was provided for cooking, or by a cigarette.[27]

Their deaths prompted an outpouring of sympathy and outrage in Ireland. Thousands lined the streets of Dublin to greet the bodies when they were returned. *The Irish Times* claimed that the poverty experienced by the dead men and their families was "beyond comprehension" for most Irish people.[28] The Irish Embassy in London responded to news of the fire by dispatching the minister for Justice, P. J. Ruttledge, and his wife, who were in London, to Scotland. Officials in the Department of External Affairs were extremely sensitive about how the story would be presented in Britain. They feared that British newspapers would suggest that the young men had been drinking or that outrage in Ireland at descriptions of their living and working conditions would provoke hostility, and might even result in restrictions being imposed on Irish immigrants, as was currently being demanded in England and in Scotland.

The government's response was to appoint an interdepartmental committee of civil servants to investigate the matter, which was chaired by Seán Moylan, TD and parliamentary secretary at the Department for Industry and Commerce. Reports of interdepartmental committees were not normally published, but on this occasion it was decided that the report should be made public in deference to public demand. This decision was controversial. J. P. Walshe, secretary of the Department of External Affairs, told R. C. Ferguson, assistant secretary in Industry and Commerce (the department responsible for the committee) that "those who wish to fire stones at us on the other side are already amply provided with ammunition. Moreover I hardly think there is any real need to expose those particular wounds. You know what nasty things have already been said by the British Press from time to time about these poor people, and I am very much afraid that the publication of Part I of the Report [the section dealing with the living and working conditions of seasonal migrants] would provoke new outbursts. The quieter we keep about this unfortunate aspect of our relations with the neighbouring island the better."[29]

Examining "this unfortunate aspect of our relations with the neighbouring island" was a risky undertaking for de Valera's government, because it prompted questions about the circumstances that forced teenagers and adults from the western seaboard to endure such hardship in Scotland for several months each year. An editorial in *The Irish Times* asked readers, "If any citizen of the Irish Free State is unmoved by the awful light of the tragedy thrown on the conditions of Achill, can his pride remain unmoved against the degradation of his countrymen in the eyes of neighbouring nations?"[30] Pride and saving face were sentiments that this newspaper shared with senior civil servants.

The interdepartmental inquiry may have given the government some temporary protection against accusations of inaction, but the

report confirmed that there was very little that they could do to miti-
gate the conditions experienced by Irish migrant workers or to make
it unnecessary for them to travel. Responsibility for setting minimum standards of pay and conditions for migrant agricultural
workers rested with the Scottish authorities. A fatal accident inquiry
following a similar fire in Ayrshire thirteen years earlier, in which
nine migratory workers lost their lives, had recommended tighter
regulations of the buildings used to house seasonal workers, and
these were implemented by an act passed in 1925.[31] The inquest into
the deaths at Kirkintilloch recommended that all accommodation
used by seasonal workers should be inspected and approved by local
authorities. The Scottish Housing (Agricultural Population) Act,
1937, which was passed in response to this recommendation, provided grants for the erection of new buildings to replace unsatisfactory or unsafe dwellings, and it introduced a requirement that there
should be separate entrances in houses where sleeping areas formed
part of the premises—the inquest determined that at Kirkintilloch
the main exit from the shed had been locked and access was blocked
by stored farm equipment.[32]

The quality of housing in Scotland was a matter for the Scottish
local authorities and the Westminster parliament. Dáil Éireann could
have introduced regulations preventing boys and girls in their early
teens from emigrating or controls over gangs of seasonal workers,
but it failed to do so. The interdepartmental committee noted that
"short of restrictions on the liberty of migrants of so serious a character that they should not be attempted," they were "unable to suggest any effective means" of improving the conditions of migrant
laborers. The only recommendations under this heading were for improvements in the boat service between Ireland and Scotland, and a
recommendation that the migratory workers organize themselves
to achieve better conditions. Their recommendations for improving economic conditions in Achill and other areas of migrant labor
amounted to a reprise of schemes that had either been recommended
or implemented in the past by the Congested Districts Board and the
commission on the Gaeltacht: land restructuring, drainage, turf and
mineral development, and so on.[33] The only positive outcome to the
disaster was the opening of a technical school in Achill.[34]

Kirkintilloch brought no long-term change in the provisions that the Irish government made for emigrants. At the time, many Irish families were living in squalid, overcrowded housing with leaking roofs and no sanitary facilities, as were many Scottish families, so while conditions in Kirkintilloch were appalling, and beyond the imagination or experience of most readers of *The Irish Times,* they were probably not beyond the comprehension of rural smallholders and slum dwellers in Ireland and Scotland. One of the most revealing aspects of the report of the interdepartmental committee was the lack of information about the extent of seasonal migration. The most recent statistics had been collected in 1918, part an annual series that began in 1880. The collection of agricultural statistics was suspended during the Anglo-Irish war; when it resumed in 1923, the questions on migratory workers was dropped.[35] Despite Kirkintilloch, the series was not resumed. The Irish authorities appear to have been more concerned about the possible damage to Ireland's image in Britain than with the circumstances that sent young boys and girls to work as seasonal laborers in Scotland. Seasonal migration continued after the Kirkintilloch fire; in 1941 and 1942 the Irish government was forced to modify its controls over emigration following pressure from communities that were heavily dependent on the income from seasonal migration. Complaints about the living conditions of Irish potato pickers in Scotland were still being made in the early 1960s.[36]

During the war years, the British Ministry of Labor provided an extensive range of services for essential workers, including travel vouchers, subsidized hostels, and canteens, which made it easier for Irish emigrants to adjust to life in Britain. Many wartime jobs were in areas without a strong Irish community, with the result that few emigrants could find temporary housing with settled relatives, as often happened in the United States. When the war ended, the Ministry of Labor continued to arrange short-term accommodation for workers recruited through the Irish employment exchanges, as did a number of major employers, such as the General Electric Company in Birmingham and the Ford Motor Company in Dagenham.[37] When Stanley Lyon traveled to Britain in 1948 to collect evidence about the conditions of Irish emigrants on behalf of the Commission on Emigration, he commented that "the amount of welfare and social help given to the public by the Ministry of Labour was to me surprising"; he noted the "very elaborate social amenities, . . . billiard tables, canteens etc.," that employers such as Firestone and Ford provided for their workers at no charge. Lyon visited several hostels, but he does not appear to have checked other accommodation, although he notes in passing that the housing shortage prevented many London Irish emigrants from marrying, and many Irish workers at the Ford plant were trying to find accommodation close to their jobs so that they could bring their wives and families to England.[38]

"Fifteen in One Room": Eamon de Valera and the Living Conditions of Irish Emigrants in the English Midlands

In August 1951 Eamon de Valera gave a speech to a Fianna Fáil jubilee dinner in Galway, in which he claimed that fifty workers were living in one house in Birmingham, fifteen of them in one room, each paying a weekly rent of £2. In one instance men and women shared a room—the women who worked on night shift slept in the room during the day, the men slept there at night. He claimed that "avaricious landlords" were exploiting the housing shortage in the Midlands, and that the prestige of "our people suffers by the suggestion that 'anything is good enough for the Irish.'" But "the saddest part of all" was that work was available at home in conditions that were "infinitely better" from the point of view of health and morals; wages on offer in Ireland for many occupations were higher than in England. "There is no doubt that many of those who emigrate could find employment at home at as good, or better, wages—and with living conditions far better—than they find in Britain. Moreover, not only do they fail to improve their own circumstances by being abroad, but they leave enterprises for the development of our natural resources without sufficient labor to enable progress to be made as rapidly as we would all desire."[39]

The advance preparations to ensure that this speech was widely reported in Ireland and in Britain were worthy of a modern public relations agency. On 22 August, one week before the Galway dinner engagement, de Valera asked Frank Aiken, the minister for Foreign

Affairs, to instruct the Irish ambassador in London to make suitable representations to the British government about housing conditions for Irish emigrants in Britain, and he directed the Government Information Bureau to prepare a summary of evidence concerning the living and working conditions of Irish emigrants so that they would be in a position to respond to queries following this speech.

As anticipated, the speech was widely reported in Ireland and in national and local newspapers throughout England, who had been tipped off. According to a memorandum prepared by the Government Information Bureau, presumably for circulation to British journalists, de Valera did not normally speak from a prepared script, and consequently it was not possible to issue the actual text; the attached notes indicated "in general the topics to which he will refer and the lines on which he will deal with them."[40] On 30 August, the day after de Valera delivered the speech, the London embassy relayed word that it had been reported in *The Times, Guardian, Daily Telegraph, News Chronicle, Daily Mail, Daily Worker, Daily Mirror,* and the *Birmingham Post*. Every British newspaper that carried the story cited de Valera's statement about fifteen Irish workers sharing one room, and his claim that working and living conditions at home were "infinitely better" than those on offer in Britain. One Irish emigrant newspaper claimed that de Valera's denunciation of housing conditions in Midland cities "almost created an international incident."[41] Conor Cruise O'Brien, who monitored the story on behalf of the Department of External Affairs, noted, after a number of telephone calls from British newspapers, that the mayors in English Midland cities were "up in arms." The aftershocks of the speech can be found in the letters pages of Irish and English newspapers and in the comments and protests from local authorities in the Midlands and Irish emigrant communities. The report of fifteen men sharing one room elicited varied responses—one Irish emigrant reported that he had found twenty men sharing a room.[42] An unnamed "worker on behalf of a religious organization" confirmed de Valera's description of men and women sleeping in rotation in one room in Coventry; the same social worker reported that seven Irishmen were accommodated in two double and three single beds squeezed into an attic space four feet by four feet eight inches in the Sparkbrook area of

Birmingham—the weekly rent was 36s each.[43] One columnist in an Irish emigrant newspaper described six to eight families drawing water from a communal tap.[44] At the time there was a severe housing shortage in Britain; according to the 1951 census there were 13.12 million private households, but only 12.08 million private dwellings.[45] The housing shortage was especially acute in Midland cities that had suffered heavy bombing, such as Coventry, Wolverhampton, and Birmingham, and were now attracting record numbers of immigrants.

Reports of the squalid living conditions of Irish immigrants in Britain are eerily reminiscent of the descriptions given by Engels or Mayhew one hundred years earlier. Some of the comments in the English press repeated nineteenth-century claims that Irish emigrants were responsible for the squalid conditions, but most elected representatives in the Midlands refuted the wilder allegations of overcrowding. The Mayor of Coventry sent de Valera a telegram expressing hurt and indignation; and landladies in Midland cities dispatched letters of protest. A statement issued by the British Ministry of Labor noted that the accommodation provided for migrant workers, who were recruited by the ministry, was carefully vetted, with a maximum of two people to a room. Others, including a number of Irish emigrants, claimed that de Valera had exaggerated the degree of overcrowding; some pointed out that English and Scottish workers were also living in overcrowded conditions.[46] The most ironic commentary on de Valera's speech is Enda Delaney's discovery that there was a significant increase in the number of applications to the British Ministry of Labor liaison office in Dublin for jobs in Britain immediately after the speech.[47]

As Britain reverted to a peacetime economy, the elaborate wartime network of official canteens and hostels gradually closed down.[48] Irish emigrants, who had come to rely on these services, found it difficult to fend for themselves. A. E. C. W. Spencer suggested that Irish emigrants grudged spending money on food because they had never paid for food in Ireland.[49] The Midlands lacked a tradition of Irish settlement, so it took time to develop Irish networks that could supply short-term accommodation, and the housing shortage probably delayed this process. There were allegations that many of the landlords who exploited Irish lodgers and tenants were Irish, and also that some men wished to keep their rents to a minimum to leave more money for beer.[50] The pub was often the only alternative to spending the evening in an overcrowded and unheated bedroom.[51] De Valera did not mention discrimination against Irish immigrants, but at the time there were reports of landlords specifying "no coloured; no Irish."[52] *The Irish Democrat,* a left-wing emigrant newspaper, carried numerous reports of discrimination, but the majority related to employment rather than accommodation.[53] Yet at this time Irish workers were more likely to experience discrimination with respect to accommodation than employment. The housing shortage meant that landlords could select their tenants; a shortage of workers meant that employers had no such discretion.

A statement issued by the Government Information Bureau emphasized that de Valera had not made this speech "irresponsibly." His purpose was to warn young people who "might be tempted to go to Britain" without any guarantee of proper accommodation.[54] However, the claim that emigrants were abandoning well-paid jobs and superior living conditions was widely disputed, and as a columnist in one emigrant newspaper said, " 'Yes, Mr. de Valera,' but what now." Several correspondents referred to the poor housing standards in Ireland; one specifically mentioned that there were overcrowded tenements within walking distance of Dáil Éireann.[55] An article in *The Irish Democrat* suggested that "Mr. de Valera with his self-satisfied orations about "frugal comfort" at home and how badly the Irish emigrants are overcrowded in Birmingham (as indeed they are) should visit the poorer cottages of Connemara and see how six, eight or even ten are trying to live in three small rooms."[56] The *Daily Mail* quoted a comment from the Midlands Branch of the Ulster Association that "those who live in these overcrowded conditions are usually those brought up in Ireland in similar conditions."[57] While this remark was designed to denigrate Irish emigrants, it contained an element of truth. Most emigrants in the early 1950s were unaccustomed to running water, indoor toilets, bathrooms, or electricity, and bed linen was a luxury in many Irish homes at the time.[58] It is not altogether surprising that many settled for very low standards or that they might have fallen foul of English landladies for failing to keep bathrooms or living quarters in an acceptable condition.[59] Yet individual emigrants and emigrant associations resented de Valera's intervention. Reverend Patrick Smith, president of the Coventry United Irish Societies, expressed regret that de Valera had made this speech, and he associated himself with a protest by the mayor of Coventry. One man who worked as a bank porter complained that his workmates teased him about sharing a room with fourteen others.[60]

Although the Irish embassy in London, acting on de Valera's instructions, presented the British authorities with a formal démarche about the living conditions of Irish emigrants, it received no formal response. By November 1952, reports from the Irish embassy in London indicated that overcrowding was becoming less of a problem, because the postwar housing drive was beginning to have an impact. Seán Nunan of the Department of External Affairs cautioned that it would be a mistake for the Irish authorities to adopt the position that the British authorities were failing in their duty to house Irish emigrants: the difficulties that Irish emigrants experienced reflected a general housing shortage. In January 1953 F. H. Boland, the Irish ambassador in London, visited Birmingham and reported that housing conditions were much improved, but only because a recession in local industries had reduced the number of new immigrants.[61]

At this point the Irish authorities appear to have lost interest in emigrant housing, until 1956 when Seán Murphy, the secretary of External Affairs, contacted Boland to seek further information following a report in *The Times* that Irish emigrants were sharing accommodation with "coloured" emigrants. Murphy reported that "we were somewhat perturbed" by the story. "Whether the situation is as bad as in 1951 is I imagine doubtful, but even then there was little evidence of Irish people sharing with coloured people in overcrowded lodging houses. This seems to be a new development."[62] It probably was. In 1951 there approximately 74,500 people of color in England and Wales, compared with 472,000 natives of the Irish Republic.[63] This comment suggests that the Irish authorities may have been more concerned about questions of cultural assimilation and the image that Irish emigrants presented to outsiders than with actual living conditions.

De Valera's controversial Galway speech was prompted by a report written by Maurice Foley, a "whole-time investigator" employed by a Catholic voluntary organization, the Young Catholic Workers' Association (YCWA). Foley later became a Labor MP, serving as undersecretary of state at the Home Office with responsibility for immigration from 1966 to 1970. Foley was primarily interested in the impact of life in English cities on the morals and religious practice of Irish emigrants. He claimed that their reputed high earnings were only achieved by long hours of overtime and that for many emigrants, overtime offered an escape from poor living conditions. He contrasted the lives of Irish people at home and in the English Midlands: between life in the countryside and in the city, between home and hostel, and between a Catholic and "other traditions . . . in his home surroundings, the Irishman is not called upon to exercise the same missionary spirit which is necessary in countries such as ours. Hence their Catholicity in the main tends to be far more one of acceptance of the Christian doctrine and the personal living of it, rather than the missionary spirit and desire to share it with others."

For an Irish emigrant, practicing the Catholic religion in Midland cities was "comparable to uprooting a hot-house plant and its replantation on a windswept hill." The arrival of 50,000 Irish emigrants offered immense possibilities for English Catholicism: "50,000 potential apostles? An enrichment for the church." But this potential was not being realized. Emigrants commonly sacrificed the comfort of "good digs" in order to live together as a group; there was a "constant floating of boys and girls from one place to another" in search of cheaper lodgings, closer to their work or their friends. Many survived on a diet of tea and buns, and some men spent most of their money in pubs, succumbing to tuberculosis or gastric ulcers in consequence.

Foley also described situations that highlighted, in particular, the moral dangers facing women: female "clippies" who worked late shifts and became friendly with male bus drivers; a barman who fathered several children by different "Irish girls"; the pregnant Irish clippie who continued working until she collapsed on the bus and died, as did her child; single pregnant women arriving from Ireland; others who became pregnant in Britain—the majority by "Irish

boys"; Irish women who had abortions; wives in Ireland who contacted priests or the police seeking information about errant Irish
husbands (who were often found to be cohabiting with other
women); the "small but appreciable number" of Irishmen arrested
for drunkenness; and the many Irish emigrants who no longer practiced their religion.[64]

De Valera presented a very bowdlerized version of Foley's report
in his Galway speech. He did not mention extramarital pregnancies
or men in second unions. Instead, he spoke about Ireland's distinctive national culture and the golden age of the early-Christian era
when Ireland had made a major contribution to western civilization.
He suggested that modern Ireland should aim at working in "the
same spiritual field and to win distinction in that field rather than in
the material," but one wonders whether his audience grasped how this
might relate to fifteen men living in one room, or how Irish newspapers would have reacted if he had mentioned abortion, broken
marriages, and pregnant single women.

Protecting Irish Women

Foley was not the first person to warn about the moral dangers that
Britain posed for Irish emigrants, especially women. In a Lenten pastoral issued in 1933, the archbishop of Tuam, Dr. Gilmartin, claimed
that a number of agencies who recruited Irish girls to work in England were "traps, in order that our Irish girls may be enticed into
houses of ill-fame, and very often terrible tragedies follow." He urged
young women to consult their parish priest before answering these
advertisements.[65] Gilmartin returned to this theme in 1937, when he
warned that "foolish girls" who left home without investigating the
source of these advertisements and consulting their parish priest or
curate "run terrible risks."[66]

The 1931 *Irish Catholic Directory* noted the death of Father Anthony Grogan, who for over thirty years had been charged with
meeting "all" emigrants landed from Ireland at Ellis Island, on the
instructions of the archbishop of New York.[67] It was relatively easy to
monitor the arrival of new emigrants to the United States because
they were subject to stringent immigration controls. Contacting

newly arrived emigrants to Britain was a much more difficult task, given the multiple points of entry and the absence of passport or visa controls. By the late 1920s, a number of organizations had emerged to assist young female emigrants; whether this was a new problem, or one that had suddenly come to public attention is unclear, but the League of Nations' concern with the trafficking of women and children may have been a factor in their emergence. The Port and Station Work Society of Liverpool, a vigilance organization that sought to prevent the international trafficking of women and children, provided assistance to Irish women from at least 1929.[68] The International Catholic Girls Protection Society opened a hostel for intending emigrants in Dublin's Mountjoy Square and their workers began to visit the city's railway stations seeking out girls who were traveling alone.[69] By the late 1930s, members of the Catholic Young Men's Society of Ireland (CYMS) were visiting the North Wall in Dublin, the terminal for ships to Liverpool, speaking to intending emigrants, and having learned their destination, supplying them with a list of suitable lodgings and the name and address of the local branch of the CYMS. They also arranged for CYMS members in England to meet emigrants at their destination and to take them to accommodation "in keeping with their Catholic Faith."[70] But these arrangements were ad hoc and not coordinated.

The introduction of wartime travel restrictions brought an end to free movement between Britain and Ireland. From September 1939, intending emigrants had to obtain a travel permit from the Irish authorities. In July 1942 the newly appointed archbishop of Dublin, John Charles McQuaid, established the Catholic Social Welfare Bureau with a view to coordinating and improving the range of Catholic welfare services in the Dublin area.[71] The first section of the Catholic Social Welfare Bureau to be established was the Emigrants' Section. Although the bureau claimed that its mandate was the "service of the emigrant in the widest interpretation of the phrase," it concentrated on religious and moral welfare. When the Catholic Social Welfare Bureau was established, many people contacted it looking for jobs in Britain, but although the Catholic hierarchy had warned intending emigrants to be cautious about offers of jobs or accommodation in Britain, the bureau was not an employment agency and it did not provide financial assistance, although in emergencies it might arrange for this to be given by the Society of Saint Vincent de Paul.[72]

Although the Catholic Social Welfare Bureau was established to assist all emigrants, from the beginning it showed much greater interest in women. In a speech at the official opening on 17 June 1942, McQuaid stated that the "chief activity" of the bureau would be the care of emigrants, especially women and girls. The Emigrants Section was based at 18 Westland Row, opposite the railway station that was the terminus for trains from the west of Ireland and the starting point for the boat trains to Dun Laoghaire. Intending emigrants could drop into the office, which was open from ten in the morning until eleven at night. During the war, when trains and boats were often seriously behind schedule, the bureau arranged overnight accommodation in Dublin for emigrants on outward or return journeys. Although McQuaid saw the Catholic Social Welfare Bureau as a mechanism for ensuring that welfare services would remain under the control of the Catholic church rather than the state, he was not content to rely exclusively on voluntary agencies. On 4 July 1942, approximately three weeks after the bureau was established, McQuaid met de Valera to discuss possible cooperation between church and state on emigration. He met Gerald Boland, the minister for Justice, on July 6; on the following day the secretary of the Department of Justice traveled to All Hallows College in Drumcondra to meet Dr. McQuaid. The archbishop asked the government to raise the minimum age for granting an exit permit to an unaccompanied traveler from twelve to sixteen years, and he urged the Department of Justice to require all lodging houses and every person or agent who recruited domestic servants for jobs outside Ireland to be registered. He also requested that the bureau be supplied with the names and addresses of all persons who were granted travel permits and that the application form for travel permits be redesigned to include the names and addresses of the person offering employment as well as the type of employment. McQuaid wished in particular to be in a position to identify domestic servants and probationer nurses, further evidence of his determination to monitor female emigrants.[73]

According to McQuaid's notes, Daniel Costigan (a senior official in the Department of Justice) "saw no trouble" with these requests. McQuaid subsequently met de Valera, Boland, and Joseph Walshe, the secretary of the Department of External Affairs, at Iveagh House, and according to McQuaid's notes of this meeting, de Valera agreed to supply the Catholic Social Welfare Bureau with a slip containing the relevant details of all emigrants; this new form would be included in future in all the police forms submitted by intending emigrants. There was also agreement on registering lodging houses and emigrant agencies, and the ministers gave a commitment to negotiate with the British government to raise the minimum age for unaccompanied emigrants to sixteen years. McQuaid informed the meeting that bureau workers had recently met two girls, aged fourteen and a half and fifteen, who were waiting at Westland Row station for a man who did not appear until the following day.

McQuaid's notes indicate that the Department of Justice informed him on 14 August that they were agreeable to meeting all his requests, except the order requiring employment agencies that recruited emigrant workers to be registered.[74] But a minute of the Iveagh House meeting in the files of the Department of the Taoiseach gives no indication of any government commitment to supply the Catholic Social Welfare Bureau with the personal details of intending emigrants; the same file shows that officials were dubious about the need for a register of hotels and lodging houses used by emigrants when they stayed overnight in Dublin, perhaps because, as the file noted, the bureau would find overnight accommodation for intending emigrants.[75] In the event, the Catholic Social Welfare Bureau was not given the personal details of intending emigrants; they had to rely on voluntary efforts to track them.

When the Irish hierarchy met on 22 June 1943, the bishops recommended that all priests should be reminded of the need to warn congregations about the dangers to the faith and morals of young women emigrants,[76] but if priests followed this advice, the warnings proved ineffective, because the number of female emigrants continued to rise (likewise the proportion who were under twenty-two years of age). In 1941 a total of 3,272 women obtained travel permits;

this rose to 14,448 in 1942 and 19,003 in 1943, when 36 percent of permits were issued to women under twenty-two, a higher proportion than in 1941 or 1942. Although government regulations prohibited men and women aged less than twenty-two years from emigrating, exemptions were granted for those going to religious orders or professional training (including nursing) and in cases of family hardship:[77] The high proportion of women emigrants under twenty-two years of age suggests that exemptions were granted without much difficulty, despite the fact that at least two secretaries of government departments, Costigan (Justice) and Walshe (External Affairs), appear to have shared McQuaid's concerns about young female emigrants.

The Department of External Affairs took advantage of the temporary lull in emigration in the run-up to the D-Day landings to review the regulations governing emigration, with a view to tightening them. One official (probably Walshe) expressed concern over the "steady increase" in the number of permits being granted to women, and the "deep public uneasiness" over the large numbers of women emigrants in their teens and early twenties. He reported that the British police had returned several young female emigrants to Ireland, because they were too young and too immature, adding, "One would want to be a very insensitive person not to feel the humiliation of such cases." He recommended that additional restrictions be imposed on young women emigrants, either by setting a quota for women under the age of twenty-two or by stringently enforcing the existing controls. This official believed that many women emigrants were motivated by factors other than economics, and he dismissed the idea that male and female emigrants should be treated in an identical manner, citing Article 6 of the Women and Children's Convention of the League of Nations—to which Ireland was a signatory—where the contracting parties agreed, in cases where they had not already done so, to introduce regulations to ensure the protection of women and children seeking employment in another country. As to the argument that the state could not override parental wishes and that young people should be permitted to emigrate if they had parental approval, he claimed similar arguments had been advanced by opponents of the nineteenth-century factory acts, which restricted the working rights and hours of women and children. A revised form of this memorandum, which was submitted to cabinet, noted that the employment of young persons was "a responsibility of the State. Where the pagan sociologist—like the statute of the ILO [International Labor Organization]—assumes educational and physical development as the limits of that responsibility, people in this country think rather of moral and social considerations." People who were quite prepared to admit the necessity for men with families to emigrate if they cannot find work in Ireland "cannot see any present or future good in allowing young people, particularly girls, to go straight from the severe, but salutary restraints of their home environment into the hectic wartime atmosphere of British cities and towns, for the sake of earning high rates of wages which they have neither the experience nor the knowledge of the world to be able to spend to their moral and material advantage, and which, being purely temporary can only sow the seed of grave future discontent."[78]

Although the Irish authorities tightened restrictions on emigration during the summer of 1944, no additional controls were imposed on women. When the British authorities decontrolled female employment in July 1946, which meant that women were free to travel to Britain in search of work or to find jobs through private advertisements or recruitment agents (though they still required a travel permit) the Irish government made no effort to prevent this relaxation. On 25 June, less than a week before the changes were due to come into effect, de Valera instructed that McQuaid should be informed of this, and that the government had concluded "provisionally" that the only practicable control was to require parental permission before issuing travel permits to minors.[79] There is no evidence that McQuaid or his fellow bishops protested at this decision. Although the memorandum from the Department of External Affairs expressed the view that the state had a responsibility to prevent young people, particularly girls, from emigrating, even if this involved overriding parental wishes, Catholic social teaching emphasized that responsibility rested with the family, not with the state. In January 1946 the Conference of Irish Superiors of Convent Secondary Schools had invoked parental rights in their opposition to compulsory medical inspections of school children, and McQuaid supported their decision.[80] The primacy of parental rights was also central to the church's later opposition to the Mother and Child Scheme. The Catholic hierarchy could hardly turn around and demand that the state override parental wishes in order to prevent young women from emigrating.

The proportion of emigrants who were women continued to rise in the years immediately following the end of World War II. Many British women who had been conscripted into the labor force during the war returned to the home and had to be replaced, whereas demobilized male soldiers were seeking civilian jobs. In the summer of 1946 the Irish authorities lifted the ban on recruitment advertisements imposed in 1942 for jobs in Britain, but the cabinet instructed the Department of Industry and Commerce to investigate the possibility of regulating agencies recruiting workers for Britain.[81] Employment agencies became a major target for those wishing to prevent, or at least restrict, female emigration. On 7 October 1947 the Catholic hierarchy issued a press statement concerning the "recent excessive increase in emigration" and warning of the dangers to faith and morals of "our young emigrants," and they passed a resolution for "private transmission to the Taoiseach." Although the statement ostensibly applied to both men and women, in practice it was directed at women: "The Bishops view with grave alarm the continuous drain on the womanhood and future motherhood of the country as the result of the present wave of emigration and they consider it contrary to the spiritual and temporal welfare of the nation that foreign agents should be allowed to enter the country to attract girls with promises of lucrative employment the fulfilment of which no one in this country could control."[82]

As I noted in chapter 4, this letter was not answered until February 1948, by which time the Fianna Fáil government had been succeeded by the first Inter-Party government. The new taoiseach, John A. Costello, acknowledged that the large number of young women emigrants was causing "particular anxiety," but he firmly stated that "the denial to individuals of the opportunity to seek a livelihood or a career abroad would, in the Government view, be the restriction of a fundamental human right which could only be justified in circumstances of great national emergency." Costello also indicated that the government did not believe that emigration agencies were a major factor in encouraging emigration.[83] All the available evidence suggests that most young women (and men) emigrated with parental approval, even encouragement. Furthermore, a report prepared by the Department of External Affairs in August 1947 dismissed allegations that women emigrants were being exploited by English employers. Women emigrants were free to change jobs, and jobs were readily available in Britain, so it was unlikely that they would remain in a position that offered poor pay and working conditions. It concluded that the dangers to female emigrants were "mainly moral and social." Whereas men commonly went in groups to factories or building sites, where arrangements were in place for their moral and religious welfare and "often for the maintenance of an Irish atmosphere," women who became domestic servants in English homes faced a moral atmosphere that "young and inexperienced girls are only too often unfitted to withstand."[84]

The evidence collected by Stanley Lyon on behalf of the Commission on Emigration confirms that the primary concerns about female emigrants related to morality not to material circumstances. Lyon's report on Irish female emigrants in England is littered with moral judgments and stereotypes, whereas his comments about men were much less judgmental. Although he did not identify any particular shortcomings among the women that he met in the Lucas lamp factory in Birmingham, he described them as "a poorish type."[85] When he visited the Adelphi dance hall he was horrified to notice that many men and some girls were under the influence of drink; he described the women as coming from "very low stratums of life," noting that the men came "mostly from the west." Elsewhere he recorded that the men were "all of good type," the girls of "much lower class." Lyon was not alone in this. An official of the British Ministry of Labor in Lancashire informed him that Irishmen gave little trouble, but Irish girls were either very good or very bad; there was no middle way.[86] Lyon reported that many Irishmen working in Britain believed "it would be far better if girls were not allowed to leave Ireland until they had at least reached twenty-one years of age. . . . There is a great temptation in the path of those young girls who suddenly find themselves in England with no restrictions as to late hours of associations. Many of the unwary got into bad company soon after arrival and the sequel was bad."[87] Father Walsh, a Catholic priest in Southampton, reported that the small number of Irishmen living in the area were mostly "of a good type," although they drifted away from their religion rather easily. He was much more critical of Irish women, describing them as of "a distinctly lower type except those who go for nursing"; he claimed that they were careless about religion and morals.[88]

Father Walsh was not alone in singling out trainee nurses. At the time the British Ministry of Labor's Irish office interviewed all applicants for trainee nursing positions in Britain; candidates who were accepted had their fare paid. According to the matron of Highgate Hospital, the interviews ensured "a strong and suitable type of student," who was attentive to her religious duties. Nursing, like domestic service, was viewed as a career that would equip women to become wives and mothers. But whereas domestic servants lived and worked in isolation from other emigrants, Irish nurses tended to congregate in certain hospitals, living and working in a middle-class, feminine, and protected variant of a McAlpine's building site, although this point was never made explicitly. It was often implied that probationer nurses were better equipped to emigrate because of their superior social and educational background. Yet even trainee nurses were subject to occasional censure. Some matrons claimed that they were "now being drawn from a lower type"; this was particularly true of psychiatric nurses.[89]

Statements about the sexual behavior and the religious practices of female emigrants were colored by attitudes toward assimilation. Many of the Irish women who emigrated to the United States before 1929 became servants in prosperous Protestant households and, it would appear, adopted the mores of their employers, transmitting them to their families when they married.[90] Domestic service became a mechanism, then, for assimilating Irish emigrants into American society without necessarily abandoning the Catholic religion. In Ireland domestic service was regarded as a suitable career for young women because it was compatible with the ideology of domesticity, and it appeared to provide suitable training for future wives and mothers.[91] By the late 1940s the status of domestic service had declined both in Britain and Ireland, but abandoning domestic service only left these young women open to further strictures. Lyon claimed that women who were initially hired as domestic servants often moved to other jobs such as waitressing or factory work. "A certain social distinction (or, better perhaps lack of social stigma) attaches to these occupations, permitting a higher holding of the head, especially when affairs of the heart crop up. The metropolitan boy-friend is apparently allergic to the domestic servant."[92] Ultimately the concerns that were expressed about women emigrants reflected fears about sexuality, assimilation, and the abandonment of religious practice.

"Pregnant from Ireland"

The emigration of pregnant single women was the most sensitive and contentious aspect of female emigration; it prompted calls for the Irish government to appoint a social worker to care for emigrants in Britain, and it also gave rise to tensions between the Catholic church in England and in Ireland. By the early 1930s, perhaps earlier, the Irish authorities were aware that pregnant single women were traveling to Britain and that some Irish women became pregnant shortly after their arrival.[93] The report on the Criminal Law Acts in 1931 noted that it was difficult to determine the true rate of illegitimate births in Ireland because many pregnant Irish women fled to Britain.[94] The report of the Department of Local Government and Public Health for 1932 noted complaints from English Catholic charities about the number of pregnant Irish single women who were giving birth in Britain.[95] Officials of the Department met representatives of British Catholic organizations at the offices of the Irish High Commission in London to plan a scheme for the repatriation of Irish single mothers and their babies.[96] The Irish authorities drew a very firm line on this issue: only women whose babies were conceived in Ireland were eligible for assistance.[97] Although Irish officials preferred to leave charitable agencies with the primary responsibility for pregnant emigrants, the English Catholic church and some British officials pressed the government to take a more active role. The archbishop of Westminster, Cardinal Hinsley, wrote to de Valera in 1939 expressing concern about the numbers of single pregnant Irish women traveling to Britain and suggesting that a social worker should be attached to the office of the Irish High Commission in London to arrange their repatriation.[98] In 1942 the Birmingham Medical Officer of Health, Dr. Newsholme, sent Helen Murtagh, a Birmingham city councillor and a member of that city's public health committee, to Dublin to discuss the problems that pregnant Irish women posed for Birmingham's health and welfare services. Many Irish women were arriving in Birmingham in distress. Murtagh, a Catholic, met McQuaid and he arranged that she meet de Valera and the ministers for Justice and Local Government and Public Health. She also spent two days with Alice Litster, the official in the Department of Local Government and Public Health responsible for unmarried mothers. In an undated letter to McQuaid written from Dublin's Shelbourne Hotel, Helen Murtagh promised that when she returned to Birmingham she would ask Bishop Griffin (bishop of Birmingham) to approach Cardinal Hinsley to ensure that every Irish baby was baptized before leaving England and to enlist his efforts in preventing newspapers such as the *Universe* (an English Catholic paper) giving exaggerated reports (presumably about Irish pregnant women in Britain). She also gave a commitment to try to ensure that, where possible, Irish women who became pregnant would be reinstated in "their situations." This approach to Cardinal Hinsley reflected concern in the Department of Local Government and Public Health and in the Dublin archdiocese about the unsympathetic attitude of social workers in the archdiocese of Westminster toward pregnant Irish women and their children. Murtagh's visit appears to have resulted in improved arrangements in Birmingham for the repatriation of Irish mothers and their babies, with the cooperation of the Catholic Social Welfare Bureau and the Department of Local Government and Public Health.[99] But most pregnant Irish women did not wish to be repatriated; they regarded England as a refuge.

England offered many attractions unavailable to pregnant single women in Ireland: anonymity, escape from the sanction of parents and neighbors, and the option of adoption as well as that of leaving the mother and baby home shortly after the birth. Legislation providing for adoption was not introduced in Ireland until 1952—the delay was due to objections from the Catholic church—although some private adoptions took place before that date.[100] Of the 4,170 children born out of wedlock in 1953 who were chargeable to Irish public assistance authorities, 2,284 were boarded out. The remainder were placed in institutions. Conditions in mother and baby homes in Britain were undoubtedly less severe than in Ireland. In order to gain admission to one of the five Irish mother and baby homes that were supported by public assistance authorities and run by religious orders, an expectant mother had to apply to her local authority, although the application could be made on her behalf by a voluntary organization. Little is known about the administrative procedures, but if a means test on a woman's family was required (and I suspect that it was because there are detailed, county-by-county files on these cases in the National Archives),[101] her privacy would have been compromised.

In the absence of adoption, mothers generally remained in the mother and baby home for two years after the birth, caring for their child until he or she was sent to an institution or boarded out. A memorandum by the Department of Health claimed that there were no legal powers preventing a mother from leaving before that time, but as she would have been required to either leave with her baby, or make arrangements for its care, in practice she had little choice.[102] When in the mid-1950s Halliday Sutherland visited a children's home at Tuam run by the Bon Secours Sisters, he noted that mothers remained for one year after the birth. During that time they cared for their baby and carried out domestic work without pay. At the end of the year, a mother could either take her baby or leave the child at the home with a view to it being adopted. Children who were not adopted were transferred to an industrial school at the age of seven, as were many boarded-out children. Sutherland describes how the children vied for his attention, hoping that he might be an adoptive parent. "At the Dogs' Home, Battersea, every dog barks at the visitor in the hope that it will be taken away."[103]

Stanley Lyon believed that the number of pregnant Irish women arriving in Britain was rising. At the West Hill Sacred Heart convent for unmarried mothers, an estimated seven of eight patients were Irish. English mothers, according to Lyon, were often eager to keep their babies, perhaps putting them in an institution for a few years, but most Irish women, the majority aged twenty-four to

twenty-eight, wanted "to get the job over and leave the child anywhere." Over a twenty-five-day period in October 1948, a total of 48
pregnant Irish women, average age twenty-five, had applied to the
Crusade of Rescue—an English Catholic charity that worked closely
with the Catholic Rescue and Protection Agency in South Anne
Street in Dublin. Many of these women were described as "of the
cheeky type."[104] At the Sacred Heart convent in West Hill, 85 of the 89
children baptized between March and September 1948 were born to
Irish girls, who were reported to be pregnant when they arrived in
England.[105] A female welfare officer in a Lancashire office of the British Ministry of Labor claimed that some Irish doctors passed women
who were in relatively advanced stages of pregnancy as fit for employment in England, presumably so that they would have their fare
paid. If a woman was so advanced in pregnancy that she was unable
to take up a job on arrival in England, the ministry would contact her
parents or the local clergy to arrange her return to Ireland. Some of
the evidence collected by Lyon suggested that the majority of women
became pregnant in Ireland. But the Birmingham Catholic Maternity and Child Welfare Council claimed that of 114 who applied to
them for assistance known to be Irish, 43 had become pregnant in
Ireland, 65 in England, and in 6 cases the details were not known.
Over 60 percent of these women came from rural areas. Very few
were reported to be in their teens.[106]

Pregnant Irish women continued to travel to Britain throughout
the 1950s.[107] Of the 3,291 women who applied for assistance to the
Westminster Crusade of Rescue between 1950 and 1953, more than
half, or 1,693, were Irish.[108] A report presented to a meeting of British
voluntary agencies noted that "a girl has little chance of going free
under almost two years" from Irish mother and baby homes.[109] This
was tantamount to serving a prison sentence for pregnancy out of
wedlock; it also meant that it was extremely difficult for a woman to
conceal a pregnancy or rebuild a normal life. Cardinal Griffin, now
archbishop of Westminster, told Lyon that Irish girls who became
pregnant had "too great a fear" of the Irish clergy and that "too narrow a view" was taken of the offence in Ireland.[110]

Practically none of the information that Lyon collected in Britain
featured in the report of the Commission on Emigration, and there

is no indication that it was ever read by ministers or civil servants. The report noted that the commission did not inquire "whether the arrangements generally for the care of unmarried mothers and their children in this country are satisfactory because we do not think it is our direct concern."[111] The investigation of facilities for single mothers in Ireland consisted of a memorandum prepared by the Department of Health and the evidence given by Frank Duff, the founder of the Legion of Mary, on the Legion's Regina Coeli Hostel for mothers and babies. Despite its limitations, Regina Coeli provided the most sympathetic services for single mothers in Ireland at the time.[112] The Commission on Emigration dismissed the question of Irish single mothers by noting that "for us as a Population Commission, the significance of the problem of illegitimacy rests primarily on the loss by emigration of many unmarried mothers who find it preferable for one reason or another, to emigrate rather than to face all the circumstances of an illegitimate pregnancy and confinement in this country."[113] The word "confinement" was doubly appropriate in this instance in the light of the facilities provided for unmarried mothers in Ireland at this time.

Emigrant Welfare: The Role of the London Embassy

Cardinal Hinsley's letter to de Valera in 1939 requesting the appointment of a welfare officer at the Irish High Commission in London was the first of many such requests. In 1944 Henry Gray, the secretary of the Catholic Social Welfare Bureau, suggested that a female welfare liaison officer should be stationed at the Irish High Commission to deal *"particularly"* with Irish girls "in trouble [probably a euphemism for pregnant] or otherwise in serious difficulties in England." This officer would be available for consultation by clergy, local authorities, and welfare organizations, which would arrange the girls' repatriation and see that they were received by relatives, if appropriate. In the longer term, Gray expressed the hope that the liaison might assist with other problem cases, such as Irish girls who, having served a short prison sentence, were deported from England without any arrangements for their aftercare in Ireland; mothers deported with young infants; and women who needed psychiatric care. He was fearful that the end of the war would see an increasing number of single mothers repatriated, as some were employed in war industries and their babies had been placed in government nurseries, which were expected to close when the war ended.[114]

This putative welfare officer was only to be concerned with women. Many Irish men were deported, having served a prison sentence; others, having been convicted of petty crimes, were served with deportation orders by magistrates; and some Irishmen in Britain suffered from psychiatric and physical illness, including serious accidents at work. However, there was no suggestion that men might require the services of a welfare officer. The men who feature in the welfare files of the Catholic Social Welfare Bureau tended to be husbands who were no longer sending money to their families or men who had contracted registry office marriages.

Gray's request is unusual because it originated in Ireland; most demands for the appointment of a welfare officer came from individuals and organizations in Britain. In 1952 Mary Byrne, a social worker at Martin's House in London (an association that rehabilitated "fallen Irish women") and daughter of independent TD and long-time Lord Mayor of Dublin Alfie Byrne, contacted the minister for External Affairs to press for the appointment of a welfare officer in London. The Department of Finance had dismissed the proposal, claiming that it was not the function of the state to assume responsibility for the economic, spiritual, or moral welfare of Irish citizens resident abroad; the appointment of a welfare officer would imply that the government accepted such an obligation, and they would then come under continuous pressure from organizations interested in emigrant welfare to extend the services and even to provide financial aid to emigrants in distress. The Department of External Affairs, however, was more sympathetic. While not accepting that the state was responsible for the welfare of Irish citizens resident abroad, they claimed that the state had a duty to protect their interests and to provide protection to those who needed it.

But having given the proposal qualified support, they identified a number of difficulties. The Irish ambassador in London, F. H. Boland, noted that the people who were most concerned about emigrant welfare were the Catholic clergy, but "as is only natural," they were more concerned about spiritual than material welfare. According to Boland, the clergy were especially concerned to counteract the influence of the Connolly Clubs,[115] and their first priority was to keep the Irish together, believing that this would reduce the risk that they would cease to practice their religion. In another report written around this time, Seán Nunan, secretary of the Department of External Affairs, noted that although Catholic clergy in England took a great interest in emigrant housing, their views did not necessarily coincide with those of the embassy. Priests were eager that Irish emigrants should live together rather than take digs with English families, although this might provide better accommodation, because they believed that an Irish environment would best preserve their religion. Nunan cited the satisfaction expressed by one priest that 150 immigrant men were living in three small houses near Southwark Cathedral. The houses were extremely overcrowded, but the canon was content, because the landlord was a Catholic of good character and the houses were close to the cathedral.[116]

Boland cautioned that many emigrants tended to avoid centers and services that were too closely identified with the Catholic clergy. "Valuable as support and co-operation of the clergy can be, however, problems arise if activities intended to appeal to Irish people are identified too closely with clerical endeavour."[117] His observations are confirmed by a 1960 report by A. E. C. W. Spencer, who remarks on the "incipient anti-clericalism" of some Irish emigrants, which in extreme cases might manifest itself in membership of the Communist Party, the Connolly Clubs, or "bitter public criticism of the priests," but usually took the form of "attempts to avoid the priests, shyness with priests, and general lack of co-operation."[118] If the government decided to provide some form of welfare services for emigrants, Boland cautioned against creating expectations among charitable organizations that the state would assume responsibility for all or part of the cost of Irish relief in Britain. Having weighed the merits of the case, Boland came down in favor of a welfare officer, whose primary role should be to liaise with the voluntary agencies and coordinate their work. The Department of Health concurred, but they also cautioned that some Irish girls in trouble did not contact these agencies.[119]

Rapid decision making was not a feature of Irish governments in the early 1950s, and the appointment of an emigrant welfare officer was no exception. Nothing had happened by the summer of 1953 when the Department of External Affairs received a report on the welfare of Irish girls in Britain prepared by Elizabeth Fitzgerald, president of the archdiocese of Westminster branch of the Catholic Women's League. Before submitting the report to External Affairs, she sent a copy to John Charles McQuaid for his approval.[120] This report seems to have been designed to put pressure on the government. According to the British Vigilance Association and the National Committee for the Suppression of Traffic in Persons, "hordes" of young women between the ages of fourteen and twenty were arriving at Euston Station. In the year ending 31 March 1953, the association had encountered seventy women and girls, ranging in age from fourteen to forty-five, who arrived from Ireland without money, without friends, and without any immediate prospects of employment. Many had no luggage. The association believed that just one-quarter to one-third of those who arrived in such circumstances came to their notice.[121] They expressed particular concern that teenage girls could emigrate without restrictions. A high proportion of these girls became a charge on voluntary services or on the state; some "drifted to the streets"; and some featured in police cases.[122] Mrs. Fitzgerald was especially concerned at the numbers of "young, ignorant and untrained girls" arriving from Ireland to "swell the ranks of unmarried mothers." English Catholic charities were unable to cope with the numbers seeking assistance; consequently, many expectant mothers were cared for by "non-catholic and undenominational societies," and their babies were adopted by non-Catholic families. She suggested that the solution was to provide better services in Ireland.[123]

The adoption of the children of Irish Catholic mothers by non-Catholics was essentially a matter for the Catholic church rather than the state, but the government could not so easily evade other matters in this report. Fitzgerald cited instances where agencies recruited girls for jobs in England but failed to supply them with the address of their employer before they left Ireland and failed to meet them on arrival. She also cited a case of a young woman hired as a mother's helper who arrived only to discover that her employer was a single man; girls hired as domestic servants who were dismissed shortly after arriving in England because they were untrained, unemployable, or "indescribably dirty"; two "unemployable" girls aged fifteen and nineteen who arrived in London with a total of 1s. 9d. and no contact address; parents sending fourteen-year-old daughters to England to take jobs as ward maids, with instructions to send home half their earnings. She quoted a letter from a father, complaining that his daughters, aged fourteen and sixteen, had ceased sending him remittances six or seven weeks after they emigrated. This man reported that an older daughter had previously emigrated to England, but had already got into trouble; he feared that the younger daughters would have a similar fate, because they were "troublesome and stubborn." Fitzgerald demanded that all agencies recruiting domestic workers be licensed by the minister for Justice, that there be a ban on the emigration of young women under sixteen years, and that sixteen-year-olds should only be permitted to emigrate if they had a prearranged job.[124]

Having considered Mrs. Fitzgerald's report at their meeting on 13 October 1953, the Irish hierarchy decided to ask the government to take action to minimize the "grave moral dangers to which young female emigrants were exposed." They specifically requested controls on the activities of domestic employment agencies and the reintroduction of travel permits, which had lapsed in 1951, with all applicants required to obtain a letter from a parish priest or a Catholic curate. McQuaid met the minister for External Affairs, Frank Aiken, to press these demands.[125]

Irish officials remained reluctant to impose controls over the recruitment and emigration of young women. Alice Litster, an official in the Department of Health who was extremely knowledgeable about Irish women emigrants in Britain, believed that the onus rested with employers in England to ensure that they did not recruit anybody whose welfare might be impaired by being hired, because they were too young or for any other reason. She expressed fears that restricting the activities of employment agencies might give rise to other abuses, and she suggested that parents had a responsibility to ensure that their children did not accept jobs outside Ireland that threatened their moral welfare.[126] This reference to parents hints at a fundamental obstacle to state controls over the emigration of young persons. Most young women emigrated with parental consent and were expected to send money home. Given that the primacy of the family and parental rights was guaranteed in the Constitution, any attempt to prevent young people who had parental approval from leaving Ireland would have been open to constitutional challenge. It might also have contravened the right to emigrate, a right that Pope Pius XII had reiterated on several occasions.[127]

The *Report of the Commission on Emigration* suggested that it would be desirable to have some safeguards against misleading recruitment advertisements, but it conceded that it would be difficult to make these effective; the best approach would be for government departments to keep Irish newspapers "informed in these matters."[128] The commission was marginally more assertive in its recommendation that "some type of social bureau [should be established] in Great Britain to look after the welfare of our emigrants there"; this could be done through a central committee consisting of representatives of Irish societies and experienced individuals, and "if it were considered necessary," the state should provide "an initial grant of reasonable amount to help to establish a bureau."[129]

This paragraph was obviously drafted with considerable care. Although it is only a "suggestion," the message is clear: the state should assume some responsibility for emigrant welfare. Many Commonwealth countries had appointed welfare officers at their London legations, as had a number of foreign countries with large numbers of citizens working in England. A welfare officer could have intervened in specific cases such as the welfare of young people. The (British) Youth Employment Service had the power to send home under escort any British boy or girl who had run away from home, but it could not exercise these powers in respect of Irish runaways.[130]

In June 1955, at the request of the Catholic hierarchy, McQuaid met Liam Cosgrave, the minister for External Affairs, to press for the appointment of a welfare officer and for legislation to control employment agencies. He reported to his fellow bishops that Cosgrave had been "very sympathetic" and had immediately approached the government seeking approval for the establishment of an interdepartmental committee aimed at "working out a solution. . . . [I]t is hoped that legislation will soon be presented to control the agencies."

The controls would be modeled on those operated by London County Council.[131] Did any member of the hierarchy see the irony in this statement?

But despite McQuaid's confident predictions, the government failed to impose controls on employment agencies or to appoint a welfare officer. The only statutory provision regulating the activities of employment agencies was a clause in the 1907 Public Health (Amendment) Acts permitting a local authority to take steps to prevent fraud and immorality by agencies recruiting female domestic servants. Dublin and Cork were the only Irish local authorities to have adopted these powers.[132] In June 1956 the interdepartmental committee reported that new legislation would be necessary to control the activities of employment agencies, and this was not warranted at present, because only a small proportion of total emigrants (approximately 700 every year) were recruited through agencies.[133] If the recruitment of Irish emigrant workers had been controlled by foreigners, as was often alleged, the government might have shown a greater willingness to regulate their activities, but the market was dominated by Hynes Universal Employment Agency of Upper O'Connell Street. In 1952 the chairman of the Catholic Social Welfare Bureau, Monsignor Cecil Barrett, contacted Mrs. Hynes to express concern at reports that she was sending young women to jobs in Britain without first providing them and their families with the name and address of their employer. Mrs. Hynes acknowledged that she had begun doing this when travel permits were abolished, in order to safeguard her business interests, but she agreed to abandon the practice.[134] The Catholic Social Welfare Bureau persuaded Independent Newspapers, the country's largest newspaper group, to insert a notice in the jobs columns warning intending emigrants that they should confirm if facilities for religious duties were available before they accepted a job offer, and the hierarchy pressed Irish newspapers not to publish advertisements for lodgings in Britain without first consulting the Catholic Social Welfare Bureau to see if the lodgings were suitable.[135]

The interdepartmental committee on emigrant welfare reported that the Department of External Affairs believed that emigrants' needs were being adequately met by the voluntary agencies, and in attaching a welfare officer, the embassy would only duplicate these services.[136] When Fianna Fáil returned to office in 1957, this decision was reviewed. The Irish ambassador in London reported that in recent years there had been a considerable expansion in the number of Irish associations and that the most effective emigrant services were provided by a combination of ecclesiastical authorities, voluntary organizations, and the embassy, though it is unclear what role it envisaged for the latter.[137]

The English and Irish Hierarchies and Ireland's Spiritual Empire

The Irish Center in London in Camden Town was officially opened in September 1955 by the archbishop of Armagh, Cardinal D'Alton. It provided temporary accommodation for up to fifty persons, a hall, and a canteen. The resident chaplain, Reverend Thomas McNamara, had previously been in charge of two emigrant hostels in the London area.[138] The archbishop of Westminster, Dr. Griffin, was the driving force behind the center. Eighty-three percent of the initial funding was raised in Britain, mainly by the archdiocese of Westminster and the dioceses of Southwark and Brentwood, with the balance apparently coming from the Irish hierarchy. Irish centers also opened in Birmingham and Manchester in 1957 and 1960. The Birmingham center was financed by the local diocese plus a generous donation from McQuaid, and it was directed by a priest.[139]

Archbishop McQuaid had been conscious for some time of the need for Irish centers. In 1948, H. J. Gray, the secretary of the Catholic Social and Welfare Bureau had sent McQuaid an outline of a scheme to assist Irish emigrants. The proposal, which was drafted by M. J. Shaw (another member of the Catholic Social and Welfare Bureau), opened with the statement that "we in Ireland have a duty to help our emigrants in England to retain, in the first place, the heritage of the Catholic Faith, and in the second place, the heritage of their Irish Nationality." Successive governments had done "practically nothing" about this, Shaw stated, probably because of fears that they would be accused of encouraging emigration. The Irish hierarchy had been equally inactive. He conjectured, "I suspect that they do not wish to admit that some at least of our emigrants are losing the Faith in England, which admission would be a slur on their pas- . toral work on behalf of the emigrants while they were still in their diocese in Ireland." As a first step, Shaw recommended that a network of emigrant bureaus should be opened in English Catholic dioceses that attracted large numbers of emigrants, beginning with Birmingham. The bureaus would assist emigrants in finding suitable lodgings and put them in contact with Irish organizations such as the Gaelic Athletic Association and the Gaelic League. He expressed the hope that these organizations could provide a nucleus for study circles and discussion groups designed to promote the Catholic religion and enable emigrants "to resist the fallacious but attractive arguments of the Communists." The plan envisaged that every Irish diocese would appoint a priest who would be responsible for emigrants, with "a sensible diplomatic priest" of the Dublin archdiocese acting as coordinator between the British and Irish operations. Gray suggested that Archbishop McQuaid try to secure support for these proposals from sympathetic bishops who might help him "soften the ground," but he acknowledged that many Irish bishops were suspicious of the Catholic Social and Welfare Bureau because it was run by laymen.[140]

In 1950 the English hierarchy approached the Irish embassy with proposals for an Irish center, which had been drawn up in agreement with the Irish hierarchy, and McQuaid made a parallel appeal to then taoiseach John A. Costello, but no government aid was forthcoming.[141] Maurice Foley, the author of the report that prompted de Valera's 1951 Galway speech, contacted the Department of External Affairs in 1953 seeking financial support for a center in Birmingham. But Boland cautioned that if this request were met, other British cities would demand similar assistance. As the proposed center would cater only for Catholics, and it would give priority to promoting spiritual rather than material welfare, it "raises the difficult question to what extent the State would be justified in assuming responsibilities in the spiritual sphere." The Irish hierarchy had established a committee to discuss the question of establishing Irish centers with the English hierarchy,[142] and Boland advised that the matter should be left in their hands. Foley responded to a letter from External Affairs, which had advised him to contact the Irish hierarchy, with a curt statement that he had sent his petition for financial assistance to the government, not to the hierarchy.[143]

During 1952 separate plans were mooted for a national collection in Ireland and among the Irish in Britain to raise funds for an organization to assist Irish emigrants that would not be under direct church control. Boland reported that there was very little organization at present among the Irish in Britain; the activities of existing Irish societies and groups such as the Gaelic League hardly extended beyond the occasional social and an annual Saint Patrick's Day dinner, and their finances were "extremely shaky." The Anti-Partition League was an exception, but he recommended that the league should not be used as the basis for a new emigrant organization, "for fear of distracting the energies of its local branches from their present task."[144]

The only institutions catering specifically to Irish people in Britain in the early 1950s were the Irish Club in London, founded in 1947, the National University of Ireland Club (NUI), and the Ulster Club. Although the Irish Club and the NUI Club claimed to be nonpolitical and nonsectarian, their membership was overwhelmingly Catholic and nationalist, and the Ulster Club was restricted to those of Ulster birth or descent who were interested in Ulster, which effectively meant unionist and Protestant. A Catholic priest based in Middlesex remarked that the Irish Club was too expensive and too smart to meet the needs of "the poorer types" of emigrants;[145] a comment that would equally apply to the NUI Club and the Ulster Club. The major social event in the Irish Club's calendar was the annual Saint Patrick's Day dance. In 1954 the club president was Lord Killanin and the guest speaker was Fine Gael Senator E. A. McGuire. Eamon de Valera made a brief appearance just before midnight, accompanied by the Irish ambassador, F. H. Boland.[146] De Valera told those present that every exile was an envoy for Ireland; every Irishman an ambassador for his country.

The Irish Times reported that in speaking of emigration, de Valera referred not only to saints and scholars but to the plain people of Ireland all over the world. But on Saint Patrick's night the plain people of Ireland in Britain were probably attending functions organized by the county associations or celebrating in pubs or Irish ballrooms, like the Galtymore in Cricklewood, that had sprouted up in London and other centers with large emigrant communities. County associations provided informal networks for those seeking work or accommodation. A council of the Irish county associations was established in the late 1950s to act as an umbrella organization; this followed the New York model.[147]

But the Catholic church was probably the only group with sufficient resources to establish and run Irish centers without government support. P. McGrath, of the Irish Immigrants' Association in Coventry, owner of a dance hall and lodging house, contacted the Department of External Affairs on several occasions seeking funding for an emigrants advice center in Coventry. He presented de Valera with records of the money that he had raised to provide emergency accommodation for emigrants, and his request was supported by a local Oblate priest who worked closely with the Irish community. When McGrath received the standard reply that Irish centers were a matter for the clergy, he retorted that the Catholic church in England was finding it difficult to raise sufficient money to provide Catholic schools (presumably to educate the children of Irish emigrants), and they should also not be expected to finance Irish centers.[148] A request for government assistance in providing hostels and advice bureaus in the Midlands by Anthony Toner, a member of the Legion of Mary who was involved in running Irish information bureaus in Birmingham and Coventry, was dismissed using the convenient argument that if the government provided financial support, they might be open to charges of religious discrimination.[149] Monsignor Barrett informed McQuaid that although McGrath "means well and is a decent poor fellow," he had tried to dissuade him and others who had formed a committee to assist emigrants in finding jobs and accommodation in England from their efforts, because Barrett believed that they had failed to grasp the magnitude of the task.[150] Dr. Cornelius Lucey appears to have been the only leading church figure to denounce publicly the government's failure to provide hostels and other assistance to young emigrants.[151] The Irish hierarchy and the government (regardless of its composition) were of one mind: emigrant services should be under church control. But which hierarchy, the English or the Irish?

The opening of the Irish centers was part of a concerted campaign by the Catholic hierarchies in England and Ireland to improve services for emigrants. Some days before the official opening of the center in Camden Town, Cardinal Griffin carried out an official blessing ceremony at the Irish Club in Eaton Square, and in the course of his speech he remarked that 1955 was the year when English Catholics made a concerted effort to address the problems arising from Irish immigration.[152] This may have been in response to the upsurge in emigration, or it may reflect pressure from Rome. A majority of migrants and emigrants in postwar Europe were probably Catholic.[153] In 1951 Pope Pius XII established the International Catholic Migration Commission in Geneva to coordinate services for emigrants, with a particular emphasis on creating links between the countries of emigration and immigration.[154] The Catholic church believed that emigration presented opportunities as well as challenges, and they wished to use emigrants to expand Catholicism in countries of immigration. G. W. Kampschoer, the secretary of the International Catholic Migration Commission, told the 1954 Congress at Breda that the history of Irish emigration offered "the best proof for the influence of emigration in the international Catholic field."[155] The commission urged that emigrants should be prepared to face challenges to their faith. H. J. Gray, the secretary of the Catholic Social Welfare Bureau, informed the Breda conference that Irish emigrants could cope with such challenges; he believed that special arrangements for Irish immigrants were unnecessary and impracticable. Irish emigration to Britain could be

> a considerable asset to the Church in that country, just as Irish emigration has been a help in the past both in Great Britain and U.S.A.
>
> Most emigrants leave home under pressure of individual economic circumstances and can be relied upon to be prepared to maintain the high standards of Catholicity to which they were accustomed at home (although there is, of course, a minority who emigrate in search of less stringent codes of conduct).
>
> [The] available evidence demonstrates beyond question that there is very little leakage from the Church amongst Irish emigrants but it is recognized by the Church authorities in both Ireland and Britain that there are many aspects of Irish emigration to Great Britain that

involve grave dangers and especially moral dangers, it must, however be recognized, also, that the absolute cleavage of home ties which is a normal characteristic of emigration is not generally a feature of Irish emigration to Great Britain and that this circumstance (along with the presence in Great Britain of many priests and a large body of Catholic lay-people of Irish birth or extraction) goes far towards securing the welfare of new emigrants.

In the absence of any population pressure in favour of emigration and in circumstances in which emigration is spontaneous and facile, deliberate planning to secure the proper training and placement of emigrants appears to be impracticable, however desirable it might be from a Catholic standpoint.

Prevailing material circumstances (and the extent of the emigration flow) are apparently insuperable obstacles to the provision of special machinery for the reception of Irish emigrants in Great Britain, and their integration into the community.

Gray suggested that the British and Irish hierarchies should make emigrant welfare "a major claim on the normal parochial structure of the two countries." He called for closer liaison between the two hierarchies, suggesting (predictably) that this task could be undertaken by the Emigrants' Section of the Catholic Social Welfare Bureau.[156] Such equanimity about religious practice among the Irish in Britain appears to have been common in Ireland: an article in *Christus Rex* suggested that "up to June 1950 it was debatable whether any religious problem was created by emigration from Ireland—that is among the emigrants."[157] However, in June 1950 Dr. Beck, coadjutor bishop of Brentwood, addressed the Maynooth Union on the religious problems arising from Irish emigration to Britain.[158] By 1952 the English hierarchy had appointed a committee to consider the matter, and in the following year the Irish hierarchy appointed a committee to liaise with them.[159] McQuaid wrote to Cardinal Griffin in May 1954 asking if it would be acceptable for him to send "two sensible people—a man and a woman" from the Emigrants' Section of the Catholic Social Welfare Bureau to London to examine the position of emigrants. Hubert Daly, a member of the Legion of Mary, spent several months in England; having met Cardinal Griffin, the bishops of Southwark and Brentwood and a number of priests in the greater London area, he reported his findings to McQuaid, but if he supplied a written report it has not come to light.[160]

In 1955 Cardinal Griffin and the Irish hierarchy issued pastoral letters on emigration. The pastoral letter issued by the Irish bishops urged Irish parents to use the home to prepare their children for emigration. Irish missionary priests began to conduct missions among the Irish in Britain in September 1955.[161] The Irish hierarchy assumed that these would be directed exclusively at Irish Catholics, but the English hierarchy insisted that they should be parochial missions, because they were keen to integrate emigrants into English Catholic life; they feared that separate missions would promote isolation.[162] When Reverend Aedan McGrath, a member of the Columban Order who had recently been released from prison in China, was appointed to coordinate the missionary work of the Legion of Mary among the Irish in Britain, Cardinal Griffin insisted that he work under the English national director of the Legion of Mary rather than the Irish director.[163] The first emigrant chaplains were appointed in 1957; these were priests who had been released by Irish dioceses for temporary service in English dioceses, working with the Irish community.[164]

These initiatives appear to have fallen far short of what Rome regarded as desirable. In 1958 Cardinal Mimmi, the member of the Roman Curia responsible for migration, wrote to Cardinal D'Alton about "the difficult problem of Irish emigration to England." Mimmi indicated that there was an urgent need to devise a well-organized plan to meet the spiritual needs of Irish emigrants, in cooperation with the English hierarchy. As a first step he suggested carrying out a statistical survey of Irish emigrants—their occupations, the process of emigrating, and their origins and destinations. Although the cardinal welcomed the efforts of the Irish hierarchy, including the initiation of an annual "Emigration Day" (first held on 15 August 1955), he indicated that it was not sufficient to appoint missionary priests to the Irish community in England; chapels, schools, and hostels were also necessary to create "a favourable climate." McQuaid dismissed this letter as "a strange idealistic document, which seems to me to be impractical."[165] The bishop of Ferns, Dr. Staunton, who was chairman of the emigrant mission, commented that "Cardinal Mimmi seemed to think our emigrants were small communities like the

Italians"—a remark that indicates at least equal ignorance on both parts. Dr. Staunton pointed out that if the Irish hierarchy undertook to provide chapels, schools, and hostels for the Irish community in England, they would be undertaking a commitment to provide facilities for one-quarter of the Catholic population of England and Wales.[166] When Cardinal Mimmi gave the closing address at the Fourth National Congress of Diocesan Delegates for Emigration in Spain in September 1959, he remarked that "had all the Irish people, who have emigrated to England throughout the centuries, kept their faith, perhaps the number of Catholics in the latter country would be twelve millions instead of the three millions they now number."[167] In the course of a letter to Cardinal D'Alton concerning Mimmi's remarks, McQuaid noted that on two occasions he had informed the papal nuncio, "in very clear terms, exactly what is being done for our emigrants, what is being said about us in Rome for years and what are our feelings about the failure to appreciate the true position."[168]

Cardinal Mimmi's intervention may have prompted the English and the Irish hierarchies to compile more comprehensive reports on Irish emigrants. The Catholic Social Welfare Bureau commissioned a statistical report based on their case files from Reverend Conor Ward, who had recently completed his doctoral degree in sociology at Liverpool University. In 1959 the Catholic Social Welfare Bureau dealt with 7,598 emigrants; almost equal numbers of men and women. In 56 percent of cases, the first contact was made by port workers, on the trains from Dublin to Dun Laoghaire, or on the boats at the North Wall and Dun Laoghaire;[169] 19 percent were contacted through information provided by a priest in Ireland; 16 percent made direct contact with the bureau. A total of 1,068 were classified as "special cases." Of these, 284 concerned the "moral welfare of youth," 293 were "marriage problems," 162 concerned "the nonpractice of religion," 71 involved missing persons, and the remainder were unclassified. Matters such as the "non-practice of religion," the 112 register office marriages, or the 53 classified as "mixed marriage difficulties," were only of concern to the church, but the bureau handled 128 cases of "desertion and other matrimonial problems." Twelve special cases were described as "coloured association." The 284 cases classified as "moral welfare of youth" presumably included pregnant single women, though women only accounted for 178 of the total. In 38 percent of cases, the files recorded complete success; the success rate was greatest for recent emigrants.[170]

In 1959 the archdiocese of Westminster asked the Newman Demographic Survey, a Catholic social survey group based in London, to prepare a report on arrangements to promote the welfare of Irish immigrants in England and Wales, which would be presented at the International Catholic Migration Commission conference in Ottawa in 1960.[171] A first draft of the report, by A. E. C. W. Spencer, was presented to an invited audience in London in June 1959.[172] Writing some days later to Dr. Conor Ward, who had been present, Spencer commented that "John Hickey[173] remarked at lunch-time that it had been the most depressing morning of his life." Spencer added, "I had often been warned about this by the English clergy but had always taken these warnings with a grain of salt." Spencer's report was subjected to a barrage of criticism from Monsignor Barrett, H. J. Gray and Father McElroy, an Irish Columban priest working in England. They were particularly exercised by a section describing "the characteristics of the immigrants from Ireland," which included several pages on "the home environment of the emigrant."[174] Spencer claimed that to understand the problem of integrating Irish emigrants into English Catholic society it was essential to understand the society from which they came. He began by highlighting the importance of the family farm, citing a statement by the American Jesuit sociologist Reverend Alexander Humphreys that "practically all activities are domestic in character."[175] According to Spencer, the centrality of the family farm meant that Irish parents exercised a strong authority over their children, and this authority lasted longer than in any other rural society because of the late age of marriage. He implied that the relationship between the Irish laity and the Catholic church mirrored the relationship between Irish rural parents and their children; most rural Catholics accepted church teaching without question. The high level of church attendance in Ireland was due to social pressures to conform; he also noted the "general absence of 'Sex Education.'" Spencer summarized the main characteristics of Irish emigrants as follows: "lack of self-discipline, and self-control, an undeveloped sense of responsibility toward work-mates, employers and non-Catholics, [because in Ireland such relationship often took place within the family] a social inferiority complex, a lack of articulateness about religion, a sense of ignorance about sex, and a view of clergy-laity relationships that polarises at either complete acceptance of priestly authority in *all* matters, or equally complete rejection of *any* priestly authority."

In England, he suggested, pressures to conform worked against attending Mass; Irish emigrants who viewed priests as father figures rebelled against them; they rejected the warnings that they had been given about the moral dangers in England, dropping their guard and abandoning the basic tenets of Catholic belief.[176] In his report to McQuaid, Barrett noted that the Irish church had only agreed to this report on condition that it examined the position in Britain, "and would not enter significantly into a study of the social or religious background and home environment of the migrants, their attitudes and intentions and the arrangements for promoting their welfare existing in Ireland." He dismissed Spencer's views on the Irish background as "grossly untrue," and suggested that this section of the report should be excised. Barrett had prepared an alternative draft, which substituted a eulogy on the spiritual and moral values of the Irish people: "It is generally acknowledged that in the good Irish Catholic home the parents, themselves imbued with Ireland's tradition of deep faith, piety and obedience to the laws of the Church, instill in their children from an early age a knowledge and love of God, an appreciation of virtue and a ready acceptance of the teaching mission of the Church."

Where Spencer had suggested that Ireland suffered from a latent anti-clericalism that was only kept in check by pressures to conform, Barrett wrote that "Irish reverence for the priesthood is deeply rooted in the Irish Catholic heritage, the strength of Irish faith, and the long distances travelled on foot to attend Sunday mass." Spencer's paragraph deploring the lack of sex education was replaced by a statement that "Irish children grow up in an atmosphere where purity and chastity are reverenced . . . [and] without significant exposure to the naturalistic theories of sex education." Spencer referred to the low educational standard of most Irish emigrants; Barrett claimed that their formal scholastic attainments were not "significantly different" to those of comparable social groups in England.[177] Whereas Spencer argued that Irish social structures accounted for the problems that Irish emigrants experienced in Britain, including the failure to practice their religion, Barrett suggested that responsibility for any shortcoming in morals and religious practice rested with English society. McQuaid informed Cardinal Godfrey that a substantial section of Spencer's report was "so unscientific, in that it is based on personal impressions, unsupported by established facts, that in my view, it ought to be eliminated." He asked the cardinal to intervene. Monsignor Worlock telephoned Barrett some days later and reassured him that the report would not be sent to Geneva until it had been approved by both Dublin and Westminster.[178] Spencer offered to delete the entire section relating to Ireland, other than a brief statistical summary, but this did not satisfy Barrett, who pressed for his version to be substituted.[179] While the dispute over Spencer's report was still unresolved, Monsignor Worlock discovered that a report on "The Irish Rural Immigrant and British Urban Society" by J. V. Hickey, another member of the Newman Demographic Survey, had already been submitted to Munich for a conference that would be held in association with the Eucharistic Congress. When Barrett read Hickey's paper, he described it as "much more acceptable than Spencer's," although he pressed for revisions.[180] On 14 June, McQuaid informed Cardinal Godfrey that "Geneva is now safe. Munich is still to be feared." He expressed doubts about the value of "these Demographic Surveys" in advancing "the supernatural work of the apostolate." McQuaid conceded that "they can usefully absorb the activity of laymen. They are no substitute for the traditional hard work of pastoral visitation, preaching and hearing Confession."[181]

Spencer's report was not presented at the International Catholic Migration Commission conference at Ottawa. Hickey's report may have reached Munich in a revised form, but there is no evidence that it was published.[182] In a 1958 report on the Irish in Britain, the Irish ambassador to Britain, Cornelius Cremin, remarked that there has been much controversy concerning the faithfulness of the Irish immigrant to the practice of his religion. The consensus of opinion was that while there is a not inconsiderable wastage, the majority do keep up their religious practice fairly conscientiously. Indeed, despite defects (which are often unduly publicized) the great majority of the Irish in Britain are hard working and well behaved, and the evidence of parochial clergy strongly suggests that the moral laxity of the remainder is frequently a temporary phase that passes with the years, marriage, and the normal growth of responsibility. Cremin concluded that "adaptation and acceptance—[of Irish emigrants in Britain] have, in recent years been relatively easy"; the fact that the great majority of Irish emigrants were Catholic did not necessarily operate to their disadvantage because the prevailing attitude in England was now one of indifference to religion. "Resentment of the Irish on religious grounds is far more likely to be found amongst their English co-religionists than amongst non-Catholics, the ostensible reason being the allegedly non-intellectual and narrow nature of the Irish Church but jealousy of their distinctive position as a select minority and mere social snobbery also play a part."[183]

Cremin's assessment is borne out by the disagreement concerning Spencer's report. But while acknowledging the social and cultural snobbery of English Catholicism, it is equally important to concede the reluctance of the Irish hierarchy to see Irish Catholics through the eyes of others. Although the Irish hierarchy did considerably more to assist emigrants than the Irish state, both can be accused of denouncing the dangers of emigration for their own purposes and simultaneously failing to address them, whether these concerned pregnant Irish teenagers, fifteen men sleeping in one room, or nonattendance at mass, and they both dismissed criticism by outsiders of Irish emigrants as either exaggerated or unfounded. When Barrett returned a copy of Mrs. Fitzgerald's report on Irish female emigrants to McQuaid in September 1953, he commented that "there is a tendency, among undenominational workers in England especially, to generalise too freely from isolated cases."[184] In 1955 the Catholic Women's Federation of secondary schools, with an address at 91 Lower Baggot Street in Dublin, sent a letter to the Irish hierarchy in connection with employment bureaus recruiting Irish emigrants, where they referred to "the bad reputation which our people and country receive. Cases which have appeared in the press, while perhaps reported with a certain bias, contain facts that do not redound to our credit."[185] A similar concern with image can be found in reports from the London

Embassy. In June 1957 the ambassador noted that "while criticism in the Press and elsewhere of the behavior of Irish immigrants is in many instances, well founded, the extent of the problem is undoubtedly exaggerated. Publicity, which attaches to misbehavior of individual immigrants gives rise to and helps to perpetuate an impression that the behavior of the Irish in Britain as a class is generally reprehensible. It is seldom that the decent and law-abiding immigrants, who constitute the vast majority, gain any prominence.[186] Yet the reports of "misbehavior" and the "bad reputation" of Irish emigrants highlighted the darker side of emigrant life. Moreover, they exposed the shortcomings of some of the most deeply cherished and revered icons of Irish society—the family, the church, and the church-dominated educational system—to the unflattering scrutiny of outsiders.

Caring for "Social Casualties": Emigrant Services in the 1960s

During the 1960s there was growing concern over the negative images presented by Irish emigrants. There was a sharp fall in the numbers emigrating; by 1969 net emigration was in the region of five thousand—which was commonly regarded as equivalent to "voluntary" emigrants. However, there was a growing impression during the 1960s that a higher proportion of emigrants than before were problem cases. In its report for 1969–70, the Catholic Social Welfare Bureau cautioned that "improving employment opportunities within the country can substantially reduce the outflow of the more stable elements in the community without having atall [sic] as much effect on the level of emigration of those who, because of lack of skills or other inadequacies of temperament or character, stand most in need of help and guidance and often least realise their need."[187] Economic growth had little impact on pregnant single women, absconding husbands, or those who simply wanted to get away from Ireland. The 1960s brought a greater awareness of the darker side of emigration and, indeed, a more open attitude toward social problems in general. British newspapers and television documentaries featured stories of Irish single mothers and homeless Irish in England.[188] As a by-product of the growing concern with race relations in the United Kingdom, researchers investigating the living and working conditions of immigrants of color commonly collected data about the Irish in Britain.[189] The opening of Telefís Éireann in December 1961 brought television coverage of emigrant lives into Irish homes. The practice of sending Irish priests to Britain for two or three years and then recalling them to their home diocese created a network throughout Ireland of clergy with a knowledge and interest in emigration. In 1966 the hierarchy approved the establishment of the Emigrant Chaplains' Association, consisting of current and former chaplains, and they were given their own session at the Irish hierarchy's annual Easter Emigrant Congress. Monsignor Barrett warned McQuaid that "the chaplains are building up a grievance and it would be most inadvisable of us to attempt to sweep it under the carpet."[190] By 1970 there were thirty-five emigrant bureaus operating in sixteen counties, including Derry, Antrim, and Armagh, although many of the bureaus were not regarded as effective.[191]

Other factors that may have contributed to a greater interest in emigrants and emigrant welfare were the emergence of social inquiry as a specific discipline in Ireland and a greater awareness of civil rights and social justice. Television brought coverage of the American civil rights movement into Irish homes, and the Northern Ireland civil rights movement gave the term a more immediate relevance. Pope John XXIII was another key influence; so, too, was the rediscovery of the 1916 Proclamation during the fiftieth anniversary of the Rising in 1966. When the minister for Labor, Patrick Hillery, presented the government with a lengthy paper urging radical changes in the treatment of emigrants, he referred to the papal encyclical *Mater et Magistra* and the commitment given in the 1916 Proclamation to cherishing all the children of the nation equally.[192]

Despite this increased consciousness of emigrants' needs, their welfare continued to be left to voluntary agencies and British social services. In 1961 Reverend T. McNamara of the Marian Welfare Agency, which provided hostel accommodation for Irish girls in London, informed Lemass that there were increasing demands on its services.[193] The 1961 British census revealed that many Irish emigrants in London lived in overcrowded conditions: 50 percent shared accommodation, 32 percent at a density of more than one and a half persons per room. The comparable figures for immigrants of color were 74 percent and 52 percent, respectively, and for those born in England, 30 percent and 8 percent.[194] In December 1961 the *Irish Independent* reported that there were approximately 5,000 homeless Irish people in London.[195] Slum clearance programs had reduced the supply of private rented houses and flats, and the 1957 Rent Act, which decontrolled private rented property, had resulted in higher rents and often the eviction of the existing tenants.[196] An emigrant chaplain from the diocese of Limerick, Father Eamonn Casey, launched the Catholic Housing Aid Scheme in 1961 to assist homeless families. The association bought houses and converted them into flats for family accommodation; 131 homeless families were rehoused in 1965–66; some families were given assistance to buy their own homes, and others were moved to better and cheaper accommodation outside London.[197] Although there was a general housing crisis in Britain, Irish emigrants faced particular difficulties. Their migratory pattern of work, especially on building sites, meant that they often failed to establish their place on a local authority housing list. Married men with a wife and family in Ireland were ineligible for priority housing on the basis of family need, so some took the desperate step of bringing their family to England and forcing the local authority to house them because they were homeless.[198] Although the 1966 British census recorded a significant improvement in housing conditions in the worst London boroughs,[199] in 1968 Sister Joseph of the Crispin Street Convent of Mercy in East London informed the minister for External Affairs, Frank Aiken, that her community was providing emergency accommodation for 6 homeless families who had been evicted because they had children. An official in the Department of External Affairs admitted, some months later, that housing was the greatest difficulty facing Irish emigrants in Britain.[200]

An employment agency catering for Irish emigrants, the Marian Employment Agency, opened at the Catholic church premises at Quex Road in Kilburn in 1963; it opened a second office at the Irish Center in Camden Town in 1964. The agency, which was licensed by Camden Borough Council—no adequate licensing system yet existed in Ireland—was careful to protect itself against the charge of promoting emigration. Advertisements placed in Irish newspapers advised that anybody who was "happily employed in Ireland" should stay there, but if somebody "must come to England," the Marian Agency would help to arrange work and accommodation.[201] Between 1964 and 1968 they handled an average of three thousand inquiries every year. During the summer of 1966 the agency was overrun by striking bank clerks who came to London in search of work. A representative of the Marian Agency, who addressed the 1966 Emigrants' Conference in Limerick, reported that it was becoming more difficult for Irish emigrants without qualifications to find work because many British employers were demanding O Levels (an examination after three years of second-level schooling) as a minimum qualification; this reflected the fact that a higher proportion of British children were staying on at school because their parents no longer required them to supplement family income. He also reported that some emigrants with second-level qualifications who took laboring jobs when they first arrived in Britain found it extremely difficult to break into white-collar jobs.[202]

The report of the London Irish Center for 1967 noted that some emigrants "seem to suffer from a lot of wishful thinking and a lack of common sense" concerning their prospects in England and the pitfalls of emigration.[203] Many arrived not knowing what type of work they wanted or might be capable of attaining, because there was no career guidance service in Ireland. They urged that Irish children should be persuaded to stay at school or learn a trade.[204] Damien Hannan claimed that having only primary schooling "must damage the migrants' chances of successfully adapting to life in British cities."[205] The Irish Center reported a sharp increase in the number of individuals under the age of eighteen who were contacting them because of difficulties finding work. The Marian Agency received a steady flow of letters from young men and women under eighteen years of age, who were eager to emigrate and were under the impression that they could earn large wages in England. Most claimed to have parental permission. The agency cautioned that they had little prospect of earning large wages because British employment laws restricted overtime work for those under eighteen years of age.[206]

The Irish Center appointed a full-time welfare officer in 1962.[207] By 1964 the center employed two full-time welfare officers, who worked closely with Camden Social Services.[208] The decision to appoint professional welfare officers, despite the fact that the center was in financial difficulty, was taken because the voluntary workers could no longer cope with the demands placed on them. Almost half the women arriving at the center were described as destitute or practically destitute, and voluntary workers were often called to attend the juvenile courts.[209] The number of cases handled by the center rose steadily: 1,494 in 1967 and in 1968, 1,905 individual cases plus 37 families. Less than 20 percent of those who sought assistance in 1968 were women.[210]

Unmarried mothers had not disappeared; in 1965 the Catholic Protection and Rescue Services repatriated 195 unmarried mothers from Britain,[211] and 145 mothers were repatriated in 1969.[212] But a repertoire of established services existed to cater for unmarried mothers. When an extraordinary meeting of the Irish hierarchy in November 1964 at the Irish College in Rome (the bishops were attending the Second Vatican Council) considered a report by emigrant chaplains on the care of emigrants, the bishops noted that "it was hard to see what more could be done than what was being done already" to provide for unmarried mothers.[213] A paper on "The Unmarried Mother and Her Child" presented at the 1969 Easter Emigrant Congress claimed that the services in Ireland were superior to those in England—women who could not prove one year's residence in a local authority area in Britain were ineligible for free hospital treatment. But Canon Harvey, the administrator of the (British) Crusade of Rescue, expressed fears that many Irish girls were opting for abortion. An Act passed in 1967 had considerably extended access to legal abortion in Britain, and he believed that this accounted for the decline in the number of women who were contacting the Crusade of Rescue—550 in 1967 and 428 in 1968, a break with the previous upward trend. He reported that "English non-catholic social workers are convinced that the social pressures in Ireland are such as to automatically entitle a P.F.I. (Pregnant from Ireland) to abortion facilities."[214] But the only action that the conference recommended was to ensure "that the excellent facilities available for unmarried mothers in Ireland are made more widely known."[215] In 1969, 122 women who gave Irish addresses had abortions in Britain; by 1971 the number had increased to 577, which was greater than the numbers who had contacted the Crusade of Rescue during the mid-1960s.[216]

There was also a growing concern about husbands who deserted their wives and families, leaving them without financial support, and also women and children fleeing violent husbands.[217] In 1966 the Catholic Housing Aid Society introduced a new program to provide accommodation for "fatherless families"; by 1969 they were housing an average of four families every week, although not all were Irish.[218] Former inmates of psychiatric hospitals accounted for over 10 percent of all cases assisted by the Irish Center in London 1964.[219] In the same year the Easter Emigrant Congress passed a resolution urging the Irish hierarchy, in cooperation with the English hierarchy, to tackle "the rehabilitation of Irish emigrants who become social casualties in Britain"—down-and-outs, former inmates of mental hospitals, and "borstal [reformatory] boys."[220] As the Irish Center in London did not provide systematic data on welfare cases until 1962, it is difficult to determine whether these were new problems or matters that were only coming to attention at this time, but during the 1960s many long-term psychiatric patients were discharged into the community, and some made their way to England, perhaps because of the inadequate support services in Ireland or because of the stigma associated with psychiatric illness.

Both the British and the Irish legal systems used emigration and repatriation as a means of ridding themselves of petty criminals. In 1964 the Irish bishops deplored the practice of district justices remitting court fines on social delinquents on condition that they emigrated, and they considered approaching the government to urge that this practice be dropped, although there is no evidence that they did.[221] By this time London magistrates were no longer offering Irishmen convicted of minor crimes the option of returning to Ireland in lieu of a prison sentence,[222] but there were many Irish-born inmates in English prisons and reformatories, and many former inmates of Irish industrial schools had settled in England. Richard Hauser of the Center for Group Studies, a voluntary nondenominational agency that helped migrants to the United Kingdom, particularly prisoners, wrote to McQuaid in 1964 offering to provide a training course for Christian Brothers working in industrial schools to enable them to prepare boys for life after their discharge. Hauser remarked that the brothers had expressed an initial interest in his proposal, but they apparently changed their minds. He continued:

> The most unfortunate we think are sometimes those, who deprived of mother's love from early childhood onwards, live in institutions such as industrial schools etc., deprived of normal family love, unable to learn the necessities of life like handling of money and moving freely in society. They cannot be expected to handle themselves well especially if under serious pressure in what is, after all, a doubly strange environment. It is clear that they do easily get into trouble and some of the names of such schools are well known to anybody working in British prisons and Borstal establishments. During my last trip to Ireland I made it clear in interviews and on television that the fault for this does not lie with those Brothers who under grave difficulties handle this task in your Arch-Diocese, but they were the first to say that they may need help and further training.

It is no surprise that McQuaid rejected this offer.[223] Hauser was not the only person who was concerned about these boys. In 1967 the Emigrant Chaplains' Association commissioned one of their members to report on what was happening to, and what could be done for, boys from reformatories in Ireland who came to England. The chaplains opened a center for homeless boys in London in 1970 with financial assistance from the Irish bishops and Camden Borough Council; it was staffed by a social worker, youth leaders, and a chaplain.[224] Many former inmates of industrial schools settled in England.[225] The reasons are obvious: England provided anonymity, the opportunity to slough off the stigma of being a former inmate of an industrial school, and escape from the Irish society that placed them there. And it was easier to find work.

Henry Gray, the long-serving secretary of the Emigrants' Section of the Catholic Social Welfare Bureau expressed unease at the amount of attention being given to problem emigrants. He warned the 1965 Episcopal Conference on Emigration that it was "important not to encourage our emigrants to feel that in some way they have a stigma attached to them or that 'Irish emigrants are a problem.'" A report on emigrant missions in Britain noted that many people had objected that "the very existence of the Mission Scheme was a slur on

the Irish in England."[226] In 1969 an official of the Department of External Affairs claimed that "the vast bulk of Irish people in Britain
are not in need of assistance. They are probably at least as well off as
Irish people in Ireland are, and they have the whole welfare system of
Britain to cushion them from distress. The only problem cases are
the misfits, e.g. destitute minors, unmarried mothers and handicapped persons, green or inexperienced persons arriving from Ireland without financial or other arrangements. The Embassy already
covers the cost of repatriating them, and the numbers are small."[227]

The Role of the Government

While the above comment is partly correct, it should also be seen as
yet another attempt to justify the lack of government assistance for
welfare services in Britain. The only major concession made in this
respect was the appointment in 1961 of "an officer whose work will
be to promote Irish associations in the various towns one of whose
objects will be the organisation of the healthy pastimes, amusements
and care of young Irish people in England."[228] The person appointed
to this job, which sounded like a youth club leader, was T. Feehan.
Born in Ireland and a graduate of the National University of Ireland,
Feehan had worked as a school teacher in England before becoming
the organizing secretary of the Anti-Partition of Ireland League in
Britain.[229] This background gave him extensive contacts throughout
the Irish community, which were not confined to church circles. Feehan was not a welfare officer: the word did not feature in the statement announcing his appointment. Furthermore, he was a man, and
all previous references to a welfare officer had assumed that a woman
would be appointed. In later documents the job description was
given as Local Advisory Officer at the embassy in London with "the
special task of organising Irish groups to help themselves."[230] He secured an agreement that the Irish Center, the Irish Girls Hostel, the
Irish Hostels Development Society, and the Irish Welfare Fund Committee would operate under one committee. One of his tasks was to
ensure that emigrant organizations reported to committees that were
representative of the Irish community, so that power did not rest in
the hands of an individual priest.[231] Yet while asserting the right to

interfere in the running of these agencies, the government was not prepared to provide financial assistance.

It is scarcely a coincidence that Feehan's appointment was followed by renewed demands for a government subsidy for the Irish Center in London. In the autumn of 1961 Father McNamara, the chaplain at the Irish Center, asked the Irish embassy for a contribution toward the cost of appointing a full-time welfare officer, or a once-off grant to enable the center to reduce its capital debt. The Department of External Affairs restated its long-standing opposition to Irish public funds being used to assist Irish organizations in Britain, justifying this opinion with an assertion that Irish people in Britain were at least as well off as those in Ireland and should therefore be in a position to finance their own activities, including welfare services. Furthermore, if the government came to the assistance of the London Center, other Irish organizations would demand comparable treatment.[232] These statements were forwarded to Lemass, prompting a note on the file that "the Department of External Affairs themselves . . . have, I'm afraid, gone somewhat off the rails."[233] In a more considered response to the same matter, the Irish ambassador in London, Hugh McCann, expressed fears that "the receipt of Government assistance might lead to attempts by outsiders to fetter their discretion. . . . [F]reedom of action by bodies which are entirely voluntary, as distinct from government agents, permits them to concentrate their assistance into channels where they know the most good will be done." Yet McCann reported that when Irish organizations in Britain attempted to raise funds from private sources, the initial reaction of those approached was "what are the government doing about it." He claimed that the Irish "in this country" (presumably Britain) had not been generous in supporting a fund-raising campaign. As the Irish Center in London was strongly representative of Irish interests in the city, he suggested that the argument that assisting the center would open the floodgates did not really apply, although the government would obviously come under pressure to provide similar assistance to centers in Birmingham and Manchester. In the end, however, McCann advised that a grant from the Irish hierarchy might provide "a possible alternative" to government assistance.[234]

When Lemass met Father McNamara in December 1961, he informed him that any decision was a matter for the minister for External Affairs, who was in New York. Lemass also suggested that there might be constitutional difficulties in providing funding to Catholic agencies. A decision on financial assistance to the London Center was deferred on countless occasions during 1962 and 1963.[235] Lemass's indecisiveness is utterly out of character; if he had been determined to assist the Irish Center he would have found some means of doing so.

Lemass's government also maintained the long-standing policy of refusing to restrict emigration to those over age eighteen, despite renewed calls for such action from the Irish hierarchy and TDs. Lemass replied that the land border with Northern Ireland made any restrictions impracticable. He also queried whether such legislation would be constitutional; if it was, it would discourage young people who went to Britain from returning to Ireland. He informed the hierarchy that the government had "recently" provided the embassy with funds to repatriate Irish citizens "whenever the Ambassador is satisfied that, because of extreme youth or mental infirmity, they should be returned to Ireland"; this would assist the cases that caused the greatest concern.[236] Although this statement reiterated long-standing government policy, there were now additional reasons for not departing from this position. If the Irish government introduced travel documents to control migration between Ireland and Britain, even for those under eighteen, it might open the way for Britain to impose restrictions on Irish immigration at a time when restrictions were being introduced on Commonwealth immigration.[237] The numbers repatriated by the Irish embassy remained tiny: thirty-seven in the first year 1965; fewer than a hundred in 1968.[238]

By 1965 the London Irish Center was planning a major extension that would entail a three-fold increase in its existing debt of £26,000 and a corresponding rise in current spending.[239] Minister for External Affairs, Frank Aiken, and John Leydon, the former secretary of the Department of Industry and Commerce, persuaded the National Bank (of which Leydon was a director) to agree to a £50,000 loan, but the government refused to provide financial support. As justification for this decision, External Affairs claimed that Irish centers were first and foremost clubs—their administrative standards were lax, there was a danger that they might lose a lot of money, and their welfare functions were only incidental.[240] But this would not preclude the government from paying all or part of the salary of a welfare officer, or contributing toward the cost of hostel accommodation. By the late 1960s the department's attitude had, if anything, hardened. When Dublin City Councillor Seán D. Loftus wrote to Aiken asking for a government subvention for the Marian Employment Agency, Aiken expressed his admiration for the agency's work, but went on to state that "it is by such voluntary effort and by the spirit of self-reliance . . . that the needs of the situation can best be met."[241]

External Affairs was no longer the only department with an interest in emigrants. A speech given by the minister for Labor, Dr. Patrick Hillery, at the opening of a new labor exchange at Cahirciveen in July 1968 appeared to signal a major change in government policy. Hillery indicated that the Department of Labor (established in 1966) planned to transform old-style labor exchanges into modern placement centers, where all applicants would be provided with jobs or training. His remarks about emigration and emigrant services must be read in this context. Dr. Hillery described emigration as "a fact of life"; it would continue for some time, despite the best efforts by the government to create employment. In a dramatic break with the past, he then stated that "as Minister for Labour I believe that I have a degree of responsibility to those members of the country's work force who cannot for the time being at least be absorbed at home"; there was "some responsibility on the community" to ensure that those who were forced to emigrate were "equipped for life overseas."

The speech was warmly welcomed by the newspapers; the position is well summarized by the title of an editorial in *The Irish Times,* "Better Late . . ."[242] Hillery's speech appears to have been something of a kite-flying exercise because it was not followed by any formal announcement of measures to assist emigrants. In November he informed the Dáil that the matter required "certain government decision," adding that at Cahirciveen "I expressed some personal views which had to be—" Before he could complete the sentence, Fine Gael deputy Richie Ryan added the word "retracted." The Dáil record gives no indication that Dr. Hillery attempted to finish his sentence or refute this remark. Labor deputy Steve Coughlan ended this exchange by noting that the late Donogh O'Malley "would make the decision, announce it and then the Government would have to back it"[243]—a reference to O'Malley's 1966 announcement of free secondary education, which had not been discussed or approved by the cabinet.[244]

On 29 November 1968, three weeks after this exchange, Dr. Hillery presented the cabinet with proposals to integrate emigrant services with the Department of Labor's training and placement services. The long-term objective would be to make the department's placement and guidance facilities available to those who were "obliged to seek work abroad"; in the interim he proposed to provide an annual grant of £10,000–£15,000 to domestic voluntary agencies catering for emigrants and to impose controls on private employment agencies and advertisements seeking to recruit emigrant workers. He recommended that An Chomhairle Oiliúna—the state training agency—should provide training facilities for workers, irrespective of whether or not they intended to emigrate (though priority should be given to domestic needs), and that arrangements should be made with the British authorities for the mutual recognition of educational and training qualifications. The state should also provide financial assistance to voluntary organizations that assisted Irish emigrants in Britain (though no sum was specified): money would be allocated to these agencies and to Irish-based voluntary organizations by "a representative council" (presumably of the various emigrant organizations). He ruled out measures to control juvenile emigration, both for practical reasons and "recognising people's personal right to freedom of movement," but recommended that the matter be kept under review. He also set out the underlying principles behind this new policy on emigrants:

- The 1916 Proclamation gave a commitment to "cherishing all the children of the nation equally"; to honor this, the less privileged should receive "as adequate a preparation for emigration as the better-off and highly qualified."
- Principles of social justice imposed a duty on the community to protect the moral and material interests of young people who have to emigrate.
- Improved services would help to maintain contact with emigrants who might wish to return to Ireland at a later date; improved services

would promote their social advancement and contribute to "improving the image of Ireland abroad."

Anticipating claims that these measures would encourage emigration, the memorandum suggested that they "represent a recognition of basic facts" and the principle of equal opportunity. On the latter point, it noted that "as all citizens, irrespective of whether or not they intend emigrating, should have the right of access to services provided by the State (e.g. education), the same principle should apply to industrial training, . . . that those who cannot benefit from higher education should at least have the opportunity of fitting themselves, by suitable training, for employment."[245]

The radical nature of this memorandum cannot be overstated. It was the first acknowledgment by a government minister that emigrants had rights and that the state had a responsibility toward emigrants. It also raised the thorny issue of equality of opportunity and the state's responsibility in that regard. It must be read in the context of the recent expansion in provisions for second- and third-level education;[246] most emigrants and intending emigrants had no formal educational qualifications. On a more practical level, the reciprocal recognition of British and Irish qualifications, and proposals that the Irish employment service seek jobs in Britain for those who were unable to find work in Ireland, implied a further integration of the two economies and the two states—a process that was already in train with the 1965 Anglo-Irish Trade Agreement.

Given the dramatic change in government policy that these proposals represented, it is not surprising that they encountered strong opposition within the cabinet, especially from the ministers for Finance and External Affairs. The latter was concerned lest any formal arrangement between the British and Irish employment and training services would give the British authorities the option of exercising controls over Irish emigration "to their own advantage." External Affairs asserted that "the maintenance of freedom of travel and concomitant mobility of labour between the two countries [is] of great importance to Ireland in present circumstances"; they cautioned that Britain had imposed restrictions on Irish exports in contravention of the 1965 Anglo-Irish Trade Agreement.

Acknowledging that "appropriate education and training should be given to all who must seek employment, including those who may emigrate," External Affairs were determined that government assistance should stop at the boundaries of the state. When Irish workers traveled to another country their welfare became the responsibility of the state that benefited from their labor and their taxes. If the government provided funds for welfare services in Britain, the demand for these services would escalate and the burden on Irish taxpayers "could become intolerable." The Irish Center in London was "already looking for £100,000." Further, these centers were "church-operated," many people would be unwilling to use them, and there might be a possible constitutional objection to providing financial assistance. Spending Irish tax revenue on welfare work outside the country was "unsound in principle" and would reduce the amount available for economic development and measures to create employment at home; Britain provided a comprehensive welfare system to which Irish people had equal entitlement, and any additional needs should be met by voluntary services; if the Irish government provided financial assistance to the voluntary agencies this would lead to a drying up of voluntary effort among the Irish community in Britain, a community that "is probably better off financially than their relatives at home." Any emigrant who could not get by in Britain was free to return home "and share in the social assistance which the Irish economy has been able to provide for its necessitous members in Ireland. If assistance provided out of Irish revenue is spent in Ireland it will benefit the Irish economy."[247]

Finance's response was more muted. They wanted the employment service to defer making provisions for intending emigrants until it had proved that it could meet Irish manpower needs. Increased provision for education, including a planned raising of the school-leaving age and the introduction of a career guidance service for second-level students, would meet the educational needs of intending emigrants. It, too, objected to state funds being provided for voluntary services.[248]

When the matter came before the cabinet on 3 January 1969, the item was postponed, and it was postponed at nineteen subsequent cabinet meetings. The number of postponements is highly unusual for a Fianna Fáil cabinet and suggests that ministers were very divided on this issue.[249] On 26 March Hillery reminded Lynch that the item had been on the cabinet agenda for almost four months and, in the meantime, many more recent submissions had been disposed of. The cabinet eventually considered the proposals on 28 March, when they decided that

1. As a long-term objective the placement and guidance facilities of the Employment Service should be made available to persons who wish to return to Ireland.
2. No action should be taken to control the emigration of persons under 18 years of age by means of formal regulations, but that the matter should be kept under review.
3. Steps should be taken to control private employment agencies and the activities of foreign agencies and firms recruiting here for work abroad.
4. The voluntary cooperation of the press should be sought to prevent misleading advertising.
5. Arrangements should be made with the British authorities to secure mutual recognition of educational and training certificates and qualifications.[250]

These decisions were a defeat for the Department of Labor. Items 2, 3, and 4 confirmed the existing position; 5 was uncontroversial; the commitment given under item 1 was long term and it applied to returning emigrants and not, as in the Department of Labor submission, to those "obliged to seek work abroad." By 1969 attracting returning emigrants, particularly those with skills and expertise, formed part of the government's economic and social program. Jackson's study of Skibbereen emigrants suggested that returning emigrants faced a number of difficulties including a housing shortage and restrictive practices by some craft unions. The difficulties were most acute for Irish women who had trained as nurses or teachers in England; their career prospects in Ireland were limited by a number of factors, including religious control of hospitals and schools, an Irish language requirement for teaching jobs, and a marriage ban that applied to most jobs in nursing, teaching, and social work.[251]

Hillery's Cahirciveen speech had created expectations that the government was about to announce funding for emigrant services.

When this did not happen, the Emigrant Chaplains' Association, stepped up their campaign. On 15 March 1969 *The Irish Times* published a letter from Reverend Joseph Nolan, the Chairman of the Irish Emigrant Chaplains' Association protesting at the Department of External Affair's refusal to assist Irish centers in Birmingham, Manchester, and London. "There is no disputing our responsibility towards our emigrants. Other countries help their emigrants, even countries with less of a problem and less pretensions to caring for *all* their citizens. . . . The truth is that Mr. Aiken can continue to refuse aid because emigrant welfare is not an issue with us. We do not care about it in the same way as we care for those in need at home, for free education, or economic development. Yet it is in no way a less important issue than these." Father Nolan called on the public to make an issue of this.[252]

On 26 March, two days before the cabinet discussed the proposals submitted by the Department of Labor, Aiken introduced a supplementary estimate for the Department of External Affairs in Dáil Éireann, which included an additional £3,000 for repatriating or otherwise assisting Irish citizens overseas, though this money appears to have been needed to meet requests from continental embassies, not from Britain.[253] The Fine Gael leader Liam Cosgrave used the debate to criticize the government's failure to assist welfare and information centers for the Irish in Britain, and he called for restrictions to be introduced on emigrants under 18 years of age.[254] Aiken repeated the familiar departmental line that these matters should be left to voluntary efforts, but he gave a positive response to the proposal from Labor TD James Tully for the formation of an all-party group to discuss what measures should be introduced to meet the needs of emigrants. He continued: "We all have the same emotional approach to any human being in need wherever he may be or whatever his class, race or creed. We all have the same emotion and would like to help but we want to help our people in Britain in a way that will not discourage them from getting out and helping themselves. We do not want to turn them into mendicants, hanging around centers where they will get additional funds to those they have got from the British Social Services Bureaux."[255]

This final sentence prompted angry responses in Britain and in Ireland. The director of the Irish Center in Birmingham wrote to

Aiken: "I consider it a personal insult to my Superiors and myself. Your remarks and their obvious implications are accepted as insulting, and are resented by all attached to our Irish Centre in Birmingham." He sent a copy of his letter to Lynch, asking "if these are the official views of the Government or the personal views of the Minister? If the latter I think it should be made known publicly, and then the very bitter feelings caused here may be reduced."[256]

It is difficult to determine whether the public reaction to Aiken's speech prompted a change of mind within the cabinet. However, on 2 April, "on the recommendation of the Minister for Labour," it was agreed in principle "that a sum of money should be made available to assist designated voluntary emigration bureaux within the state in meeting their expenditure on advisory services to intending emigrants."[257] A sum of £10,000 was eventually agreed. This concession retained the principle that assistance should be confined to Ireland. The modest grant was not announced until 21 April, several weeks after the annual Easter Emigrants Conference, which was attended in an observer capacity by Jack Agnew, the assistant secretary of the Department of Labor, and Brian Gallagher, assistant secretary of the Department of External Affairs. Both men had to sit through speeches condemning the government for failing to recognize its "responsibility towards our emigrants." The criticism directed at Frank Aiken was particularly pointed. One speaker condemned his Dáil statement as indicating "an appalling ignorance of professional welfare services that were both needed and provided."[258] Gallagher defended the government's refusal to fund services for emigrants in Britain, but his reference (quoted above) to "misfits and ne'er do wells" was unlikely to have improved relations between the emigrant chaplains and the government. In the report on the congress that he presented to the Department of External Affairs, Gallagher claimed that "it seemed to me from the handclap which I got when leaving that a number of the former Chaplains were not unimpressed with the strength of the arguments I had put before them."[259] However, the report presented to the hierarchy told a different story: it claimed that Gallagher had offered "pretty strong arguments, but most of the former Chaplains were not impressed." Jack Agnew received a better reception, because he indicated that the Department of Labor was

considering providing assistance to emigrant advisory bodies in Ireland, and he expressed some optimism that the government would
provide aid for emigrant welfare services in Britain.[260] Agnew and
two colleagues from the Department of Labor met Barrett and Gray
of the Catholic Social Welfare Bureau the following month to discuss
how the £10,000 earmarked for emigrant services in Ireland should
be disbursed. The Department of Labor wanted the money to be
allocated by a broadly based, nonstatutory committee that would include representatives of trade unions. They suggested that the hierarchy's Emigrant Advisory Committee might undertake the job, presumably with some additional members, but Monsignor Barrett of
the Catholic Social Welfare Bureau (which were not represented on
the committee) expressed fears that accepting a government grant
would curtail the independence of the voluntary agencies on the
grounds that inspections carried out by the department might jeopardize the confidentiality of individual cases and the insistence on
standards acceptable to the department might offend the ethos of
the Catholic Social Welfare Bureau. He also criticized the "apparent
belief" that a grant of £10,000 could "work miracles." There was a
feeling in the Department of Labor, he believed, "that nothing is
being done at the moment but under its mantle all will be cured."[261]

When Patrick Hillery became minister for External Affairs after
the 1969 general election, major changes in the department's policy
toward emigrants might have been anticipated, but this did not happen. By December 1970 the only service for emigrants provided by
the Irish embassy in London was the repatriation of emigrants—
those who were destitute, unfit for work because of ill health, or who
might not qualify for British health services and national insurance
because they had recently arrived in the United Kingdom as well as
young persons, expectant unmarried mothers, and unmarried mothers whose children were under the age of six months. In addition, the
embassy maintained close contact with the children's departments of
British local authorities, with Irish welfare centers, and with diocesan
welfare societies, and it reimbursed the voluntary organizations for
the cost of repatriating Irish citizens "in the categories referred to
above."[262] In March 1971 Dr. Hillery reaffirmed the department's policy of not providing financial assistance to Irish centers.[263]

By 1970 and 1971 the Department of External Affairs was preoccupied with negotiations for Ireland's accession to the EEC and the crisis in Northern Ireland. The latter event added a new dimension to relations with emigrants. In October 1969 Fianna Fáil representatives Ruairí Brugha and John Nash reported to Hillery on a conference of the United Ireland Association in Britain, where criticism was expressed about the uninformed speeches that government ministers made on visits to Britain and their ignorance of the feelings and problems experienced by Irish emigrants. The conference criticized the London embassy for failing to provide them with information when violence broke out in Northern Ireland in August 1969. Brugha and Nash reported that "some elements" had called meetings to collect money for arms and to arrange volunteers. They recommended that a survey be carried out "and recommendations made on our communications with emigrants in Britain and elsewhere. The aim should be to establish how best our emigrants and their close interest in Ireland can best be harnessed to help solve our unity problem and also to expand our Irish markets." In his reply, Hillery lamented that "[Irish] radio is not heard there, with the result that information was coming via the BBC." He asked the minister for Posts and Telegraphs to investigate the possibility of improving radio transmission to Britain.[264]

The agenda had swung once again from the needs of Irish emigrants to how these emigrants might best serve the needs of the Irish state—both political and economic. In January 1972, following a disastrous tourist season that was blamed on the Northern Ireland crisis, an "ethnic tourism" campaign was launched in Britain; the Irish in Britain were likewise targeted in export drives.[265] Similar campaigns had been launched in the United States during the 1950s and the early 1960s with mixed success.[266] There was also a strong focus on returning emigrants: the London embassy kept emigrants informed of job opportunities in Ireland, and it provided relevant information for those wishing to return to Ireland.[267] In December 1969 Con Murphy, the chairman of the Irish hierarchy's Emigrant Advisory Committee, informed Hillery that the committee was strengthening lines of communication between the Irish in Britain and their home districts. Murphy believed that similar links should

be established with all the Irish overseas, "to advise them of investment opportunities here, skills required here and so on." He recommended that the term emigrant should be dropped as there was "too
much of the 'pathetic Irish' about it. I wish we could call them 'the
Irish abroad' or 'the overseas Irish.'"[268] There is a sense that emigrants
were being repackaged to fit the image of a modern progressive Ireland. When the United States introduced new legislation governing
immigration in 1968, including the end of national quotas, officials at
the Irish embassy in Washington were extremely sanguine about the
impact on Irish immigration. One official minuted that "once the
global quota system comes into operation the essential factors in
immigrants' selection will be the fitness of the individual concerned
and/or the fact of his relationship to a person already a U.S. citizen. . . .
[T]he comparatively high level of education of our people and the
fact of their being English speaking will, it is expected to a large extent meet the first factor." Because of this and the large numbers of
Irish people with relatives who were American citizens he expected
that Irish immigration to the United States would be largely undis-
turbed.[269] In reality, the number of immigrants plummeted. Most
applicants had only primary schooling—a far cry from "the comparatively high level of education." Yet the collapse in Irish immigration
attracted very little attention in Ireland, because it was widely believed that the era of mass emigration had ended. In March 1972 Jack
Lynch told the Dáil that a net increase of 50,000 jobs was expected by
1978, offering "the first real prospect, since independence, of achieving full employment and ending involuntary emigration."[270]

By 1971 Ireland was no longer a predominantly rural and agrarian society, and the population patterns that were characteristic
of postfamine Ireland—high emigration, few marriages, and large
families—were disappearing. The future seemed bright. EEC membership was expected to bring a substantial increase in investment by
multinational companies (providing jobs for school-leavers, former
farm workers, and returning emigrants) and secure markets and
higher incomes for Ireland's farmers, although the Mansholt Plan to
restructure agricultural holdings might threaten the survival of
small farms in the west of Ireland. The population was rising, the
marriage boom was continuing, and the number of births was on

the increase. Rural Ireland had seen off the apparent threat posed by the Buchanan report and was taking advantage of free second-level education, free school transport, and new opportunities for college education. If the Irish state continued to refuse financial assistance for emigrant services in the United Kingdom, there was some evidence that it was becoming less necessary to emigrate: the introduction in 1970 of a Deserted Wife's Allowance and an Unmarried Mothers Allowance in 1973 indicated a greater willingness to assist those in personal difficulties, and perhaps more importantly, to acknowledge their existence, although the rising numbers of Irish women who were traveling to England for abortions suggested a sad continuity with the past. After 1973 unemployment replaced emigration as the major human problem, while feminism, the rise in births outside marriage, marital breakdown, and the growing gap between Catholic church teaching on marriage, contraception, and abortion shifted debates on Irish population and family to new issues.

Statistical Appendix

Population of Ireland 1841–2002

	Republic of Ireland (26 counties)	Northern Ireland (6 counties)	Total Ireland
1841	6,528,800	1,646,300	8,175,100
1851	5,111,600	1,440,800	6,552,400
1861	4,402,100	1,396,900	5,799,000
1871	4,053,200	1,359,100	5,412,300
1881	3,870,000	1,304,800	5,174,800
1891	3,468,700	1,236,000	4,704,700
1901	3,221,800	1,236,900	4,458,700
1911	3,139,700	1,250,500	4,390,200
1926	2,972,000	1,256,500	4,228,500
1936–37*	2,968,400	1,279,700	4,248,100
1946	2,955,100		
1951	2,960,600	1,370,900	4,331,500
1956	2,898,300		
1961	2,818,300	1,426,000	4,243,300
1966	2,884,000	1,484,800	4,368,800
1971	2,978,200	1,536,000	4,514,200
1979	3,368,200		
1981	3,443,400	1,532,600	4,976,000
1986	3,540,600		
1991	3,525,700	1,573,300	5,099,000
1996	3,626,100		
2001–2**	3,917,200	1,685,200	5,602,400

*The census in the Irish Free State was taken in 1936; the Northern Ireland census in 1937.

** The Northern Ireland census was taken in 2001; the Irish government postponed their census from 2001 to 2002 in order to reduce the chances of spreading foot-and-mouth disease.

Ireland: Average Annual Births, Deaths, Natural Increase, and Estimated Net Migration for Each Intercensal Period, 1871–2002 (thousands)

	Births	Deaths	Natural Increase	Population Change	Estimated Net Migration
1871–1881	104	72	32	-18	-50
1881–1891	84	64	20	-40	-60
1891–1901	74	59	15	-25	-40
1901–1911	71	53	18	-8	-26
1911–1926	65	49	16	-11	-27
1926–1936	58	42	16	-0.4	-17
1936–1946	60	43	17	-1.3	-19
1946–1951	64	40	24	1	-24
1951–1956	63	36	27	-12	-39
1956–1961	61	34	26	-16	-42
1961–1966	63	33	29	13	-16
1966–1971	63	33	30	19	-11
1971–1979	69	33	35	49	14
1979–1981	73	33	40	38	-3
1981–1986	67	33	34	19	-14
1986–1991	56	32	24	-3	-27
1991–1996	50	31	18	20	2
1996–2002	54	31	23	49	26

Note: The figures have been rounded up and down, so arithmetically they may not necessarily tally.

Source: Statistical Abstract of Ireland; Statistical Yearbook of Ireland.

Notes

1. The Pathology of Irish Demographic History

1. K. H. Connell, in *The Population of Ireland, 1750–1845* (Oxford, 1950), 120, writes of "a pathological rate of population-growth."

2. *The Irish Times,* 8 September 2004.

3. Unless otherwise stated, when I use the term Ireland I am referring to the Republic of Ireland; article 4 of the 1937 Constitution says that "The name of the State is Éire, or in the English language, Ireland."

4. In 1871 the population of today's Irish Republic was 4,053,000; in 1881 it was 3,870,000. The population of Northern Ireland is higher today than at the time of the famine.

5. In 1700 more than one-quarter of the population was of English or Scottish origin. L. M. Cullen, *The Emergence of Modern Ireland, 1600–1900* (London, 1981), 15, 51–55, 84–87; *The Irish Times,* 8 September 2004.

6. The first population census was taken in 1821; the 1841 census was the first that is recognized as reasonably accurate.

7. Ireland's dependency rate remained high until the 1990s. Tony Fahey and John FitzGerald, *Welfare Implications of Demographic Trends* (Dublin, 1997), 2–5, 11–23.

8. Liam Kennedy, *People and Population Change* (Dublin, 1994), 2.

9. Cormac Ó Gráda, *A Rocky Road: The Irish Economy since the 1920s* (Manchester, 1997), 210.

10. Enda Delaney, *Demography, State, and Society: Irish Migration to Britain, 1921–1971* (Liverpool, 2000), 5 –21, and "Placing Post-War Irish Migration to Britain in a Comparative European Perspective, 1945 –81," in Andy Bielenberg, ed., *The Irish Diaspora* (London, 1999), 331–56.

11. Timothy W. Guinnane, *The Vanishing Irish: Households, Migration, and the Rural Economy in Ireland, 1850–1914* (Princeton, N.J., 1997), xv.

12. Ibid., 3 –7, 27 –29, 97 –98, 249; Michael Anderson and Donald J. Morse, "High Fertility, High Emigration, Low Nuptiality: Adjustment Processes in Scotland's Demographic Experience, 1861–1914," pt. 1, *Population Studies* 47, no. 1 (1993): 5 –25, and pt. 2, *Population Studies* 47, no. 2 (1993): 319 –43.

13. This is a major theme of Simon Szreter in *Fertility, Class, and Gender in Britain, 1860–1914* (Cambridge, 1996).

14. This point is emphasized in the *Commission on Emigration and Other Population Problems, 1948–54 Reports*, P. 2541, R. 38, 3.

15. "What is migration in other countries is emigration with us, and the mind of the country, brooding upon the dreary statistics of this perennial drain, naturally and longingly turns to schemes for the rehabilitation of rural life—the only life it knows." Horace Plunkett, *Ireland in the New Century* (London, 1905), 39.

16. Silvana Patriarca, *Numbers and Nationhood: Writing Statistics in Nineteenth-Century Italy* (Cambridge, 1996), 1–3.

17. T. W. Grimshaw, "Statistical Survey of Ireland, from 1840 to 1888," *JSSISI* 9 (1888): 322.

18. James F. Meenan, "Preliminary Report Notes on the Census of Population in Northern Ireland, 1937," *JSSISI* 15 (1936 –37): 69.

19. Michael Kennedy, in *Division and Consensus: The Politics of Cross-Border Relations in Ireland, 1926–1969* (Dublin, 2000), shows that this was true of all socioeconomic issues.

20. Northern Ireland Census of Population 1926, xxiv.

21. Liam Kennedy, *People and Population Change*, 20; David Fitzpatrick, *The Two Irelands, 1912–1939* (Oxford, 1998), 215 –16.

22. Kerby Miller, *Emigrants and Exiles: Ireland and the Irish Exodus to North America* (New York, 1985), chapter 3, quotations from 103 –5.

23. Ibid., 245.

24. William Joseph O'Neill Daunt: *Eighty-Five Years of Irish History, 1800–1885*, vol. 1 (London, 1996), 111–12.

25. George O'Brien, "Historical Introduction" to E. J. Riordan, *Modern Irish Trade and Industry* (London, 1920), 51.

26. *Cork Examiner*, 8 June 1891, quoted at greater length in Arnold Schrier, *Ireland and the American Emigration, 1850–1900* (Chester Springs, Penn., 1997 edition), 54.

27. Ronan Fanning, et al., eds., *Documents in Irish Foreign Policy*, vol. 1 (Dublin, 1998), 3; 1125/15, Gavan Duffy Papers. The document was attached to a letter by Arthur Griffith dated 23 January 1919.

28. Fanning, et al., vol. 1, no. 13; DFA, FS, Paris, 1919, 20, NAI.

29. Liam Kennedy, "The Economic Thought of the Nation's Lost Leader: Charles Stewart Parnell," in *Colonialism, Religion, and Nationalism in Ireland* (Belfast, 1996), 75–102.

30. Robert Kane, *The Industrial Resources of Ireland* (Dublin, 1844); Dáil Éireann, *Commission of Inquiry into the Resources and Industries of Ireland, 1920–22*; Plunkett, *Ireland in the New Century*, 248–49, on the potential of turf.

31. *Census of Population Ireland 1841*, viii–ix.

32. *Census of Population Ireland 1871, General Report*, 12.

33. Jeffrey Williamson, "Economic Convergence: Placing Post-Famine Ireland in Comparative Perspective," *Irish Economic and Social History* 21 (1994): 5–27; William Neilson Hancock, "On the Condition of the Irish Labourer," *Dublin Statistical Society*, vol. 1, 1848.

34. Grimshaw, "Statistical Survey of Ireland," 331.

35. Denis Caulfield Heron, "Historical Statistics of Ireland," *Dublin Statistical Society* 3 (1862), as quoted in Mary E. Daly, *The Spirit of Earnest Inquiry: The Statistical and Social Inquiry Society of Ireland, 1847–1997* (Dublin, 1997), 40.

36. W. F. Bailey, "Ireland since the Famine: A Sketch of Fifty Years' Economic and Legislative Changes—Presidential Address," *JSSISI* 11 (1902–3): 129.

37. J. J. Spengler, *France Faces Depopulation* (Raleigh, N.C., 1936); Richard A. Soloway, *Demography and Degeneration: Eugenics and the Declining Birthrate in Twentieth-Century Britain* (Chapel Hill, 1995 edition), chapters 1–3.

38. L. Paul-Dubois, *Contemporary Ireland* (Dublin, 1908), 356–58. This account reflects the belief, which was common in the historiography of postfamine population until perhaps the 1970s, that there was relatively

little emigration from the west of Ireland in the decades immediately after the famine. S. H. Cousens, "Emigration and Demographic Change in Ireland, 1851–1861," *Economic History Review* 14, no. 4 (1961): 275–88, and "The Regional Variations in Population Change in Ireland, 1861–1881," *Economic History Review* 17, no. 2 (1964): 301–21. Cormac Ó Grada, in "A Note on Nineteenth-Century Emigration Statistics," *Population Studies* 25 (1975): 143–49, shows that this was not the case.

39. Tom Garvin, *Nationalist Revolutionaries in Ireland, 1858–1928* (Oxford, 1987), 72.

40. Lawrence McBride, *The Greening of Dublin Castle: The Transformation of Bureaucratic and Judicial Personnel in Ireland, 1892–1922* (Washington, 1991), 10–20.

41. John Francis Maguire, *The Irish in America* (London, 1868), 233.

42. Patrick Maume, *The Long Gestation: Irish Nationalist Life, 1891–1918* (Dublin, 1999), 50–51.

43. Paul-Dubois, *Contemporary Ireland*, 364–65.

44. Bailey, "Ireland since the Famine," 134–35. According to Joe Lee, "only the consolation of the church to the celibate victims of economic man prevented lunacy rates, which quadrupled between 1850 and 1915, from rising even more rapidly." J. J. Lee, *The Modernisation of Irish Society, 1848–1918* (Dublin, 1973), 6. The most extreme attempt to link psychiatric illness with celibacy is found in Nancy Scheper-Hughes, *Saints, Scholars, and Schizophrenics: Mental Illness in Rural Ireland* (Berkeley, 1979). Research by Catherine Cox suggests that the rise in admissions to mental hospitals after the famine reflected the increased supply of beds; most patients were admitted on the initiative of family members. Catherine Cox, "Managing Insanity: Carlow Lunatic Asylum, 1832–1922," Ph.D. thesis, UCD, 2004.

45. Paul-Dubois claimed that emigration had resulted in "the survival of the unfittest" in Ireland. *Contemporary Ireland*, 355; On eugenics, see Greta Jones, "Eugenics in Ireland: The Belfast Eugenics Society," *IHS* 28, no. 109 (May 1992): 81–95.

46. See, for example, D. B. Quinn, *The Elizabethans and the Irish* (Ithaca, N.Y., 1966); Edward MacLysaght, *Irish Life in the Seventeenth Century*, 3rd edition (Dublin, 1979).

47. Connell, *The Population of Ireland*, 39–42, 49–52; Michael Drake, "Marriage and Population Growth in Ireland, 1780–1845," *Economic History Review* 16, no. 2 (1963): 301–13; Guinnane, *Vanishing Irish*, 82–84.

48. Connell, *The Population of Ireland*, 85.

49. Plunkett, *Ireland in the New Century*, 56–57. The argument that slavery destroyed family life for Blacks originated with sympathetic abolitionists

in the 1880s, but it later acquired racist overtones. The debate is examined in Herbert G. Gutman, *The Black Family in Slavery and Freedom, 1750–1925* (New York, 1976).

50. Miller, *Emigrants and Exiles*, 481–85; David Fitzpatrick, *Oceans of Consolation: Personal Accounts of Irish Migration to Australia* (Ithaca, N.Y., 1994).

51. See chapter 4.

52. Plunkett, *Ireland in the New Century*, 116.

53. On Plunkett, the Catholic church, and the co-operative movement, see Liam Kennedy, "The Early Response of the Irish Catholic Clergy to the Co-Operative Movement," in *Colonialism, Religion, and Nationalism in Ireland*, 117–35; Plunkett, *Ireland in the New Century*, 94–121.

54. Schrier, *Ireland and the American Emigration*, 57.

55. In addition to the works already mentioned by L. Paul-Dubois and Horace Plunkett, see Filson Young, *Ireland at the Cross-Roads: An Essay in Explanation* (London, 1903); M. J. F. McCarthy, *Priests and People in Ireland* (London, 1902).

56. Jacques Verrière, *La Population de l'Irlande* (Paris, 1979), 474. Verrière cites Thomas Newenham (1805), Edward Wakefield (1812), and Sir John Anderson (1823).

57. K. H. Connell, "Catholicism and Marriage in the Century after the Famine," in *Irish Peasant Society: Four Historical Essays* (Oxford, 1968), 113–60.

58. Aideen Foley, " 'No Sex Please, We're Catholic': The Influence of the Catholic Church on Declining Marriage Rates in Ireland between the Famine and the First World War," M. Litt. thesis, UCD, 1999.

59. The Irish Folklore Commission was established in 1935. There is substantial contemporary evidence of the Catholic clergy's opposition to traditional peasant practices such as wakes and patterns, but most of this relates to prefamine Ireland.

60. *Irish Ecclesiastical Record* (1897): 109.

61. Schrier, *Ireland and the American Emigration*, 63.

62. Robert E. Kennedy, in *The Irish: Emigration, Marriage, and Fertility* (Berkeley, 1973), provides a comprehensive analysis of statistical trends and much more.

63. Liam de Paor, "Ireland's Identities," *Crane Bag* 3, no. 1 (1979): 25.

64. Delaney claims that "no government file relating to emigration is extant for the period from 1921 to 1939," *Demography, State, and Society*, 58. This is not entirely correct; there are files relating to assisted emigration and to changes in American immigration quotas, but emigration was not a major concern for government at this time.

2. Saving Rural Ireland

1. See, for example, Guinnane, *Vanishing Irish*, 3.

2. D. H. Akenson has suggested that this was not true of Irish emigrants to the United States. *Small Differences: Irish Catholics and Irish Protestants, 1815–1922* (Kingston, Ont., 1988), 107. For the contrary view, which commands more general support, see David N. Doyle, "The Remaking of Irish-America, 1845–80," in W. J. Vaughan, ed., *A New History of Ireland*, vol. 6 (Oxford, 1996), 745–58.

3. Meenan, "Preliminary Notes on the Census of Population in Northern Ireland, 1937," 69.

4. In 1951 30.9 percent of men aged thirty-five to thirty-nine living in towns were single, compared with 53.3 percent of rural males. In the case of women aged thirty-five to thirty-nine, the comparable figures were 30.8 percent of urban women and 26.5 percent of rural women. These patterns were consistent regardless of age. *Census of Population 1951*.

5. *Bunreacht na hÉireann 1937*, article 45 V.

6. *Commission on Emigration and Other Population Problems, 1948–54 Reports*, P. 2541 R. 84 para. 474.

7. Ferdinand Braudel, *The Identity of France*, vol. 1, *History and Environment* (London, 1988), 676–78. See the many nostalgic accounts of rural life, such as Flora Thompson's *Lark Rise to Candleford* (first published 1948, reprinted 1973 and on many subsequent occasions) or, in Ireland, Alice Taylor's *To School through the Fields: A Country Childhood* (Dingle, 1991), *Quench the Lamp* (Dingle, 1990), and many others.

8. Martin Wiener, *English Culture and the Decline of the Industrial Spirit, 1850–1980* (Cambridge, 1981).

9. Pilgrim Trust, *Men without Work: A Report Made to the Pilgrim Trust* (Cambridge, 1938).

10. Feliks Gross, *Il Paese: Values and Social Change in an Italian Village* (New York, 1974), 43; Paul Ginsbourg, *A History of Contemporary Italy: Society and Politics, 1943–1988* (London, 1990), 218.

11. DT, S16877 X/62, European Economic Community, NAI.

12. Quoted in F. S. L. Lyons, *Culture and Anarchy in Ireland, 1890–1939* (Oxford, 1979), 5.

13. Garvin, *Nationalist Revolutionaries in Ireland*, 53, 103.

14. Daniel Corkery, *The Hidden Ireland: A Study of Gaelic Munster in the Eighteenth Century* (Dublin, 1925), 19–20.

15. Daniel Corkery, "Of Visions National and International," *Irish*

Stateman, 2 Mar. 1924, as cited in Peter Hart, *The IRA and its Enemies: Violence and Community in Cork, 1916–1923* (Oxford, 1998), 143.

16. Hart, *The IRA and Its Enemies: Violence and Community in Cork, 1916–1923,* 151–59.

17. Maguire, *The Irish in America,* 216 –18.

18. This image was probably accurate; see Cormac Ó Gráda and Joel Mokyr, "Heights and Living Standards in the United Kingdom, 1815 –1860," *Explorations in Economic History* (April 1996): 1–27.

19. DT, S13109 A, Commission on Youth Unemployment, NAI. The books were offered to the Commission on Youth Unemployment.

20. *Commission on Vocational Organisation,* Report, 1944, para. 544.

21. Mary E. Daly, *Dublin: The Deposed Capital. A Social and Economic History, 1860–1914* (Cork, 1984), 3, 244.

22. Colm A. Barry, "Irish Regional Life Tables," *JSSISI* 16 (1941–42): 10.

23. R. C. Geary, "The Mortality from Tuberculosis in Saorstát Éireann: A Statistical Study," *JSSISI* 14 (1929 –30): 67; Irish emigrants to Britain had a high morbidity from tuberculosis for the same reason. John Jackson, *The Irish in Britain* (London, 1963), 65; Greta Jones, *"Captains of All These Men of Death": The History of Tuberculosis in Nineteenth- and Twentieth-Century Ireland* (London, 2001), 188 –90.

24. Lindsey Earner-Byrne, "'In Respect of Motherhood': Maternity Policy and Provision in Dublin City, 1922–1956," Ph.D. thesis, UCD, 2001, 114 –22.

25. Gerard Fee, "The Effects of World War II on Dublin's Low-Income Families, 1939 –1945," Ph.D. thesis, UCD, 1996, 55 –76, 153 –98.

26. By comparison, the Catholic parishes in Italian cities provided a range of services. See Paul Ginsbourg, *A History of Contemporary Italy: Society and Politics, 1943–1988* (London, 1990), 168 –70.

27. See *Christus Rex* 7 (1953); 8 (1954); 12 (1958); *The Furrow* 8 (1957); 11 (1960).

28. *Royal Commission on the Poor Law. Report on Ireland, 1909* (command. 6153), 21.

29. *Irish Catholic Directory* (1934): 586.

30. Reverend H. Murphy, "The Rural Family: The Principles," *Christus Rex* 6 (1952): 3 –9.

31. Edward Cahill, *The Framework of a Christian State* (Dublin, 1932), 331–33.

32. DT, S10816, Muintir na Tíre, NAI.

33. "Human Values in the Rural Community: Declaration of Principles

Issued by the Union Internationale d'Etudes Sociales, Malines," *Christus Rex* 5 (1951): 121–23.

34. DT, S17032 I/95, Small Western Farms, NAI.

35. Alexander J. Humphreys, *New Dubliners: Urbanization and the Irish Family* (London, 1966), 27–33.

36. Alexander J. Humphreys, "Migration to Dublin: Its Social Effects," *Christus Rex* 9 (1955): 192–99. Many of Humphreys's assumptions concerning rural stability and the self-sufficiency of the family are not supported by historical research.

37. Reverend H. Murphy, "The Rural Family," 20. A scheme along these lines was developed in Belgium in the late nineteenth century, prompted by Catholic social teaching. Instead of building working-class accommodation in the city, workers in Brussels lived in nearby villages, in cottages that they owned, and commuted to work on heavily subsidized trains. Janet Polasky, "Transplanting and Rooting Workers in London and Brussels: A Comparative History," *Journal of Modern History* 73 (September 2001): 528–60.

38. PDDE, vol. 72, 6 July 1938, col. 309.

39. S5111/7, S5111/8, NAI.

40. Mary E. Daly, *The Buffer State: The Historical Roots of the Department of the Environment* (Dublin, 1997), 174–76.

41. DIC, Trade and Industry Division, TID 43/63, NAI; Mary E. Daly, *Industrial Development and Irish National Identity, 1922–1939* (Syracuse, N.Y., 1992), 106–16.

42. Mary E. Daly, *The Buffer State,* chapters 4 and 9.

43. Mary E. Daly, *The First Department: A History of the Department of Agriculture* (Dublin, 2002), 66–70, 97.

44. Sean Fitzpatrick, "Donnchadh Ó Briain. Requests and Representations: An Unsung Life of Fidelity to Fianna Fáil," M.A. thesis, UCD, 1995, 19–25. The other common requests relate to pensions.

45. Minutes of parliamentary party, 14 June 1933, 8 March 1934, 19 December 1934, 27 October 1938, 8 December 1938, P 176/439, Fianna Fáil Papers, UCDA; Richard Dunphy, *The Making of Fianna Fáil Power in Ireland, 1932–48* (Oxford, 1995), 155.

46. *Commission on Emigration,* paras. 104–5.

47. Mary E. Daly, *The First Department,* 247. Statistics on the number of women engaged in farming are almost meaningless because they exclude farmers' wives, the largest category.

48. See Bernadette Whelan, *Ireland and the Marshall Plan, 1947–1957* (Dublin, 2000).

49. For details, see Mary E. Daly, *The First Department,* 281–330.

50. *Commission on Emigration,* addendum no. 2, 200.

51. PDDE, 2 July 1947, cols. 705 –11.

52. *Commission on Emigration,* para. 72 and tables 14 and 15. Ireland had the lowest density of total population to total area after Norway and Sweden and the fourth lowest number of agricultural workers per square mile of agricultural land. Paragraph 14 showed that between 1841 and 1951 the population of Ulster (three counties) had fallen by 66 percent, Connacht by 67 percent, Munster 62 percent, and Leinster, excluding Dublin city and county, by 60 percent.

53. Patrick Noonan, "Why Few Irish Marry," in *The Vanishing Irish: The Enigma of the Modern World,* ed. John A. O'Brien, 48 (New York, 1954).

54. Rural Depopulation Memorandum, 4 December 1946, 67/262, Seán MacEntee Papers, UCDA.

55. *Commission of Inquiry into Banking Currency and Credit* (1934 –38), R. 38, Third Minority Report; Eithne McDermott, *Clann na Poblachta* (Dublin, 1998), 61.

56. Joseph Hanly, *The National Ideal: A Practical Exposition of True Nationality Appertaining* (Dublin, 1931), 224, 227. A paper to the Statistical and Social Inquiry Society of Ireland by J. P. Beddy, comparing the economies of Ireland and Denmark, had to be reprinted in January 1944 in response to popular demand. Mary E. Daly, *"The Spirit of Earnest Inquiry"* 123 –24.

57. Mary E. Daly, "The Economic Ideals of Irish Nationalism: Frugal Comfort or Lavish Austerity?" *Éire-Ireland* 29, no. 4 (Winter 1994): 77 –100.

58. Index of Memoranda: Mellifont Conference on Depopulation and Council of National Action, MS 8305/14, Marsh Papers, Papers of the Commission on Emigration, TCD. Muintir na Tíre (people of the countryside) was founded in 1931 by Canon Michael Hayes, as a voluntary organization dedicated to promoting rural life and rural communities.

59. When the war ended, the net external assets of the Irish commercial banks stood at £159.5 million. This sum had accumulated during the war because of British restrictions on sales of goods to Ireland. The repatriation of these sterling assets to Ireland, where they would be used to finance various forms of public investment, was frequently suggested during these years as the solution to Ireland's economic difficulties. In reality these sterling assets were the property of the commercial banks, not the state.

60. Patrick Noonan, "Why Few Irish Marry," 49. In 1961 only 9,017 of the 419,465 residents of Connacht were born outside the state, and 7,099 were born in Britain or in Northern Ireland. Many of these were probably the spouses or children of returned emigrants.

61. MS 8305/2 34M, Marsh Papers.

62. Tony Varley and Chris Curtin, "Defending Rural Interests Against Nationalists in Twentieth-Century Ireland: A Tale of Three Movements," in John Davis, ed., *Rural Change in Ireland* (Belfast, 1999), 67.

63. J. J. Lee, *Ireland, 1912–1985 Politics and Society* (Cambridge, 1989), 73.

64. Joseph Brennan, first secretary of the Department of Finance, was born in west Cork; his successor J. J. McElligott was a native of county Kerry; likewise brothers Sean and Maurice Moynihan, secretaries to the government; Francis Meyrick, secretary of the Department of Agriculture, was a Dubliner, but his successor Daniel Twomey was from west Cork.

65. Mary E. Daly, *The First Department*, 180.

66. Ibid., 269–71.

67. David Seth Jones, "Divisions within the Irish Government over Land Distribution Policy, 1940–70," *Éire-Ireland* 36, nos. 3/4 (Fall/Winter, 2001): 87–92. There was a similar division of opinion in the first inter-party government (102–4).

68. PDDE, 2 July 1947, cols. 705–7.

69. MS 8307/14, oral evidence from Land Commission, Waddell and O'Brien, Marsh Papers.

70. Dunphy, *The Making of Fianna Fáil Power in Ireland*, 155; David Seth Jones, "Divisions within the Irish Government over Land Distribution Policy," 96–101.

71. Mary E. Daly, *The First Department*, 268–70.

72. MS 8307/14, oral evidence from Land Commission, Waddell and O'Brien, Marsh Papers.

73. Mary E. Daly, *The First Department*, 279–86.

74. PDDE, 2 July 1947, col. 708.

75. DT, S14638 I, Proposals by the OEEC for the Liberalization of European Trade, NAI.

76. As quoted in Paul Rouse, *Ireland's Own Soil: Government and Agriculture in Ireland, 1945–1963* (Dublin, 2000), 175.

77. DT, S15161, Glass-House Crops, NAI.

78. *Irish Press*, 30 May 1955, cited in Diarmaid Ferriter, "'A Peculiar People in Their Own Land': Catholic Social Theory and the Plight of Rural Ireland, 1930–55," Ph.D. thesis, UCD 1996, 242.

79. John A. O'Brien, *The Vanishing Irish*, 29. See the second quotation at the beginning of this chapter.

80. Para. 384.

81. *Commission on Emigration*, paras. 473–75.

82. Ibid., Geary and McCarthy, addendum no. 2, 199–200; Meenan, Minority Report, para. 18; Dr. Lucey, Minority Report, paras. 338–47.

83. *Commission on Emigration,* para. 372.

84. Minutes of National Executive, 9 December 1957, 8 September 1958, P176/345, Fianna Fáil Papers, UCDA.

85. *Irish Catholic Directory* (1953): 641–42.

86. S8301, Summaries of evidence to Commission on Emigration, S1(a) Congested Districts, M 34, Marsh Papers.

87. C. S. Andrews, *Man of No Property* (Dublin, 1982), 72.

88. Mary E. Daly, *The First Department,* 72–73.

89. MS 8307/16, Evidence from Department of Lands, Forestry Division, Marsh Papers; *Commission on Emigration,* paras. 361–64.

90. DT, S14249 A/2, NAI.

91. DE, General Files, D/E G 316/3, Part 2, NAI.

92. Mary E. Daly, *The First Department,* 530–32.

93. MS 8305/2 34, memorandum from M. J. Molloy, Marsh Papers.

94. MS 8307/2, Transcripts of Evidence, Marsh Papers.

95. MS 8307/22, Transcripts of Evidence, Marsh Papers.

96. *Commission on Emigration,* paras. 437–40; Mary E. Daly, "'Turn on the Tap': The State, Irish Women, and Running Water," in Maryann Gianella Valiulis and Mary O'Dowd, eds., *Women and Irish History: Essays in Honour of Margaret MacCurtain* (Dublin, 1997), 206–19.

97. MS 8306, Rural Surveys, S2 Kilkenny, Marsh Papers.

98. MS 8306, Rural Surveys S17 Portarlington, S19 Tullow, Marsh Papers.

99. MS 8306, Rural Surveys, S18 Newbridge, Marsh Papers.

100. Mary E. Daly, *Industrial Development and Irish National Identity,* 106–16, 141–42. Also information from Frank Casey, former managing director of the Industrial Credit Company.

101. MS 8306, Rural Surveys, S21, Marsh Papers.

102. MS 8306, Rural Surveys, S13, Drogleda, Marsh Papers.

103. *Commission on Emigration,* paras. 472, 385–404.

104. Denis I. F. Lucey and Donald R. Kaldor, *Rural Industrialization: The Impact of Industrialization on Two Rural Communities in Western Ireland* (London, 1969), 29.

105. *Commission on Emigration,* paras. 405 and 410.

106. DT, S10816, Muintir na Tíre, NAI. This argument is not sustained by statistics. The only Irish city to achieve sustained growth for over a century was Belfast.

107. Peter Flora, *State Economy and Society in Western Europe, 1915–1977: A Data Handbook,* vol. 2, *The Growth of Industrial Societies and Capitalist Economies* (Frankfurt, 1987), chapter 7.

108. DT, S10816, Muintir na Tíre, NAI.

109. *Commission on Emigration,* paras. 298, 438–40.

110. MS 8305/28, memorandum submitted by Micheal O Cíosóg, survey of Connemara, Marsh Papers.

111. MS 8305/5, memorandum from Seán Hogan, Smithstown, Bunratty, Marsh Papers.

112. MS 8307/5, Transcripts of Evidence, Marsh Papers.

113. *Commission on Emigration,* Minority Report, paras. 207, 26 –31.

114. MS 8300/5/1, memoranda, Marsh Papers.

115. J. F. Gravier, *Paris et le Désert Français* (Paris, 1947).

116. MS 8301 M. 76 Summary of evidence to Commission on Emigration, Marsh Papers.

117. DT, S14880, Emergency Preparations, NAI.

118. DE, General Files, G271/1, Commission on Population, NAI.

119. A motorway running north from the city toward Belfast was first planned in the 1940s, but has not yet been completed. By contrast, the state picked up almost the entire cost of road works in western counties.

120. Mary E. Daly, *The Buffer State,* 351–56.

121. DE, General Files, G271/1, NAI.

122. *Commission on Emigration,* para 31.

123. Ibid., paras. 409, 29; DT, S14249/A2, Commission on Emigration, NAI.

124. DT, S14249 A/2, Commission on Emigration, NAI.

125. DT, S14249 B, Commission on Emigration, NAI.

126. Under the Northern Ireland Development Acts of 1945 to 1953, the proposed location of the industry was taken into account, but no formal regional discrimination in terms of grants or other incentives applied. By 1959 an estimated 36,800 jobs had been created under the Northern Ireland Acts. *Ulster Year Book, 1957–59* (Belfast, 1959).

127. The research carried out in county Clare formed part of a wider research program in Ireland, beginning in 1931, by the Department of Anthropology at Harvard University, which was designed to provide case material for a comparative sociology. Most anthropological research carried out before that time had examined primitive societies; Ireland was selected because it was a more modern society (the terms are theirs not mine), but one that blended old and new. In addition to examining the social anthropology of rural Ireland, Harvard scholars were involved in several major archaeological excavations and a racial survey of the physical anthropology of the ancient and current inhabitants of Ireland directed by Earnest Hooton and C. Wesley Dupertuis, which was published in 1955. See Earnest A. Hooton and C. Wesley Dupertuis, *The Physical Anthropology of Ireland* (Cambridge, Mass., 1955). For a detailed account of the background

to this research program and a critique of their work, together with a comprehensive bibliography of publications relating to these studies, see Conrad Arensberg and Solon T. Kimball, *Family and Community in Ireland*, third edition (Ennis, 2001), with a new introduction by Anne Byrne, Riccas Edmondston, and Tony Varley.

128. Conrad Arensberg, *The Irish Countryman* (Gloucester, Mass., 1959; first edition 1937), 24.

129. Kevin O'Neill, *Family and Farm in Pre-Famine Ireland: The Parish of Killashandra* (Madison, Wis., 1984), 100–102, 130–54.

130. Cited in Terence Brown, *Ireland: A Social and Cultural History, 1922–79* (London, 1980), 200.

131. Damien Hannan, *Displacement and Development: Class, Kinship, and Social Change in Irish Rural Communities* (Dublin, 1979), 59.

132. In 1932 the Irish government stopped making repayments to Banlain on land purchase annuities. Britain retaliated by imposing tariffs on Irish agricultural produce. The dispute was settled in 1938.

133. DE, SS3, Report of the Committee on Water and Sewerage and Other Functions of Sanitary Authorities, 1958, NAI.

134. MS 8307/5, Evidence from Dr. Moran, Marsh Papers.

135. PDDE, 2 July 1947, cols. 732–34.

136. Robert Cresswell, *Une communauté Rurale de l'Irlande* (Paris, 1969), 85. The *Dundalk Democrat* carried advertisements throughout 1956 selling electrical goods to families who had just been connected to the electricity network.

137. DT, S13058 C, NAI; Mary E. Daly, "'Turn on the Tap,'" 206–19.

138. Peter Hall, *Cities in Civilization* (London, 1998), 407–10.

139. The number of tractors increased from 10,100 in 1949 to 43,700 in 1960, and to 84,300 by 1970. I remember waiting for a bus in Carrickmacross some time in the late 1960s or early 1970s and seeing one passenger being left at the bus by tractor.

140. Arensberg and Kimball, *Family and Community in Ireland*, 107.

141. John M. Mogey, *Rural Life in Northern Ireland* (Oxford, 1947), 84–86.

142. MS 8305/2 34 (emphasis in the original), Marsh Papers.

143. DT, S 8670C, Interdepartmental Committee on Islands, NAI.

144. 8305/29, memoranda, Blasket Islands and Dingle Peninsula, Marsh Papers.

145. DT, S10816, Muintir na Tíre, NAI.

146. Jude McCarthy, "'From Herod to Pilate': State-Aided Island Migrations, 1930–60," M.A. thesis, UCD, 1997, 90.

147. Caitríona Clear, *Women of the House: Women's Household Work in Ireland, 1922–1961* (Dublin, 2000), 316–18.

148. MS 8306 S5, Rural Surveys, Clonmel, Arklow, and Wexford, Marsh Papers.

149. MS 8301 M36, Summaries of evidence, county Leitrim Vocational Education Committee, Marsh Papers.

150. See for example, Mogey, *Rural Life in Northern Ireland*, 55–57.

151. Anne O'Dowd, *Meitheal: A Study of Co-operative Labour in Rural Ireland* (Dublin, 1981).

152. Arensberg and Kimball, *Family and Community in Ireland*, 173–74, 177–94.

153. Arensberg, *Irish Countryman*, 124–25.

154. MS 8301 M74, Marsh Papers.

155. I am indebted to Patrick Travers for this information.

156. Rosemary Harris, *Prejudice and Tolerance in Ulster: A Study of Neighbours and "Strangers" in a Border Community* (Manchester, 1972), 65, 75, 89, 91, 114.

157. John H. Whyte, *Church and State in Modern Ireland, 1923–1970* (Dublin, 1971), 28.

158. *Irish Catholic Directory,* passim; David Fitzpatrick, *The Two Irelands, 1912–1939* (Oxford, 1998), 228; Thekla Beere, "Cinema Statistics in Saorstát Éireann," *JSSISI* 15 (1935–36): 83.

159. DT, S13058 A, B, C, Village Halls, and DE, General Files, G 326/1–4, National Development Fund, NAI; Mary E. Daly, *The Buffer State*, 415–20.

160. Patrick McNabb, "Social Structure," in Jeremiah Newman, ed., *The Limerick Rural Survey, 1958–1964* (Tipperary, 1964), 228–29.

161. P 67/282, MacEntee Papers, UCDA.

162. Arensberg and Kimball, *Family and Community in Ireland*, 222–23.

163. Desmond Farley, *Social Insurance and Social Assistance in Ireland* (Dublin, 1964), 55. From 1935 smallholders in possession of land valued at £4 or more were refused benefit between March and October, and men living in rural areas without family dependents were disqualified from claiming benefit between June and October in an effort to ensure adequate supplies of rural labor during peak farming seasons.

164. Geary, "The Future Population of Saorstát Éireann," *JSSISI* 15 (1935–36): 25.

165. Jude McCarthy, "'From Herod to Pilate,'" 81.

166. Statement by the President, 10 August 1933, P 176/451, Fianna Fáil Parliamentary Party Minutes, Fianna Fáil Papers, UCDA.

167. Mary E. Daly, *The Buffer State*, 266.

168. Harris, *Prejudice and Tolerance in Ulster,* 54–55.

169. R. C. Geary, "The Future Population of Saorstát Éireann," 25.

170. Arensberg, *The Irish Countryman,* 49–52.

171. Cited in Mary E. Daly, *The Buffer State,* 408.

172. D Ag, AGI G 1093/1938, Agricultural Wages Act, NAI; PDDE, 2 July 1947, col. 722.

173. Patrick McNabb, "Demography," in Newman, *Limerick Rural Survey,* 173.

174. Michael Murphy, "Financial Results on Mixed Dairy Farms in 1937–38," *JSSISI* 16 (1938–39): 105–30; "Financial Results on Sixty-One West Cork Farms in 1940–41," *JSSISI* 16 (1941–42): 60–87; "Financial Results on Mixed Dairy Farms in 1942–43 as Compared with 1937–39," *JSSISI* 17 (1943–44): 269–308; R. O'Connor, "Financial Results on Twenty Farms in Mid-Roscommon in 1945–46," *JSSISI* 18 (1948–49): 79–108; "Financial Results on Twenty-Five Farms in Mid-Roscommon in 1948–49," *JSSISI* 18, pt. 3 (1949–50): 270–92.

175. D Ag, AGI G764/1946, Harvest labor scheme, NAI.

176. MS 8301, Summary of oral evidence, Marsh Papers.

177. Dónal Mac Amhlaigh, *Dialann Deorai* (Dublin, 1960), 1; Rural Surveys, S5, Marsh Papers.

178. 8305/4, Transcripts of Evidence, Marsh Papers.

179. MS 8306, Rural Surveys, S3, Marsh Papers.

180. Ibid., Rural Surveys, S6.

181. Evidence to the Brennan Commission on the Civil Service in the 1930s showed that although the lowest grades, such as writing assistant, only specified primary schooling, many of the women who were appointed to these jobs had secondary school qualifications. Commission of Inquiry into the Civil Service, 1932–34, Minutes, MS 956, 43, NAI. In *Ireland, 1912–1985,* 197, Lee cites other evidence given to the Brennan Commission showing that in 1931–32 there were fifteen applications for every vacant post as writing assistant and similar competition for higher grade posts.

182. MS 8301 M 74, Summary of evidence of Micheál Ó Cíosóg, Marsh Papers.

183. MS 8306, Rural Surveys, S21, Marsh Papers.

184. MS 8307/20, Oral evidence from the Department of Education: T. Ó Raiftearaigh, P. A. Mc Kenna, Dr. O'Sullivan, Marsh Papers. There is no suggestion that the sample of schools was scientific; they were schools where the manager proved to be cooperative. One-third were boarding schools, and the average number of leaving certificate students in each girls' school was only five, which Ó Raiftearaigh, then the assistant secretary

with responsibility for secondary education, suggested was the average number.

185. MS 8306, Rural Surveys, S22, Marsh Papers; McNabb, "Social Survey," 204.

186. Rural Surveys, S8, Marsh Papers; DT, S13431 B, Second Homes on Family Farms, NAI.

187. MS 8307/20, Marsh Papers.

188. Cited in Very Reverend Martin Brenan, "Rural Education: The Principles," *Christus Rex* 7 (1953): 94.

189. MS 8307–8/21, Oral evidence, Department of Education, Marsh Papers.

190. Ibid., MS 8305/25, memoranda from the chief executive officers of vocational education committees.

191. Ibid., MS 8307–8/21.

192. Ibid., MS 8308/31, Evidence concerning vocational education.

193. Ibid., MS 8305/2 34.

194. Ibid., MS 8304/8; Reverend Thomas Counihan, S.J., "Addendum no. 1," *Commission on Emigration*, 193.

195. DT, S14310, Cabinet Economic Committee, 1948, emigration, NAI.

196. MS 8307–8/21, Marsh Papers.This was not a new phenomenon. Mary O'Brien, the daughter of a prosperous dairy farmer in county Limerick was taught at her convent school to give orders to imaginary footmen and butlers and to curtsey when presented to the lord lieutenant. Mary Carbery, *The Farm by Lough Gur* (Cork, 1978 edition), 102.

197. *Economic Development,* Department of Finance (T. K. Whitaker) (1958) F. 58, chapter 11, para. 14, 114.

198. MS 8305/4, Marsh Papers.

199. Harris, *Prejudice and Tolerance in Ulster,* 32–42; Henri Mendras, *The Vanishing Peasant: Innovation and Change in French Agriculture* (Cambridge, Mass., 1970), 91–92.

200. *Commission on Emigration,* 176–78; paras. 446, 447, 452.

201. Minutes of the National Executive, 1955–57, P/176/ 347 and 348, Fianna Fáil Papers, UCDA.

202. DT, S17032 A, Small Farms: Development of Pilot Areas, NAI.

203. Arensberg and Kimball, *Family and Community in Ireland,* 153, 170–72.

204. Ibid., 53 –55.

205. DT, S13431, Second Homes on Family Farms: McFall to de Valera in 1943, NAI.

206. Arensberg and Kimball, *Family and Community in Ireland,* 55.

Despite an extensive search of the Dáil Web site, I have failed to locate this quotation and wonder if it actually exists.

207. MS 8301 T18, Summary of evidence to Commission on Emigration, evidence given by Gaeltacht Services Section, Department of Lands; 8301 R22, Marsh Papers.

208. Arensberg and Kimball, *Family and Community in Ireland,* 54.

209. DT, S12117 A, Cabinet Committee on Family Allowances, 1939, NAI.

210. McNabb, "Social Structure," 214.

211. Macra na Feirme was founded in 1944 to promote education and social activities for young men and women engaged in farming.

212. Cresswell, *Une Communauté Rurale,* 527.

213. McNabb, "Social Structure," 215, 237, 245–46.

214. McNabb, "Social Structure," 231.

215. Mendras, *The Vanishing Peasant,* 89–90.

216. See Arensberg and Kimball, *Family and Community in Ireland,* chapter 14, "The Framework of Relationship," 299–306.

217. DT, S13431, NAI.

218. E. Banfield, *The Moral Basis of a Backward Society* (Glencoe, Ill., 1958); C. Tullio-Altan, *Il Nostra Italia* (Milano, 1986); Ginsbourg, *A History of Contemporary Italy,* 2–3.

219. Cresswell, *Une Communauté Rurale,* 505; Michael Shiel, *The Quiet Revolution: The Electrification of Rural Ireland* (Dublin, 1984), 180–82; Mary E. Daly, " 'Turn on the Tap.' "

220. DT, S 10816, Muintir na Tíre, NAI.

221. Arensberg and Kimball, *Family and Community in Ireland,* 305.

3. Marriages, Births, and Fertility

The quote from Reverend T. H. McFall that opens this chapter is taken from S13431 A, Second Homes on Family Farms, NAI.

1. Guinnane, *The Vanishing Irish,* 6, 21.

2. From 1923 to 1937, the official name of the state was the Irish Free State or Saorstát Éireann.

3. Geary, "Future Population of Saorstát Éireann," 20–23.

4. Guinnane, *The Vanishing Irish,* 204–6; David Fitzpatrick, "Irish Farming Families before the First World War," *Comparative Studies in Society and History* 25, no. 2 (1983): 339–74.

5. *Census of Population 1926,* vol. 10, 117–18; Cormac Ó Gráda, *Ireland: A New Economic History, 1780–1939* (Oxford, 1994), 216–17.

6. Hannan, *Displacement and Development,* 41, 209.

7. *Census of Population 1926,* vol. 10, 113.

8. S9178, 1936 Census Summary, vol. 5, pt. 2, NAI.

9. Arensberg and Kimball, *Family and Community in Ireland,* 99–101.

10. Ibid., 103.

11. Pat Hudson and Steve King, "Two Textile Townships, c. 1660–1820: A Comparative Demographic Analysis," *Economic History Review* 53, no. 4 (November 2000): 737.

12. Hannan has suggested that the Ulster counties of Donegal, Monaghan, and Cavan had a different pattern than Connacht and west Munster, despite apparent similarities in farm structures. *Displacement and Development,* 44–45.

13. According to Peter Gibbon, "On every score—the family, the mutual aid system and its politics, their account ranges from the inaccurate to the fictive." "Arensberg and Kimball Revisited," *Economy and Society* 2, no. 4 (1973): 491. But I tend to support Hannan's claim that Arensberg and Kimball's account "is a safe base from which to start analysing changes in farming and communal systems in the west of Ireland." *Displacement and Development,* 50.

14. Hannan, *Displacement and Development,* 100; Liam Kennedy, "Farm Succession in Modern Ireland: Elements of a Theory of Inheritance," in John Davis, ed., *Rural Change in Ireland* (Belfast, 1999), 116–42; Fitzpatrick, "Irish Farming Families before the First World War," 339–74.

15. See the information on the careers of past pupils of the Swinford convent school in chapter 2.

16. Arensberg, *The Irish Countryman,* 61–62.

17. Donna Birdwell-Pheasant, "The Early Twentieth-Century Irish Stem Family: A Case Study from County Kerry," in Marliyn Silverman and P. H. Gulliver, eds., *Approaching the Past: Historical Anthropology through Irish Case Studies* (New York, 1992), 205–35.

18. Guinnane, *Vanishing Irish,* 230–33; Joanna Bourke, "'The Best of All Home-Rulers': The Economic Power of Women in Ireland," *Irish Economic and Social History* 18 (1991): 479–99.

19. Arensberg and Kimball, *Family and Community in Ireland,* 67.

20. Connell, *The Population of Ireland,* 57–79.

21. The archives of the Department of Irish Folklore at UCD contain surprisingly little material on attitudes to bachelors. There is one poem from Cork about a lonely bachelor (54.25), and a reference to a lonely bachelor in South Wexford who had nobody to cook his meals (54.189).

22. *Commission on Emigration,* 69.

23. MS 8302, R. C. Geary, "Level and Trend of Population," Marsh Papers. This was an early draft of sections of the report of the Commission on Emigration.

24. Arensberg and Kimball, *Family and Community in Ireland*, 122–23.

25. Arensberg, *The Irish Countryman*, 97. This statement might not withstand statistical analysis.

26. Arensberg and Kimball, *Family and Community in Ireland*, 220–22.

27. Ibid., 217, 221–22.

28. DT, Private papers, 97/9/95, Harvard University, 19 August 1932, NAI. The Irish government apparently provided some funds for the Harvard University Racial Survey carried out by Dr. Dupertuis, and the Irish-American community in Boston met part of the cost of the archaeological research. For the background to the Harvard research in Ireland, see "Introduction to the Third Edition" of *Family and Community in Ireland*, xvii–lix.

29. DT, Private papers, 97/9/95, 3 June 1943, NAI.

30. Arensberg and Kimball, *Family and Community in Ireland*, 222–23.

31. Soloway, *Demography and Degeneration*, 234–35. Roy Geary used Kuczynski's formula for net reproduction as the basis for his population projections.

32. Joseph J. Spengler, *Facing Zero Population Growth: Reactions and Interpretations, Past and Present* (Durham, N.C., 1978), 47–51; D. V. Glass, *The Struggle for Population* (Oxford, 1936), 269–70; Enid Charles, *The Twilight of Parenthood: A Biological Study of the Decline of Population Growth* (London, 1934), 45.

33. R. R. Kuczynski. "The World's Future Population," in Quincy Wright, ed., *Population* (Chicago, 1933), 302, as cited in Spengler, *Facing Zero Population Growth*, 51.

34. Geary, "The Future Population of Saorstát Éireann," 17–19.

35. Soloway, *Demography and Degeneration*, 241. The books were D. V. Glass, *The Struggle for Population;* Robert Kuczynski, *Population Movements* (Oxford, 1936); and A. M. Carr-Saunders, *World Population: Past Growth and Present Trends* (Oxford, 1936). Glass's book was commissioned by the Eugenics Society. Dorothy Porter, *Health, Civilization and the State: A History of Public Health from Ancient to Modern Times* (London, 1999), 187.

36. Mary E. Daly, *The Spirit of Earnest Inquiry*, 116–17.

37. Carr-Saunders, *World Population*, 114–16.

38. Ibid., 102.

39. Soloway, *Demography and Degeneration*, 260; Ross McKibben, *Classes and Cultures: England 1918–1951* (Oxford, 1998), 307–10.

40. Carr-Saunders, *World Population*, 102–3. The Church of England only abandoned its objections to birth control in 1930.

41. This anticipates the economic explanations favored by Gary Becker. *A Treatise on the Family* (Cambridge, Mass., 1991 edition), 138–51.

42. Carr-Saunders, *World Population*, 110–11.

43. Adrian Kelly has come to a similar conclusion with respect to policy on social security. "Social Security in Ireland, 1922–52," thesis abstract, *Irish Economic and Social History* 24 (1997): 114.

44. Halliday Sutherland, *Laws of Life* (London, 1955, cheap edition), 33; Soloway, *Demography and Degeneration*, 254.

45. Halliday Sutherland, *Irish Journey* (London, 1956), 23, 27.

46. George O'Brien, "The Coming Crisis of Population," *Studies* 25 (December 1936): 566–80.

47. John Busteed, "The Problem of Population," *JSSISI* 15 (1936–37): 47.

48. S9684 A, Population Statistics, NAI.

49. PDDE, 6 February 1936, col. 208.

50. Eoin O'Leary "The Irish National Teachers Organisation and the Marriage Bar for Women National Teachers, 1933–58," *Saothar* 12 (1987): 47–52.

51. Maurice Curtis, "Catholic Action as an Organised Campaign in Ireland, 1921–1947," Ph.D. thesis, WCD, 2000, 183–84.

52. Cormac Ó Gráda and Niall Duffy, "The Fertility Transition in Ireland and Scotland, c. 1880–1930," in S. J. Connolly, R. A. Houston, and R. J. Morris, eds., *Conflict, Identity, and Economic Development: Ireland and Scotland, 1600–1939* (Preston, 1995), 98–99.

53. John T. Noonan, Jr., *Contraception: A History of Its Treatment by the Catholic Theologians and Canonists* (Cambridge, Mass., 1965), 411.

54. Department of Justice, Censorship Files, 315/7, NAI.

55. Ibid.

56. L. M. Cullen, *Eason & Son: A History* (Dublin, 1989), 271–72.

57. Fitzpatrick, *The Two Irelands*, 228.

58. Whyte, *Church and State in Modern Ireland*, 31. My thanks to Susannah O'Riordan for her comments on this topic.

59. Cahill, *The Framework of a Christian State*, 326–31.

60. Noonan, *Contraception*, 426.

61. Ibid., 431.

62. Ibid., 506.

63. Earner-Byrne, "'In Respect of Motherhood,'" 75–77.

64. Ibid., 78–82.

65. Irish women's magazines launched during these years included *Model Housekeeping, Mother and Maid, Woman's Mirror, The Modern Girl, Ladies Home Journal, Woman's Life,* and the *Dublin Ladies Journal*. Research carried out by Catherine Conway.

66. Finola Kennedy, *Cottage to Crèche: Family Change in Ireland* (Dublin, 2001), 158–63.

67. Tony Farmar, *Holles Street 1894–1944: The National Maternity Hospital—A Centenary History* (Dublin, 1994), 99.

68. Earner-Byrne, "'In Respect of Motherhood,'" 73.

69. According to Halliday Sutherland the findings of this research was published in 1930 and 1931 respectively. *Laws of Life,* 52. But Noonan cites 1924 for Ogino and 1929 for Knaus. *Contraception,* 443.

70. "Diffusion of Knowledge Regarding the Sterile Period," *Irish Ecclesiastical Record,* 1934, vol. 43, 414–18.

71. Busteed, "The Problem of Population," 62.

72. Curtis, "Catholic Action as an Organised Campaign in Ireland, 1921–1947," 289, 305.

73. Sutherland, *Irish Journey,* 58.

74. PDSE, 18 November 1942, cols. 16–86.

75. PDSE, 18 November 1942, col. 54.

76. Sutherland, *Irish Journey,* 58.

77. S9684 A, Observations bearing upon the problem of a Declining Population, 23 January 1942, NAI. The sections given to cabinet colleagues came from chapters 9–12: "The False Law of Malthus"; "Population and Food Supplies"; "Neo-Malthusian Claims"; "The Law of Fertility." Sutherland, *Laws of Life,* 143–212.

78. Szreter questions this interpretation and suggests that instead of a single explanation based on class, that there were multiple fertility declines, determined by occupation and gender relationships. *Fertility, Class, and Gender,* 310–432.

79. Calculated from data in the summary volume of the 1911 census.

80. Timothy W. Guinnane, Carolyn Moehling, Cormac Ó Gráda, "Fertility in South Dublin a Century Ago: A First Look," University College Dublin, Centre for Economic Research (Working Paper Series WP01/26, 2001).

81. Ó Gráda and Duffy, "The Fertility Transition in Ireland and Scotland, c. 1880–1930," 92; Ó Gráda, *Ireland: A New Economic History,* 221–22.

82. Registration records may well have been incomplete. The number of births registered jumped from 56,780 in 1941 to 66,117 in 1942, a rise of 16 percent; the increase was at least partly caused by wartime food rationing and the need to register in order to qualify. *Commission on Emigration,* paras. 191–92.

83. Low fertility may have been a relatively new phenomenon among Irish Protestants. Cormac Ó Gráda, "Did Ulster Catholics Always Have Larger Families?" *Irish Economic and Social History* 11 (1972): 89–98.

84. S9178 B, 1936 Census, NAI.

85. George O'Brien, "The Coming Crisis of Population," 566–80.

86. Geary, "Future Population of Saorstát Éireann," 21–23.

87. S9178, 1936 Census, NAI.
88. S9636, Small Farmers in West Cork, Economic conditions, NAI.
89. S9645, Marriage Bounty, NAI.
90. Gisela Bock, "Antinatalism, Maternity, and Paternity in National Socialist Racism," in Gisela Bock and Pat Thane, eds., *Maternity and Gender Policy: Women and the Rise of the European Welfare States, 1880s–1950s* (London, 1991), 233–55; Chiara Saraceno, "Redefining Maternity and Paternity: Gender, Pro-natalism, and Social Policies in Fascist Italy," in Bock and Thane, *Maternity and Gender Policy,* 196–212.
91. D. V. Glass, *Population Policies and Movements in Europe* (Oxford, 1940), 350–70.
92. A study of fertility in rural Sicily concluded that "there is virtually no evidence that people in Villamaura took these measures seriously. Jane Schneider and Peter Schneider, "Going Forward in Reverse Gear: Culture, Economy, and Politics in the Demographic Transitions of a Rural Sicilian Town," in John R. Gillis, Louise A. Tilly, and David Levine, eds., *The European Experience of Declining Fertility* (Oxford, 1992), 159.
93. For a detailed discussion of the schemes introduced by French employers and their rationale, see Susan Pedersen, *Family, Dependence, and the Origins of the Welfare State: Britain and France, 1914–1945* (Cambridge, 1993), chapter 5.
94. There is an enormous literature on these topics. See for example, Glass, *Population Policies and Movements;* Bock and Thane, *Maternity and Gender;* Pedersen, *Family, Dependence, and the Origins of the Welfare State.* Irish women's groups did not embrace maternalist feminism.
95. Quoted in Cahill, *The Framework of a Christian State,* 396.
96. Glass, *Population Policies and Movements;* Bock and Thane, *Maternity and Gender Policies.*
97. PDDE, 23 November 1943, cols. 27–28.
98. Mel Cousins, "The Introduction of Children's Allowances in Ireland, 1939–1944," *Irish Economic and Social History* 26 (1999): 15–34; F. Powell, *The Politics of Irish Social Policy* (Lewiston, N.Y., 1992), 213–15; J. J. Lee, *Ireland 1912–1985,* 277–85; Catríona Clear, *Women of the House: Women's Household Work in Ireland, 1922–1961* (Dublin, 2000), 51–56.
99. PDDE, vol. 75, 30 March 1939, cols. 406–8 and col. 388; vol. 74, 1 March 1939, cols. 1204–12.
100. S11265 B, NAI.
101. Cousins, "The Introduction of Children's Allowances in Ireland," 37. At this time the army was the only state organization that paid family allowances.

102. S12117 A and B, Committee on Family Allowances, NAI.

103. This is followed by a footnote referring to Professor Pigou, as quoted by Eleanor Rathbone, in *The Ethics and Economics of Family Endowment* (London, 1927). (Emphasis in the original.)

104. S12117 A, 28 October 1939, NAI. See Lee, *Ireland, 1912–1985,* 283–84.

105. S11265 A, NAI.

106. Cahill, *The Framework of a Christian State,* especially 320–36. "The State cannot interfere in any way with the unity and integrity of the family, nor override any of the essential obligations of domestic life, nor usurp the functions which the natural law has assigned to the parents" (321).

107. S12117 B, NAI.

108. Sir Alexander Gray, *Family Endowment: A Critical Analysis* (London, 1927); Glass, *Population Policies and Movements.*

109. Glass, "Introduction to State Intervention," *Population Policies and Movements,* 86–98.

110. S11265 A, NAI.

111. S12117 B, NAI.

112. There is no evidence that any Irish women's organization actively campaigned in favor of children's allowances. Mary E. Daly, "Wives, Mothers, and Citizens: The Treatment of Women in the 1935 Nationality and Citizenship Act," *Éire-Ireland* 38, nos. 3/4 (Autumn/Winter 2003): 262–63.

113. S12117 B, NAI.

114. S9684 A, Observations bearing upon the problem of a Declining Population, 23 January 1942, NAI. The phrase comes from Sutherland, *Laws of Life,* 218.

115. Sutherland, *Laws of Life,* 206–7.

116. Brownlee subscribed to a theory of "germinal vitality," which suggested that at various times different races underwent a decline in their procreative ability. Stevenson's analysis of the fertility data in the 1911 census refuted this theory. Brownlee's theory was widely discredited. See Szreter, *Fertility, Class, and Gender,* 263, 270.

117. S9684 A, NAI.

118. *The Tablet* article was in response to the British government's decision to appoint a Royal Commission on Population. Soloway, *Demography and Degeneration,* 338.

119. S 13810, British Population, NAI. One interesting feature of this article is that it is gender neutral; there is no attempt to relate falling fertility to women's education or changes in women's lives.

120. Susannah Riordan, "'A Political Blackthorn': Seán MacEntee, the

Dignan Plan, and the Principle of Ministerial Responsibility," *Irish Economic and Social History* 27 (2000): 44–62.

121. Chiara Saraceno, "Constructing Families, Shaping Women's Lives: The Making of Italian Families between Market Economy and State Interventions," in Gillis, Tilly, and Levine, *The European Experience of Declining Fertility*, 260.

122. Earner-Byrne, "'In Respect of Motherhood,'" chapters 3 and 4 ; Ruth Barrington, *Health, Medicine, and Politics, 1900–1970* (Dublin, 1987), 137–66.

123. Undated letter from Dublin's Shelbourne, 519/1A Box 1, folder 1942, McQuaid Papers, DDA.

124. Beveridge Report, 53, as cited in Finola Kennedy, *Cottage to Crèche*, 7.

125. Mary E. Daly, "The Irish Family Since the Famine: Continuity and Change," *Irish Journal of Feminist Studies* (1999): 1–21.

126. Finola Kennedy, *Cottage to Crèche*, 137.

127. Department of Health, *National Nutrition Survey, Part 1: Dietary Survey—Dublin Sample*, K 53 –1 (1948): 16.

128. Department of Health, *National Nutrition Survey, Part 7: Clinical Survey*, K 53 –7 (1951): 11–13.

129. For a summary of some of the main arguments in the Irish debate, see Mary E. Daly, *Spirit of Earnest Inquiry*, 124 –29.

130. DLGPH, S12117 B, 16 March 1943, NAI. (Emphasis in the original.)

131. Cousins, "The Introduction of Children's Allowances," 49 –50.

132. Clear, *Women of the House*, 53.

133. PDDE, vol. 103, 23 November 1943, cols. 106, 109.

134. PDDE, 2 July 1947, col. 738.

135. S9178 B, Population Statistics, June 1939, NAI.

136. PDDE, 23 November 1943, cols. 46, 70, 187, 196.

137. Hannan, *Displacement and Development*, 206, appendix, table 3.

138. There is an extensive literature on this subject: Peter Gibbon and Chris Curtin, "The Stem Family in Ireland," *Comparative Studies in Society and History* 20, no. 3 (1978): 429 –53; Fitzpatrick, "Irish Farming Families before the First World War"; Chris Curtin, Eoin Devereux, and Dan Shields, "Replaying the 'Match': Marriage Settlements in North Galway," *Irish Journal of Sociology* 2 (1992): 85 –95.

139. Pauric Travers, "Emigration and Gender: The Case of Ireland, 1922–60," in Mary O'Dowd and Sabine Wichert, eds., *Chattel, Servant or Citizen? Women's Status in Church, State, and Society* (Belfast, 1995), 197 –98.

140. S13431 A, NAI.

141. Hannan, *Displacement and Development,* 39, 46; Guinnane, *The Vanishing Irish,* 204 –6; Fitzpatrick, "Irish Farming Families before the First World War," 339 –74.

142. *Commission on Emigration,* table 63, 84.

143. Murphy, "Financial Results on Mixed Dairy Farms in 1937 –38," 105 –30; "Financial Results on Sixty-One West Cork Farms in 1940 –41," 60 –87; "Financial Results on Mixed Dairy Farms in 1942 –43 as Compared with 1938 –39," 269 –308; R. O'Connor, "Financial Results on Twenty Farms in Mid-Roscommon in 1945 –46," 79 –108; "Financial Results on Twenty-Five Farms in Mid-Roscommon in 1948 –49," 270 –92.

144. S13431 B, NAI.

145. Arensberg and Kimball, *Family and Community,* 221.

146. S13431B NAI. Report Inter-Departmental Committee on Dower Houses, Appendix B Questionnaires submitted to Land Commission Inspectors, no. 6.

147. S13431B NAI. Report Inter-Departmental Committee on Dower Houses, Appendix B Questionnaires submitted to Land Commission Inspectors, no. 11.

148. Liam Kennedy, "Farm Succession in Modern Ireland," 124 –26.

149. Hannan, *Displacement and Development,* 52–53.

150. Clear, *Women of the House,* 172–73.

151. Harris, *Prejudice and Tolerance in Ulster,* 106 –14.

152. In 1951 Reverend C. B. Daly, a future cardinal and archbishop of Armagh, condemned "the hot air of contemporary decadence with its sexual license, companionate marriage, emancipation of women, rejection of motherhood." "Family Life: The Principles," *Christus Rex* 5 (1951): 8.

153. S13431 B, NAI. Inter-Deparmental Committee On Dower Houses, Appendix B Questionnaire no. 11.

154. S13431 B, NAI.

155. McNabb,"Demography," 227.

156. Birdwell-Pheasant, "The Early Twentieth-Century Irish Stem Family"; *Report by the Inter-Departmental Committee on the Problems of Small Western Farms,* 1962, A 52, Pr. 6540.

157. Mary E. Daly, *The First Department,* 416 –21. The scheme was part of a wider proposal for farm apprenticeships.

158. These children were orphaned or dependent on single persons, grandparents, or fathers not resident in the state.

159. *Census of Ireland 1926,* vol. 9, 143 –46, 97 –100.

160. Mary E. Daly, *Industrial Development and Irish National Identity, 1922–39,* 125.

161. *Report Commission on Youth Unemployment,* 1952, R.82 para. 9.

162. Women trade unionists frequently responded to attacks on "pin money girls" and single women in the labor force by noting that many of these women were supporting family members.

163. S9178 A, NAI.

164. S9178 A, NAI.

165. Julian Jackson, *France: The Dark Years, 1940–1944* (Oxford, 2001), 103–4.

166. Soloway, *Demography and Degeneration,* 9, 169, 309, and 313.

167. S9178 A, NAI. The list of possible members of the commission included economists George O'Brien and Liam Ó Buachalla; Professor Farnham or another medical practitioner; Father Cahill or Father Hayes, the founder of Muintir na Tíre, or another clergyman nominated by the Catholic hierarchy; Mrs. Gavan Duffy; Thomas Johnson and Senator Sean Campbell representing labor and trade union interests; Fianna Fáil TD Erskine Childers, who appears to have been the token Protestant, Senator Michael Tierney (UCD president); plus representatives of the Departments of Local Government, Agriculture, Industry and Commerce, and Education.

168. Enda Delaney has also remarked on the similarity. *Demography, State, and Society,* 190.

169. SS4 (b), synopsis of evidence prepared by Dr. Lucey regarding the causes of the low marriage rate, Marsh Papers.

170. Stanley Lyon, "Some Observations on Births in Dublin in the Years 1941 and 1941, *JSSISI* 17 (1942–43): 144–67; "Natality in Dublin in the Years 1943, 1944 and 1945," *JSSISI* 18 (1947–48): 57–77.

171. Report of the Royal Commission On Population, 1948–1949, Cmd. 76 95,

172. 5300/57/2, memorandum submitted by Luce, Marsh, and Collis concerning chapter 9, Marsh Papers. This does not appear among the addenda, notes, and reservations in the published report, though it may have been the genesis of the reservation submitted by Collis and Marsh as well as a separate one submitted by Luce.

173. *Commission on Emigration,* Reservation no. 6.

174. *Commission on Emigration,* paras. 157, 164, 165, 169. The only available statistics concerned age of marriage by male occupation in 1945–46. These were tabulated by occupation, but not by place of residence.

175. *Commission on Emigration,* p. 945, paras. 200–202.

176. Ibid., 99–100, paras. 211–12.

177. Ibid., table 75, Families Classified According to the Numbers of Dependent Children, p. 100, para. 212.

178. On the Catholic social services council, see Earner-Byrne, "'In Respect of Motherhood,'" chapter 3; Feeney's report is cited in Clear, *Women of the House,* 122–23.

179. *Commission on Emigration,* p. 80, para. 166.

180. *Commission on Emigration,* p. 180, para. 438.

181. *Commission on Emigration,* pp. 96–97, para. 204. Dr. Luce would have preferred to omit all references to religion from the report. MS 8300/24, Luce to Marsh, 6 July 1949, Marsh Papers.

182. MS 8300, handwritten notes by Marsh concerning chapter 9, Marsh Papers; Noonan, *Contraception,* 426.

183. MS 8300, Amendments to Reports, p. 214, Marsh Papers.

184. MS 8300, 17 October 1952, Marsh Papers.

185. MS 8300/92, Beddy to Collis, 8 March 1954, Marsh Papers.

186. *Commission on Emigration,* Reservation no. 1, 220.

187. *Commission on Emigration,* Reverend A. A. Luce, Reservation no. 6, 230–31.

188. Lee, *Ireland 1912–1985,* 383; *Commission on Emigration,* Alexis Fitzgerald, Reservation no. 2, 222–23.

189. *Commission on Emigration,* Minority Report, 340–41, paras. 210–11. Lucey adhered to the paragraph numbers in the majority report.

190. *Commission on Emigration,* Counihan addendum no. 1, 191–97.

191. 8302, Level and Trend of Population, folio 182, p. 117, in proof report 117/182, Marsh Papers.

192. Ibid.

193. *Commission on Emigration,* para. 220.

194. *Iris Oifigiúl,* 21 October 1949, 1751; *Iris Oifigiúl,* 10 January 1950, 65; Paul Blanshard, *The Irish and Catholic Power* (London, 1954), 105.

195. Reverend C. B. Daly, "Family Life: The Principles," 11.

196. Reverend Charles J. Kelly (Catholic Social Guild, Scotland), "The British Population Report," *Christus Rex* 4, no. 4 (1949): 16. Reverend Kelly was much more sanguine about the findings of the Royal Commission than Cathal Daly.

197. Reverend C. B. Daly, "Family Life," 13.

198. Noonan, *Contraception,* 445–46.

199. Cormac Ó Gráda, *A Rocky Road,* 194. In Brittany *Foyers Rayonnants,* a book written by a Catholic priest, Abbé Dantec, presented a positive account of the safe period. It sold 200,000 copies. Catholic rural organizations, such as the Jeunesses agricoles chrétiennes (JAC) and the female counterpart, the JACF, organized lectures on marriage, conjugal relations and the safe period. Martine Segalen, "Exploring a Case of Late French

Fertility Decline: Two Contrasted Breton Examples," in Gillis, Tilly, and Levine, *The European Experience of Declining Fertility,* 240–44. In Quebec the Dominican Fathers were the first to publicize the safe period; the method was subsequently promoted by Catholic Action groups in marriage preparation classes and classes giving moral and spiritual guidance to families. Diane Gervais and Danielle Gauvreau, "Women, Priests, and Physicians: Family Limitation in Quebec, 1940–1970," *Journal of Interdisciplinary History* 34, no. 2 (Autumn 2003): 301.

200. George Alter, "Theories of Fertility Decline: A Nonspecialists's Guide to the Current Debate," in Gillis, Tilly, and Levine, *The European Experience of Declining Fertility,* 13–27; Szreter, *Fertility, Class, and Gender,* 50–55, 403–24; Simon Szreter, Robert A. Nye, and Franz von Poppel, "Fertility and Contraception during the Demographic Transition: Qualitative and Quantitative Approaches," in "Before the Pill: Preventing Fertility in Western Europe and Quebec," *Journal of Interdisciplinary History* 34, no. 2 (Autumn 2003): 141–54.

201. Guinnane, Moehling, and Ó Gráda, "Fertility in South Dublin."

202. Calculations made using data given in J. F. Knaggs, "Natality in Dublin in the Year 1955," *JSSISI* (1957–58): 41–42; 50.

203. John A. O'Brien, *The Vanishing Irish,* 33.

204. John A. O'Brien, "The Irish Enigma," *The Vanishing Irish,* 7, 36–39. The claim of a low marriage rate among Irish-Americans is unproven. See Marc C. Foley and Timothy W. Guinnane, "Did Irish Marriage Patterns Survive the Emigrant Voyage? Irish-American Nuptiality, 1880–1920," *Irish Economic and Social History* 26 (1999): 15–34.

205. By 1954 male emigration exceeded female emigration.

206. John A. O'Brien, *The Vanishing Irish,* 9–10, 33.

207. Arland Ussher, "The Boundary between the Sexes," in John A. O'Brien, *The Vanishing Irish,* 153–56. On Ussher, see Brown, *Ireland: A Social and Cultural History,* 76.

208. Seán Ó Faoláin, "Love among the Irish," in John A. O'Brien, *The Vanishing Irish,* 111.

209. José Cutileiro, *A Portuguese Rural Society* (Oxford, 1971), 93–99.

210. Arensberg and Kimball, *Family and Community,* 201.

211. Ibid., 206.

212. Arensberg and Kimball, *Family and Community,* 207.

213. "The second Missioner was hearing Confessions during the sermon [on sexual behavior] and the transformation he was effecting in the minds of the penitents was astonishing. Men who had forgotten what they were born for came out of the confessional, in the words of Charlie Trainor,

'ready to bull cows.' This was the effect the Mission was having on all minds." Patrick Kavanagh, *Tarry Flynn* (London, 1975 edition), 44.

214. Arensberg and Kimball, *Family and Community*, 199.

215. Tim Ryan's *Albert Reynolds, The Longford Leader: An Unofficial Biography* (Dublin, 1994), 16–30, is a useful source of information on carnivals and dance halls during the 1950s and 1960s.

216. *Commission on Emigration*, 80–81, para. 167.

217. Stanley Lyon, "Natality in Dublin in the Years 1943, 1944, and 1945," 66.

218. See the short stories and novels of Seán Ó Faoláin, William Trevor, and Brian Moore.

219. *Commission on Emigration*, p. 70, para. 148.

220. Arensberg and Kimball, *Family and Community*, 202.

221. Seán Ó Faoláin, "Love among the Irish," in John A. O'Brien, *The Vanishing Irish*, 108.

222. Cresswell, *Une Communauté Rurale de l'Irlande*, 484.

223. For example, M. Molloy, MS 8305/2 34, and Louie Bennett, MS 8307/8, Marsh Papers.

224. Rural Surveys, S21, Swinford; Oral evidence to commission, Molloy 8307/13, Marsh Papers. Caroline Brettell, writing about southern Europe, noted that the dowry "appears to have greater significance in societies where a woman's role as wife and mother is emphasized more than her role as economic producer or where there are few alternatives to marriage and child rearing." "Property, Kinship and Gender: A Mediterranean Perspective," in David L. Kertzer and Richard P. Saller, eds., *The Family in Italy: From Antiquity to the Present* (New Haven, Conn., 1991), 341.

225. Paul Vincent Carroll, "The Mystical Irish," in John A. O'Brien, *The Vanishing Irish*, 60.

226. John A. O'Brien, "The Vanishing Irish," 41–42.

227. Reverend Jerome Dennehy, "The Rural Community," *Christus Rex* 12 (1958): 265–69.

228. Arensberg and Kimball, *Family and Community in Ireland*, 153.

229. Brendan M. Walsh, "Trends in Age of Marriage in Postwar Ireland," ESRI Reprint Series, vol. 9, no. 2 (May 1972).

230. Con Gillman, "Recent Marriage Patterns in Ireland," *Christus Rex* 23, no. 1 (January 1969): 49.

231. Walsh, *Some Irish Population Problems*, 2.

232. Gillman, "Recent Marriage Patterns," 52.

233. Until 1957 the only information on age of marriage was the special inquiry into the age of marriage under one year's duration that was included in the 1946 population census. From 1957 marriage certificates gave the age

of the bride and groom. Until then the age was only given if either was under twenty-one years. Walsh, "Trends in Age of Marriage in Postwar Ireland," 187–88.

234. On this issue with regard to Britain, see Szreter, *Fertility, Class, and Gender*, 578.

235. Walsh, *Some Irish Population Problems*, 14.

4. The Irish State and Its Emigrants

1. *Documents in Irish Foreign Policy*, vol. 1, edited by Ronan Fanning, Michael Kennedy, Dermot Keogh, and Eunan O'Halpin (Dublin, 1998), gives many instances where Ireland's fledgling diplomatic service used the Irish overseas community to promote the case for independence.

2. Memorandum by Seán MacBride to Paul Hoffman, administrator for Economic Cooperation, transmitted FLCA Mission R Ireland 24 May 1948, 890 500, recovery 5 –2548, US National Archive Washington.

3. Although not published until 1932, the book was commissioned by the Cosgrave government. The committee consisted of Michael Tierney, TD (future president of UCD), chairman, F. T. Cremins, Kevin O'Sheil, W. J. Williams (professor of education at UCD), and Bulmer Hobson, the editor.

4. *Census of Population 1936*, preliminary report, 7–9. Between 1911 and 1926, the population of the Irish Free State fell by 168,000. The 1926 census claimed that a loss of 70,000 could be attributed to the British withdrawal, and 27,400 to Irish soldiers who were killed during the 1914–18 war. For a more detailed analysis of these figures see Enda Delaney, *Demography, State, and Society*, 37–38.

5. DT, S9178 A, NAI; *Census of Population 1936*.

6. J. G. Hughes, "Estimates of Annual Net Migration and their Relationship with Series on Annual Net Passenger Movement in Ireland, 1926 –76," (ESRI, August 1977), table 1. My thanks to Gerry Hughes for supplying me with a copy.

7. S9178 A, NAI.

8. Thomas J. Archdeacon, *Becoming American: An Ethnic History* (London, 1983), 175; Francis P. Cavanaugh, "Immigration Restriction at Work Today: A Study of the Administration of Immigration Restriction by the United States," Ph. D. thesis, Catholic University of America, Washington, D.C., 1928, 20–21. My thanks to David Doyle for drawing the latter work to my attention. In 1924 the Irish minister in Washington, Timothy Smiddy, although not yet accredited, worked hard to ensure a separate Irish quota under the 1924 act; under the original arrangement, Ireland would have been included in the United Kingdom quota. S3292, NAI.

9. R. S. Walshaw, *Migration to and from the British Isles: Problems and Policies* (London, 1941), 70–73. Walshaw's data do not tally with Hughes or with net passenger movements. It is unclear how he derived his figures.

10. Matthew J. O'Brien, "Transatlantic Connections and the Sharp Edge of the Great Depression," *Éire/Ireland* (Spring/Summer 2002): 48. In "Immigration Restriction at Work Today," Cavanaugh stated that many Irish men and women were deported during the 1920s having failed medical examinations—often because they were suffering from tuberculosis or heart disease caused by rheumatic fever. The files of the Department of Foreign Affairs in the National Archives list many Irish men and women deported during the 1920s, but these are not open to researchers.

11. Patrick J. Blessing, *The Irish in America: A Guide to the Literature and Manuscript Collections* (Washington, 1982), table 13, 308; Archdeacon, *Becoming American*, 175. Estimates of net emigration derived from the Census of Population suggest that emigration reached 197,000 during the period 1951–56 and 212,000 in the years 1956–61. Robert E. Kennedy, *The Irish*, 212–13.

12. Although an estimated 520,359 people of Irish birth (thirty-two counties) were resident in the United States in 1950, this represented a drop of more than 40 percent over the previous twenty years; in 1930 there were 923,642 American residents of Irish birth.

13. DFA, P 115/I, Report on the Irish in the New York Consular Area, by John M. Conway and Eamonn Gallagher, NAI.

14. Ultan Cowley, *The Men Who Built Britain: A History of the Irish Navvy* (Dublin, 2001).

15. Jackson, *The Irish in Britain;* MS 8306 S24B, Stanley Lyon, Report survey of living and employment conditions of Irish workers in Great Britain, Marsh Papers.

16. Mark Wyman, *Round-Trip to America* (Ithaca, N.Y., 1993): 11.

17. David Fitzpatrick, "'A Peculiar Tramping People': The Irish in Britain, 1801–70," in W. J. Vaughan, ed., *A New History of Ireland,* vol. 5 (Oxford, 1990), 626.

18. 1901 and 1911 census returns, NAI.

19. P 35/157, Imperial Conference on empire migration, Patrick McGilligan Papers, UCD.

20. During the 1950s local newspapers frequently noted emigrants returning on holidays or their departure for England at the end of the summer. See, for example, *Dundalk Democrat,* 5 May 1956, Carrick Gossip, "Home on Holiday"; *Dundalk Democrat,* 12 January 1957, Castleblaney News, "Emigrants, Good-bye for Another Twelve Months," as emigrants

spending their Christmas vacation at home parted once more with friends and relatives.

21. John Healy, *The Death of an Irish Town* (Cork, 1968), 25–26. The 1946 census recorded 424,945 married men and 451,331 married women. This was the highest discrepancy; in 1951 there were 448,786 married men and 464,072 married women; in 1961 there were 453,603 married men and 468,228 married women.

22. MS 8306 S 24A and B, Employment and Living Conditions in Great Britain, reports by Stanley Lyon, Marsh Papers.

23. Sharon Lambert, "Irish Women's Emigration to England, 1922–1960: The Lengthening of Family Ties," in Alan Hayes and Diane Urquhart, eds., *Female Experience: Essays in Irish Women's History* (Dublin, 2000), 152–67. Lambert claims that the strength of family ties meant that the Irish women emigrants in Lancashire that she interviewed did not assimilate into British society. But for a remarkable account of an Irish woman who became totally assimilated to the extent of changing her name and concealing her Irish background, see Blake Morrison, *Things My Mother Never Told Me* (London, 2002).

24. On self-sufficiency, see Mary E. Daly, *Industrial Development and Irish National Identity, 1922–39.*

25. DFA, 2002/19/75, NAI.

26. Mary E. Daly, *Spirit of Earnest Inquiry,* 124–28.

27. P 35/157, Imperial Conference, 27 August 1926, McGilligan Papers, UCDA.

28. DT, S11582 A, NAI.

29. Opposition was especially vocal in Scotland, an area with a strong tradition of Irish immigration; the 1920s and 1930s saw an escalation of sectarian prejudice directed at Irish Catholic immigrants, which coincided with rising unemployment. Richard B. McCready, "Revising the Irish in Scotland: The Irish in Nineteenth- and Early-Twentieth-Century Scotland," in Andy Bielenberg, ed., *The Irish Diaspora* (London, 2000), 61; Delaney, *Demography, State and Society,* 84–93. As Irish citizens were British subjects with similar rights to those born in the United Kingdom, it would have been difficult to impose restrictions. Mary E. Daly, "Irish Nationality and Citizenship since 1922," *IHS* 32, no. 127 (May 2001): 377–407.

30. Seán Glynn, "Irish Immigration to Britain, 1911–1951: Patterns and Policy," *Irish Economic and Social History* 8 (1981): 61–67.

31. Tracey Connolly, "Emigration from Ireland to Britain during the Second World War," in Bielenberg, *Irish Diaspora,* 51–53. Many had deserted from the Irish army.

32. Jackson, *The Irish in Britain*, 98–104; Tracey Connolly, "Emigration from Ireland to Britain during the Second World War," 51–64; Cowley, *The Men Who Built Britain;* Margaret Gowing, "The Organisation of Manpower in Britain during the Second World War," *Journal of Contemporary History* 7, nos. 1/2 (1972): 147–67.

33. P 35/157 Imperial Conference, 27 August 1926, McGilligan Papers, UCDA.

34. DT, S3517, S9627, Emigration, government policy, NAI.

35. *Commission on Emigration,* appendix 6, Note on Travel Permits, Identity Cards, and Passports, NAI; Tracey Connolly, in "Emigration from Ireland to Britain during the Second World War," 52, claims that many Irish people who traveled on visitors' visas took up work in Britain.

36. DT, S11980 A, Invasion or Isolation of Ireland, Interdepartmental Committee on Emergency Problems, NAI; Cowley, *The Men Who Built Britain,* 113. Most of these agents were Irishmen who had been working in England for some years.

37. Gowing, "The Organisation of Manpower in Britain," 148–49.

38. DT, S11980, Interdepartmental Committee on Emergency Problems; S11582 A, Irish Labor, Emigration to Great Britain and Northern Ireland, NAI.

39. DT, S11582 A, NAI.

40. On the shortage of raw materials, see Mary E. Daly, *The Buffer State,* 275–77.

41. DT, S15398 A, Department of Social Welfare, 19 January 1948, NAI.

42. John Jackson, *The Irish in Britain,* 100. Jackson had access to British Ministry of Labor records. See footnote 2, 176.

43. DT, S11582 A, April 1941, NAI. Initially workers were given a guarantee that they would not be liable for conscription for two years, when they would be free to return to Ireland, but in the autumn of 1941 Britain agreed to give any worker recruited under this program a permanent waiver.

44. DT, S15398 A, NAI.

45. Tracey Connolly, "Emigration from Ireland to Britain," 55.

46. DT, S11582 A, 24 March 1941, NAI.

47. DE Files, Box 748, TA 183, Emigration to Great Britain and Northern Ireland, NAI.

48. Mary E. Daly, *The First Department,* 235–46; *The Buffer State,* 265–68.

49. Mary E. Daly, *The First Department,* 243.

50. Mary E. Daly, *The Buffer State,* 267.

51. DT, S11582 A, NAI.

52. Mary E. Daly, *The First Department,* 241–44.

53. DT, S12882, Planning for postwar situation, general file, NAI; Lee, *Ireland 1912–85,* 226 –29; Mary E. Daly, *The Buffer State,* 283 –85.

54. DT, S11582 B, NAI; *Commission on Emigration,* appendix 7.

55. Import restrictions led to a surplus in the balance of payments.

56. DT, S11582 A, NAI.

57. Lee, *Ireland 1912–1985,* 227.

58. Tracey Connolly, "Emigration from Ireland to Britain," 57; Frank McCourt, *Angela's Ashes: A Memoir of a Childhood* (London, 1996), 216 –23.

59. *The Bell* 7, no. 1 (October 1943): 57 –59.

60. Mary E. Daly, *The Buffer State,* 283.

61. DT, S12882 A, NAI; cited by Lee, *Ireland 1912–1985,* 227.

62. For details, see Mary E. Daly, *The Buffer State,* 279 –95.

63. James B. Wolf, in "'Withholding Their Due': The Dispute between Ireland and Great Britain over Unemployment Insurance Payments to Conditionally Landed Irish Wartime Volunteer Workers," *Saothar* 21 (1996): 39 –45, suggests that Britain's refusal to pay unemployment insurance payments to workers who returned to Ireland when the war ended meant that most of these workers chose to remain in Britain.

64. Ian R. G. Spencer, *British Immigration Policy since 1939: The Making of Multi-Racial Britain* (London, 1997), 20–38.

65. *Royal Commission on Population, 1948–49,* Report, Cmnd. 7695, paras. 326 –28.

66. DT, S11582 B, S15398 A, Views of the Hierarchy on Emigration, NAI.

67. Local Surveys, S10, Cork, Marsh Papers.

68. Rural Surveys, S5, Wexford, Clonmel, and Arklow, and S6, Killarney, Tralee, Marsh Papers.

69. DT, S11582 B, NAI.

70. Zig Layton-Henry, *The Politics of Immigration: Immigration, "Race," and "Race" Relations in Post-War Britain* (Oxford, 1992), 28 –29. Dónal Mac Amhlaigh worked with Ukrainians and Poles in Northampton in 1951. *Dialann Deoraí,* 6.

71. British officials used this argument to suggest that it was preferable to recruit displaced persons from Europe, who would be likely to return home, rather than immigrants from the colonies, who would be more likely to remain in Britain. Spencer, *British Immigration Policy,* 40.

72. E. P. Thompson, *The Making of the English Working Class* (London, 1963), 439.

73. *Royal Commission on Population,* para. 329; Spencer, *British Immigration Policy,* 83, citing a cabinet meeting, 11 July 1956, and 61, citing a 1953 working party.

74. Mary E. Daly, "Irish Nationality and Citizenship since 1922," 388 –90.

75. In an interview in 1987, Seán MacBride, minister for External Affairs in the 1948 –51 Inter-Party government, indicated that the decision to declare a republic and to leave the Commonwealth was taken in the knowledge that the British Nationality Act protected the position of Irish citizens in the United Kingdom. Ian McCabe, *A Diplomatic History of Ireland, 1948– 49: The Republic, the Commonwealth, and NATO* (Dublin, 1991), 37, 58 –59, 73 –81.

76. Board of Trade 11/8221, Anglo-Irish Trade Talks, NAEW.

77. Treasury 236/777, Anglo-Irish Trade Negotiations, 18 June 1948, NAEW.

78. Treasury 236/778, Anglo-Irish Trade Negotiations, memorandum, 29 June 1948, NAEW.

79. The figures are published in tables 96 and 97 of the *Commission on Emigration,* 128 –29.

80. Pauric Travers, "Emigration and Gender," 190, 197; S14310 A, Cabinet Economic Committee, emigration, NAI.

81. DT, S15398, 15 December 1947, NAI.

82. McDermott, *Clann na Poblachta,* 54.

83. DT, S15398, S11582 B, DEA memorandum, August 1947, NAI.

84. DT, S11582 B, NAI.

85. MacDermott, *Clann na Poblachta,* 56.

86. On the Mellifont group, see chapter 2.

87. *The Irish Times,* 30 January 1948, 2 February 1948.

88. "How It Goes in County Monaghan," *The Irish Times,* 30 January 1948.

89. *The Irish Times,* 23 January 1948.

90. David McCullagh, *A Makeshift Majority* (Dublin, 1998), 32.

91. Patrick Lynch, "The Irish Economy since the War, 1946 –51," in K. B. Nowlan and T. D. Williams, eds., *Ireland in the War Years and After, 1939–51* (Dublin, 1969), 187 –93; "More Pages from an Irish Memoir," in Richard English and Joseph Morrison Skelly, eds., *Ideas Matter: Essays in Honour of Conor Cruise O'Brien* (Dublin, 1998), 133.

92. Memorandum by Sean McBride to Paul Hoffman, administrator for Economic Cooperation, transmitted 24 May 1948, 890 500, recovery 5 – 2548, National Archives, Washington D.C.

93. Mary E. Daly, *The Buffer State,* 333 –35.

94. Figures from *Statistical Abstract;* J. P. Digby, "Emigration—The Answer," *The Bell* 17, no. 8 (November 1951): 34 –35.

95. Kieran A. Kennedy and Brendan R. Dowling, *Economic Growth in Ireland: The Experience since 1947* (Dublin, 1975), 217 –18.

96. Charles Bean and Nicholas Crafts, "British Economic Growth since 1945"; Nicholas Crafts and Gianni Toniolo, "Postwar Growth: An Overview," in Nicholas Crafts and Gianni Toniolo, eds., *Economic Growth in Europe since 1945* (Cambridge, 1996), 1–37, 138.

97. DT, S14249 A, Commission on Emigration, NAI.

98. PDDE, 2 July 1953, col. 530. The exchange was prompted by de Valera's assertion that his government had actually tackled emigration as opposed to setting up a commission to look into the matter; de Valera claimed that he knew nothing about the proposal. The files suggest otherwise.

99. DT, S15398 A, Emigration, Views of the Hierarchy on Emigration, NAI.

100. Minutes of the Hierarchy, McQuaid Papers, DDA.

101. *Commission on Emigration*, 1.

102. For a summary of this evidence by geographical region, see Delaney, *Demography, State, and Society*, 169–76.

103. Rural Surveys, S1, Beddy, Marsh Papers.

104. Rural Surveys, S10, Cork Exchange, Report by Lucey and McCarthy, Marsh Papers.

105. MS 8305/3, Athlone Committee on Emigration, Marsh Papers. The survey was carried out by a local group, which obtained from the Gardai the names of all who had been given permits to emigrate and then followed up on these people. Five hundred seventy-eight permits were granted and 490 of these were traced.

106. Rural Surveys, S10, Lucey and McCarthy, Marsh Papers.

107. Rural Surveys S1, Beddy, Mayo, and Sligo, Marsh Papers.

108. Rural Surveys, S5, Honohan, Marsh Papers.

109. Rural Surveys, S4, Marsh Papers.

110. MS 8305/5, memorandum, Sean Hogan, Smithstown, Bunratty, 24 June 1948, Marsh Papers.

111. MS 8306/6 Rural Surveys, Marsh Papers.

112. MS 8305/2 34, M. Molloy from Milltown, Co. Galway; Marsh Papers.

113. MS 8305/15, memorandum submitted to the Commission on Emigration jointly on behalf of the Mellifont Conference and the Council of National Action, signed by Joseph Hanly, retired civil servant, Captain R. Segrave Daly, farmer Co. Wexford, James Anglin, farmer and member of Wexford County Council, and Frank Coyle, farmer and member of Monaghan Co.Co., Marsh Papers. A "nonpolitical conference" was held at Mellifont in October 1947 to discuss the question of rural depopulation. It was chaired by Hanly and his memorandum was forwarded to the Catholic hierarchy.

114. MS 8304/41, memoranda by members of the commission; Aodh de Blacam, "Emigration: The Witness of Geography. An Essay on T. W. Freeman's *Ireland: Its Physical, Historical Social and Economic Geography*," Marsh Papers.

115. During the 1948 election campaign when he stood as a candidate for Clann na Poblachta in county Louth, he alleged that eighteen English families who had no interest in Ireland or its traditions had recently purchased land that could have supported one hundred Irish families. *The Irish Times*, 19 January 1948.

116. Rural Surveys, S2, Marsh Papers.

117. MS 8305/8, Keogh, Marsh Papers.

118. Rural Surveys, S4, Marsh Papers.

119. Delaney, *Demography, State, and Society*, 176.

120. *Commission on Emigration*, paras. 290–303.

121. MS 8305/12, Richard Orpen, Monksgrange, Enniscorthy, Marsh Papers.

122. S19, Marsh Papers.

123. MS 8305/3, Athlone Committee on Emigration, Marsh Papers.

124. S24B, Marsh Papers.

125. S20, Marsh Papers.

126. MS 8301 T 18, evidence given by Gaeltacht Services Section, Department of Lands, Marsh Papers.

127. Lambert, "Irish Emigration to England, 1922–1960," 152–67.

128. MS 8307/3, Transcript of evidence given by the Irish Housewives' Association, Marsh Papers.

129. MS 8301, Summary of evidence concerning wages, conditions of employment, etc., by Ruaidhri Roberts, Marsh Papers. It may be significant that this evidence is not cited in the report or any of the appendices.

130. DT, S11582 B, NAI.

131. S6, Marsh Papers.

132. S11, Marsh Papers.

133. S20, Marsh Papers.

134. DT, S11582 B, 1947, NAI.

135. MS 8307/3, Transcript of evidence given by the Irish Housewives' Association, Marsh Papers. There was a strong racist component in the most militant anti-emigration rhetoric at this time.

136. MS 8307/11, Evidence, Irish Nurses' Organization, Marsh Papers.

137. MS 8307/20, Evidence of witnesses from Department of Education, Marsh Papers.

138. S24 B, Marsh Papers.

139. MS 8307/11, Evidence, Irish Nurses' Organization, Marsh Papers.

140. *Commission on Emigration,* para. 306.

141. Ibid., para. 308.

142. Ibid., para. 310.

143. Ibid., para. 313.

144. Ibid., para. 309.

145. Ibid., para. 312.

146. Ibid., paras. 315 –16.

147. Ibid., paras. 320–21.

148. Ibid., paras. 323 –28.

149. Addendum no. 2, 201–3.

150. John E. Spencer, "R. C. Geary: His Life and Work," in Denis Conniffe, ed., *Roy Geary, 1896–1983: Irish Statistician* (Dublin, 1997), 28.

151. *Commission on Emigration,* Reservation no. 2.

152. Ibid., Reservation no. 9, 238.

153. DT, S9684 A, Population Statistics, NAI.

154. *Commission on Emigration,* Minority Report of Mr. James Meenan, 369 –71, paras. 6 –12.

155. *Commission on Emigration,* para. 312.

156. Ibid., para. 433.

157. *Commission on Emigration,* Reservation no. 3, R. C. Geary and M. D. McCarthy. On 27 September 1955 *The Irish Times* reported that many Dublin building workers went to Britain, despite the fact that basic rates were similar in Dublin, because Britain offered better opportunities for overtime and bonus payments. In Ireland the trade union restricted overtime to conserve the available work.

158. This was probably true of many skilled trades and industries that were highly unionized. However, it did not apply in the case of farmers' sons or to the majority of emigrants from rural Ireland and small towns.

159. DT, S14249 A/2, Honohan, 28 August 1951, NAI. (Emphasis in the original.)

160. *Commission on Emigration,* para. 465.

161. *Commission on Emigration,* para. 479.

162. MS 8307/13, Marsh Papers.

163. John A. O'Brien, "The Vanishing Irish," in *The Vanishing Irish,* 15 –45.

164. Paul Vincent Carroll, "The Mystical Irish," 56, 62.

165. Mary E. Daly, "Nationalism, Sentiment, and Economic Relations between Ireland and Irish America in the Postwar Years," *Éire-Ireland* 37, nos. 1/2 (Spring/Summer 2002): 79 –82.

166. O'Donnell made this point in a letter to *The Irish Times,* 12 May 1954.

167. DT, S14249 A/2, NAI.

168. *The Irish Times,* 10 May 1954.

169. Ibid., 11 May 1954.

170. Ibid., 10 May 1954.

171. Ibid., 11 May 1954.

172. S5, Marsh Papers.

173. *The Irish Times,* 10 May 1954.

174. Ibid., 10 September 1955; MS 8305/2 34, Marsh Papers.

175. DT, S16325 A, 7 March 1957, NAI. This was a reference to the sample Passenger Card Inquiry that the Central Statistics Office introduced in 1951. For details see "Statistics of Emigration and Passenger Movements," *Irish Trade Journal and Statistical Bulletin* (June 1951): 76–84.

176. DT, S14249 B, NAI.

177. DT, 97/6/611, Irish labor: emigration, NAI.

5. The Vanishing Irish

1. *Belfast Telegraph,* 24 August 1961.

2. *The Irish Times,* 22 August 1961.

3. "Analyst," "Emigration and Unemployment: The Labour Surplus," *The Irish Times,* 7 February 1956.

4. *Census of Population 1956,* Preliminary Report; *Irish Trade Journal and Statistical Bulletin* (June 1956): 97.

5. *The Irish Times,* 12 February 1958.

6. Analyst, "Emigration since 1951: A New Peak in 1957," *The Irish Times,* 12 February 1958.

7. Garret FitzGerald, *Planning in Ireland* (Dublin, 1968), 16.

8. *The Irish Times,* 15 July 1954.

9. *The Irish Times,* 12 May 1954, 13 May 1954.

10. *Roscommon Herald,* 16 June 1956; *Nationalist and Leinster Times,* 18 August 1956; *Dundalk Democrat,* 3 August 1957.

11. *The Irish News,* 2 June 1956.

12. Minutes of the Meetings of the Hierarchy, 19 June 1956, McQuaid Papers, DDA.

13. *Roscommon Herald,* 23 November 1957.

14. *Roscommon Herald,* 14 April 1956.

15. *Nationalist and Leinster Times,* 28 April 1956.

16. *The Irish Times,* 20 June 1956. FitzGerald had anticipated these findings in six articles on emigration and employment that were published in *The Irish Times* between 21 January and 9 February 1956.

17. PDDE, 13 March 1956, vol. 155, cols. 333 –37. Kennedy and Dowling, *Economic Growth in Ireland* , 220–21; Ronan Fanning, *The Irish Department of Finance, 1922–25* (Dublin, 1978), 501–2; Maurice Moynihan, *Currency and Central Banking, 1922–1960* (Dublin, 1975), 420–27; FitzGerald, *Planning in Ireland,* 14; Mary E. Daly, *Buffer State,* 372–76. The crisis was largely self-inflicted; in Feburary 1955 Sweetman decided not to raise Irish interest rates in line with Britain. Patrick Honohan and Cormac Ó Gráda,"The Irish Macroeconomic Crisis of 1955 –56: How Much Was Due to Monetary Policy," *Irish Economic and Social History* 25 (1998): 52–80.

18. PDDE, vol. 159, 25 July 1956, cols. 1613 –14.

19. FitzGerald, *Planning in Ireland,* 15 –17; James McGilvray, *Irish Economic Statistics* (Dublin 1968), 106 –67, 61. In 1958 net agricultural output, which stood at 108.5 in 1957, fell to 96.9.

20. *The Dundalk Democrat,* 19 May 1956.

21. *The Dundalk Democrat,* 7 July 1956.

22. *Irish Press,* 2 January 1957.

23. DT, S16325, 9 January 1958, ref to Cmnd. 336, Third Report, British Overseas Migration Board, NAI.

24. *The Irish Times,* 12 February 1958.

25. *The Irish Times,* 18 January 1957.

26. *The Irish Times,* 18 January 1957; *The Kerryman,* 28 July 1956, 5 October 1957. Other newspapers such as *The Nationalist* and *Leinster Times* highlighted the fact that jobs were scarce in England (9 January 1957).

27. *Roscommon Herald,* 14 April 1956.

28. *Roscommon Herald,* 28 April 1956; *Dundalk Democrat,* 20 April 1957.

29. *Dundalk Democrat,* 7 January 1956.

30. DT, S11582 G, NAI.

31. *Dundalk Democrat,* 7 September 1957, 14 September 1957; *Roscommon Herald* 21 September 1957.

32. *The Kerryman,* 31 March 1956, 29 December 1956.

33. DT, S16325 B, NAI.

34. See, for example, *Dundalk Democrat,* 14 April 1956, "*Ballybay News,* . . . 'the roll of shame.'"

35. *Roscommon Herald,* 2 November 1957.

36. *The Irish Times,* 22 June 1957.

37. *The Irish Times,* 11 February 1958. But many building workers moved frequently, and they failed to establish a right to local authority housing.

38. *Nationalist and Leinster Times,* 28 January 1956, concerning emigration of unemployed Carlow sugar workers.

39. *Dundalk Democrat,* 20 October 1956.

40. *Dundalk Democrat,* 3 August 1957.

41. *Sunday Independent,* 3 June 1956.

42. Maurice Manning, *James Dillon: A Biography* (Dublin, 1999), 152.

43. *Sunday Press,* 3 June 1956.

44. *Irish Press,* 2 June 1956. The flight from the land was never confined to poorer areas. In fact, during the 1930s the rate of decline of the agricultural labor force was greater in Leinster than in Connacht or Ulster. The Commission on Emigration emphasized that the rate of population decline since the famine had been remarkably similar in all regions.

45. *Irish Press,* 16 June 1956.

46. *Irish Independent,* 2 June 1956, "A New Challenge."

47. *Irish Independent,* 2 June 1956, Roger Hampton.

48. *The Irish Times,* June 2, 1956, "The Vanishing Irish."

49. *Belfast Telegraph,* 4 June 1956.

50. *Belfast Newsletter,* 4 June 1956.

51. PDDE, vol. 158, 19 June 1956, cols. 463–64.

52. Ibid., vol. 158, 25 July 1956, col. 1692.

53. Ibid., vol. 158, 25 July 1956, cols. 1697–98, citing para. 480 in *Commission on Emigration.*

54. PDDE, vol. 158, 25 July 1956, col. 1699.

55. Ibid., vol. 158, 26 July 1956, cols. 1902–5, 1924–26. De Valera's response anticipates the Tallaght strategy that Alan Dukes, the leader of Fine Gael, adopted in 1987 when he offered his party's support to a minority Fianna Fáil government in its efforts to surmount a major economic crisis.

56. PDDE, vol. 158, 26 July 1956, col. 1921.

57. Ibid., vol. 158, 25 July 1956, cols. 1700–1701.

58. Ibid., vol. 158, 26 July 1956, cols. 1911–12.

59. *Roscommon Herald,* 16 June 1956.

60. PDDE, vol. 158, 19 June 1956, cols. 463–64.

61. Moynihan, *Currency and Central Banking in Ireland,* 409–10; S15551 A, National Development Fund, memorandum, 28 July 1953, NAI; Mary E. Daly, *The Buffer State,* 419.

62. *The Irish Times,* 12 October 1955.

63. *The Irish Times,* 12 October 1955.

64. John F. McCarthy, "Ireland's Turnaround: Whitaker and the 1958 Plan for Economic Development," in John McCarthy, ed., *Planning Ireland's Future: The Legacy of T. K. Whitaker* (Dublin, 1990), 24–25.

65. John F. McCarthy, "Ireland's Turnaround," 28.

66. John Horgan, *Sean Lemass: The Enigmatic Patriot* (Dublin, 1997), 174.

67. John F. McCarthy, "Ireland's Turnaround," 34–37.

68. Ibid., 24; *The Irish Times*, 12 October 1955. The absence of any reference to foreign investment is rather puzzling, since during the mid-1940s he had made efforts to remove the restrictions on overseas investment. By the 1950s he seems to have lost interest in this matter, perhaps because of opposition from Irish industrialists and officials in the Department of Industry and Commerce.

69. John F. McCarthy, "Ireland's Turnaround," 25–29. This was a continuation of the philosophy of the 1932 and 1934 Control of Manufactures Acts, where licenses were only granted to firms manufacturing products not already being made in Ireland. Mary E. Daly, "'An Irish-Ireland for Business'? The Control of Manufactures Acts, 1932 and 1934," *IHS* 94 (November 1984): 246–72.

70. *The Kerryman*, 8 October 1956; *Dundalk Democrat*, 6 October 1956.

71. *Dundalk Democrat*, 19 October 1957.

72. *The Kerryman*, 18 February 1956, 19 May 1956, 7 September 1956.

73. *Roscommon Herald*, 14 January 1956, editorial; *Nationalist and Leinster Times*, 4 February 1956, 28 April 1956; *The Kerryman*, 21 July 1957, 13 October 1957.

74. *Dundalk Democrat*, 15 December 1956, 8 June 1957.

75. *The Irish Times*, 24 January 1957.

76. *The Irish Times*, 15 February 1957, 12 February 1957.

77. Garret FitzGerald, "Foreword," in John F. McCarthy, *Planning Ireland's Future*, 6–7.

78. John F. McCarthy, "Ireland's Turnaround," 34.

79. *The Irish Times*, 23 February 1957.

80. *The Irish Times*, 11 February 1957.

81. *The Irish Times*, 23 February 1957.

82. *The Irish Times*, 23 February 1957.

83. *The Irish Times*, 18 January 1957. An editorial in *The Irish Times* on the same day was more enthusiastic of these proposals than in 1955, though it noted the lack of attention given to forestry and fisheries.

84. Mike Milotte, *Communism in Modern Ireland: The Pursuit of the Workers' Republic since 1916* (Dublin, 1984), 228.

85. *The Irish Times*, 14 May, 15 May, 17 May 1957.

86. *The Irish Times*, 20 May 1957, address to a Fianna Fáil meeting at Bettystown.

87. *The Irish Times*, 23 May 1957.

88. Milotte, *Communism in Modern Ireland*, 228.

89. *The Irish Times*, 8 May 1957.

90. DT, S16325 A, NAI.

91. DT, S16325 B, NAI.

92. DT, S16325 B, NAI.

93. Kennedy and Dowling, *Economic Growth in Ireland*, 222–23.

94. *The Irish Times*, 13 May 1957.

95. *Belfast Newsletter*, 4 June 1956.

96. *The Kerryman*, 24 August 1957.

97. *Dundalk Democrat*, 25 August 1956.

98. *The Kerryman*, 26 January 1957.

99. *The Irish Times*, 9 May 1957, reported a speech by Brian Faulkner, Unionist chief whip, in which he referred to the fact that the population of Northern Ireland had increased by 114,000 over the past twenty years, and there were more people at work.

100. *The Irish Times*, 11 February 1957.

101. Quoted in Ronan Fanning, "The Genesis of Economic Development," in John McCarthy, *Planning Ireland's Future*, 95–96.

102. *The Irish Times*, 20 May 1957.

103. *Economic Development*, chapter 1, para. 12.

104. *The Nationalist*, 29 September 1956, 26 January 1957; *Roscommon Herald*, 13 April 1957.

105. There is an enormous literature on this subject: see John F. McCarthy, *Planning Ireland's Future*; Fanning, *Finance*, chapter 11; Lee, *Ireland, 1912–1985*, 341–59.

106. Analyst, "Emigration since 1951, II: A New Peak in 1957," *The Irish Times*, 12 February 1958; Kennedy and Dowling, *Economic Growth in Ireland*, 222.

107. *The Irish Times*, 27 May 1959.

108. See DT, S16325 B, NAI; *Irish Independent*, 11 May 1959, for a claim by the president of the National Organization of Ex-Servicemen that the flight from the land was developing into the flight from the nation.

109. Patrick McNabb, *Limerick Rural Survey: (First) Interim Report (Migration)* (Tipperary, 1960).

110. Speech, 25 October 1960, on S16325 B, NAI.

111. Mary E. Daly, *The First Department*, 258–64, 372, 385–86.

112. DT, S16325 B, NAI.

113. DT, S16325 B, NAI. All data for Irish entrants to British national insurance are seriously flawed by the number of Irish workers who were "on the lump" and not registered for national insurance and by the fact that many long-term emigrants registered and claimed benefits under one name, only to return the following year and register under a different name. HO 344/190, NAEW.

114. Spencer, *British Immigration Policy,* 95.

115. DT, 97/6/310, Irish Labor, Emigration, 1961, NAI.

116. DT, 97/6/310, NAI.

117. HO 344/190, NAEW. A further reason may have been that the information, drawn from a survey of Irish immigrants and Ministry of Pensions records, was regarded as "to some extent inconsistent." The information was given in a written reply on 18 November 1963. Hansard, vol. 684, written questions, cols. 48–52.

118. Spencer, *British Immigration Policy,* 166.

119. DT, S16697 A, Census 1961, NAI.

120. Cornelius O'Leary, *Irish Elections, 1918–1977: Parties, Voters, and Proportional Representation* (Dublin, 1979), 61. O'Donovan, a member of the economics department at UCD, was then a Fine Gael senator. He had previously served as a TD and a parliamentary secretary; he was subsequently elected as a Labor TD.

121. *Nationalist and Leinster Times,* 26 August 1961.

122. PDDE, 2 August 1961, col. 2565.

123. *Sunday Press,* 13 August 1961.

124. *Sunday Press,* 27 August 1961.

125. *Irish Independent,* 25 August 1961.

126. *Dundalk Democrat,* 26 August 1961.

127. *Roscommon Herald,* 26 August 1961.

128. *Sunday Press,* 27 August 1961.

129. *Dundalk Democrat,* 19 August 1961.

130. *Dundalk Democrat,* 19 August 1961; *Nationalist and Leinster Times,* 19 August 1961.

131. *Roscommon Herald,* 26 August 1961.

132. *Nationalist and Leinster Times,* 9 September 1961.

133. *Irish Press,* 18 August 1961.

134. PDDE, 2 August 1961, cols. 2567–77. On cross-border trade, see Michael Kennedy, *Division and Consensus,* 183–91.

135. PDDE, 2 August 1961, col. 2563–67.

136. Susan Baker, "Nationalist Ideology and the Industrial Policy of Fianna Fáil: The Evidence of the *Irish Press,*" *Irish Political Studies* 2 (1987): 52–56.

137. PDDE, 2 August 1961, col. 2576.

138. This is somewhat at variance with the views of Eamon de Valera, who believed that independence at a lower standard of living was preferable to economic and political dependency on Britain. In 1928 he told Dáil Éireann that it was necessary to settle for the "plain furniture" of an independent

cottager, noting that "we cannot have the furniture that we might have in a lord's mansion." PDDE, 13 July 1928.

139. S16325 A, 12 May 1961, NAI.

140. *The Irish Times,* 13 May 1961.

141. *Belfast Newsletter,* 18 August 1961.

142. *Belfast Telegraph,* 24 August 1961.

143. *Impartial Reporter,* 31 August 1961.

144. *Impartial Reporter,* 14 September 1961.

145. Hughes, "Estimates of Annual Net Migration," chart 1.

146. This point was made in the *Irish Independent,* 12 September 1961.

147. Aiken, "FF Made Country Ready for EEC," and MacEntee, "Membership of the EEC Vital to Our Survival," *The Irish Times,* 15 September 1961; report of election broadcast on Radio Éireann, *The Irish Times,* 12 September 1961.

148. *Irish Independent,* 1 September 1961; *The Irish Times,* 13 September 1961.

149. *Irish Independent,* 18 September 1961, 22 September 1961.

150. Manning, *James Dillon,* 316 –17; *The Kerryman,* 23 September 1961.

151. *Nationalist and Leinster Times,* 2 September 1961.

152. *Nationalist and Leinster Times,* 23 September 1961.

153. *The Kerryman,* 28 October 1961.

6. 1961–1971

1. Tobin, *The Best of Decades: Ireland in the 1960s.*

2. *Time,* 12 July 1963.

3. NIEC, *Full Employment,* Report no. 18 (1967), para. 18.

4. DT, 96/6/206, Muintir na Tíre, NAI.

5. The phase was used in Michael D. McCarthy, "Some Irish Population Problems," *Studies* (Autumn 1967): 245.

6. Department of Finance, *Third Programme: Economic and Social Development, 1969–72,* Prl. F 52/7 (1969), para. 6.

7. Jeremiah Newman, "Social Provision and Rural Centrality," 250.

8. Michael D. McCarthy, "Some Ireland Population Problems," 238.

9. Mary E. Daly, *The First Department,* 499.

10. Helena Sheehan, *Irish Television Drama: A Society and Its Stories* (Dublin, 1987), 107.

11. The phrase probably originated with John Healy, *The Irish Times* columnist. It first appeared in Dail Éireann on 12 April 1967, col. 1582, on eight occasions during 1968, and three during 1969. Examples include a reference by opposition deputies to "mohaired executive types wandering

the corridors of Leinster House," 20 November, col. 847, or "the mohair boys who have so much to lose and who had not a seat to their trousers," a reference to TDs in PDDE, 12 February 1969, col. 834.

12. Varley and Curtin, "Defending Rural Interests against Nationalists in Twentieth-Century Ireland," 69.

13. Healy, *The Death of an Irish Town*, 8.

14. Suzanne Berger, in *Peasants against Politics: Rural Organization in Brittany, 1911–1967* (Cambridge, Mass., 1972), 72, notes a similar phenomenon in Brittany around that time. "What this generation desired above all was to enter modern life, and, as one of these men put it, 'no longer to feel out of place in a century of machines, no longer to have the inferiority complex vis-à-vis the city population who did benefit from progress.'"

15. National Industrial and Economic Council, established in 1963. For some background, see Mary E. Daly, *The First Department*, 444–47.

16. The Commission on Emigration, established in 1948, reported in 1954; the Commission on Youth Unemployment, established in May 1943, reported in 1951. *Commission on Youth Unemployment*, R. 82.

17. Newman, *Limerick Rural Survey, 1958–64*, vii.

18. It would not be possible to list the relevant studies carried out by the staff of An Foras Talúntais, but examples include the *West Cork Resource Survey* (May 1963) and Rosemary Fennell, "Industrialisation and Agricultural Development in the Congested Districts," in An Foras Talúntais, *Economic Research Series*, no. 2 (Dublin, 1962).

19. W. J. L. Ryan, "The Methodology of the Second Programme for Economic Expansion," *Second Programme for Economic Expansion*, part 2, appendix 5, table 1 (1964); *JSSISI* 21, pt. 2 (1963–64): 122.

20. Department of Finance, *Third Programme*, 9, 28–29.

21. John Jackson, *Report on the Skibbereen Social Survey* (Dublin, 1967), 3.

22. Ibid., 17.

23. Damien Hannan, *Rural Exodus: A Study of the Forces Influencing Large-Scale Migration of Irish Rural Youth* (London, 1970), 237, 246–47.

24. Ibid., 250.

25. Ibid., 242; Jackson, *Report on the Skibbereen Social Survey*, 41.

26. Hughes, "Estimates of Annual Net Migration."

27. NIEC, *Full Employment*, para. 146, also 7. The National Industrial and Economic Council was established in 1963, with members nominated by the government, trade unions, employers' organizations, state companies, and the Federation of Irish Industries to prepare reports on key issues

relating to economic development. See James F. Meenan, *The Irish Economy since 1922* (Liverpool, 1970), 157.

28. Ibid., 28, and para. 54.

29. Garret FitzGerald. Dublin, 1968. *Planning in Ireland*, 192–93. Plans to expand second-level schooling were well underway by 1963–64 with the proposed establishment of comprehensive schools, and the numbers attending second-level schools were rising sharply.

30. W. J. L. Ryan, "The Methodology of the Second Programme," 122.

31. DT, 97/6/213, Census of Population 1966, NAI.

32. NIEC, *Full Employment*, para. 26.

33. Department of Finance, *Third Programme*, 27–28.

34. Department of Education, *Investment in Education: Report of the Survey Team Appointed by the Minister for Education in October 1962* (1966), Education. 56, 24–30.

35. Brendan M. Walsh, *Some Irish Population Problems*, 2.

36. Brendan M. Walsh, "Ireland's Demographic Transition, 1958–70," *Economic and Social Review* 1 (1969): 260–63.

37. Clement Merlens. "Birth Regulations," *Studies* 52 (1963): 231–48.

38. Joseph Fuchs, "The Pill," *Studies* 53 (1964): 352.

39. *Women's Way* was first published in 1963.

40. Peter Lennon, "Sex and the Irish," *The Irish Times*, 31 October 1966.

41. *The Irish Times*, 2 October 1968.

42. Walsh, "Ireland's Demographic Transition," 261.

43. *The Irish Times*, 2 October 1968.

44. Walsh, *Some Irish Population Problems*, 16.

45. For Irish fertility post-1970, see D. A. Coleman, "The Demographic Transition in Ireland in International Context," in *The Development of Industrial Society in Ireland*, ed. J. H. Goldthorpe and C. T. Whelan, 53–78 (Oxford, 1992).

46. *Second Programme for Economic Expansion*, part 2, para. 227.

47. For specific examples, see Mary E. Daly, *The First Department*, 372–80, 441–503.

48. Ibid., 455–56.

49. DT, S11563 C/63, Farm Incomes, NAI.

50. Manning, *James Dillon*, 314.

51. *Sligo Champion*, 16 May 1964. In reality, there were considerable subsidies on agricultural rates and fertilizer plus guaranteed prices for many products, including wheat, barley, and milk.

52. For details, see Mary E. Daly, *The First Department*, 459–70, 492–96.

53. Ibid., 502.

54. Ibid.

55. *Mater et Magistra*, paras. 123–25.

56. DT, S16105 C/61, Farm Apprenticeship, NAI; John Horgan, *Sean Lemass*, 322; S17303/62, National Farmers' Association, application for technical assistance, NAI.

57. Newman, *Limerick Rural Survey*, appendix B, Index of Social Provision, 310.

58. John Jackson, *Report on the Skibbereen Social Survey*, 27.

59. Newman, "Social Provision and Rural Centrality," in *Limerick Rural Survey*, 273.

60. *Western People*, 23 December 1961.

61. Mary E. Daly, "'Turn on the Tap,'" 484–88.

62. Colin Buchanan and Partners, *Regional Studies in Ireland*, 35. The other significant variables were rural density and the proportion of people living in settlements.

63. An Foras Talúntais, *West Cork Resource Survey*, C-97–98, 1963.

64. Mary E. Daly, *The First Department*, 502.

65. Hannan, *Rural Exodus*, 248.

66. McNabb, "Migration," in *Limerick Rural Survey*, Newman, *Limerick Rural* Survey, 182.

67. *West Cork Resource Survey*, C-83.

68. DT, S17032 A/61, Small Farms Committee, NAI.

69. DT, S17032 A/61, Address by Seán F. Lemass to the Annual General Meeting of the Irish Countrywomen's Association, Mansion House, Dublin, 11 April 1961, NAI.

70. This section should not be regarded as a comprehensive account of the report of the interdepartmental committee.

71. *Report by the Inter-Departmental Committee on the Problems of Small Western Farms*, 11.

72. DT, S17032E, NAI. In 1961, 62 percent of holdings in Connacht were less than thirty acres.

73. DT, S17032 E, NAI.

74. DT, S17032 B/62, NAI; E. A. Attwood, "Agriculture and Economic Growth in Western Ireland," *JSSISI* 20, pt. 5 (1961–62): 172.

75. *The Irish Times*, 20 November 1961.

76. David Seth Jones, "Divisions within the Irish Government over Land Distribution Policy, 1940–70," 95.

77. DT, S17032 E, exchange between Smith and Moran, January 1963, NAI.

78. Department of Lands, "The Irish Land Acts, Their History and Development," *Report of the Irish Land Commission, 1 April 1963–31 March 1964,* appendix A, 42.

79. S17032 F, NAI.

80. See an editorial in the *Western People,* 4 March 1961; a report in the *Western People,* 24 June 1961, of a protest meeting allegedly attended by 250,000 indignant farmers "less than 200 yards away from where Michael Davitt founded the Land League"; Louis P. F. Smith, "Foreign Land Buying in Ireland," *Christus Rex* 18 (July 1964): 181–86.

81. PDDE, 11 June 1963, col. 771.

82. Varley and Curtin, "Defending Rural Interests," 70.

83. Vincent Tucker, "Images of Development and Underdevelopment in Glencolumbkille, County Donegal, 1830–1970," in John Davis, ed., *Rural Change in Ireland* (Belfast, 1999), 111. See also, M. J. Costello, "Agriculture in the West of Ireland,." *Studies* 56 (1967): 337–48.

84. *Irish Press,* 11 June 1963.

85. DT, S17032 C, press cutting from *Irish Independent,* 7 June 1962, NAI.

86. Farm organizations such as the National Farmers' Association and the Irish Creamery Milk Suppliers' Association were relatively weak in the west of Ireland.

87. Healy, *The Death of an Irish Town,* 64.

88. Mary E. Daly, *The First Department,* 429–31.

89. *Western People,* 16 November 1963.

90. Varley and Curtin, "Defending Rural Interests," 75.

91. Department of Agriculture, *Report on Pilot Areas Development (by) the Inter-Departmental Committee on the Problems of Small Western Farms* (1964), Agriculture 52/1.

92. Mary E. Daly, *The First Department,* 429–30.

93. DT, S17032 I/95, NAI.

94. DT, S17032 I/95, 17 June 1964, Dr. Fergus to Lemass, NAI.

95. DT, S17032 I/9, NAI.

96. John J. Scully, *Agriculture in the West of Ireland: A Study of the Low Farm Income Problem* (1971), Agriculture 67.

97. *Longford News,* 14 September 1963, press cutting on S17032 G., NAI.

98. Healy, *The Death of an Irish Town,* 17.

99. *Longford News,* 14 September 1963, as on S17032 G., NAI.

100. John Healy, "Problems and Prospects of Rural Ireland," *Christus Rex* 22 (October 1968): 314.

101. Hannan, *Rural Exodus,* 249.

102. PDDE, 3 December 1963, col. 389, Fianna Fáil TD Pádraig Faulkner.

103. Fennell, "Industrialisation and Agricultural Development in the Congested Districts"; Mary E. Daly, *The First Department,* 427.

104. Hannan, *Rural Exodus,* 251–52.

105. Lucey and Kaldor, *Rural Industrialization,* 195–97. This was a study of two communities with long-established factories: Scarriff, county Clare, and Tubbercurry, county Sligo.

106. Foreword by Michael P. Fogarty to Lucey and Kaldor, *Rural Industrialization,* 9.

107. Ibid., 10.

108. Ibid., 97.

109. *Third Programme,* 169–70.

110. Flann O'Brien, *The Best of Myles* (London, 1968), 383.

111. Department of Finance, *Economic Development,* para. 9.

112. Mary E. Daly, *The Buffer State,* 483–84, 488–91.

113. Ibid., 446–49

114. Garret FitzGerald, *Planning in Ireland,* 114.

115. Tony Fahey, "Housing and Local Government," in Mary E. Daly, ed., *County and Town: One Hundred Years of Local Government in Ireland* (Dublin, 2001), 125–26.

116. Fahey, "Housing and Local Government," 126.

117. Berna Grist, "The Planning Process," in Mary E. Daly, *County and Town,* 130–40.

118. C. E. V. Leser, "Problems of Industrialisation in Developing Countries and Their Implications for Ireland," *JSSISI* 21, pt. 6 (1967–68): 1.

119. DT, 97/6/90, Statement of Government Policy on the Report of the Committee on Development Centres and Industrial Estates . . . And the Comments of the National Industrial Economic Council on the Report, August 1965, NAI.

120. DT, 97/6/90, August–September 1965, NAI.

121. Nathaniel Lichfield and Associates, *Report and Advisory Outline Plan for the Limerick Region* (Dublin: Stationery Office, 1967).

122. Myles Wright, *The Dublin Region: Advisory Regional Plan and Final Report,* vols. 1–2 (Dublin: Stationery Office, 1967).

123. DT, 98/6/695, Hillery to Limerick Junior Chamber of Commerce, 24 November 1967, NAI.

124. Buchanan and Partners, *Regional Studies,* paras. 280–88.

125. Ibid., paras. 278–79.

126. Ibid., table 23.

127. Ibid., paras. 351–56.

128. NIEC, *Full Employment,* para. 151.

129. DT, 2000/6/338, Office of the Minister for Local Government, Memorandum for the Government, 10 January 1969, Growth Centres and Regional Planning and Development, NAI.

130. I have not located a copy of the memorandum from the minister for Agriculture and Fisheries. What I have written is based on the comment by the minister for Local Government on that memorandum. DT, 2000/6/338, 13 January 1969, NAI.

131. In November 1967 Lynch had announced that the Department of Lands would move to Castlebar and the Department of Education to Athlone.

132. DT, 2000/6/338, NAI.

133. GC 12/179, Cabinet Minutes, 9 May 1969, NAI.

134. 2000/6/339, Government Information Bureau statement, 19 May 1969, NAI.

135. National Industrial Economic Council, *Report on Physical Planning* (Prl. 641), 1969.

136. Ibid., paras. 13 –14, 17.

137. Ray MacSharry and Padraic White, *The Making of the Celtic Tiger: The Inside Story of Ireland's Boom Economy* (Cork, 2000), 300.

138. Press cuttings on DT, 2000/6/339, NAI.

139. Seán Treacy, PDDE, 9 July 1969, col. 295.

140. *Western People*, 24 May 1969.

141. Desmond Roche, "Local Government," in Frank Litton, ed., *Unequal Achievement: The Irish Experience, 1957–82* (Dublin, 1982), 135 –36.

142. Cornelius O'Leary, *Irish Elections*, 61.

143. PDDE, 28 February 1968, vol. 232, col. 1947.

144. PDDE, Martin Corry, 7 March 1968, col. 320.

145. Cornelius O'Leary, *Irish Elections*, 69. The fact that this referendum was coupled with a second attempt by Fianna Fáil to replace the system of elections by proportional representation with a British-style straight vote was a major factor in the defeat, as were claims by opposition deputies that both amendments were prompted by a cynical attempt to remain in office.

146. *The Irish Times*, June 1969; the announcement of new industries was made on 12 June 1969.

147. PDDE, Mr. Hogan, 18 December 1969, col. 1865.

148. Roche, "Local Government," 136.

149. Industrial Development Authority, *Reports (on) Regional Industrial Plans 1973–77*, 1972; *Jobs to the People: A Summary of the Industrial Development Authority's Regional Plans, 1973–77*, 1972.

150. Arthur Maltby and Brian McKenna, *Irish Official Publications: A*

Guide to Republic of Ireland Papers with a Breviate of Reports, 1922–72 (Oxford, 1980), 338 –39.

151. MacSharry and White, *The Making of the Celtic Tiger,* 301.

152. Hannan, *Rural Exodus,* 256.

153. Mary E. Daly, *Industrial Development and Irish National Identity,* 106 –16.

154. PDDE, 20 May 1969, col. 1348. Sir Anthony Esmonde, speaking about the Buchanan report: "The people in Kilkenny will not be allowed to have their own hospital; they will have to go to Waterford. There will be an industrial centre in Waterford."

155. PDDE, 19 February 1970, col. 1282. "Mr. O. J. Flanagan asked the minister for Industry and Commerce if he will comment on the Buchanan report, which makes no mention of any worthwhile industrial development in the counties of Laois and Offaly; and if he will make a statement in relation to the industrial prospects of both counties having regard to the fact that they have been omitted from this report."

156. MacSharry and White, *The Making of the Celtic Tiger,* 299.

157. Mancur Olson, *The Rise and Fall of Nations* (New Haven, Conn., 1976), 31.

7. "A Ticket to London Is a Ticket to Hell"

The phrase "a ticket to London is a ticket to hell" was allegedly used by Redemptionist missionaries in sermons warning against the dangers of emigration. A. E. C. W. Spencer, "The Religious Arrangements for the Integration of Irish Catholic Immigrants," pp. 66, 68, DDA.

1. Blanshard, *The Irish and Catholic Power,* 262.

2. PDDE, 24 November 1948.

3. PDDE, 24 November 1948, cols. 354, 392–93.

4. 19 January 1962. Speech to Minister of the Member States of the European Economic Community, Government Information Service (915) 1/216, NAI.

5. There are no accurate figures on remittances from the United Kingdom, but statistics on emigrant remittances and legacies can be found in the annual *Statistical Abstract.* 1958 was the first occasion that the value of merchandise exports exceeded remittances and legacies.

6. DT, S5111/1–4, Broadcast Messages by President, NAI. These files contain copies of Saint Patrick's Day addresses and correspondence from Irish Americans relating to some of these broadcasts. After 1937 the practice was for the president of Ireland to broadcast at Saint Patrick's Day, with a Christmas broadcast by the taoiseach. For a flavor of Cosgrave's 1931 broadcast, see

Mary E. Daly, "Nature and Nationalism in Modern Ireland," in Howard Clark and Judith Devlin, eds., *European Encounters: Essays in Memory of Albert Lovett* (Dublin, 2003), 316 –35.

7. Mary E. Daly, "Irish Nationality and Citizenship since 1922," 377 –407.

8. Seán Cronin, *Washington's Irish Policy* (Dublin, 1986), 166.

9. DFA, Washington Files, D22-I, Visit of Taoiseach John A. Costello to the United States, 1956, NAI. Costello originally planned to refuse an invitation to the Saint Patrick's Day dinner of the Friendly Sons of Saint Patrick in Philadelphia in order to attend a dinner at Yale University, but Irish officials persuaded him to change his mind.

10. Mary E. Daly, "Nationalism, Sentiment, and Economic Relations between Ireland and Irish America," 82–85.

11. DFA, Washington Files, P115/1, Paul Keating, 21 July 1954 and 13 August 1954, NAI.

12. DFA, P115/1, 13 August 1954, NAI.

13. In 1954, however, *The Sunday Press* ran a series of stories under the heading, "If You Are Thinking of Emigrating, Think Again," giving the hard-luck stories of Irish emigrants in Canada, the United States, and Australia, though not Britain. *The Sunday Press,* 24 January 1954; 21 February 1954; 28 February 1954; 18 March 1954.

14. Mary Corcoran, *Irish Illegals: Transients between Two Societies* (Westport, Conn., 1993).

15. Walshaw, *Migration to and from the British Isles,* 33. The big exception to this was, of course, immediately following the great famine, when reports of high mortality on emigrant ships (the so-called "coffin ships") led to a significant tightening of regulations governing passenger shipping.

16. MS 8300/8, memorandum from Department of External Affairs, copy of note prepared by the office of the Australian High Commissioner concerning emigration to Australia, Marsh Papers.

17. DT, S14249 A, Commission on Emigration, letter dated 19 November 1948, NAI.

18. DFA, C/6/A1, 14 August 1959, NAI.

19. DT, S3308, Emigration and Immigration, international conference, 1 February 1924, NAI.

20. DT, S11582 B, NAI. This attitude was consistent with the overall government attitude at the time, showing a general reluctance to sign on to European-wide agreements.

21. DT, 2002/19/75, Irish emigrants and assistance to persons emigrating for work, NAI.

22. DT, 2002/19/74, Irish emigrants and assistance to persons emigrating

for work; Ministry of Labor, Memorandum for Government, 29 November 1968, NAI.

23. Wyman, *Round Trip,* 93 –94.

24. A. E. C. W. Spencer, "The Religious Arrangements for the Integration of Irish Catholic Immigrants," 55 (1960), Diocesan Agencies Newman Demographic Survey, DDA.

25. Fitzpatrick, *The Two Irelands,* 216.

26. A. E. C. W. Spencer, "The Religious Arrangements for the integration of Irish Catholic Immigrants," pp. 24 –25, DDA.

27. DFA, 202/49, report by Dulanty, NAI.

28. *The Irish Times,* 20 September 1937.

29. DFA, 202/49, Kirkintilloch fire, NAI.

30. *The Irish Times,* 20 September 1937.

31. *Irish Labour News,* 22 September 1937.

32. *Irish Independent,* 19 October 1937.

33. *Report of the Inter-Departmental Committee on Seasonal Migration to Great Britain,* 1937 –38, R. 655/1 P. 3403.

34. MS 8307/20, Evidence, Department of Education, Dr. O'Sullivan, Marsh Papers.

35. *Report of the Inter-Departmental Committee on Seasonal Migration,* 10; Mary E. Daly, *Spirit of Earnest Inquiry,* 101–3. The first data on migratory laborers were collected as part of the 1841 census.

36. PDDE, volume 191, 3 August 1961, Irish Workers in Scottish Potato Fields, col. 2689; DT, 97/6/310, Irish Labor, Emigration, 26 June 1961, motion of Donegal Co. Council, and DEA, memorandum 17/8/61, NAI; Heather Holmes in "Sanitary Inspectors and the Reform of Housing Conditions for Irish Migratory Potato Workers in Scotland from 1945 to the 1970s," *Saothar* 24 (1999): 45 –58, shows that Scottish local authorities made considerable efforts to improve housing conditions for migratory workers in later years.

37. S24, Employment and Living Conditions of the Irish in Britain, Marsh Papers.

38. S24A, S24B, Marsh Papers.

39. DT, S11582 C, NAI.

40. Ibid.

41. *The Irish Democrat,* January 1952.

42. *The Irish Democrat,* February 1952.

43. *The Birmingham Post,* 30 August 1951. The unnamed social worker was probably Maurice Foley, the source of de Valera's information.

44. *The Irish Democrat,* October 1951.

45. S. Alderson, *Britain in the Sixties: Housing* (London, 1962), 13.

46. *Birmingham Post,* 1 September 1951.

47. Delaney, *Demography, State, and Society,* 195.

48. DT, 2002/19/75, NAI.

49. A. E. C. W. Spencer, "The Religious Arrangements for the Integration of Irish Catholic Immigrants," p. 30, DDA.

50. *Birmingham Post,* 30 August 1951; S11582 C, statement by Councillor W. F. Smith, NAI; *Birmingham Post,* 1 September 1951.

51. See the comments of Kevin Casey, who managed Irish pubs in London, in Catherine Dunne, *An Unconsidered People: The Irish in London* (Dublin, 2003), 10.

52. John Jackson, *The Irish in Britain,* 63.

53. *The Irish Democrat,* "No Irish Need Apply," 18 March 1952.

54. Government Information Bureau statement as reported in *The Birmingham Post,* 31 August 1951.

55. *The Irish Times,* 4 September 1951, 12 September 1951.

56. *The Irish Democrat,* October 1952.

57. S11582 C, NAI.

58. Thrifty housewives often made sheets out of flour bags.

59. John Jackson, *The Irish in Britain,* 102.

60. *Birmingham Post,* 31 August 1951.

61. DT, S11582 D, NAI.

62. DT, S11582 F, NAI.

63. E. J. B. Rose and Associates, *Colour and Citizenship: A Report on British Race Relations* (London, 1969), 72.

64. DT, S11582 C, NAI.

65. *Irish Catholic Directory* (1934): 607.

66. *Irish Catholic Directory* (1938): 584.

67. *Irish Catholic Directory* (1931): 627.

68. Earner-Byrne, "'In Respect of Motherhood,'" 239.

69. Annual reports of the society, DDA. My thanks to Maurice Curtis for making me aware of this reference.

70. Report by John Costelloe of the CYMS, 519/1A, Box 1, folder 1942, DDA.

71. Deirdre McMahon, "John Charles McQuaid, Archbishop of Dublin, 1940–72" in James Kelly and Daire Keogh, eds., *History of the Catholic Diocese of Dublin* (Dublin, 2000), 355–61.

72. Report on the Catholic Social Welfare Bureau prepared for the International Catholic Migration Congress, 1954, DDA.

73. 519/1A, Box 1, folder 1942, DDA.

74. Ibid.

75. DT, S11582 A, NAI.

76. Minutes of the Hierarchy, 22 June 1943, McQuaid Papers, DDA.

77. DT, S11582 A, NAI.

78. DT, S11582 B, NAI.

79. Ibid.

80. Barrington, *Health, Medicine, and Politics,* 172.

81. DT, S15398 A, Emigration, Views of the Hierarchy, NAI.

82. Minutes of the Hierarchy, 7 October 1947, McQuaid Papers, DDA.

83. DT S15398 A, Emigration, Views of the Hierarchy, NAI.

84. DT S11582 B, NAI.

85. S24B, Report, survey of living and employment conditions of Irish workers in Great Britain, Marsh Papers.

86. Ibid.

87. S24C, Stanley Lyon, The Irish Emigrant in Great Britain, General Report, Marsh Papers.

88. S24A, Interim Report on Survey in Great Britain, Marsh Papers.

89. S24B, Marsh Papers.

90. Hasia Diner, *Erin's Daughters in America: Irish Immigrant Women in the Nineteenth Century* (Baltimore, 1983), 80–94.

91. Mona Hearn, *Below Stairs: Domestic Service Remembered in Dublin and Beyond, 1830–1922* (Dublin, 1993), 3.

92. S20, Interviews with returned female emigrants, Marsh Papers.

93. Earner-Byrne, "'In Respect of Motherhood,'" 238–56.

94. Sandra McAvoy, "The Regulation of Sexuality in the Irish Free State, 1929–1935," in Elizabeth Malcolm and Greta Jones, eds., *Medicine, Disease, and the State in Ireland, 1650–1940* (Cork, 1999), 258–59.

95. Annual Report of DLGPH, 1931–32, 129.

96. The diplomatic offices of Commonwealth countries were known as High Commissions; the Irish representative in London was raised to the status of ambassador after Ireland left the Commonwealth in 1949.

97. Earner-Byrne, "'In Respect of Motherhood,'" 241.

98. Ibid., 243–44.

99. 519/1A, Box 1, folder 1942, DDA.

100. For details, see Whyte, *Church and State in Modern Ireland,* 183–93, 274–77.

101. These records are not open.

102. *Commission on Emigration,* appendix 4, Arrangements by Public Assistance Authorities for the Accommodation of Unmarried Mothers and Their Children, 263–65.

103. Sutherland, *Irish Journey,* 76–77.

104. S24A, Marsh Papers.

105. S24B, Marsh Papers.

106. Ibid.

107. "Helping Those Young Pregnant Girls Became My Mission in Life," in Dunne, *An Unconsidered People,* 151–63, gives the recollections of an Irish woman member of the Legion of Mary in London.

108. Sutherland, *Irish Journey,* 85–86. The figures in Sutherland's book do not tally, but there is no reason to assume that the arithmetical error distorts the overall picture.

109. DT, S11582 D, NAI.

110. S24B, Marsh Papers.

111. *Commission on Emigration,* para. 218. Although an adoption act was not passed until 1952, private adoptions were carried out before that date, but details remain obscure.

112. Catholic Social Welfare Bureau (1), Helen Murtagh to McQuaid, DDA.

113. *Commission on Emigration,* para. 219.

114. Catholic Social Welfare Bureau, Emigrant Folder, DDA. (Emphasis in the original).

115. The objectives of the Connolly Association were to win support for the ending of partition and to work closely with the British trades unions and labor movement for the interests of Irish emigrants in Britain. Although it claimed to have no affiliation with any political party, it was generally regarded as a communist front. John Jackson claims that "there would appear, however, to be little weight in these charges." *The Irish in Britain,* 125–26.

116. DT, S11582 D, S11582 E, NAI.

117. DT, S11582 E, NAI.

118. A. E. C. W. Spencer, "The Religious Arrangements for the Integration of Irish Catholic Immigrants," pp. 22–23, DDA.

119. DT, S11582 E, NAI.

120. Minutes of the Hierarchy, letter from Elizabeth Fitzgerald, 25 August 1953, McQuaid Papers, DDA.

121. DT, S11582 D, NAI.

122. DT, S11582 E, NAI.

123. Minutes of the Hierarchy, McQuaid Papers, DDA.

124. DT, S11582 E, NAI.

125. Minutes of the Hierarchy, 13 October 1953, DDA; DT, S11582 F, NAI.

126. Catholic Social Welfare Bureau, Emigrants' Section, 104th meeting, 28 May 1954, DDA.

127. "The Catholic Attitude to Emigration," *Christus Rex* 9 (1955): 61.

128. *Commission on Emigration,* para. 327.

129. Ibid., para. 328. The commission distinguished between recommendations and suggestions.

130. Used by Redemptorist missionaries in sermons warning against the dangers of emigration. A. E. C. W. Spencer, "The Religious Arrangements for the Integration of Irish Catholic Immigrants," pp. 66, 68, DDA.

131. Minutes of the Hierarchy, 11 October 1955, DDA.

132. DFA, 2002/19/75, memorandum, Department of Labor, November 1968, paras. 29–30, NAI.

133. DT, S11582 G, NAI.

134. Catholic Social Welfare Bureau, Emigrants' Section, 92nd meeting, 24 January 1952, DDA. Mrs. Hynes claimed that if young women were given advance notice of their future place of employment, some of them might refuse to take up jobs in isolated areas and private houses.

135. Ibid., 87th meeting, 26 April 1951; Minutes of the Hierarchy, 21 June 1955, DDA.

136. DT, S14249 D, NAI.

137. DT, S16325 A, NAI.

138. *The Irish Times,* 28 September 1955.

139. *The Irish Times,* 20 June 1957; Catholic Social Welfare Bureau, "Twenty-Five Years of Service," p. 9, DDA.

140. Catholic Social Welfare Bureau Folder, DDA.

141. DFA, 2002/19/74, NAI.

142. Minutes of the Meeting of the Hierarchy, 23 June 1953, considering a letter from Cardinal Griffin asking that a liaison committee be established consisting of members of the English and Irish hierarchies, DDA.

143. DT, S11582 E, NAI.

144. DT, S11582 F, NAI.

145. John Jackson, *The Irish in Britain,* 130–31.

146. *The Irish Times,* 19 March 1954.

147. Dunne, *An Unconsidered People,* 85; John Jackson, *The Irish in Britain,* 128–30; A. E. C. W. Spencer, "The Religious Arrangements for the Integration of Irish Catholics," 49–50; Mac Amhlaigh, *Dialann Deoraí,* 27, 128–31.

148. Spencer noted that in the late 1950s, about five Irish Catholics were reaching parenthood in England and Wales for every twelve native Catholics; by 1962–64 the proportion would have increased to seven or eight Irish Catholics for every ten or eleven native Catholics. The Catholic share of live births had increased from 12 percent on the eve of World War II to 15.5 percent in

1958. He estimated that the cost of providing Catholic schools would amount to approximately £100 million in the 1960s, and there was an urgent need for church building to accommodate enlarged or new Catholic communities. "The Religious Arrangements for the Integration of Irish Catholic Immigrants," p. 47, DDA; DT, S16325 A, NAI.

149. DT, S16325 A, NAI.

150. Catholic Social Welfare Bureau, Emigrants' Section, 6 August 1957, DDA.

151. *The Irish Times*, 27 April 1959.

152. *The Irish Times*, 9 September 1955.

153. "The Catholic Attitude to Emigration," *Christus Rex* 60.

154. International Catholic Migration Commission, Migration, Informative Series, No. 4., Catholic Migration Activities, DDA

155. Quoted in "The Catholic Attitude to Emigration," *Christus Rex* 66.

156. Catholic Social Welfare Bureau, Emigrants' Section, "The Extent and General Nature of Emigration from Ireland," Minutes of 104th meeting, 28 May 1953, paper prepared for Breda Conference, DDA.

157. Reverend Peadar Arnold, "Emigration: Some Suggestions?" *Christus Rex* 5 (1951): 260, quoted in A. E. C. W. Spencer, "The Religious Arrangements for the Integration of Irish Catholics," p. 73c, DDA.

158. *The Furrow*, September 1950. However, in May 1948 seventy priests met in Westminster Cathedral to discuss the problems facing newly arrived Irish emigrants. Kieran O'Shea, *The Irish Emigrant Chaplaincy Scheme in Britain, 1957–82* (Naas, 1985).

159. A. E. C. W. Spencer, "The Religious Arrangements for the Integration of Irish Catholic Immigrants," p. 73d, DDA.

160. Minutes of Catholic Social Welfare Bureau, Emigrants' Section, 1954, DDA; O'Shea, *The Irish Emigrant Chaplaincy Scheme in Britain*, 12.

161. Minutes of the Hierarchy, 21 June 1955, and Report on Missions to Irish Emigrants in Britain Conducted by Irish Missionaries from June 1956 to June 1957, DDA; O'Shea, *Irish Emigrant Chaplaincy Scheme*, 18–31.

162. Diocesan Agencies Newman Demographic Survey, letter to Cardinal Mimmi drafted by Reverend James Staunton, thebishop of Ferns, concerning provisions for Irish emigrants in Britain, DDA.

163. Minutes, June 1955, McQuaid Papers, DDA.

164. Catholic Social Welfare Bureau, "Twenty-Five Years," p. 9, DDA; O'Shea, *Irish Emigrant Chaplaincy Scheme*, 37–39.

165. Cardinal Mimmi to Cardinal D'Alton. Handwritten note by McQuaid on a copy of the letter, 27 November 1958, Emigrants Section, McQuaid Papers, DDA.

166. Diocesan Agencies Newman Demographic Survey, Report by Dr. James Staunton, June 1959, DDA.

167. Ibid., translation of Cardinal Mimmi's speech given 26 September 1959, supplied to McQuaid, DDA. The translation tallies with the printed Spanish version, which is also in the archives.

168. Newman Demographic Survey, McQuaid to D'Alton, 1 February 1960, DDA.

169. In January 1956 Monsignor Barrett suggested establishing a special presidium of the Legion of Mary in Dun Laoghaire to work exclusively in the port. Catholic Social Welfare Bureau, Emigrants' Section, 20 January 1956, Barrett to McQuaid, DDA.

170. Catholic Social Welfare Bureau, Survey of Irish Emigrant Cases, 1959, DDA. My thanks to Professor Conor Ward for supplying me with this document and for discussing his work with the Catholic Social Welfare Bureau.

171. Newman Demographic Survey, Report to the Clergy on the parish register returns for the year ending 31 December 1959, marked "Not for Publication. For Information of the Clergy Only," DDA.

172. The conference was chaired by Professor Michael Fogarty (who subsequently became the director of the Economic and Social Research Institute in Dublin). A long excerpt of this report, together with the comments of Monsignor Barrett, will be published in a forthcoming edition of *Analecta Hibernica*.

173. Hickey was another sociologist and the author of a paper called "The Irish Rural Emigrant and British Urban Society."

174. A. E. C. W. Spencer "The Religious Arrangements for the Integration of Irish Immigrants." The numbering of the copy of Spencer's Papers DDA is complicated; some numbered pages are missing, but the text seems to be complete and there are numbered pages 73a to 73f.

175. This was a quotation from Humphreys, "Migration to Dublin: Its Social Effects," *Christus Rex* 9 (1955): 192–99.

176. A. E. C. W. Spencer, "The Religious Arrangements for the Integration of Irish Catholic Immigrants," 13–24, DDA. (Emphasis in the original).

177. Catholic Social Welfare Bureau, Comments on First Draft of Report by Newman Demographic Survey on "The Religious Arrangements for the Integration of Irish Catholic Immigrants in England and Wales," submitted to McQuaid on 3 June 1960, DDA.

178. McQuaid to Westminster, 5 June 1960, DDA.

179. Spencer suggested that a brief statement should be inserted, expressing regret at the lack of information on the background of Irish immigrants. Barrett claimed that Professor Michael Fogarty wished to use the

report and this statement to support an application to the Ford Foundation for a £100,000 research grant. Barrett to Dr. Kampschoer, 25 July 1960, DDA.

180. Barrett to McQuaid, 18 June 1960, DDA. I have not located a copy of Hickey's paper in the DDA.

181. McQuaid to Godfrey, 14 June 1960, DDA.

182. International Catholic Migration Commission, *4th Conference of the ICMC, Ottawa, 1960: The Integration of the Catholic Immigrant* (Geneva, 1960); John Hickey, in his *Urban Catholics: Urban Catholicism in England and Wales, 1829 to the Present Day* (London, 1967), does not include any paper that might correspond to the Munich paper in the bibliography.

183. Report by Cornelius Cremin on the Irish in Britain, January 1958, on S16325 B, NAI.

184. Catholic Social Welfare Bureau, Emigration Files, Barrett to McQuaid, 12 September 1953, DDA.

185. Minutes of the Hierarchy, 3 June 1955, McQuaid Papers, DDA.

186. DT, S16325 A, NAI.

187. Cited in Owen R. Sweeney, "The Apostolate to Irish Emigrants in Britain: A Report to the Irish Hierarchy" (May 1970): 2, copy in Minutes of the Hierarchy, 1970, folder 2, DDA.

188. S16325 B, NAI.

189. Rose and Associates, *Colour and Citizenship.*

190. Catholic Social Welfare Bureau, Barrett to McQuaid, 22 March 1966, DDA.

191. Sweeney, "The Apostolate to Irish Emigrants," 16–17.

192. DFA, 2002/19/75, Persons Emigrating to England, assistance, NAI.

193. DT, S16325 B, NAI.

194. Rose and Associates, *Colour and Citizenship,* 139, 146.

195. *Irish Independent,* 5 December 1961.

196. Rose and Associates, *Colour and Citizenship,* 234; Rodney Lowe, *The Welfare State in Britain since 1945* (second edition, London,1999), 250, 259–60.

197. Minutes of the Hierarchy, April 1967, report on missions in England, DDA.

198. A. E. C. W. Spencer, "The Religious Arrangements for the Integration of Irish Catholic Immigrants," 68.

199. Rose and Associates, *Colour and Citizenship,* 139.

200. DFA, 2002/19/75, NAI.

201. Sweeney, "The Apostolate to Irish Emigrants in Britain," 14.

202. DFA, 2002/19/74, Irish Centres and Assistance for Irish Persons, Emigrating for Work, NAI.

203. DFA, 2002/19/75, NAI.

204. DFA, 2002/19/75, NAI.

205. Hannan, *Rural Exodus*, 254–55.

206. Report in DFA, 2002/19/74, NAI.

207. *Irish Press*, 16 February 1962.

208. DFA, 2002/19/74, has a copy of the Annual Report of the London Irish Center, 31 October 1964, NAI.

209. S16325 B, NAI; also DFA, 2002/19/74.

210. DFA, 2002/19/75, Annual Report of the London Irish Center, 31 October 1969, NAI.

211. Report by Barrett, 5 March 1966, DDA.

212. Sweeney, "The Apostolate to Irish Emigrants in Britain," 14.

213. Minutes of the Hierarchy, Extraordinary General Meeting, 10 November 1964, DDA.

214. DFA, 2002/19/75, Report on Easter Emigrant Conference by DEA, NAI.

215. Sweeney, "The Apostolate to Irish Emigrants in Britain," 14.

216. PDDE, 2 November 1972, vol. 263, col. 514, Parliamentary Question by Dr. John O'Connell to Minister for Health Erskine Childers.

217. DFA, 2002/19/75, NAI.

218. Minutes of the Hierarchy, Report on Missions in England, April 1967, DDA; Sweeney, "The Apostolate to Irish Emigrants in Britain," 18. Fifty percent of families assisted by the Catholic Housing Aid Scheme were Irish.

219. DFA, 2002/19/74, Report by Reverend Owen Sweeney, NAI.

220. Sweeney, "The Apostolate to Irish Emigrants in Britain," 6, citing 1964 Emigrant Conference.

221. Minutes of the Hierarchy, Extraordinary General Meeting, 10 November 1964, DDA. I have found no evidence that they did so.

222. DFA, 2002/19/75, NAI.

223. Catholic Social Welfare Bureau, Emigrants Section, DDA. The fact that Hauser was Jewish was one reason why the offer was rejected.

224. Sweeney, "The Apostolate to Irish Emigrants in Britain," 19.

225. Mary Raftery and E. O'Sullivan, *Suffer the Little Children: The Inside Story of Ireland's Industrial Schools* (Dublin, 1999).

226. Henry J. Gray, "The Emigrant in England: Service by an Irish Bureau in the Care of Emigrants," paper presented to 1965 Easter Emigrant Conference, Minutes of the Hierarchy, 1965, DDA; Report on Missions for Emigrants by Irish Missioners in England and Wales, Easter 1965–66 and 1966–67.

227. DFA, 2002/19/75, NAI.

228. PDDE vol. 191, 11 July 1961, Col. 671.

229. *Irish Independent,* 26 July 1961.

230. See, for example, Department of Labor, Memorandum for Government, proposals in relation to official policy on emigration to Great Britain, 28 November 1968, in DFA, 2002/19/75, NAI. The wording recalls Horace Plunkett's description of the co-operative movement.

231. DFA, 2002/19/74, NAI.

232. DT, S16325 B, NAI. This material can also be found on DFA, 2202/19/74, Irish Centers and Assistance for Irish Persons Emigrating for Work.

233. DT, 97/6/310, Irish Labor, emigration, NAI. Lemass gave a personal donation of £1 10s.

234. DFA, 2002/19/74, NAI.

235. DT, 97/6/310, NAI.

236. Minutes of the Hierarchy, 27 April 1965, Lemass letter dated 12 January 1965, DDA.

237. This point was argued very forcefully by the DFA in November 1968 in response to proposals by the Minister for Labor. DFA, 2002/19/75, NAI.

238. PDDE, 27 March 1969, col. 1247. The figures did not include unmarried mothers.

239. Minutes of the Hierarchy, Extract from Father Sweeney's letter, 29 March 1965, DDA.

240. DFA, 2002/19/74, NAI.

241. DFA, 2002/19/75, NAI.

242. *The Irish Times,* 20 July 1968.

243. PDDE, vol. 236, 7 November 1968, col. 2366.

244. T. Ryle Dwyer, *Nice Fellow: A Biography of Jack Lynch* (Cork, 2001), 119–20.

245. DFA, 2002/19/75, NAI; also on DT, 2000/6/561.

246. In 1967 free second-level education and school transport was made available to all; the late 1960s saw the opening of regional technical colleges, which provided third-level education, and a major expansion in grants for students in higher education.

247. DFA, 2002/19/75, Memorandum for Government, 13 December 1968, NAI.

248. Ibid.

249. DT, 2000/6/561, NAI. This is the largest number of postponements by a Fianna Fáil cabinet that I have seen in my research, but the first and second Inter-Party governments quite commonly postponed cabinet discussions of contentious issues.

250. DT, 2000/6/561, NAI.

251. John Jackson, 44–46.

252. *The Irish Times,* 15 March 1969 (emphasis in the original).

253. PDDE, Aiken statement, 26 March 1969, cols. 1202–3.

254. PDDE, 27 March 1969, cols. 1223–24.

255. Ibid., col. 1248.

256. DT, 2000/6/561, NAI.

257. Ibid.

258. DT, 2000/6/561, and DFA, 2002/19/74, NAI.

259. DFA, 2002/19/74, NAI.

260. Report of 15th annual Emigrant Congress, DDA.

261. Meeting, Department of Labor and Catholic Social Welfare Bureau, 27 May 1969, DDA.

262. PDDE, 15 December 1970, cols. 915–16. The reply was given by Brian Lenihan, on behalf of the minster for External Affairs.

263. PDDE, 24 March 1971, col. 1212.

264. DT, 2000/6/561, NAI.

265. PDDE, 8 June 1972, col. 1188.

266. Mary E. Daly, "Nationalism, Sentiment, and Economics," 74–92.

267. PDDE, 15 December 1970, col. 916.

268. DT, 2000/6/561, 8 December 1969, NAI.

269. DFA, Washington Files, C 32 Irish Immigration, NAI.

270. PDDE, 21 March 1972, col. 1918.

Bibliography

Manuscript Sources

Archbishop's House Drumcondra,
Dublin Diocesan Archives
John Charles McQuaid Papers
National Archives of Ireland
Department of Agriculture Files
Department of an Taoiseach Files
Department of the Environment Files
Department of Foreign Affairs Files
Government Information Service Files
National Archives of England and Wales, Kew
Board of Trade Files
Home Office Files
Treasury Files
National Library, Manuscripts Room
Commission of Inquiry into the Civil Service, 1932–34. Minutes and Evidence.

Trinity College Dublin, Manuscripts Room
Arnold Marsh Papers. Papers of the Commission on Emigration.
University College Dublin
  ARCHIVES
Fianna Fáil Papers
Seán MacEntee Papers
Patrick McGilligan Papers
  DEPARTMENT OF IRISH FOLKLORE
Irish Folklore Archives

Newspapers and Periodicals

Belfast Newsletter
Belfast Telegraph
The Bell
The Birmingham Post
Christus Rex
Dundalk Democrat
The Furrow
Impartial Reporter
Irish Catholic Directory
The Irish Democrat
Irish Ecclesiastical Record
Irish Farmers' Journal
Irish Independent
Irish Labour News
The Irish News
Irish Press
The Irish Times
The Kerryman
The Nationalist
Nationalist and Leinster Times
Roscommon Herald
Sligo Champion
Sunday Press
Western People

Official Publications: Ireland

An Foras Forbartha, Colin Buchanan, and Partners. *Regional Studies in Ireland*. Dublin, 1969.
An Foras Talúntais. West Cork Resource Survey C 97–98. 1963.

Belfast/Good Friday Agreement. 1998.

Bunreacht na hÉireann 1937.

Census of Population 1926.

Census of Population 1936.

Census of Population 1946.

Census of Population 1951.

Census of Population 1956.

Census of Population 1961.

Census of Population 1966.

Census of Population 1971.

Census of Population 2002.

Commission of Inquiry into Banking Currency and Credit. 1938. Reports and Minutes of Evidence. P. 2628 R. 38.

Commission on Emigration and Other Population Problems, 1948–54, Reports. P. 25411 R. 63.

Commission on Vocational Organisation. Report. 1944. R. 77.

Commission on Youth Unemployment. 1952. R. 82.

Dáil Éireann. *Commission of Inquiry into the Resources and Industries of Ireland, 1920–22.* R. 10.

Department of Agriculture. *AgriFood 2010, Main Report.* 2000. A. 104.

Department of Agriculture. *Reports on Pilot Areas Development (by) the Inter-Departmental Committee on its Problems on Small Welsh Farms.* 1964. A. 52/1.

Department of Education. *Investment in Education: Report of the Survey Team Appointed by the Minister for Education in October 1962.* 1966. E. 56.

Department of Finance (T. K. Whitaker). *Economic Development.* 1958. F. 58.

Department of Finance. *Programme for Economic Expansion.* 1958. F. 57.

Department of Finance. *Second Programme for Economic Expansion.* Part 1. 1963. F. 57/1.

Department of Finance. *Second Programme for Economic Expansion.* Part 2. 1964. F. 57/2.

Department of Finance. *Third Programme: Economic and Social Development, 1969–72.* 1969. F. 57/7 .

Department of Health. *National Nutrition Survey. Part I. Dietary Survey—Dublin Sample.* 1948. K. 53 –1.

Department of Health. *National Nutrition Survey. Part VII. Clinical Survey.* 1952. K. 53 –7.

Department of Lands. "The Irish Land Acts, Their History and Development." *Report of the Irish Land Commission.* 1 April 1963 –31 March 1964.

Department of Local Government. *Ireland Is Building.* 1950. K. 55.

Department of Local Government and Public Health. *Annual Reports.*
Industrial Development Authority Reports (on) Reported Industrial Plans.
    1972, 1973 –77.
Iris Oifigiúl.
Irish Trade Journal and Statistical Bulletin.
Lichfield, Nathaniel, and Associates. *Report and Advisory Outline Plan for
    the Limerick Region.* Dublin, 1967.
National Industrial and Economic Council. *Full Employment.* Report No.
    18. 1967.
National Industrial and Economic Council. *Report on Physical Planning.*
    1969. Prl. 641.
*Report by the Inter-Departmental Committee on the Problems of Small West-
    ern Farms.* 1962. A. 52, Pr. 6540.
*Report of the Inter-Departmental Committee on Seasonal Migration to Great
    Britain.* 1937–38.
Scully, John J. *Agriculture in the West of Ireland: A Study of the Low Farm In-
    come Problem.* 1971. A. 67.
Statistical Abstract.
Wright, Myles. *The Dublin Region: Advisory Regional Plan and Final Report.*
    2 vols. Dublin, 1967.

Published Debates

Dail Éireann
Seanad Éireann
(These are now available on the Web site www.oireachtas-debates.gov.ie)

Official Publications: Northern Ireland

Census of Population 1926.
Census of Population 1937.
Census of Population 1951.
Census of Population 1961.
Census of Population 1991.
Ulster Yearbook.

Official Publications: United Kingdom

Census of Population Ireland 1841.
Census of Population Ireland 1851.
Census of Population Ireland 1861.
Census of Population Ireland 1871.
Census of Population Ireland 1881.

Census of Population Ireland 1891.
Census of Population Ireland 1901.
Census of Population Ireland 1911.
Royal Commission on the Poor Law: Report on Ireland. 1909.
Royal Commission on Population. 1948–49. Report, Cmnd. 7695.
Hansard Parliamentary Debates.

Books and Articles

Akenson, D. H. *Small Differences: Irish Catholics and Irish Protestants, 1815–1922.* Kingston, Ont., 1988.
Alderson, S. *Britain in the Sixties: Housing.* London, 1962.
Alter, George. "Theories of Fertility Decline: A Nonspecialist's Guide to the Current Debate." In *The European Experience of Declining Fertility,* ed. John R. Gillis, Louise A. Tilly, and David Levine, 13–27. Oxford, 1992.
Anderson, Michael, and Donald J. Morse. "High Fertility, High Emigration, Low Nuptiality: Adjustment Processes in Scotland's Demographic Experience, 1861–1914." *Population Studies* 47, no. 1 (1993): 5–25; 47, no. 2 (1993): 319–43.
Andrews, C. S. *Man of No Property.* Dublin, 1982.
An Foras Talúntais. *West Cork Resource Survey.* May 1963.
Anon. "Diffusion of Knowledge Regarding the Sterile Period." *Irish Ecclesiastical Record* 43 (1934): 414–18.
Archdeacon, Thomas J. *Becoming American: An Ethnic History.* London, 1983.
Arensberg, Conrad. *The Irish Countryman.* Gloucester, Mass., 1959. First published 1937.
Arensberg, Conrad M., and Solon T. Kimball. *Family and Community in Ireland.* Second edition. Cambridge, Mass., 1968.
———. *Family and Community in Ireland.* Third edition, with a new introduction by Anne Byrne, Riccas Edmondston, and Tony Varley. Ennis, 2001.
Attwood, E. A. "Agriculture and Economic Growth in Western Ireland." *JSSISI* 20, pt. 5 (1961–62): 172–95.
Bailey, W. F. "Ireland since the Famine: A Sketch of Fifty Years' Economic and Legislative Changes—Presidential Address." *JSSISI* 11 (1902–3): 129–56.
Baker, Susan. "Nationalist Ideology and the Industrial Policy of Fianna Fáil: The Evidence of the Irish Press." *Irish Political Studies* 2 (1987): 57–66.
Banfield, E. *The Moral Basis of a Backward Society.* Glencoe, Ill., 1958.
Barrington, Ruth. *Health, Medicine, and Politics, 1900–1970.* Dublin, 1987.
Barry, Colm A. "Irish Regional Life Tables." *JSSISI* 16 (1941–42): 1–18.

Bean, Charles, and Nicholas Crafts. "British Economic Growth since 1945." In *Economic Growth in Europe since 1945*, 131–72. Cambridge, 1996.

Becker, Gary. *A Treatise on the Family.* Cambridge, Mass., 1991. First published 1981.

Beddy, J. P. "A Comparison of the Principal Economic Features of Eire and Denmark." *JSSISI* 17 (1943–44): 189–220.

Beere, Thekla. "Cinema Statistics in Saorstát Éireann." *JSSISI* 15 (1935–36): 83–110.

Berger, Suzanne. *Peasants against Politics: Rural Organization in Brittany, 1911–1967.* Cambridge, Mass., 1972.

Bielenberg, Andy, ed. *The Irish Diaspora.* London, 2000.

Birdwell-Pheasant, Donna. "The Early Twentieth-Century Irish Stem Family: A Case Study from County Kerry." In *Approaching the Past: Historical Anthropology through Irish Case Studies,* ed. Marilyn Silverman and P. H. Gulliver, 205–35. New York, 1992.

Blanshard, Paul. *The Irish and Catholic Power.* London, 1954.

Blessing, Patrick J. *The Irish in America: A Guide to the Literature and Manuscript Collections.* Washington, D.C., 1982.

Bock, Gisela. "Antinatalism, Maternity, and Paternity in National Socialist Racism." In *Maternity and Gender Policy: Women and the Rise of the European Welfare States, 1880s–1950s,* ed. Gisela Bock and Pat Thane, 233–55. London, 1991.

Bock, Gisela, and Pat Thane, eds. *Maternity and Gender Policy: Women and the Rise of the European Welfare States, 1880s–1950s.* London, 1991.

Boserup, Ester. *Population and Technology.* Chicago, 1981.

Bourke, Joanna. "'The Best of All Home-Rulers': The Economic Power of Women in Ireland." *Irish Economic and Social History* 18 (1991): 479–99.

Braudel, Ferdinand. *The Identity of France: History and Environment.* London, 1988.

Brenan, Martin. "Rural Education: The Principles." *Christus Rex* 7 (1953): 387–99.

Brettell, Caroline. "Property, Kinship, and Gender: A Mediterranean Perspective." In *The Family in Italy: From Antiquity to the Present,* ed. David L. Kertzer and Richard P. Saller, 340–54. New Haven, Conn., 1991.

Brown, Terence. *Ireland: A Social and Cultural History, 1922–79.* London, 1980.

Buchanan, Colin, and Partners. *Regional Studies in Ireland.* Dublin, 1969. First edition 1938.

Busteed, John. "The Problem of Population." *JSSISI* 15 (1936–37): 49–68.

Cahill, Edward. *The Framework of a Christian State.* Dublin, 1932.

Carbery, Mary. *The Farm by Lough Gur*. Cork, 1978.

Carroll, Paul Vincent. "The Mystical Irish." In *The Vanishing Irish: The Enigma of the Modern World*, ed. John A. O'Brien, 54–64. New York, 1954.

Carr-Saunders, A. M. *World Population: Past Growth and Present Trends*. Oxford, 1936.

Charles, Enid. *The Twilight of Parenthood: A Biological Study of the Decline of Population Growth*. London, 1934.

Clear, Caitríona. *Women of the House: Women's Household Work in Ireland, 1922–1961*. Dublin, 2000.

Coleman, D. A. "The Demographic Transition in Ireland in International Context." In *The Development of Industrial Society in Ireland*, ed. J. H. Goldthorpe and C. T. Whelan, 53–78. Oxford, 1992.

Connell, K. H. "Catholicism and Marriage in the Century after the Famine." In *Irish Peasant Society: Four Historical Essays*. Oxford, 1968.

———. *The Population of Ireland, 1750–1845*. Oxford, 1950.

Conniffe, Denis, ed. *Roy Geary, 1896–1983: Irish Statistician*. Dublin, 1997.

Connolly, Linda. *The Irish Women's Movement: From Revolution to Devolution*. Cork, 2002.

Connolly, S. J., R. A. Houston, and R. J. Morris. *Conflict, Identity, and Economic Development: Ireland and Scotland, 1600–1939*. Preston, 1995.

Connolly, Tracey. "Emigration from Ireland to Britain during the Second World War." In *The Irish Diaspora*, ed. Andy Bielenberg, 51–64. London, 2000.

Coogan, Tim Pat. *Wherever Green Is Worn: The Story of the Irish Diaspora*. London, 2000.

Corcoran, Mary. *Irish Illegals: Transients between Two Societies*. Westport, Conn., 1993.

Corkery, Daniel. *The Hidden Ireland: A Study of Gaelic Munster in the Eighteenth Century*. Dublin, 1925.

Costello, M. J. "Agriculture in the West of Ireland." *Studies* 56 (1967): 337–48.

Coughlan, Anthony, and Roy Johnston. *The Case against the Common Market*. Dublin, 1967.

Cousens, S. H. "Emigration and Demographic Change in Ireland, 1851–1861." *Economic History Review* 14, no. 4 (1961): 275–88.

———. "The Regional Variations in Population Change in Ireland, 1861–1881." *Economic History Review* 17, no. 2 (1964): 301–21.

Cousins, Mel. "The Introduction of Children's Allowances in Ireland, 1939–1944." *Irish Economic and Social History* 26 (1999): 15–34.

Cowley, Ultan. *The Men Who Built Britain: A History of the Irish Navvy*. Dublin, 2001.

Crafts, Nicholas, and Gianni Toniolo. "Postwar Growth: An Overview." In *Economic Growth in Europe since 1945,* ed. Nicholas Crafts and Gianni Toniolo, 1–37. Cambridge, 1996.

Creswell, Robert. *Une Communauté Rurale de l'Irlande.* Paris, 1969.

Cronin, Seán. *Washington's Irish Policy.* Dublin, 1986.

Cullen, L. M. *Eason & Son: A History.* Dublin, 1989.

———. *The Emergence of Modern Ireland: 1600–1900.* London, 1981.

Curtin, Chris, Eoin Devereux, and Dan Shields. "Replaying the 'Match': Marriage Settlements in North Galway." *Irish Journal of Sociology* 2 (1992): 85–95.

Cutileiro, José. *A Portuguese Rural Society.* Oxford, 1971.

Daly, C. B. "Family Life: The Principles." *Christus Rex* 5 (1951): 1–19.

Daly, Mary E. *The Buffer State: The Historical Roots of the Department of the Environment.* Dublin, 1997.

———. *Dublin, The Deposed Capital: A Social and Economic History, 1860–1914.* Cork, 1984.

———. "The Economic Ideals of Irish Nationalism: Frugal Comfort or Lavish Austerity?" *Éire-Ireland* 29, no. 4 (Winter 1994): 77–100.

———. *The First Department: A History of the Department of Agriculture.* Dublin, 2002.

———. *Industrial Development and Irish National Identity, 1922–1939.* Syracuse, N.Y., 1992.

———. "The Irish Family since the Famine: Continuity and Change." *Irish Journal of Feminist Studies* 3, no. 2 (1999): 1–21.

———. "'An Irish-Ireland for Business?' The Control of Manufactures Acts, 1932 and 1934." *IHS* 24, no. 94 (November 1984) 246–72.

———. "Irish Nationality and Citizenship since 1922." *IHS* 32, no. 127 (May 2001): 377–407.

———. "Nationalism, Sentiment, and Economic Relations between Ireland and Irish America in the Postwar Years." *Éire-Ireland* 37, nos. 1/2 (Spring/Summer 2002): 74–92.

———. "Nature and Nationalism in Modern Ireland." In *European Encounters: Essays in Memory of Albert Lovett,* ed. Howard Clark and Judith Devlin, 316–35. Dublin, 2003.

———. *The Spirit of Earnest Inquiry: The Statistical and Social Inquiry Society of Ireland, 1847–1997.* Dublin, 1997.

———. "'Turn on the Tap': The State, Irish Women, and Running Water." In *Women and Irish History: Essays in Honour of Margaret MacCurtain,* ed. Maryann Gianella Valiulis and Mary O'Dowd, 206–19. Dublin, 1997.

———. "Wives, Mothers, and Citizens: The Treatment of Women in the 1935 Nationality and Citizenship Act." *Éire-Ireland* 38, nos. 3/4 (Winter 2003): 244–63.

———, ed. *County and Town: One Hundred Years of Local Government in Ireland*. Dublin, 2001.

Davis, John. ed. *Rural Change in Ireland*. Belfast, 1999.

Delaney, Eamonn. *An Accidental Diplomat*. Dublin, 2001.

Delaney, Enda. *Demography, State, and Society: Irish Migration to Britain, 1921–1971*. Liverpool, 2000.

———. "Placing Post-War Irish Migration to Britain in a Comparative European Perspective, 1945–81." In *The Irish Diaspora*, ed. Andy Bielenberg, 331–56. London, 2000.

Dennehy, Jerome. "The Rural Community." *Christus Rex* 12 (1958): 265–69.

De Paor, Liam. "Ireland's Identities." *Crane Bag* 3, no. 1 (1979): 354–61.

Digby, J. P. "Emigration—The Answer." *The Bell* 17, no. 8 (November 1951): 34–35.

Diner, Hasia. *Erin's Daughters in America: Irish Immigrant Women in the Nineteenth Century*. Baltimore, 1983.

Doyle, David N. "The Remaking of Irish-America, 1845–80." In *A New History of Ireland*, vol. 6, ed. W. J. Vaughan, 745–58. Oxford, 1996.

Drake, Michael. "Marriage and Population Growth in Ireland, 1780–1845." *Economic History Review* 16, no. 2 (1963): 301–13.

Dunne, Catherine. *An Unconsidered People: The Irish in London*. Dublin, 2003.

Dunphy, Richard. *The Making of Fianna Fáil Power in Ireland, 1932–48*. Oxford, 1995.

Dwyer, T. Ryle. *Nice Fellow: A Biography of Jack Lynch*. Cork, 2001.

English, Richard, and Joseph Morrison Skelly, eds. *Ideas Matter: Essays in Honour of Conor Cruise O'Brien*. Dublin, 1998.

Fahey, Tony. "Housing and Local Government." In *County and Town: One Hundred Years of Local Government in Ireland*, ed. Mary E. Daly, 120–29. Dublin, 2001.

Fahey, Tony, and John FitzGerald. *Welfare Implications of Demographic Trends*. Dublin, 1997.

Fanning, Ronan. "The Genesis of Economic Development." In *Planning Ireland's Future: The Legacy of T. K. Whitaker*, ed. John McCarthy, 74–111. Dublin, 1990.

———. *The Irish Department of Finance, 1922–58*. Dublin, 1978.

Fanning, Ronan, Michael Kennedy, Dermot Keogh, and Eunan O'Halpin, eds. *Documents in Irish Foreign Policy*. Vol. 1. Dublin, 1998.

Farley, Desmond. *Social Insurance and Social Assistance in Ireland*. Dublin, 1964.

Farmar, Tony. *Holles Street 1894–1944: The National Maternity Hospital—A Centenary History*. Dublin, 1994.

Fennell, Rosemary. "Industrialisation and Agricultural Development in the Congested Districts." In An Foras Talúntais, *Economic Research Series*, no. 2. Dublin, 1962.

FitzGerald, Garret. "Foreword." In *Planning Ireland's Future: The Legacy of T. K. Whitaker*, ed. John McCarthy, 5–10. Dublin, 1990.

——. *Planning in Ireland*. Dublin, 1968.

FitzGerald, John. "The Story of Ireland's Failure—and Belated Success." In *Bust to Boom? The Irish Experience of Growth and Inequality*, ed. Brian Nolan, Philip J. O'Connell, and Christopher T. Whelan, 27–57. Dublin, 2000.

Fitzpatrick, David. "Irish Farming Families before the First World War." *Comparative Studies in Society and History* 25, no. 2 (1983): 339–74.

——. *Oceans of Consolation: Personal Accounts of Irish Migration to Australia*. Ithaca, N.Y., 1994.

——. " 'A Peculiar Tramping People': The Irish in Britain, 1801–70." In *A New History of Ireland*, vol. 5, ed. W. J. Vaughan, 623–60. Oxford, 1996.

——. *The Two Irelands, 1912–1939*. Oxford, 1998.

Flora, Peter. *State, Economy, and Society in Western Europe, 1915–1977: A Data Handbook*. Vol. 2. *The Growth of Industrial Societies and Capitalist Economies*. Frankfurt, 1987.

Foley, Marc C., and Timothy W. Guinnane. "Did Irish Marriage Patterns Survive the Emigrant Voyage? Irish-American Nuptiality, 1880–1920." *Irish Economic and Social History* 26 (1999): 15–34.

Freeman, T. W. *Ireland: Its Physical, Historical, Social, and Economic Geography*. London, 1950.

Fuchs, Joseph. "The Pill." *Studies* 53 (Winter 1964): 352–67.

Garvin, Tom. *Nationalist Revolutionaries in Ireland, 1858–1928*. Oxford, 1987.

Geary, R. C. "The Future Population of Saorstát Éireann." *JSSISI* 15 (1935–36): 15–36.

——. "The Mortality from Tuberculosis in Saorstát Éireann: A Statistical Study." *JSSISI* 14, no. 67 (1929–30): 67–103.

Gervais, Diane, and Danielle Gauvreau. "Women, Priests, and Physicians: Family Limitation in Quebec, 1940–1970." *Journal of Interdisciplinary History* 34, no. 2 (Autumn 2003): 293–315.

Gibbon, Peter. "Arensberg and Kimball Revisited." *Economy and Society* 2, no. 4 (1973): 479–98.

Gibbon, Peter, and Chris Curtin. "The Stem Family in Ireland." *Comparative Studies in Society and History* 20, no. 3 (1978): 429–53.

Gillis, John R., Louise A. Tilly, and David Levine, eds. *The European Experience of Declining Fertility*. Oxford, 1992.

Gillman, Con. "Recent Marriage Patterns in Ireland." *Christus Rex* 23, no. 1 (January 1969): 49–53.

Ginsbourg, Paul. *A History of Contemporary Italy: Society and Politics, 1943–1988*. London, 1990.

Glass, D. V. *Population Policies and Movements in Europe*. Oxford, 1940.

———. *The Struggle for Population*. Oxford, 1936.

Glynn, Seán. "Irish Immigration to Britain, 1911–1951: Patterns and Policy." *Irish Economic and Social History* 8 (1981): 56–69.

Goldthorpe, J. H., and C. T. Whelan, eds. *The Development of Industrial Society in Ireland*. Oxford, 1992.

Gowing, Margaret. "The Organisation of Manpower in Britain during the Second World War." *Journal of Contemporary History* 7, nos. 1/2 (1972): 147–67.

Gravier, J. F. *Paris et le Désert Français*. Paris, 1947.

Gray, Sir Alexander. *Family Endowment: A Critical Analysis*. London, 1927.

Grimshaw, T. W. "Statistical Survey of Ireland, from 1840 to 1888." *JSSISI* 9 (1888): 321–62.

Grist, Berna. "The Planning Process." In *County and Town: One Hundred Years of Local Government in Ireland,* ed. Mary E. Daly, 130–40. Dublin, 2001.

Gross, Feliks. *Il Paese: Values and Social Change in an Italian Village*. New York, 1974.

Guinnane, Timothy W. *The Vanishing Irish: Households, Migration, and the Rural Economy in Ireland, 1850–1914*. Princeton, N.J., 1997.

Guinnane, Timothy W., Carolyn Moehling, and Cormac Ó Gráda. "Fertility in South Dublin a Century Ago: A First Look." University College Dublin, Center for Economic Research, Working Papers Series WP01/26. Dublin, 2001.

Gutman, Herbert G. *The Black Family in Slavery and Freedom, 1750–1925*. New York, 1976.

Hall, Peter. *Cities in Civilization*. London, 1998.

Hancock, William Neilson. "On the Condition of the Irish Labourer." *Dublin Statistical Society* 1 (1848): 211–22.

Hanly, Joseph. *The National Ideal: A Practical Exposition of True Nationality Appertaining*. Dublin, 1931.

Hannan, Damien. *Displacement and Development: Class, Kinship, and Social Change in Irish Rural Communities*. Dublin, 1979.

———. *Rural Exodus: A Study of the Forces Influencing Large-Scale Migration of Irish Rural Youth*. London, 1970.

Harris, Rosemary. *Prejudice and Tolerance in Ulster: A Study of Neighbours and "Strangers" in a Border Community*. Manchester, 1972.

Hart, Peter. *The IRA and Its Enemies: Violence and Community in Cork, 1916–1923*. Oxford, 1998.

Hayes, Alan, and Diane Urquhart, eds. *Female Experience: Essays in Irish Women's History*. Dublin, 2000.

Healy, John. *The Death of an Irish Town*. Cork, 1968.

———. "Problems and Prospects of Rural Ireland." *Christus Rex* 22 (October 1968): 302–16.

Hearn, Mona. *Below Stairs: Domestic Service Remembered in Dublin and Beyond, 1830–1922*. Dublin, 1993.

Heron, Denis Caulfield. "Historical Statistics of Ireland." *Dublin Statistical Society* 3 (1862): 235–68.

Hickey, John. *Urban Catholics: Urban Catholicism in England and Wales, From 1829 to the Present Day*. London, 1967.

Holmes, Heather. "Sanitary Inspectors and the Reform of Housing Conditions for Irish Migratory Potato Workers in Scotland from 1945 to the 1970s." *Saothar* 24 (1999): 45–58.

Honohan, Patrick, and Cormac Ó Gráda. "The Irish Macroeconomic Crisis of 1955–56: How Much Was Due to Monetary Policy." *Irish Economic and Social History* 25 (1998): 52–80.

Hooton, Earnest A., and C. Wesley Dupertuis. *The Physical Anthropology of Ireland*. Cambridge, Mass., 1955.

Horgan, John. *Irish Media: A Critical History since 1922*. London, 2001.

———. *Seán Lemass: The Enigmatic Patriot*. Dublin, 1997.

Hudson, Pat, and Steve King. "Two Textile Townships, c. 1660–1820: A Comparative Demographic Analysis." *Economic History Review* 53, no. 4 (November 2000): 706–41.

Hughes, J. G. "Estimates of Annual Net Migration and Their Relationship with Series on Annual Net Passenger Movement in Ireland, 1926–76." Unpublished paper, ESRI. Dublin, August 1977.

Humphreys, Alexander J. "Migration to Dublin: Its Social Effects." *Christus Rex* 9 (1955): 192–99.

———. *New Dubliners: Urbanization and the Irish Family*. London, 1966.

Industrial Development Authority. *Reports (on) Regional Industrial Plans, 1973–77*. Dublin, 1972.

———. *Jobs to the People: A Summary of the Industrial Development Authority's Regional Plans, 1973–77*. Dublin, 1972.

International Catholic Migration Commission. *Fourth Conference of the ICMC, Ottawa, 1960: The Integration of the Catholic Immigrant*. Geneva, 1960.

Jackson, John. *The Irish in Britain*. London, 1963.

———. *Report on the Skibbereen Social Survey*. Dublin, 1967.

Jackson, Julian. *France: The Dark Years, 1940–1944*. Oxford, 2001.

Pope John XXIII. *Mater et Magistra: A Re-evaluation of the Social Question in the Light of Christian Teaching*. Encyclical Letter. 1961.

Jones, David Seth. "Divisions within the Irish Government over Land Distribution Policy, 1940–70." *Éire-Ireland* 36 (Fall/Winter 2001): 83–110.

Jones, Greta. *"Captains of All These Men of Death": The History of Tuberculosis in Nineteenth- and Twentieth-Century Ireland*. London, 2001.

———. "Eugenics in Ireland: The Belfast Eugenics Society." *IHS* 28, no. 109 (May 1992): 81–95.

Kane, Robert. *The Industrial Resources of Ireland*. Dublin. 1844.

Kavanagh, Patrick. *Tarry Flynn*. London, 1975.

Kelly, Adrian. "Social Security in Ireland, 1922–52." Thesis abstract. *Irish Economic and Social History* 24 (1997): 114.

Kelly, Charles J. "The British Population Report." *Christus Rex* 4, no. 4 (1949): 10–21.

Kelly, James, and Daire Keogh, eds. *History of the Catholic Diocese of Dublin*. Dublin, 2000.

Kennedy, Finola. *Cottage to Crèche: Family Change in Ireland*. Dublin, 2001.

Kennedy, Kieran A., ed. *From Famine to Feast: Economic and Social Change in Ireland, 1847–1997*. Dublin, 1998.

Kennedy, Kieran A., and Brendan R. Dowling. *Economic Growth in Ireland: The Experience since 1947*. Dublin, 1975.

Kennedy, Liam. *Colonialism, Religion, and Nationalism in Ireland*. Belfast, 1996.

———. "Farm Succession in Modern Ireland: Elements of a Theory of Inheritance." In *Rural Change in Ireland*, ed. John Davis, 116–42. Belfast, 1999.

———. *People and Population Change*. Dublin, 1994.

Kennedy, Liam, and Leslie Clarkson. "Irish Population History, 1700–1921." In *An Historical Geography of Ireland*, ed. B. J. Graham and L. J. Proudfoot. London, 1993.

Kennedy, Michael. *Division and Consensus: The Politics of Cross-Border Relations in Ireland, 1926–1969*. Dublin, 2000.

Kennedy, Robert E. *The Irish: Emigration, Marriage, and Fertility*. Berkeley, 1973.

Kenny, Kevin. *The American Irish: A History.* New York, 2000.

Kertzer, David L., and Richard P. Saller, eds. *The Family in Italy: From Antiquity to the Present.* New Haven, Conn., 1991.

Knaggs, J. F. "Natality in Dublin in the Year 1955." *JSSISI* 20 (1957–58): 37–55.

Kuczynski, Robert. *Population Movements.* Oxford, 1936.

Lambert, Sharon. "Irish Women's Emigration to England, 1922–1960: The Lengthening of Family Ties." In *Female Experience: Essays in Irish Women's History,* ed. Alan Hayes and Diane Urquhart, 152–67. Dublin, 2000.

Layton-Henry, Zig. *The Politics of Immigration: Immigration, "Race," and "Race" Relations in Post-War Britain.* Oxford, 1992.

Lee, J. J. *Ireland, 1912–1985: Politics and Society.* Cambridge, 1989.

———. *The Modernisation of Irish Society, 1848–1918.* Dublin, 1973.

Leser, C. E. V. "Problems of Industrialisation in Developing Countries and Their Implications for Ireland." *JSSISI* 21, pt. 6 (1967–68): 1–30.

Litton, Frank, ed. *Unequal Achievement: The Irish Experience, 1957–82.* Dublin, 1982.

Lowe, Rodney. *The Welfare State in Britain since 1945.* Second edition. London, 1999.

Lucey, Denis I. F., and Donald R. Kaldor. *Rural Industrialization: The Impact of Industrialization on Two Rural Communities in Western Ireland.* London, 1969.

Lynch, Patrick. "The Irish Economy since the War, 1946–51." In *Ireland in the War Years and After, 1939–51,* ed. K. B. Nowlan and T. D. Williams, 187–93. Dublin, 1969.

———. "More Pages from an Irish Memoir." In *Ideas Matter: Essays in Honour of Conor Cruise O'Brien,* ed. Richard English and Joseph Morrison Skelly, 109–22. Dublin, 1998.

Lyon, Stanley. "Natality in Dublin in the Years 1943, 1944, and 1945." *JSSISI* 18 (1947–48): 57–77.

———. "Some Observations on Births in Dublin in the Years 1941 and 1942." *JSSISI* 17 (1942–43): 144–67.

Lyons, F. S. L. *Culture and Anarchy in Ireland, 1890–1939.* Oxford, 1979.

Mac Amhlaigh, Dónal. *Dialann Deoraí.* Dublin, 1960.

MacLysaght, Edward. *Irish Life in the Seventeenth Century.* Third edition. Dublin, 1979.

MacSharry, Ray, and Padraic White. *The Making of the Celtic Tiger: The Inside Story of Ireland's Boom Economy.* Cork, 2000.

Maguire, John Francis. *The Irish in America.* London, 1868.

Malcolm, Elizabeth, and Greta Jones, eds. *Medicine, Disease, and the State in Ireland, 1650–1940.* Cork, 1999.

Maltby, Arthur, and Brian McKenna. *Irish Official Publications: A Guide to Republic of Ireland Papers with a Breviate of Reports, 1922–72.* Oxford, 1980.

Manning, Maurice. *James Dillon: A Biography.* Dublin, 1999.

Maume, Patrick. *The Long Gestation: Irish Nationalist Life, 1891–1918.* Dublin, 1999.

McAvoy, Sandra. "The Regulation of Sexuality in the Irish Free State, 1929–1935." In *Medicine, Disease, and the State in Ireland, 1650–1940,* ed. Elizabeth Malcolm and Greta Jones, 253–66. Cork, 1999.

McBride, Lawrence. *The Greening of Dublin Castle: The Transformation of Bureaucratic and Judicial Personnel in Ireland, 1892–1922.* Washington, D.C., 1991.

McCabe, Ian. *A Diplomatic History of Ireland, 1948–49: The Republic, the Commonwealth and NATO.* Dublin, 1991.

McCarthy, John F. "Ireland's Turnaround: Whitaker and the 1958 Plan for Economic Development." In *Planning Ireland's Future: The Legacy of T. K. Whitaker,* ed. John F. McCarthy, 11–73. Dublin, 1990.

———, ed. *Planning Ireland's Future: The Legacy of T. K. Whitaker.* Dublin, 1990.

McCarthy, Michael D. "Some Irish Population Problems." *Studies* 56 (Autumn 1967): 237–47.

McCarthy, M. J. F. *Priests and People in Ireland.* Dublin, 1902.

McCourt, Frank. *Angela's Ashes: A Memoir of a Childhood.* London, 1996.

McCready, Richard B. "Revising the Irish in Scotland: The Irish in Nineteenth- and Early-Twentieth-Century Scotland." In *The Irish Diaspora,* ed. Andy Bielenberg, 37–50. London, 2000.

McCullagh, David. *A Makeshift Majority.* Dublin, 1998.

McDermott, Eithne. *Clann na Poblachta.* Dublin, 1998.

McGilvray, James. *Irish Economic Statistics.* Dublin, 1968.

McKibben, Ross. *Classes and Cultures: England 1918–1951.* Oxford, 1998.

McMahon, Deirdre. "John Charles McQuaid, Archbishop of Dublin, 1940–72." In *History of the Catholic Diocese of Dublin,* ed. James Kelly and Daire Keogh, 355–61. Dublin, 2000.

McNabb, Patrick. "Demography." In *Limerick Rural Survey, 1958–1964,* ed. Jeremiah Newman, 158–92. Tipperary, 1964.

———. *Limerick Rural Survey: (First) Interim Report (Migration).* Tipperary, 1960.

———. "Social Structure." In *Limerick Rural Survey, 1958–1964,* ed. Jeremiah Newman, 193–247. Tipperary, 1964.

Meenan, James F. *The Irish Economy since 1922.* Liverpool, 1970.

———. "Preliminary Report Notes on the Census of Population in Northern Ireland, 1937." *JSSISI* 15 (1936 –37): 69 –80.

Mendras, Henri. *The Vanishing Peasant. Innovation and Change in French Agriculture.* Cambridge, Mass., 1970.

Mertens, Clement. "Birth Regulations," *Studies* 52 (1963): 231–48.

Miller, Kerby. *Emigrants and Exiles: Ireland and the Irish Exodus to North America.* New York, 1985.

Milotte, Mike. *Communism in Modern Ireland: The Pursuit of the Workers' Republic since 1916.* Dublin, 1984.

Mogey, John M. *Rural Life in Northern Ireland.* Oxford, 1947.

Morrison, Blake. *Things My Mother Never Told Me.* London, 2002.

Moynihan, Maurice. *Currency and Central Banking, 1922–1960.* Dublin, 1975.

Murphy, Rev. H. "The Rural Family: The Principles." *Christus Rex* 6 (1952): 3 –9.

Murphy, Michael. "Financial Results on Mixed Dairy Farms in 1937–38." *JSSISI* 16 (1938 –39): 105 –30.

———. "Financial Results on Mixed Dairy Farms in 1942–43 as Compared with 1937–39." *JSSISI* 17 (1943 –44): 269 –308.

———. "Financial Results on Sixty-One West Cork Farms in 1940–41." *JSSISI* 16 (1941–42): 60–87.

Newman, Jeremiah, ed. *The Limerick Rural Survey, 1958–1964.* Tipperary, 1964.

———. "Social Provision and Rural Centrality." In *The Limerick Rural Survey, 1958–1964,* ed. Jeremiah Newman, 248 –306. Tipperary, 1964.

Ní Bhrolcháin, Máire. "Is Ireland Underpopulated?" In *From Famine to Feast: Economic and Social Change in Ireland, 1847–1997,* ed. Kieran A. Kennedy, 23 –37. Dublin, 1998.

Nolan, Brian, Philip J. O'Connell, and Christopher T. Whelan. *Bust to Boom? The Irish Experience of Growth and Inequality.* Dublin, 2000.

Noonan, John T., Jr. *Contraception: A History of Its Treatment by the Catholic Theologians and Canonists.* Cambridge, Mass., 1965.

Noonan, Patrick. "Why Few Irish Marry." In *The Vanishing Irish: The Enigma of the Modern World,* ed. John A. O'Brien, 46 –53. New York, 1954.

Nowlan, K. B., and T. D. Williams, eds. *Ireland in the War Years and After, 1939–51.* Dublin, 1969.

O'Brien, Flann. *The Best of Myles.* London, 1968.

O'Brien, George. "The Coming Crisis of Population." *Studies* 25 (December 1936): 566 –80.

———. "Historical Introduction." In E. J. Riordan, *Modern Irish Trade and Industry*. London, 1920.

O'Brien, John A., ed. *The Vanishing Irish: The Enigma of the Modern World*. New York, 1954.

O'Brien, Matthew J. "Transatlantic Connections and the Sharp Edge of the Great Depression." *Éire/Ireland* (Spring/Summer 2002): 38 –57.

O'Connor, R. "Financial Results on Twenty Farms in Mid-Roscommon in 1945 –46." *JSSISI* 18 (1948 –49): 79 –108.

———. "Financial Results on Twenty-Five Farms in Mid-Roscommon in 1948 –49." *JSSISI* 18, pt. 3 (1949 –50): 270 –92.

O'Dowd, Anne. *Meitheal: A Study of Co-operative Labour in Rural Ireland*. Dublin, 1981.

O'Faoláin, Seán. "Love among the Irish." In *The Vanishing Irish: The Enigma of the Modern World*, ed. John A. O'Brien, 105 –16. New York, 1954.

Ó Gráda, Cormac. "Did Ulster Catholics Always Have Larger Families?" *Irish Economic and Social History* 11 (1972): 89 –98.

———. *Ireland: A New Economic History, 1780–1939*. Oxford, 1994.

———. "A Note on Nineteenth-Century Emigration Statistics." *Population Studies* 25 (1975): 143 –49.

———. *A Rocky Road: The Irish Economy since the 1920s*. Manchester, 1997.

Ó Gráda, Cormac, and Niall Duffy. "The Fertility Transition in Ireland and Scotland c. 1880–1930." In *Conflict, Identity, and Economic Development: Ireland and Scotland, 1600–1939*, ed. S. J. Connolly, R. A. Houston, and R. J. Morris, 89 –102. Preston, 1995.

Ó Gráda, Cormac, and Joel Mokyr. "Heights and Living Standards in the United Kingdom, 1815 –1860." *Explorations in Economic History* (April 1996): 1–27.

O'Leary, Cornelius. *Irish Elections, 1918–1977: Parties, Voters, and Proportional Representation*. Dublin, 1979.

O'Leary, Eoin. "The Irish National Teachers Organisation and the Marriage Bar for Women National Teachers, 1933 –58." *Saothar* 12 (1987): 47 –52.

O'Leary, Olivia, and Helen Burke. *Mary Robinson: The Authorised Biography*. London, 1998.

Olson, Mancur. *The Rise and Fall of Nations*. New Haven, Conn., 1976.

O'Neill, Kevin. *Family and Farm in Pre-Famine Ireland: The Parish of Killashandra*. Madison, Wis., 1984.

O'Neill Daunt, William Joseph. *Eighty-Five Years of Irish History, 1800–1885*. 2 Vols. London, 1886.

O'Shea, Kieran. *The Irish Emigrant Chaplaincy Scheme in Britain, 1957–82*. Naas, 1985.

Ó Súilleabháin, Seán. *A Handbook of Irish Folklore*. Dublin, 1942.

Patriarca, Silvana. *Numbers and Nationhood: Writing Statistics in Nineteenth-Century Italy*. Cambridge, 1996.

Paul-Dubois, L. *Contemporary Ireland*. Dublin, 1908.

Pedersen, Susan. *Family, Dependence, and the Origins of the Welfare State: Britain and France, 1914–1945*. Cambridge, 1993.

Pilgrim Trust. *Men without Work: A Report Made to the Pilgrim Trust*. Cambridge, 1938.

Plunkett, Horace. *Ireland in the New Century*. London, 1905.

Polasky, Janet. "Transplanting and Rooting Workers in London and Brussels: A Comparative History." *Journal of Modern History* 73 (September 2001): 528–60.

Porter, Dorothy. *Health, Civilization, and the State: A History of Public Health from Ancient to Modern Times*. London, 1999.

Powell, F. *The Politics of Irish Social Policy*. Lewiston, N.Y., 1992.

Quinn, D. B. *The Elizabethans and the Irish*. Ithaca, N.Y., 1966.

Raftery, Mary, and E. O'Sullivan. *Suffer the Little children: The Inside Story of Ireland's Industrial Schools*. Dublin, 1999.

Rathbone, Eleanor. *The Ethics and Economics of Family Endowment*. London, 1927.

Riordan, Susannah. "'A Political Blackthorn': Sean MacEntee, the Dignan Plan, and the Principle of Ministerial Responsibility." *Irish Economic and Social History* 27 (2000): 44–62.

Roche, Desmond. "Local Government." In *Unequal Achievement: The Irish Experience, 1957–82,* ed. Frank Litton, 133–46. Dublin, 1982.

Rose, E. J. B., and Associates. *Colour and Citizenship: A Report on British Race Relations*. London, 1969.

Rouse, Paul. *Ireland's Own Soil: Government and Agriculture in Ireland, 1945–1963*. Dublin, 2000.

Ryan, Tim. *Albert Reynolds, The Longford Leader: An Unofficial Biography*. Dublin, 1994.

Ryan, W. J. L. "The Methodology of the Second Programme for Economic Expansion." *Second Programme for Economic Expansion*. In *JSSISI* 21, pt. 2 (1963–64): 120–44.

Saorstát Éireann Irish Free State Official Handbook. Dublin, 1932.

Saraceno, Chiara. "Constructing Families, Shaping Women's Lives: The Making of Italian Families between Market Economy and State Interventions." In *The European Experience of Declining Fertility,* ed. John R. Gillis, Louise A. Tilly, and David Levine, 251–69. Oxford, 1992.

——. "Redefining Maternity and Paternity: Gender, Pro-Natalism, and Social Policies in Fascist Italy." In *Maternity and Gender Policy: Women and the Rise of the European Welfare States, 1880s–1950s,* ed. Gisela Bock and Pat Thane, 196–212. London, 1991.

Sauvy, Alfred. *General Theory of Population.* London, 1969.

Scheper-Hughes, Nancy. *Saints, Scholars, and Schizophrenics: Mental Illness in Rural Ireland.* Berkeley, 1979.

Schneider, Jane, and Peter Schneider. "Going Forward in Reverse Gear: Culture, Economy, and Political Economy in the Demographic Transition of a Rural Sicilian Town." In *The European Experience of Declining Fertility,* ed. John R. Gillis, Louise A. Tilly, and David Levine, 146–74. Oxford, 1992.

Schrier, Arnold. *Ireland and the American Emigration, 1850–1900.* Chester Springs, Penn., 1997.

Scully, John. "The Pilot Areas Development Programme." *JSSISI* 21, pt. 6 (1967–68): 51–71.

Segalen, Martine. "Exploring a Case of Late French Fertility Decline: Two Contrasted Breton Examples." In *The European Experience of Declining Fertility,* ed. John R. Gillis, Louise A. Tilly, and David Levine, 227–50. Oxford, 1992.

Sheehan, Helena. *Irish Television Drama: A Society and Its Stories.* Dublin, 1987.

Shiel, Michael. *The Quiet Revolution: The Electrification of Rural Ireland.* Dublin, 1984.

Silverman, Marilyn, and P. H. Gulliver, eds. *Approaching the Past: Historical Anthropology through Irish Case Studies.* New York, 1992.

Smith, Louis P. F. "Foreign Land Buying in Ireland." *Christus Rex* 18 (July 1964): 181–86.

Solomons, Michael. *Pro-Life? The Irish Question.* Dublin, 1992.

Soloway, Richard A. *Demography and Degeneration: Eugenics and the Declining Birthrate in Twentieth-Century Britain.* Chapel Hill, N.C., 1995.

Spencer, Ian R. G. *British Immigration Policy since 1939: The Making of Multi-Racial Britain.* London, 1997.

Spencer, John E. "R. C. Geary: His Life and Work." In *Roy Geary, 1896–1983: Irish Statistician,* ed. Denis Conniffe, 3–28. Dublin, 1997.

Spengler, Joseph J. *Facing Zero Population Growth: Reactions and Interpretations Past and Present.* Durham, N.C., 1978.

——. *France Faces Depopulation.* Raleigh, N.C., 1936.

Sutherland, Halliday. *Irish Journey.* London, 1956.

——. *Laws of Life.* Cheap edition. London, 1955.

Szreter, Simon. *Fertility, Class, and Gender in Britain, 1860–1914*. Cambridge, 1996.

Szreter, Simon, Robert A. Nye, and Franz von Poppel. "Fertility and Contraception during the Demographic Transition: Qualitative and Quantitative Approaches," introduction to "Before the Pill: Preventing Fertility in Western Europe and Quebec." *Journal of Interdisciplinary History* 34, no. 2 (Autumn 2003): 141–54.

Taylor, Alice. *Quench the Lamp*. Dingle, 1990.

———. *To School through the Fields: A Country Childhood*. Dingle, 1991.

Thompson, E. P. *The Making of the English Working Class*. London, 1963.

Thompson, Flora. *Lark Rise to Candleford*. London, 1948.

Tobin, Fergal. *The Best of Decades: Ireland in the 1960s*. Dublin, 1984.

Travers, Pauric. "Emigration and Gender: The Case of Ireland, 1922–60." In *Chattel, Servant, or Citizen? Women's Status in Church, State, and Society*, ed. Mary O'Dowd and Sabine Wichert, 187–99. Historical Studies, 19. Belfast, 1995.

Tucker, Vincent. "Images of Development and Underdevelopment in Glencolumbkille, County Donegal, 1830–1970." In *Rural Change in Ireland*, ed. John Davis, 84–115. Belfast, 1999.

Tullio-Altan, C. *Il Nostra Italia*. Milano, 1986.

Ussher, Arland. "The Boundary between the Sexes." In *The Vanishing Irish: The Enigma of the Modern World*, ed. John A. O'Brien, 150–63. New York, 1954.

Varley, Tony, and Chris Curtin. "Defending Rural Interests against Nationalists in Twentieth-Century Ireland: A Tale of Three Movements." In *Rural Change in Ireland*, ed. John Davis, 58–83. Belfast, 1999.

Vaughan, W. J., ed. *A New History of Ireland*. Vols. 5–6. Oxford, 1996.

Verrière, Jacques. *La Population de l'Irlande*. Paris, 1979.

Walsh, Brendan M. "Ireland's Demographic Transition, 1958–70." *Economic and Social Review* 1 (1969): 251–75.

———. *Some Irish Population Problems Reconsidered*. ESRI, paper no. 42. Dublin, 1968.

———. "Trends in Age of Marriage in Postwar Ireland." ESRI Reprint Series 9, no. 2 (May 1972).

Walshaw, R. S. *Migration to and from the British Isles: Problems and Policies*. London, 1941.

Whelan, Bernadette. *Ireland and the Marshall Plan, 1947–1957*. Dublin, 2000.

Whyte, John H. *Church and State in Modern Ireland, 1923–1970*. Dublin, 1971.

Wiener, Martin. *English Culture and the Decline of the Industrial Spirit,*
  1850–1980. Cambridge, 1981.
Williamson, Jeffrey. "Economic Convergence: Placing Post-Famine Ireland
  in Comparative Perspective." *Irish Economic and Social History* 21 (1994):
  5–27.
Wilson, Andrew J. *Irish America and the Ulster Connection 1968–1995.* Belfast, 1995.
Wolf, James B. "'Withholding Their Due': The Dispute between Ireland
  and Great Britain over Unemployment Insurance Payments to Conditionally Landed Irish Wartime Volunteer Workers." *Saothar* 21 (1996):
  39–45.
Wyman, Mark. *Round Trip to America: The Immigrants Return to Europe,*
  1880–1930. Ithaca, N.Y., 1993.
Young, Filson. *Ireland at the Cross-Roads: An Essay in Explanation.* London,
  1903.

Unpublished Theses

Cavanaugh, Francis P. "Immigration Restriction at Work Today: A Study of
  the Administration of Immigration Restriction by the United States."
  Ph.D. thesis. Catholic University of America, 1928.
Clear, Caitríona. "Women of the House: Women's Household Work in Ire-
  land 1922–1961. Discourses, Experiences, Memories." Ph.D. thesis. UCD,
  1997.
Cox, Catherine. "Managing Insanity: Carlow Lunatic Asylum, 1832–1922."
  Ph.D. thesis. UCD, 2004.
Curtis, Maurice. "Catholic Action as an Organised Campaign in Ireland,
  1921–1947." Ph.D. thesis. UCD, 2000.
Earner-Byrne, Lindsey. "'In Respect of Motherhood': Maternity Policy and
  Provision in Dublin City, 1922–1956." Ph.D. thesis. UCD, 2001.
Fee, Gerard. "The Effects of World War II on Dublin's Low-Income Fami-
  lies, 1939–1945." Ph.D. thesis. UCD, 1996.
Ferriter, Diarmaid. "'A Peculiar People in Their Own Land': Catholic Social
  Theory and the Plight of Rural Ireland, 1930–55." Ph.D. thesis. UCD, 1996.
Fitzpatrick, Sean. "Donnchadh Ó Briain, Requests and Representations: An
  Unsung Life of Fidelity to Fianna Fáil." M.A. thesis. UCD, 1995.
Foley, Aideen. "'No Sex Please, We're Catholic': The Influence of the Cath-
  olic Church on Declining Marriage Rates in Ireland between the Famine
  and the First World War." M. Litt. thesis. UCD, 1999.
McCarthy, Jude. "'From Herod to Pilate': State-Aided Island Migrations,
  1930–60." M.A. thesis. UCD, 1997.

McHugh, James. "Voices of the Rearguard: Republican Thought in the Post-Revolutionary Era." M.A. thesis. UCD, 1983.
Rouse, Paul. "Government Policy towards Agriculture in Post-War Ireland." Ph.D. thesis. UCD, 2000.

Index

West Indies, 210

Western People, 225, 252

Westland Row station, Dublin, 278, 279

Westmeath, county, 189

Westminster, archdiocese of, 92–93; emigrants in, 285–86, 288, 296, 301–2; Spencer report, 304–7

Westport, county Mayo, 147, 252

Wexford, county, 214

Wexford town, 153, 165, 252

Whitaker, T. K., 206–7

White, Padraic, 251–52, 254, 255

White Star Line, 145

widows' pensions, 118

Wild Geese, 7

Windsor Daily Star, 189

Wolverhampton, 272

women, 5, 186; assimilation fears as emigrants, 284–85; ban on factory work urged, 34; changing role of, 36; dependency, 117–18; education, 64–65, 67–68; as emigrants, 54, 78–79, 97, 131, 156, 157, 162; Emigration Commission on, 163–64, 168–72; and Fitzgerald report on emigration, 292–93; leaving rural life, 43–44, 54; and London embassy, 289–96; as main breadwinners, 45–46; marriage ban, 87, 122, 322; and moral dangers as emigrants, 20, 143, 265, 275–85; no unemployment assistance, 59–60; numbers of emigrants, 279–80; rights of, 86; social life of, 57; status of motherhood, 106–7; trafficking of, 277, 292; unmarried emigrant mothers, 285–89, 312–13, 325; wartime employment controls, 151–52; and water schemes, 53

Women and Children's Convention, League of Nations, 280

Women's Way, 230

workers' rights, 58

Worlock, Monsignor, 306

Wright, Myles, 248

xenophobia, 36, 239

Young Catholic Workers' Association, 275–76

youth culture, 136

Youth Employment Service, British, 294

Youth Unemployment, Commission on, 117, 226

Yugoslavia, 160

History *of* Ireland *and the* Irish Diaspora

The Slow Failure: Population Decline and Independent Ireland, 1920–1973
Mary E. Daly

The Eternal Paddy: Irish Identity and the British Press, 1798–1882
Michael de Nie

Old World Colony: Cork and South Munster 1630-1830
David Dickson

Sinn Féin: A Hundred Turbulent Years
Brian Feeney

Stakeknife: Britain's Secret Agents in Ireland
Martin Ingram and Greg Harkin

New Directions in Irish–American History
Edited by Kevin Kenny

The Same Age as the State
Máire Cruise O'Brien

*The Bible War in Ireland: The "Second Reformation" and the Polarization of
Protestant-Catholic Relations, 1800–1840*
Irene Whelan